Youth in context:

frameworks, settings and encounters

Youth: perspectives and practice

This book forms part of an innovative series of structured teaching texts from The Open University, aiming to improve readers' understanding of young people's lives at a time of rapid social change, and to encourage critical and reflective practice in work with young people. The series consists of two books, *Understanding Youth: Perspectives, Identities and Practices*, edited by Mary Jane Kehily, and *Youth in Context: Frameworks, Settings and Encounters*, edited by Martin Robb. The two books form the core texts for The Open University's third-level undergraduate course, KE308 *Youth: Perspectives and Practice*.

The two books share a number of key features:

- a biographical and holistic emphasis on young people's lives and lived experience, with extensive use of young people's voices and perspectives

- a dynamic focus on change in young people's lives, including the changing experience of youth, changes in ways of working with young people, and young people as agents of change

- an emphasis on diversity and inequalities in young people's experience, for example on the basis of class, gender, ethnicity and disability.

Youth in context:

frameworks, settings and encounters

Edited by Martin Robb

The Open University

SAGE Publications
London • Thousand Oaks • New Delhi

Published by

Sage Publications
1 Oliver's Yard
55 City Road
London EC1Y 1SP

in association with

The Open University
Walton Hall
Milton Keynes MK7 6AA

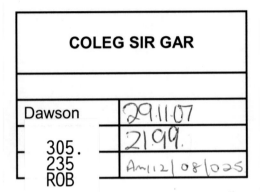
First published 2007

Edited and designed by The Open University.

Typeset by S&P Enterprises (rfod) Limited, Lydbrook, Glos.

Printed and bound in the United Kingdom by The Alden Group, Oxford.

This book forms part of an Open University course KE308 *Youth: Perspectives and Practice*. Details of this and other Open University courses can be obtained from the Student Registration and Enquiry Service, The Open University, PO Box 197, Milton Keynes MK7 6BJ, United Kingdom: tel. +44 (0)870 333 4340, email general-enquiries@open.ac.uk

A catalogue record for this book is available from the British Library.

Library of Congress Control Number: 2006924445

ISBN 978-1-4129-3066-6 (hardback)

ISBN 978-1-4129-3067-3 (paperback)

1.1

Contents

About the authors   1

Introduction   5

Part 1   Frameworks   13

    Chapter 1   Practitioners *Andy Rixon*   15

    Chapter 2   Practice *Danielle Turney*   53

    Chapter 3   Participation *Heather Montgomery*   89

Part 2   Settings   121

    Chapter 4   Neighbourhood *Sheila Henderson*   123

    Chapter 5   Education *Mary Jane Kehily*   155

    Chapter 6   Institutions *Helen Evans*   185

Part 3   Encounters   217

    Chapter 7   Risk *Claire Smith, Wendy Stainton Rogers*
    and *Stan Tucker*   219

    Chapter 8   Safeguarding *Andy Rixon* and *Danielle Turney*   251

    Chapter 9   Support *Jean Spence*   287

Acknowledgements   320

Index   321

About the authors

Helen Evans has been a Staff Tutor in the Faculty of Health and Social Care at The Open University since 2003. Her professional background is social work and her practice experience with young people spans the probation and education sectors.

Sheila Henderson is a freelance social researcher whose work has addressed many aspects of young people's lives but in particular has informed the development, delivery and evaluation of policy and practice in the field of substance use. She has a long-standing interest in youth culture, consumption, gender, identity and social change and is also interested in biographical and longitudinal qualitative methodologies. She has published widely and is Visiting Research Fellow at the Social Science Research Centre at London South Bank University.

Mary Jane Kehily is Senior Lecturer in Childhood and Youth Studies at The Open University. She has a background in cultural studies and education and has research interests in gender and sexuality, narrative and identity, and popular culture. She has published widely on these themes. Recent publications include *Sexuality, Gender and Schooling: Shifting Agendas in Social Learning* (Routledge, 2002); (edited with Joan Swann) *Children's Cultural Worlds* (Wiley/The Open University, 2003) and *An Introduction to Childhood Studies* (McGraw-Hill/Open University Press, 2004).

Heather Montgomery is Lecturer in Childhood Studies at The Open University. She is a social anthropologist who has worked in Thailand and is the author of *Modern Babylon? Prostituting Children in Thailand* (Berghahn, 2001).

Andy Rixon is Lecturer in the Faculty of Health and Social Care at The Open University. He has 16 years' experience of working in a local authority as a social worker and in training and development. His training and development work has focused particularly on multi-agency child protection training and on developing post-qualifying awards.

Martin Robb is Lecturer in the Faculty of Health and Social Care at The Open University. He is co-editor of *Relating Experience: Stories from Health and Social Care* (Routledge, 2005), *Communication, Relationships and Care* (Routledge, 2004) and *Understanding Health and Social Care* (Sage, 1998), and has published articles and book chapters on a wide range of topics, with a recent focus on issues of fatherhood, masculinity and childcare. Before joining The Open University he worked in informal and community education projects with adults and young people.

Claire Smith is Senior Researcher and Lecturer at Newman College of Higher Education in Birmingham. She has several years' experience in researching sector skills needs, including those of the childcare workforce. Her research interests lie in youth and child welfare policy, with a particular focus on safeguarding children.

Jean Spence is Lecturer in Community and Youth Work at Durham University. She has been involved in youth and community work, education, research, practice and project management for 30 years and is a long-standing member of the editorial group of the journal *Youth and Policy*. She is currently director of the *Everyday Journey* research project. Her research interests and journal publications are focused on contemporary policy and practice, the processes and history of youth work, and women's social and community activism. She has edited (with R. Gilchrist and T. Jeffs) three historical collections: *Essays in the History of Community and Youth Work* (National Youth Agency (NYA), 2001); *Architects of Change* (NYA, 2003) and *Drawing on the Past* (NYA, 2006).

Wendy Stainton Rogers has a Chair in Health Psychology at The Open University. She has a lifetime commitment to championing the welfare, rights and life opportunities of young people. Over the last 30 years she has made significant contributions to teaching in relation to safeguarding children, child welfare law in all four legislations in the UK (and the Cayman Islands!) and developing effective professional practice in work with young people, children and their families. She is currently chairing the Faculty of Health and Social Care's Foundation Degree programme in Youth Justice. Her research in this field is informed by critical theory, and is currently concerned with the ways in which the current preoccupation with 'risk factors' is leading to institutional abuse of children and young people.

Stan Tucker is Professor of Education and Policy at Newman College of Higher Education in Birmingham. He has researched and published widely in the areas of youth, child and family policy. His work on workforce reform was influential in shaping the government's Every Child Matters agenda. He has recently co-authored a major literature review on the perceptions of the roles of teaching assistants in primary and secondary schools.

Danielle Turney is Senior Lecturer in the Faculty of Health and Social Care at The Open University. She has a practice background in social work with children and young people and has taught on social work courses at qualifying and post-qualifying levels. Her current research and writing interests focus on child neglect and broader issues of policy and practice in relation to safeguarding children.

Other contributors

This book has grown out of debates and discussions in the KE308 course team at The Open University. Besides the named authors, other team members who have contributed to the development of the book include Linda Camborne-Paynter, Jo Dawson and Rachel Thomson. The Open University course team would like to thank critical readers and developmental testers for their valuable comments on earlier draft chapters, and especially Robert MacDonald who, in his capacity as external assessor, provided insightful and timely comments at every turn.

Introduction

Martin Robb

Recent years have witnessed dramatic changes in the lives of young people in the UK, as elsewhere in the world. Changes in schooling and the expansion of higher education, the loss of the traditional youth labour market, and shifts in the nature of family and intimate relationships, have combined to make transitions to adulthood more diverse, complex and unequal than in previous generations. The impact of these developments on young people's lives is explored in detail in the companion volume in this series (Kehily, 2007).

The changing experience of youth has contributed to a transformation in ways of thinking about and organising services for young people. However, developments in youth policy have also been driven by new ideological priorities. Since the mid-1990s, there has been a renewed focus on young people in social policy, with important initiatives in the fields of education, advice and guidance, and youth justice. As this book was being written, the UK government issued its Green Paper, *Youth Matters*, which claimed to offer a bold vision of 'services integrated around young people's needs' (DfES, 2005, p. 5), although it has been criticised for aiming 'to fundamentally alter the ways in which young people relate to the state and the market; to realign provision by changing from a membership to a consumerist model of youth work' (Jeffs and Smith, 2006, p. 25).

In response to these new policy agendas, services aimed at young people have undergone a number of significant changes. Examples include an increasing emphasis on inter-agency collaboration and on breaking down institutional boundaries, a renewed focus on targeting services at those deemed to be in the greatest need, and new professional and regulatory frameworks. These developments have had a major impact on the experience of practitioners across a range of services and sectors, and on the nature and focus of their interactions and relationships with young people.

In changing times such as these, there is an urgent need for educational resources that enable practitioners to reflect critically on change and its implications. This book provides a critical overview of current practice in work with young people, and offers a framework for developing a critical and transformative practice that responds to the changing and diverse needs of young people. Rather than seeing change simply as a one-way process imposed from above, the book explores it as a dialogic process, one in which dominant constructions of young people's needs are challenged and modified by the perspectives and experiences of practitioners and young people.

The model of critical practice developed in the book draws on the theoretical perspectives on youth explored in its companion volume (Kehily, 2007). That book introduced three theoretical approaches – cultural, comparative and biographical – which, taken together, offered a critical social approach to the exploration of young people's experience. Despite some differences of emphasis, what these three perspectives have in common is a focus on the dynamic and situated nature of young people's lives, and on the ways in which the social interacts with the personal. In building on these theoretical foundations, the current volume emphasises the ways in which work with young people, and the everyday experience of practitioners, is shaped by dynamic social contexts, which include competing ideas about young people and their needs, new policy agendas, and changing and diverse structures and processes.

The book takes an interdisciplinary and inter-agency approach to work with young people, identifying themes and issues that are common to a wide range of practitioners. As such, it will be an important resource for anyone working with young people, whether in mainstream youth work, education, health, social work, or advice and guidance services, and whether in the statutory or voluntary sectors. It will also be of value to those with a general interest in the changing experience of young people, and the ways in which services provided for them influence their lives.

The book is divided into three parts. The first part, 'Frameworks', provides some general building blocks for developing a critical understanding of current practice in work with young people, and for constructing a framework for critical practice. Key ideas are set out here that are taken up and developed in relation to specific practice issues and contexts later in the book.

Chapter 1 explores what it means to be a 'practitioner' with young people at a time of considerable recent change in the field. The chapter begins by taking a 'long view' of how historical factors have shaped practice, considering some of the continuing debates in the field; for example, between welfare and control. There is an examination of some of the issues with which youth practitioners have had to contend in recent times, such as a greater emphasis on targeting of services, inter-agency working and professionalism. Throughout, the chapter draws on the perspectives of both practitioners and young people, and the ways in which these offer a challenge to changes imposed from above. The discussion is set in the context of an understanding of the importance of power in shaping relationships between policy makers, practitioners and young people.

The second chapter takes up the theme of relationships as part of its exploration of the nature of 'practice' with young people. The aim of this chapter is to identify some of the key features of practice, beginning with an analysis of how it differs from other kinds of interactions, and then taking forward Chapter 1's exploration of how practice is changing, with a particular focus on changes in practice relationships. The emphasis here is on how practitioners can actively improve their own practice, and on the part played in this process by skills, values and, above all, different kinds of knowledge. The chapter includes a consideration of different models for understanding the change process, identifying the differences between reflection and reflexivity, and working towards a model of critical practice. In the process, there is a discussion of important issues such as the use of self, the links between personal biography and professional practice, and the changing relationship between experience and expertise.

The final chapter in this opening part narrows the focus to one of the key issues shaping contemporary practice: participation. This discussion builds on key elements in the previous two chapters, identifying an increased emphasis on participatory approaches as one of the key changes for practitioners in recent years, and also as a vital tool for developing a more critical and empowering practice. While broadly supportive of these developments, Chapter 3 adopts the critical approach established in the earlier chapters as it questions what is meant by 'participation' in current discussions about work with young people. Different models of participation are identified, and examples of these models are discussed. The chapter also examines the roots of the current emphasis on participation in policy and legislation, including the links with evolving ideas of citizenship. Examples are used to illustrate some of the contradictions surrounding this concept, such as the tension between partnership and protection. The final section of the chapter considers some of the limits of participation; for example, those that result from lack of social and economic power among some groups of young people.

Work with young people takes place in a wide range of social contexts, and Part 2 of the book, 'Settings', considers some of these. The emphasis here is on how settings are changing and how they shape the everyday experience of young people and practitioners. The three chapters in this part offer a spectrum of kinds of settings, beginning with one that is part of the experience of all young people – the local neighbourhood or community; and ending with those that are highly specialised and set up to respond to the needs of a minority of young people – institutional settings that remove young people from their home and community environment.

Part 2 begins with an exploration, in Chapter 4, of neighbourhood, partly because (as the chapter explains) all work with young people is based in some kind of community, and also because working with young people on their own territory has been a consistent emphasis in youth work since the 1970s, with the current policy emphasis on 'neighbourhood' only the most recent instance of this. The chapter explores some of the meanings of neighbourhood and community for young people, drawing on both classic and more recent studies and charting continuity and change in the shift of emphasis from 'community' to 'neighbourhood' in social policy. The extended discussion of what is meant by 'neighbourhood practice' explores the contested meanings of community and neighbourhood in policy and practice, using diverse examples to explore the aims and purposes of this area of practice. The final section of the chapter considers neighbourhood practice in the context of moral agendas about poor neighbourhoods, and sets these debates against young people's own experience and perspectives.

The fact that schooling is compulsory in the UK to the age of 16, and that numbers in higher education are rising, means that educational settings are another key site both for young people's everyday experience and for work with young people. Chapter 5 explores educational settings as contexts in which young people and adults interact and make meaning, tracing some of the main changes that have taken place in the education of young people in recent years and placing these in the context of social and economic change. Building on the biographical approach introduced in Chapter 2, one of the interesting features of this chapter is its extensive use of personal experience – of being on both the 'giving' and the 'receiving' ends of education – as a prism through which to examine the impact of change, and to consider continuities in experiences and ideas. The chapter includes discussions of the nature of higher education in 'new times' and of the changing role of teachers. Drawing extensively on biographical accounts from education practitioners, the chapter explores the experience of becoming a teacher, and the role of teachers as implementers of policy. This is paralleled by the use of accounts by young people of their contemporary experience of schooling. Finally, and by contrast, the chapter explores alternative sites for young people's learning, such as an informal education project for young mothers.

The last chapter in this part of the book examines settings that are part of the experience of a minority of young people – residential institutions. The focus, as in other chapters, is on change and its impact, in this case on the nature of residential work, especially (anticipating Chapter 7 on 'Risk') with young people deemed to be a risk to society. The chapter makes use of an extended case study of an institution in Northern Ireland, examining the ways in which its aims, purposes and ways of working have changed over time, as a microcosm of changing ways of thinking about residential work with young people. The history of Glenmona illustrates a continuing tension between welfare and justice models of institutional provision, and the chapter considers the extent to which a model of control has been replaced by one of care. Drawing on the work of Michel Foucault, the chapter explores the shift in emphasis from punishment to reform, in terms of changing forms of surveillance of young people. Finally, the chapter examines the implications of change for practitioners working in such settings and asks what might be the elements of good practice in this area of work, focusing on the issues of rights and participation that were first raised in Chapter 3.

If Part 2 considers how work with young people is shaped by physical settings, the third part of the book, 'Encounters', explores some of the ways in which interactions between young people and practitioners are categorised according to other criteria. The chapters in this final part examine how services for young people are currently constructed by policy, looking at how policy priorities reflect changing and competing constructions of young people and their needs. Part 3 resists a conventional division along the lines of professional boundaries (for example, youth work, social work, youth justice) and instead opts deliberately for a holistic, interdisciplinary approach that cuts across these divisions and attempts to reflect current policy concerns: hence the chapter titles 'Risk', 'Safeguarding' and 'Support'. The chapters also question these currently dominant ways of categorising young people's needs and behaviour, so that (in common with earlier chapters in the book) there is considerable dialogue and flow of ideas from one chapter to another.

Much recent media and policy debate around young people has focused on the notion of risk, and particularly on the supposed risk posed to social order by some groups of young people. The first chapter in Part 3 explores the ways in which 'risk' has come to dominate policy and practice, despite the fact that the notion appears to have little salience for young people themselves. The chapter critically analyses the discourse of risk and its implications for young people and practitioners, seeing it as part of a wider problematisation of youth and of efforts to regulate young people's behaviour. However, the chapter avoids seeing 'risk' as entirely the invention of government and the media. Instead, it offers a careful analysis of different ways of responding to risk, analysing the currently dominant retributive model, and comparing approaches rooted in an ultimately stigmatising approach, based on 'vulnerability', with alternative approaches that seek to build on the strengths of young people, their families and communities. The chapter concludes by using examples of work with homeless young people and with young mothers to elaborate what an alternative, more positive approach might look like in practice.

Chapter 8 takes up where Chapter 7 leaves off and begins by considering the risks posed *to* some groups of young people, rather than the risks posed *by* them – using examples of young people who have experienced neglect or abuse. The chapter's title uses a term – 'safeguarding' – which is increasingly common in policy and practice, and the chapter considers in detail the implications of this shift in terminology and ideas. Drawing extensively on recent research, as well as on young people's own perspectives, the chapter questions the effectiveness of existing approaches and considers some of the key issues, such as confidentiality, for practitioners working with young people 'at risk'. Following the example of the previous chapter, this chapter sets out an alternative, positive approach to safeguarding young people, one that pays attention to issues of empowerment, advocacy and the promotion of resilience.

The concluding chapter explores services that aim to offer support to all young people. The narrative of the book comes full circle, with a return to the themes of historical continuity and dramatic change which were introduced in Chapter 1. The chapter explores what is meant by 'support' in work with young people and places this in the context of the changing ways in which young people's transition to adulthood have been understood, and the historical responses of youth work practice. Although the chapter uses mainstream youth work as its central example, its discussion is of relevance to other forms of practice and includes a discussion of the emergence of hybrid services, such as Connexions. The chapter makes extensive and fascinating use of a research study which collected the first-hand accounts of youth workers, thus continuing the biographical emphasis of earlier chapters and lending a richness to its exploration of changing practice. The discussion elaborates on the point made earlier in this Introduction, and which is implicit throughout the book, that change in practice is the result of negotiation and, at times, struggle between the priorities of policy, the challenges of practitioners and the perspectives of young people. Critically analysing recent developments in supportive work with young people, the chapter makes an impassioned plea, appropriate for a closing chapter, for the values implicit in traditional youth work, and especially for a vision of work with young people which 'focuses on the creative potential of youth as a time of "being" as well as "becoming"'.

Although this book has been written for Open University students, it will be of interest to a much wider audience concerned to understand work with young people in changing times. Uniquely combining theoretical analysis with an exploration of implications for practice, and evidence from research with examples from the experience of both professionals and young people, the book provides a valuable resource for those studying or working with young people. As a teaching text, each chapter of the book includes a range of activities. These commonly call on readers to reflect on personal experience or test out ideas in relation to their own experience. Activities act as interactive learning tools that aim to consolidate the main teaching points for the chapter. They are, of course, optional for general readers. Finally, in order to help *all* readers and to make the text as accessible as possible, key terms are emboldened and explained at the point when they are first discussed.

References

DfES (Department for Education and Skills) (2005) *Youth Matters*, Norwich, The Stationery Office.

Jeffs, T. and Smith, M. (2006) 'Where is *Youth Matters* taking us?', *Youth and Policy*, vol. 91, pp. 23–40.

Kehily, M.J. (ed.) (2007) *Understanding Youth: Perspectives, Identities and Practices*, London, Sage/The Open University (Course Book).

Part 1
Frameworks

Chapter 1

Practitioners

Andy Rixon

Introduction

The main aim of this first chapter is to explore the role and identity of practitioners who work with young people and to highlight some of the issues raised by recent trends and changes in this area of practice. What are the sources of these changes? What tensions and dilemmas have they created? How are they experienced by practitioners and the young people with whom they work?

'Practice' with young people in the UK is undertaken within a wide spectrum of roles. It may not even be self-evident that there is a group of people who could be categorised as 'practitioners' in the way I am suggesting. Individual young people will come into contact with a very different range of practitioners. Some, like teachers, will be a universal experience; while others, like social workers and mental health workers, will be a more limited one. In a whole range of other settings in clubs and groups, adults, paid and unpaid, will be encountered in a much more informal way with less obviously defined labels or precise boundaries. Subsequent chapters will explore the meaning of 'practice' and will examine it in a range of settings and in different forms of encounters with young people. Here I want to identify a few of the many themes that will impact, to a greater or lesser extent, on practitioners across all these contexts.

The environment in which practitioners are working is in a constant state of change. New government policies and organisational structures and shifting views of young people themselves seem to create a continuous stream of new issues and dilemmas. However, before embarking on a discussion of the impact of recent changes, the first section of this chapter will take a historical perspective on work with young people. It will explore whether the dilemmas and contradictions in current ways of working are 'new' or whether there are continuities with policy and practice from the past.

Not all of the diverse developments currently affecting practitioners can be explored here, but Section 2 will focus on one example in some detail: that of outcome measures and targets. It will examine the impact these have and the different perspectives available to practitioners from which to understand their implications.

Within the broad definition of 'practitioner', some people also carry the label of being a 'professional'. Whether or not they have this label, or aspire to having it, will be important in shaping their identity. Being a 'professional' is not crucial in terms of the relevance of the issues raised in this chapter, or those that follow; indeed, as we will discuss in Section 3, what it means to be a professional is much contested. For young people, the labels that practitioners carry may be considerably less important than their experience of the relationship and of the service provided. Section 3 will also focus on their perspective and the shifting context in which these relationships are conducted both socially and in terms of the demand for increasingly participative ways of working.

The final theme of the chapter will be the experience of the practitioner in an increasingly inter-professional world. If all new developments assume the advantages of this way of working, why might such arrangements succeed, or fail? What impact do they have on individual professional identities?

This chapter will address the following core questions:

- What factors have shaped and now shape the role and identity of those working with young people?
- What tensions and dilemmas have some of the more recent changes created?
- What does it mean to be a 'professional'? How relevant is this to working with young people in a changing inter-professional environment?
- How do changing social relationships and the demands of working in a way that requires more sharing of professional power affect practitioners' identities?
- How can practitioners respond to the different pressures on their roles?

An example

> It's about stretching young people so they're learning about themselves. They're learning to think for themselves and to do things for themselves and to be the person that they can be.
>
> (Youth worker, quoted in Devanney and Pugh, 2005)

Many practitioners have a clear perception of their identity and the purpose of their work, whether it is trying to help young people negotiate their way through particular difficulties, offering guidance and advice, or empowering them to make decisions that will improve their lives. It is also the case that their work is often carried out in agencies subject to government policy, or in projects relying on funding focused on tackling a particular 'problem' area, such as concerns about 'antisocial behaviour', 'youth crime', or 'teenage pregnancy'. Government policy, the legislative framework and societal and media attitudes towards young people will all, to some extent, influence, restrict and define the activities of practitioners, emphasising one area of work, deprioritising another. At the very least this can create tensions within practice and challenge how workers view their work and identity. Ultimately, these factors can direct them to work in ways counter to that in which they believe young people are best helped.

The following contemporary example, based on the real experience of one voluntary sector project, will highlight some of the themes we will explore in the rest of the chapter.

Activity 1   A case study

Allow 15 minutes   Read the case study below. As you do so, make notes in response to the following questions:

- What problems or dilemmas might arise for the practitioners involved?
- What do you identify as being the source of these problems?
- What impact might there have been on the young people involved?

Positive Steps: a case study

The 'Positive Steps' community based prevention project consisted of a small group of workers drawn from different backgrounds (education, social work and youth justice) and managed by a voluntary organisation. The project was established with money from different sources of government funding, making 10–15-year-olds their target group.

The 'prevention' remit of the project was broad, aiming to achieve a range of objectives. One objective focused on reducing offending, but there were also a number of others (relating, for example, to improving health, and success at school). These objectives were to be met via a wide variety of activities including after school groups and participation projects. Consultation with local young people and the community had helped decide the nature of the work and how specific referrals were to be taken.

After one year, new criteria were introduced by the government:

- directing that 25 per cent of all funds should be spent on the one objective of crime reduction
- introducing new criteria specifying what 'counted' as preventative work from a crime prevention perspective
- specifying the way referrals were to be taken
- inviting other interventions if supported by evidence of a proven effectiveness in reducing crime.

Some of the proposals for after school groups were withdrawn to accommodate the new funding pattern, and the methods of taking referrals were changed in line with the new directive.

Comment

If you have worked in a project dependent on external funding you will be familiar with some of the themes in this example: mixed funding streams (possibly of uncertain lengths), the multi-agency nature of the project, delivery of a new initiative via the voluntary sector, the influence of changing government policy and targets, the expectation of consultation and the requirement to demonstrate 'effective' practice.

You might have noted that the project in the example was already closely linked to government policy objectives and would not have been funded otherwise. There was little flexibility, therefore, when more specific uses of the funding were dictated. However, the practitioners who joined the project may have done so because they were committed to the original, more holistic, approach to prevention delivered flexibly in a project outside of their previous statutory roles. If so, the narrowing of the perspective – more focused on 'crime prevention' – would have been problematic and a challenge to the identity they had adopted. Their different professional backgrounds may have influenced the extent to which this was experienced as a problem.

Clearly, the changes had a real impact on the services being delivered which would have a direct effect on the young people concerned even if different services emerged as a result. You may also have identified the issue of consultation – having invited the opinions of children and young people, their views were now going to be, at least partially, overruled. Research with children and young people in Scotland by Anne Stafford *et al.* (2003) has emphasised that such poor experiences of consultation can be very damaging and can create cynicism in young people as to whether practitioners are really committed to involving them in decisions that affect their lives.

The point of this example is not necessarily to argue against this sort of crime prevention or the use of specific targets, but to consider the dilemmas that are experienced by those delivering the service. Nevertheless, while this example might seem like a small shift, Bill Whyte, in an overview of research on early intervention, has argued that such crime-focused 'preventative' interventions do pose a challenge for practitioners in this area of work: 'The renewed focus on early preventative interventions aimed at reducing anti-social behaviour and youth crime has created new opportunities, new challenges, and new risks for practitioners' (Whyte, 2004, p. 4). He suggests that a balance needs to be found between a 'missed opportunity' if prevention is not engaged with and possible 'unintended consequences' of early intervention; that is, labelling young children as potential offenders (p. 4). Similarly, many of those who work with young people in 'crisis' situations will welcome the opportunity for preventative work, but will also see that this is part of an ever closer 'monitoring' and 'surveillance' of the lives of children and young people.

1 A historical perspective

The nature of the dilemmas in the example we have just discussed might seem very much a product of twenty-first century themes. Yet in a historical overview which focuses on youth and community work projects, Ruth Gilchrist *et al.* (2003) demonstrate that these kinds of inherent tensions are long standing. They identify the origins of youth work as being a response to the 'insecurities, inequalities and instability' created by social change, primarily industrialisation and the increasing mobility of the population (Gilchrist *et al.*, 2003, p. 9). In these new circumstances young people, required to be educated and in demand as labour, were also trying to assert their own place in society, creating anxiety in adults about the social order. It is as a result of such anxieties that 'youth' or 'adolescence' have in different ways come to be seen as problematic in Western societies (Kehily, 2007a). Largely in response to these perceived problems, and how they are cast, services for young people have developed. Then and now, these responses, whether via the state or via voluntary or faith groups, have offered valuable help, education and welfare, yet they have also explicitly or implicitly tended to contribute to social conformity and an orderly transition to adulthood.

1.1 Working with young people: the long view

Such a mix can be seen in early forms of provision for young people in the UK. Jean Spence (2003) cites the example of Frank Caws in Sunderland who founded the 'Sunderland Waifs Rescue Agency and Street Vendors Club' in 1902. In industrialised Sunderland as elsewhere in England there was growing concern about the condition of the poorer children and young people. It seems clear from Spence's account that Caws was genuinely moved by the situation of the young people he encountered and was inspired to act by a social conscience supported by strong evangelical Christian views. The club was to provide recreational activities, 'informal education', and 'respite from the rigours of home and street life' (Spence, 2003, p. 112). It was intended to be character changing, with young men 'coming under the influence of steady, responsible male citizens who might serve as role models' (p. 112).

Caws's perspective was a common one among similar initiatives informed by:

> the idea that the children of the unskilled working classes could only be saved from destitution if they could be shown the possibilities of inhabiting a different sort of world. If they could be taught habits of cleanliness, thrift and self discipline and most importantly, if they learned a trade capable of giving them the means to secure respectable employment.
>
> (Spence, 2003, p. 112)

Some of the themes of this early provision can be detected over a century later. For example, the stress on the importance of employment and gaining skills may be reminiscent of more recent government policies. Also, the idea that what Frank Caws was providing was 'informal education' is also one that has remained current in youth work even if the nature of the 'education' continued to be a source of debate (Jeffs and Smith, 1996).

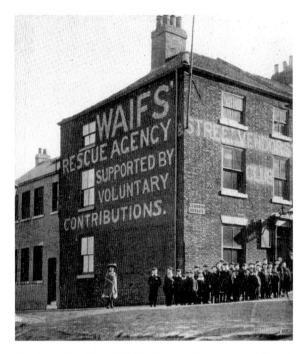

The Lampton Street Waifs Rescue Agency and Street Vendors Club in Sunderland

Activity 2   A counter attraction to the street corner

Allow 20 minutes   Read the following statements of purpose. What do they illustrate about the intentions and motivations of the organisations? Are there themes that are still identifiable today?

St Christopher's Working Boys' Club

We have long felt that in the battle against evil which is now being waged the great feature of amusement and happiness as an effective moral force has not received its true recognition. It is therefore our first aim to provide for as many of these lads as we can a cheerful, healthy place where they may spend their evenings, a counter attraction to the music hall, the street corner and the public house. Secondly, it is our aim to ourselves mix with them freely, and give them, as far as in us lies, the advantage of the better education and tone that a happier fortune has bestowed upon us. We believe that the lads can appreciate and will learn for themselves that subtle thing which is sometimes called 'good form' which is such an important feature among the higher classes. Thirdly, our aim is to teach them religion and to help them learn that the service of God is the highest service ... This is the ground for providing our work ... such things as engender light heartedness, joy and pleasure.

(St Christopher's Working Boys' Club, 1889, quoted in Booton, 1985, p. 14)

Cambridge Association for the Care of Girls

The objects of the Cambridge Association for the Care of Girls are:

(a) to help girls who live in dangerous surroundings and to give those who have once fallen an opportunity for a fresh start in life;

(b) to place young girls in service and in special cases to send young girls to homes where they may be trained for service;

(c) to provide recreation and new interests for girls.

(Cambridge Association for the Care of Girls, 1905, quoted in Booton, 1985, p. 18)

Comment

In his commentary on these historical examples, Frank Booton stresses that we need to be careful not to dismiss such statements because of their language or tone and that a closer reading can point up continuities as well as differences. Both extracts reveal an assumption that they are providing a 'preventative' service (keeping young men out of the music halls, young women from 'dangerous surroundings' or becoming 'fallen') and that there is a value placed on recreation that implies it will help with character development. Anxieties about young men hanging around on street corners are long standing and echo more recent concerns about 'antisocial behaviour' that have directed much provision. The first quotation makes explicit the intention of imposing the culture of one class on another, yet even today the idea of those working with young people providing 'role models' is not completely redundant, nor perhaps is the relevance of class. Substantial work is still done by faith based groups and organisations inspired by religious principles. Again, the belief in the value of work and training is a theme still current over a century later even if the solutions in these examples are slightly more gendered than today.

The emphasis in work with young people was not all focused on social conformity. In other historical extracts Booton demonstrates that this 'improvement' could also develop a political edge: where the need for social reform was recognised and the value of social organisation among the working class could be encouraged within the clubs. Traditions of enabling disadvantaged groups to take collective action have also persisted in some areas of work with young people even if, as Tony Jeffs and Mark Smith (2002) argue, they have been undermined by policy changes in an age of increasing individualisation. Gilchrist *et al.* (2003) believe that these competing themes, which they characterise as 'domestication and liberation' (p. 7), still go to the heart of current day-to-day practice with young people.

1.2 Welfare and control, opportunities and responsibility

A second commonly cited historical illustration of the tensions that practitioners have to work within has been to consider how policy and legislation in relation to crime and young people (particularly in England and Wales) has tended to reflect competing philosophies. One strand emphasises individual responsibility for criminal actions, requiring a control or punishment response; a second suggests that such 'delinquency' is a product of cultural and material circumstances, thereby promoting the value of a welfare or treatment response.

Landmark Acts of Parliament signpost which philosophy was in the ascendancy. The Children and Young Persons Act 1933, in raising the age of a juvenile criminal to 17 and encouraging magistrates to 'treat as well as punish', has been seen as key to advancing the welfare approach. The 1969 Children and Young Persons Act, with its emphasis on alternatives to the criminal justice system, signalled a desire to expand this welfare approach further. In emphasising the 'causes of crime' it is argued that these Acts inevitably reflected the growing concern about the cultural wellbeing of the nation's youth and a belief that a parallel expansion of service provision for young people was required (Osgerby, 1998).

In an overview of youth justice legislation, John Pitts (2005) concludes that many of the aims of this earlier legislation were never fully realised. The expansion of provision ended with the financial constraints of the 1970s, and contracted with the more explicit retreat from this welfarist perspective in the Conservative administrations of the 1980s. The policy adopted initially has been described by Pitts (2005, p. 4) as 'progressive minimalism'. Although minimising intervention was partly motivated by reducing cost, this policy did initially have the effect of keeping young people away from court through the utilisation of diversionary multi-agency panels. However, rising concern about youth crime, heightened by 'riots' in the early 1990s and the impact of the murder of two-year-old James Bulger by two ten-year-old boys, led to radical change in the political atmosphere, again signalled through the legislation:

> As a result, the key reforms embodied in the Criminal Justice Act 1991 were abandoned. In March 1993, only five months after the newly implemented Act had abolished custody for children under 15, Kenneth Clarke, the Conservative Home Secretary, promised to create 200 places for 12 to 14 year old 'persistent offenders' in new secure training centres. This *volte face* signalled a new era in which crime in general, and youth crime in particular, was to be moved back to the centre of the political stage.

(Pitts, 2005, p. 7)

Youth 'riots' in the 1990s influenced youth justice policy

In practice, there has never been an absolute division between these approaches, but rather policies that contain both perspectives. A new version of them became apparent with the publication of *No More Excuses* (Home Office, 1997) and the Crime and Disorder Act 1998. Youth justice began to reflect an emphasis on the language of prevention, individual and parental responsibility, and restorative justice. A raft of policy and legislation considerably expanded the options for intervention into the lives of young people. Preventative measures for much younger children 'at risk' increased while, simultaneously, numbers of young people in custody grew (Pitts, 2005). New powers, often civil orders such as the

Anti-Social Behaviour Order (ASBO) and local child curfews, targeted 'disorderly' as well as criminal behaviour (Muncie and Goldson, 2006). While the ASBO was introduced to apply to the whole population, the title has become particularly associated with young people and a majority of orders have been made on those under the age of 21 (Muncie and Goldson, 2006).

The youth justice system in Scotland, which has had a system of children's hearings since 1971, has often been pointed to as a model based firmly on welfare principles. While this is still the case, post devolution the picture has become more complex (McAra, 2006). There has been a growth in the use of the language of rights, responsibilities and restoration and a trend for Scotland to incorporate elements of youth justice legislation (for example, ASBOs and Parenting Orders) similar to those introduced in England:

> Paradoxically, one immediate effect of political devolution has been a greater politicisation of youth justice which seems to be eroding the difference between England and Wales and other UK jurisdictions. In all three we have seen a greater emphasis on due process, just deserts and a retreat from welfare.
>
> (Whyte, 2005, p. 19)

The impact of this welfare and control debate in an institutional setting in Northern Ireland is explored in Chapter 6, 'Institutions'.

Proposals for a new service for young people in England (DfES, 2005) demonstrated clearly that professionals in this organisation will need to continue to work with potentially competing demands, whether described as 'welfare and control' or 'opportunities and responsibilities':

> A minority of young people can get involved in behaviour that is a serious problem for the wider community, including anti-social behaviour and crime. The Government is clear that when this happens we need to respond firmly.
>
> ... This paper is therefore not just about providing more opportunities and support to young people, it is also about challenge. We need to strike the right balance between rights and responsibilities, appreciating the enormous contribution that young people can make while expecting them in return to appreciate and respect the opportunities available to them.
>
> (DfES, 2005, p. 4)

Key points

- The work undertaken with young people changes with the way young people are viewed and how their lives are defined as more or less problematic for society.

- Government policy and legislation, the structure of organisations, and sources and requirements of funding all strongly contribute to shaping the parameters of practice of work with young people.

- Historical perspectives illustrate that some themes and tensions in work with young people are long standing, although they can change as the prevailing philosophy towards young people fluctuates.

2 Measuring performance: targets and outcomes

The purpose of exploring the two historical strands discussed in Section 1 was to help illustrate continuities and connections in the themes we are exploring. Some of these themes, however, have taken on new forms, new ones have emerged and, in many areas, change has also accelerated considerably since the 1990s. Starting with the growth in use of 'targets' in this section, the rest of the chapter will return to analyse some of these more contemporary issues and their impact on practice and the identity of practitioners.

A culture of 'performance measurement' has been promoted by government, advancing the idea that quality practice (and the good use of limited resources) is best demonstrated through the achievement of specified outcomes and targets. These targets usually go beyond the identification of a general area of work with young people and require numbers, percentages and other 'hard evidence' of what work has been done. Other pressures are felt via targets imposing specific timescales; for example, for following up referrals or completing assessments and the additional procedures and paperwork that come with the need to demonstrate achievement. Many practitioners in statutory agencies will have experience of whole rafts of targets and performance frameworks, scrutinised by inspection regimes, as well as the punishments (loss of 'stars', low position in league tables, designated as 'failing') and rewards ('beacon status', the promise of less regulation) that go with them. Voluntary organisations, even if not directly part of these assessment and regulatory frameworks, are constantly pulled into them when seeking funding, as illustrated in Activity 1.

We have already discussed how focusing and refocusing on 'problem' areas and 'problem' young people can cause tensions for organisations and workers, and the drive towards outcome targets can exacerbate this further. This section does not assume that the use of targets is automatically negative, but by focusing on three issues – accountability, quality practice, and ethics – will explore some of the ways of understanding the debate.

2.1 Hitting the target

Activity 3   The impact of targets

Allow 20 minutes   Think back to your responses to Activity 1 and then analyse this more detailed example of target setting.

The government policy document *Transforming Youth Work* (DfEE, 2001) was designed to give a new profile and new funding to youth work in England. To ensure that the government's key areas of concern were focused on, the subsequent document on resources, entitled *Transforming Youth Work: Resourcing Excellent Youth Services* (DfES, 2002), came with clear performance measures and outcome targets: 'it is important that we set specific targets for the local authority youth service so that we can measure improvements in performance' (DfES, 2002, p. 16).

Read the extract below and note what you think the positives of target setting might be and what problems it might create for practitioners or young people.

Annual Youth Service Unique Targets

* 25% of the target population 13–19 reached (to reflect the cultural diversity of the community);

* Of the 25% reached in the 13–19 target population, 60% to undergo personal and social development which results in an accredited[*] outcome;

* The target population will include a locally agreed target for those assessed as not in education, employment or training (NEET) or who are at risk of, or who already fall into the following categories: teenage pregnancy, drugs, alcohol or substance abuse or offending;

* 70% of those participating in youth services expressing satisfaction with the service.

[*Contributing towards a nationally recognised award.]

(DfES, 2002, p. 16)

Comment

On the positive side you may feel these targets were completely reasonable: as the government is giving the money, it should be able to direct the areas in which it is spent. Target setting is therefore a clear way of making a service 'accountable' and demonstrating whether it is 'performing'. It could also be argued that it makes practice (in this instance what youth workers actually do) more transparent. Elsewhere in the document the voices of young people are cited: while young people want 'support' they also want to have 'outcomes from that support'; consequently, it is stressed that outcomes should not be vague, hence the link to accreditation. Other positives may be that this approach will ensure that services are delivered to those most in need and will reflect the cultural diversity of the community. Young people will be asked if they are satisfied with the service they receive (an increasing feature of government policy), which could help ensure that the youth service is involving and listening to young people.

In an article discussing this initiative, Mark Smith (2003) outlines what he sees as some of the problems of this approach (compared with his alternative vision of youth work based on the tradition of 'informal education'). He argues that targeted work in general stigmatises and pathologises 'at risk' young people and inevitably makes work with any other young people harder to justify. Crucially, the focus of the work shifts from building relationships to delivery of the targets. In relation to these specific targets, if accredited activities need to be demonstrated, workers might be under pressure to find young people who will co-operate with this or else push them into certain sorts of activity. Bureaucracy also increases as statistics are needed to demonstrate that targets are being met and the satisfaction levels of young people are being evaluated.

While the views of some young people are quoted in support of these targets, they can also experience them negatively as activities are directed towards specific areas, whether or not these are their main interest. As one young woman has said: 'But what if you want to talk about the happy things, rather than people getting battered and bullied ... We used to do happy things and now its like the Girls Group is about domestic abuse ...' (quoted in Devanney and Pugh, 2005).

While this example is drawn from youth work, teachers, social workers and practitioners in a range of other roles and settings will be familiar with some of these difficulties. The widespread experience of the growth in procedures and paperwork can lead to frustrations about the impact this has on the time to actually do face-to-face work with young people.

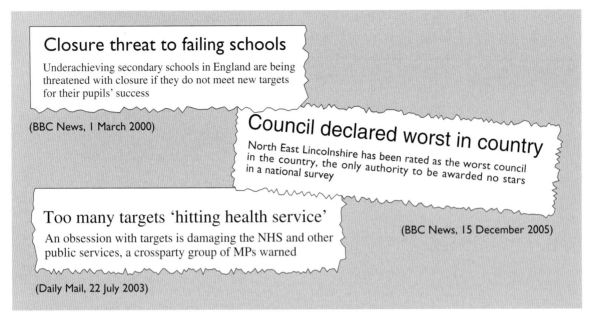

Closure threat to failing schools

Underachieving secondary schools in England are being threatened with closure if they do not meet new targets for their pupils' success

(BBC News, 1 March 2000)

Council declared worst in country

North East Lincolnshire has been rated as the worst council in the country, the only authority to be awarded no stars in a national survey

(BBC News, 15 December 2005)

Too many targets 'hitting health service'

An obsession with targets is damaging the NHS and other public services, a crossparty group of MPs warned

(Daily Mail, 22 July 2003)

The increasing influence of targets

2.2 Three perspectives

Accountability: to whom and for what?

A research project entitled *An Everyday Journey: Discovering the Meaning and Value in Youth Work* (referred to as *EJ*) explored how workers and young people understand the everyday practice experience (the research is discussed in more detail in Chapter 9, 'Support'). In discussing how the evaluation of quality practice fits with the use of outcomes and targets, workers clearly accepted the need for accountability: 'If youth work organisations take funding on the basis of achieving stated government policy targets then they must be expected to be judged on that basis' (*EJ* focus group, Devanney and Pugh, 2005). Some also believed that the profession need not be so 'insecure' that it resists some of its achievements being measured. However, practitioners and researchers alike questioned to whom they were accountable, and for what. Are practitioners only accountable to those who fund their work?

Writing on ethics and accountability in the social professions, Sarah Banks (2004) suggests that there are fundamentally two forms of accountability that will always be present: the professional (accountability to service users) and the public (accountability to the wider public for effectiveness, value for money, etc.). They are interconnected but can also be in conflict. For Banks, the increasing demand for public accountability via specific performance measures means that 'the voices, needs and rights of individual service users and their communities may get lost' (Banks, 2004, p. 151).

Another critical view is offered by Simon Bradford (2000) who sees the increasing concern for evidence of performance as the dominance of an **'instrumental' accountability** – that is, 'primarily concerned with the regulation of individuals and their work' (Bradford, 2000, p. 50) – over an 'ethical' accountability. From this perspective data is a tool for power and control, which consequently requires that work with young people must be made quantifiable. Just as young people are regulated so those working with them also need regulation.

Articulating quality

Spence (2004) offers another perspective on the potential impact of the need for the service to be accountable via these targets. The broad policy aims of the government are not necessarily incompatible with the aims of youth work, but the insistence on outcome targets could be: 'the dominant ethos in youth work is one of "process" rather than "outcome". This does not mean that outcomes are not achieved but that they cannot be prefigured' (Spence, 2004, p. 262). So while young women 'at risk' of getting pregnant can be targeted, 'preventing pregnancy cannot be a predetermined outcome' (p. 265):

> As youth workers we are not going in to stop the pregnancy rate etc. We go with a positive approach – to enhance lives. And you don't know until you start working and building relationships if the young person has issues.
>
> (Quote drawn from Joseph Rowntree Foundation commissioned research in Crimmens *et al.*, 2004, cited in Spence, 2004, p. 265)

Spence argues that relationships in this area of work depend on trust, authenticity and working from the young person's own starting point, and as such the narrow emphasis on targets can be damaging. For youth workers who see themselves as working fundamentally in a holistic way this can be a serious challenge to their professional identity.

This is not just an argument about pressure to practise in a certain way, but the frustrations of practitioners who believe that, as their work is primarily relational, this form of evaluation, via targets, does not capture the real quality of what they do. Given the demands of accountability, are there alternative ways in which practitioners can demonstrate effectiveness? The *Everyday Journey* project was one attempt to do this, to find a 'specific language' and demonstrate that quality practice is about process as well as outcomes.

Concerns about targets defining quality can be found in many other areas of work with young people. A research study in nine Scottish residential children's homes (Watson, 2003) found that workers placed a similar emphasis on quality being about the creation of good relationships that are unrelated to any form of measurement. However, while the majority of these residential workers were highly resistant to performance measures and standards, they were also not well informed about them or their rationale. David Watson suggests that this can also be problematic, as any potential contribution to quality is rejected without a clear basis for alternative definitions:

> However, failure to adopt the standards agenda does not mean that the participants were necessarily adopting a competing and challenging discourse about care. In effect, for the majority of the participants their perception of quality ... was based on their own experience and discussions with colleagues, rather than any formal professional agenda or discourse.
>
> (Watson, 2003, p. 69)

This suggests that, within the demands of the performance culture, there are arguments for practitioners to understand targets, view them critically and try to create a basis for arguing for alternative measures of quality practice. The issue of how we can think further about what constitutes quality practice will be explored in Chapter 2, 'Practice'.

An ethical dimension

Targets are not universally seen in a negative light by those working with young people. In interviews with a range of practitioners, Banks (2004) identifies a link (although not necessarily one articulated by the workers themselves) to a range of different ethical positions. Some workers could recognise that new initiatives, although heavy on targets, could highlight important areas of practice (for example, poor educational outcomes for young people looked after) and could contribute to improving services for young people.

Alongside targets, Banks sees increased procedures and form filling as the key features of the 'new' way in which professionals have to be accountable for their practice. Again, interviews with practitioners produced varying responses. For some, procedures and targets meant clarity, equity, the promotion of welfare and justice and the enhancement of rights, which Banks sees as a view drawing on utilitarian ethics. However, others clearly saw too many procedures and forms as not just inconvenient to themselves, but leading to an inflexibility and undermining of trust which they saw as bad in a moral sense. Banks links this to a different, more partialist virtue ethics or 'ethics of care'.

Again, the argument here is not necessarily that one ethical code is superior, but that these positions can be recognised and a balance created, rather than one prevailing at the expense of the other.

2.3 Challenges from practitioners

The fact that we have been focusing on the powerful impact of targets does not mean that the role and identity of the individual practitioner is wholly dictated by government policy. Some of the examples above show how practitioners can formulate their own voices and views to put alongside their 'top-down' identities. At the level of individual work with young people, decisions can still be made in their interests that may run counter to the targets that a project is set to achieve. Indeed, Mark Lymbery (2000), in analysing social work professionalism, argues that those in face-to-face contact with service users retain a degree of power over what actually happens in practice and therefore the ability to reinterpret some policies flexibly.

Earlier we discussed the historical continuity of the idea that youth work can contribute to liberation (Gilchrist *et al.*, 2003), and there are long traditions in other areas of practice of practitioners explicitly challenging policies that have been imposed by the state both on themselves and on the people with whom they work. Radical social work in the 1970s drew on Marxist ideas to attack the individualised nature of 'casework', arguing that it obscured the structural nature of social problems and that social work should instead focus on mobilising collective action (Bailey and Brake, 1975). Feminist and Black writers subsequently brought additional critiques in the 1980s, leading to the development of anti-oppressive practice that challenges all forms of inequality (Dominelli, 2002). Such perspectives have challenged assumptions behind the way existing youth provision has been structured and argued for appropriate access to services for marginalised groups; for example, provision for young black women (Parmar, 1988). Similarly, new policy developments can be challenged if they are seen not to be taking sufficient account of the voices of socially excluded young people or the forces of that exclusion: for example, racism (Kumrai and Flynn, 2006). Critical views in education too have drawn on ideas such as those of Paolo Freire (1972) that emphasise the political nature of education and role of collective action, and issues of social justice in education can still be raised in relation to current education policies (Thrupp and Tomlinson, 2005). Political perspectives can therefore still be an important source of challenge – for example, in the debate about targets – focusing attention on the key issue of the rationing of diminishing resources.

What practitioners do is mediated through their own beliefs and values. Some will also have professional or occupational codes of values or ethics that can give them another source on which to draw in order to be openly critical of the implications of legislation or policy where these are seen to run counter to the interests of young people (Banks, 2004). Banks identifies a number of these sources of challenge as alternatives to practitioners being in the position of 'reluctant conformity' (Banks, 2004, p. 189). Stanley Tucker (2004) stresses that this debate over values and beliefs must also be had in the arena of professional education and work based training, as these too significantly contribute to the shaping of identity.

Key points

- The increasing use of outcomes and targets has provided a number of challenges to practitioners.
- Considering the issues of accountability, ethics and how to define quality practice can provide different perspectives through which to view critically the debates around outcome targets.
- Dominant policy and theoretical perspectives can be challenged. Individual, political and professional values and beliefs about what work with young people should be about can influence both the shape of practice and how practitioners view themselves.

3 Professionalism and professional identity

So far I have used the terms 'practitioner' and 'professional' more or less interchangeably. However, the word 'professional' tends to carry some implied meanings even if not everyone would agree on what they were. While many of the origins of work with young people were based on the principles of voluntary work, the emergence of the state sector and creation of a variety of specialist roles made the question of professional status more acute. What is it to be 'a professional'? Is this professional identity changing? How important is the professional 'label' and how relevant is it to work with young people?

3.1 'Practitioner' or 'professional'?

Many of the debates about the emergence of the professional are summarised by Linda Finlay (2000). Historically, certain jobs, such as those of doctors and lawyers, have seemed to embody characteristics synonymous with professional status. Factors such as specialist skills and knowledge, the power to make independent judgements, formal codes of conduct, and self regulation were often cited as a defining feature of a profession. You may be aware of some of the critiques of what is sometimes described as this 'essentialist' view of the 'expert' professional, and clearly the expertise of professionals has been coming under increasing challenge and scrutiny in society. Nevertheless, these ideas have remained influential. Against these standards other jobs have been labelled as 'occupations' or accorded 'semi-professional' status: many of them jobs that relate to working with young people. To be accorded professional status (and the power that goes with it), other groups – in teaching, nursing, social work, youth work, etc. – have had to decide whether to aspire to, and have had different degrees of success in achieving, some of the characteristics of that status.

Activity 4   **Who are the professionals?**

Allow 40 minutes   If you currently work with young people, would you describe yourself as a professional and what aspects of your job made you decide? If you are not currently working in this sort of role, try to ask someone who is, or consider which job roles with young people you think are professional ones, and why. Do you think it matters?

If you can, find someone who works with young people in a different type of role (teacher, youth worker, Scout or Guide leader, etc.) and ask them the same questions. Are there any significant differences? Have things changed over time?

Comment

During my own training as a social worker in the late 1980s there was a strong feeling of ambivalence about the idea of being 'a professional'. Somehow to be a professional was to put barriers between ourselves and those we worked with. Aspiring to the professional model of the doctor did not seem to square with sitting on the floor with children or in cafés with 'juvenile offenders'. However, when giving evidence in court, for example, I wanted to be taken seriously as an 'expert' in my area of work, and in meetings with teachers and paediatricians I thought I should have equal status (and would be very irritated if I felt their views were being given more weight than mine). I acquired a formal qualification yet was uncertain about what constituted my 'expert' knowledge and probably saw social work as semi-professional. I was also aware that this view was reflected in the (not very positive) public perception of childcare social work.

Such views are by no means static. A social work colleague who qualified recently seemed surprised when I described this ambivalence. She clearly saw herself as a professional, and saw no conflict with the way she worked with young people. However, the twenty-first century has seen social work training acquire degree status, post qualifying training has increasingly become an expectation, a social care regulatory body has been established, and the term 'social worker' has become a 'protected professional title' in the Care Standards Act 2000. In addition, a strand of thinking has been emphasised: that the 'profession' is improving its expert knowledge by utilising research that provides sound evidence of what actually works in practice. All these factors may have influenced my colleague's perception of her professional identity.

Other workers gave me fascinating insights into this issue. One was surprised that her brother, a coach for a young football club, saw himself as a professional. His view was that this was a result of increased regulation: club coaches even at the teenage level are required to train to FIFA standards and may also undertake training on child protection issues, and so on. Another had one job in a school, where she described herself as 'more' of a professional in this stricter, more detached environment than in her other job in a youth club. This threw up some interesting boundary issues as some of the same young people attend the school (where they call her Mrs Monks) and the youth club (where they call her Cathy). The issue of boundaries in these relationships will be explored further in Chapter 2.

One worker in an after school club was clear that she did not view herself as a professional:

> A professional? – no I don't think so. I mean we don't have that kind of status – not qualified like the teachers in the school and definitely not the pay! ... anyway we are just trying to befriend you know and offer advice but try and make the clubs interesting places for them to come.
>
> (Personal communication)

Nevertheless, she went on to say that she was sure she worked in a 'professional' way – 'approachable', 'fair', 'trustworthy' and appropriately 'confidential' – and pointed out that the project had policies about the way they behaved at work and about what constituted 'professional', and, by implication, 'unprofessional' sorts of behaviour. Her comment perhaps brings into question the importance of having a professional label at all in the context of face-to-face work with young people.

Katie Deverell and Ursula Sharma (2000) researched the issue of professional identity among workers in newer occupational fields. In the case of HIV prevention outreach workers they discovered that, while these workers did not see themselves as professionals, they felt it was important to draw on the idea of professionalism and borrowed ethical values from counselling and social work (boundaries again being particularly significant). They were ambivalent about adopting the 'professional' label, associating it with a history of discrimination against gay men, but wanted a form of 'professionalism' that could include the value of personal relationships and the use of shared sexual identity and experience.

3.2 The ups and downs of professionalism

Critiques of professionalism have largely centred on issues of power. Self regulation can be seen not just as a characteristic of a profession but the means by which the group became one – laying claim to an area of expertise and then restricting access to it. The construction of professional groups can also be viewed as a class, race and gender issue, with a history in traditional middle class white male professions and a resistance to newer 'female' dominated areas of work. Professional language and jargon too has been seen as a way to protect the professional and disempower the service user (Finlay, 2000).

It may be that if you had questioned a teacher for Activity 4, they would have had a clear view about having professional status and being an established profession. At the same time they may also have felt that this status had changed over time or had been undermined. While some work groups are aspiring to professionalism, the concept itself has been under attack from many sources. Partly this is as a result of government policies that have stressed the importance of management and the role of external regulation, inspection and targets: a trend often described as **managerialism**. In addition, new job roles have been created which cut across existing professional groups (for example, personal advisers for young people), while others have been seen to require not 'professional' training but 'technical' training in how to perform specific tasks. This is often summarised as a process of **'deprofessionalisation'** (Malin, 2000), which some authors see as an inexorable process for all those working with young people. Karen Healy and Gabrielle Meagher (2004), writing from an Australian social work perspective, see this trend as one shared in Britain, the USA and Canada and primarily meaning: 'the fragmentation and routinization of social work and the concomitant loss of opportunities for the exercise of creativity, reflexivity and discretion in direct practice' (Healy and Meagher, 2004, p. 244).

There are alternative visions of professionalism that have attempted to incorporate some of the very reasons why many of those working with young people have previously rejected the professional label. This **'reprofessionalisation** project' proposes a more equal and empowering relationship with service users (Banks, 2004).

There are therefore different and seemingly contradictory forces impacting on the identity of professionals and the meaning of professionalism. An interesting illustration in the probation service is provided by Janet Newman and Sandra Nutley (2003). Over the course of a decade they plot the impact of the rise of the 'what works' culture (basing practice on research of what has 'proven' effectiveness: the theoretical basis for this approach is discussed in Chapter 2). The shift to this culture was initially interpreted as a force for deprofessionalisation: 'The idea of professionalism

Practitioners can experience changes in the concept of professionalism

itself is decoupled from its associations with discretion and judgement and recoupled to "what works" and the standardised practices that flow from it' (Newman and Nutley, 2003, p. 554).

Interviews with probation officers indicated a long standing resistance to changing practice, but then a gradual acceptance as it was perceived as strengthening their professional status. As one probation officer commented:

> I think probation has always been seen as much more professional than, say, social work. I think 'what works' has added to that. When we do training for magistrates on what works they are impressed because it's structured and consistent and they like that, they know exactly what the sentence is.
>
> (Quoted in Newman and Nutley, 2003, p. 559)

Newman and Nutley conclude that this is evidence that, rather than just being eroded, professional boundaries can also shift: 'creating new divisions upon which the profession might reconstruct itself' (p. 561).

Finally, this book and its companion volume (Kehily, 2007b) emphasise the importance of a **'biographical' perspective** as a way of understanding young people's experiences. From this perspective we could argue that the biographies of professionals are equally influential on the way in which they form their identity. Numerous generalisations can be made about what it means to be a professional in the twenty-first century, but there is also the construction of this meaning at an individual level. As Ivor Goodson (2003) comments in relation to the professional lives of teachers:

> teacher professionalism is complex and not definitive: there is no absolute model. Each teacher has to construct a personal professionalism that suits his or her life history, training, context

and, above all, personality. A great deal of that professionalism is learnt, constructed and necessarily sustained in the everyday working environment of the school.

(Goodson, 2003, p. 74)

The perspectives of young people

In consultation with children and young people about 'being safe', the Children's Rights Director for England (a post established by the Children Act 2004 to promote the views and interests of children and young people) summarises answers to the question of 'what staff should be trained in':

> They should be taught 'what looking after really means'. This includes having lots of key skills, having the right attitudes to children and young people, being good at communicating with young people of different ages, and accepting things like not having the right to shout at children if you feel like it. It also means treating each child as an individual, not as one of hundreds. This is a common view children and young people have given us in many of our different consultations on different subjects over the past two years.

(Morgan, 2004, p. 25)

The perspectives of young people tend to reinforce the point that it is not the professional label or professional expertise that is most important in encounters with adults seeking to 'practice' on them. Attitudes and interpersonal skills are emphasised, specialist knowledge and qualifications are secondary – useful, but not always essential.

As mentioned in the Introduction, this chapter has grouped together as practitioners an extremely diverse range of people in a way that might not be logical to young people. Even so, many commonalties emerge when young people are consulted. The *Listening to Children and Young People* project (Ahmad *et al.*, 2003) consulted 234 children and young people, aged between 10 and 20 years, on a number of issues, including their perceptions of a wide range of professional workers, such as teachers, social workers, sports coaches, Scout and Guide leaders, personal advisers and religious leaders.

Some specific groups of young people did stress particular issues relevant to their circumstances. For young people looked after by the local authority, for example, consistency and trust were among their main concerns:

> If they didn't go for a while you could learn how to trust them, but you'd learnt how to trust them and they'd disappear and then you've got to get another one and you've got to trust them again and then they disappear; it just really hassles you, you just don't want to.

(Quoted in Ahmad *et al.*, 2003, p. 59)

Across the board, however, common themes were repeated. What they wanted were professionals who treated them with respect, were able to listen and were friendly, helpful and trustworthy. For example, young people excluded from school but attending a pupil referral unit (PRU) could identify the positives in the PRU staff who were "*"laid back"*, listened before speaking, and, very importantly, were prepared to give the respondents a *"second chance"*" (Ahmad *et al.*, 2003, p. 61)

These perspectives need to be seen in relation to the complex and sometimes extremely difficult circumstances in which many practitioners are working. Some of the quotations from young people neatly sum up the complexity for some practitioners of getting the balance and boundaries right: 'They shouldn't shout, or ignore it when someone's being picked on. Should be kind. Also be a prat but not too much of one – able to muck about, but not too much' (young person with learning difficulties, quoted in Ahmad *et al.*, 2003, p. 62).

This emphasis on interpersonal skills does not negate the role of expert knowledge but puts it into context alongside forming effective working relationships with young people. This raises the question of how this can be integrated into the idea of professionalism discussed in the last subsection.

3.3 Relationships, participation and power

The interaction between practitioners and young people does not take place in a static environment. Practitioners must engage with the changing realities of young people's lives (Henderson *et al.*, 2007) and a shifting social context which brings with it changing expectations and demands. We will consider two illustrations of this here: the nature of social relationships and the demands for more participatory ways of working. The broader impact of both these themes will be explored further in Chapters 2, 'Practice', and 3, 'Participation', but the focus here is on their impact on power relationships and, in turn, the role and identity of practitioners.

Several strands of the discussion of practitioner/professional identity relate to the issue of power. The 'professional project' itself has been interpreted as work groups claiming and maintaining power for themselves. The example from probation given above (Newman and Nutley, 2003) illustrated one professional group maintaining professional power in relation to other groups in the criminal justice field. For Bradford (2000) the imposition of targets is a way of the state controlling and regulating the activities of professionals. What of the relationship between the practitioner and the young people with whom they work? Is this power dynamic changing? And, if so, what forces are acting on the relationship?

Activity 5   Power relationships

Allow 10 minutes

To begin thinking about power relationships, consider the position of a young person who wants to make a complaint to a teacher or social worker. Why might they feel powerless (or powerful)? Would it make a difference if they wanted to make a complaint to a worker in an after school club?

Comment

There is obviously a range of power dynamics at play here in addition to those between adult and child. Some practitioners have powers that derive from the state through legislation; for example, the police and social workers. Young people have little control, for instance, over whether or not they have to go to school. Research and inquiry reports have long established that young people in care do not feel they have a strong voice in the procedures in which they are involved (Dalrymple, 2005). Even practitioners with less obvious power than teachers or social workers will have an understanding of adult systems that a young person may not.

Your answers will have depended on what kind of young person you were thinking of. Feelings of powerlessness can be stronger the more marginalised (or socially excluded) someone feels within society. Many disabled young people, for example, will have experienced particular difficulties in getting their voice heard.

This does not suggest that young people have no power; many show active resistance to the powers of professionals by confrontation, non-engagement and silence. However, through this they may also be reinforcing a perception that they are 'troublesome' young people.

While power relationships remain unequal, there are processes taking place that affect this dynamic. In the previous subsection we explored some of the contradictory forces that affect professional identity. All practitioners are open to more challenge: in the courts and through inspections, inquiries into misconduct, scrutiny by the media and the demands of all of us to have a voice in decision making about our own lives. Social attitudes have been changing; there is no longer the unquestioning 'trust' or 'respect' for doctors, teachers or other professionals. This decline in trust and status can be seen as part of a broader shift in society related to major economic and technological changes.

One theme explored throughout this book and its companion volume (Kehily, 2007b) is to consider the relevance of 'late modern' theory to these debates about young people. This draws on the ideas of the sociologists

Ulrich Beck (2004) and Anthony Giddens (1995) that: 'The modes of life brought into being by modernity have swept us away from *all* traditional types of social order, in quite unprecedented fashion' (Giddens, 1995, p. 4). One specific consequence of this '**detraditionalisation**' is that being a 'professional' with a claim to 'expertise' is no longer an automatic guarantee of respect and authority. In a society where the 'hierarchical model of social class and stratification has increasingly been subverted' (Beck, 2004, p. 91), authority and respect are seen as something that must be earned rather than given.

It is argued that the effects of these changes are generational, affecting the younger generation more radically than that of their parents, and there is evidence that this requirement – for 'earned' respect – is more marked with young people. In a study of young people's values, Rachel Thomson and Janet Holland (2002) interviewed young people who were able to give examples of teachers who were not granted automatic respect or authority, but who had earned 'moral authority' through the way in which they behaved and, in particular, *how they exercised their power*:

> Our study draws attention to the importance of the moral relationship that underlies relationships of authority in young people's lives. It is clear from young people's accounts that attention to the quality of such relationships, a commitment to reciprocity and an awareness of the operations and effects of power are qualities that make the difference to young people's ability to learn, trust and develop.
>
> (Thomson and Holland, 2002, p. 114)

Another defining issue of change for practitioners in recent years has been the increasing demand on them to consult and work more meaningfully in partnership with the 'users' of their services. Consultation and participation became an essential part of the partnership ideal at the heart of the Labour government's modernisation strategies from the late 1990s, an emphasis embraced in principle in all UK jurisdictions:

> In recent years, the participation of children and young people in policy decision-making has gained unprecedented policy prominence in the UK. Children and young people are now regularly consulted by local, devolved, and national government bodies ... Children and young people's participation has never before been a more popular policy demand.
>
> (Tisdall and Davis, 2004, p. 131)

This demand for more participation is, however, not just a product of policy but, in relation to young people, a product of other drivers and social trends. Ruth Sinclair (2004, p. 107) outlines other factors that she believes have contributed to this change:

- recognition of children's rights (for example, the impact of the United Nations Convention on the Rights of the Child)
- young people being seen increasingly as 'social actors' capable of being involved in decision making
- the broader growth of the consumer movement which increasingly includes young people as 'users' of services.

While participation is described and defined in a variety of ways (Sinclair, 2004; Dalrymple, 2005), there is some agreement that it can be seen as having different 'levels'. These levels can be seen to be characterised by the degree to which power is shared and influence is meaningful, ranging from examples of one-off consultation to young people being able to take the lead and initiate change.

For practitioners across a wide spectrum of work the principle of young people having greater involvement in decision making about their own lives will be uncontroversial. A commitment to empowerment had been a feature of much individual practice before it became popular government policy and rhetoric. Nevertheless, some of these 'levels' of participation require a significant adjustment in power relationships with changing expectations that pose challenges even for practitioners who feel they are already committed to working in partnership.

In Activity 5 we could have explored the factors that affect whether the professionals involved feel powerful or powerless. The dynamics of such encounters can be complicated by the fact that some practitioners do not feel as though they have very much power. Many also work in organisational environments that do not empower them to work, in turn, in an empowering way. Organisational constraints result in individual practitioners feeling that certain aspects of the system are not within their control; there is therefore also an issue of honesty about how much power is really being shared or given away.

Key points

- The wide range of practitioners in this area of work will identify themselves differently in relation to the label of 'the professional', depending on their training, values and personal biography.
- The idea of 'the professional' is complex and contested. Different forces both internally, from within work groups, and externally, from government policy and society, are constantly shifting the nature of professionalism.
- The perspectives of young people emphasise that their key concerns are the attitudes and interpersonal skills of practitioners they encounter.
- The use of professional power remains a key concern for young people. Changing social relations and increasing demands for participative

ways of working are also raising new challenges for practitioners as power relations are questioned.

4 All joined up: partnerships and inter-professionalism

Having looked at some aspects of professional and practitioner identity, there is one further area of change that brings individual identity into sharp focus. This occurs when practitioners are required to work more closely with others from different agencies and professional cultures.

The idea that, in order to help young people and their families address complex problems, individual agencies need to work more closely together is not new. Concerted efforts have been made over many decades to encourage health and social services to work together, and 'working together' has long been a mantra in the area of child protection as successive inquiries into serious injuries and deaths have pointed to failures in communication between different agencies. Many practitioners will have palready experienced co-location with other services, 'one-stop shops' and working in multi-agency teams.

There can be little doubt, however, that this process has been accelerated since the late 1990s when the planning and delivery of services through 'partnerships' became a major plank of the Labour government's policy to modernise public services. Partnerships were to include all 'stakeholders' across professional boundaries: statutory, voluntary and private sectors, and crucially, as we have discussed, service users. An array of initiatives focusing on young people in England and Wales followed this model to tackle health concerns, social exclusion, teenage pregnancy, school non-attendance, and so on, in the shape of various strategic partnerships and action zones. This partnership approach and integration agenda has been equally positively pursued by the Scottish Executive (Glaister and Glaister, 2005).

Although collaboration rather than major structural change was stressed, nevertheless new organisations have subsequently been established. In England, the government's adoption of the recommendations of the Laming Report (Laming, 2003), following an inquiry into the death of Victoria Climbié, moved the 'working together' debate on by setting in motion major restructuring, bringing children's social services together with education – and, potentially, other agencies – into the same agency. This restructuring was backed up by other mechanisms designed to overcome the problems of multi-agency working, focusing on easier information sharing, common skills and frameworks for assessment (DfES, 2004).

Government policy on the future of working with young people also envisaged a structural change creating an integrated youth support service involving a wide range of providers, including voluntary and community groups. For those working in non statutory agencies this also creates different tensions. They have been made an essential part of partnerships, yet often do not feel sufficiently consulted over new developments (Cripps, 2005). Neither do they necessarily have the same financial or resource backing: existing power relationships have not altered (Balloch and Taylor, 2001).

The terminology – inter-professional, multi-agency, partnerships etc. – tends to be used in an overlapping way even though the terms do not mean exactly the same thing. However, the main implication is clear: that practitioners working with children and young people are increasingly working more closely with, in the same team as, or for the same organisation as, those who might previously have been seen as 'other' professionals.

What have been the implications of these changes for practitioners and their identities? Are they successful? And what messages are there for making these new collaborations work?

Services are increasingly delivered by multi-agency working

4.1 Multi-agency working?

Activity 6 The experience of a CAMHS team

Allow 10 minutes

The following quotations are taken from members of a multi-agency child and adolescent mental health team (CAMHS) who are discussing the experience of trying to set up a specialist service for 16–19-year-olds. As you read them, note down the issues and problems you think these views reveal.

> Voluntary services ... tend to be ... easier to access ... with health and social services things take a lot longer, and there seems to be issues around criteria ... access is a problem.
>
> (Primary mental health worker)

> It's a bit disjointed really ... it's down to people on the ground, individuals, rather than it being a thought out process.
>
> (Primary mental health worker)

> Agencies tend to plan in their silos ... but communications between them have traditionally been relatively poor.
>
> (Social services manger)

> ... the arguments amongst the agencies are about whose responsibility it is ... that's the issue that gets in the way.
>
> (Educational psychologist)

> We're not always clear ourselves as agencies about what we offer, that's distinct from what other organisations offer.
>
> (Non statutory families services manager)
>
> (Quoted in Richards and Vostanis, 2004, pp. 121–3)

Comment

The quotations above may seem familiar if you have worked in a similar setting; they highlight the common problems of bureaucracy in the statutory agencies, the valuable role the voluntary sector can play, lack of clear planning and protocols, and the role of communication and arguments over who is responsible (perhaps the real question often being 'who is going to pay?'). They also suggest a lack of clarity among workers themselves about their distinctiveness and boundaries. For the young people who might use this service the problems are not only between 'child and adolescent' professional groups, but also across the boundaries of child and adult care service provision.

Interestingly, the research with this team revealed a very high motivation among many of its members to establish the new service (explored further in Chapter 8, 'Safeguarding') and noted that few new resources were needed. Nevertheless, getting it underway remained highly problematic.

For Peter Reder and Sylvia Duncan (2003), in their examination of the Victoria Climbié inquiry report (Laming, 2003), not enough attention is paid to the nature of interpersonal communication. They argue that what is described as a lack of communication is often misunderstanding the nature and meaning of what was communicated across professional boundaries. They are critical of yet another restructuring proposal that assumes that:

communication between relevant professionals would improve if agency boundaries were dissolved and they all worked together within the same organizational structure. This call for reorganization fundamentally misses the point about the psychology of communication: that individuals and groups create their own boundaries based on beliefs, attitudes, work pressures, and so on. Furthermore, each episode of communication has an interpersonal dynamic of its own and clarity of understanding will not necessarily be enhanced by different organizational structures. In our view, efforts to enhance professionals' capacity to think, and therefore to communicate would be more rewarding.

(Reder and Duncan, 2003, pp. 95–6)

Research in an integrated child health service by Sue White and Brid Featherstone (2005), focusing on 'inter-professional talk', illustrated that the roles of different professionals are often 'performed' and ritualised by the way in which practitioners talk about cases, reinforcing the validity of their own views and casting other professions in a negative light. Examples include the use of stories about particular cases emphasising the incompetence of some professionals, and judgements about the length of time taken by different professional groups to complete assessments. Therefore, despite geographical proximity, certain practices served to maintain the differentiation between one part of the service and another. These authors too are sceptical about the government's reliance on the creation of new structures.

While the issues raised by the authors above are significant, they represent just two theories in a growing literature on barriers to joint working in all its forms (Cameron and Lart, 2003; Salmon, 2004). It seems clear that behind the positive rhetoric there are numerous issues, both structural and in relation to professional culture, power, trust, misunderstanding and communication, all of which pose major challenges for practitioners and potentially undermine the supposed gains to young people of this style of working.

4.2 Inter-agency learning

The uncertain professional identity noted by one practitioner in Activity 6 raises the question of whether, in a multi-professional environment, roles become more interchangeable, or whether each 'professional' is bringing distinct skills and knowledge. Do professional identities sharpen or become more blurred?

Multi-agency Youth Offending Teams (YOTs) were created in England and Wales in 1998, drawing together a range of practitioners involved in youth justice with the intention of offering a comprehensive response to the needs of young offenders. Research by Nick Frost *et al.* (2005), which included practitioners in a youth justice team, found that divisions of opinion frequently emerged that seemed to be based on different professional values. This was illustrated by an issue of whether a young offender should go on a trip abroad, social workers tending to be more exclusively focused on the needs of the young person, the police believing that it was reasonable for this to be balanced with a victim perspective. Social workers and probation officers too appeared to have divergent views on 'breaching' (returning to court young people who had not complied with the conditions of an order), with social workers seemingly less keen to breach, emphasising an approach about 'getting back on track', probation officers stressing the public interest and the importance of enforcing the rules.

While drawing out the inevitable stresses and strains of such conflicts, the researchers also found that this team appeared to be able to cope with this difference and working relationships were reported as being positive. Their analysis draws on a conceptual framework, developed by Etienne Wenger (1998), of a 'social' learning theory. This suggests that such a team can be viewed as a '**community of practice**' – a team that can combine the knowledge that individual practitioners bring to it with knowledge created *in* practice by the interaction between, and shared experience of, team members. A culture can then develop which allows for both 'the containment of difference' (Frost *et al.*, 2005, p. 190) and the modification of models of practice. Wenger emphasises that this theory of learning has important implications for individual identity. Interestingly, the view is reported from one practitioner in the YOT team (a youth support worker) that over time they observed the views of probation officers and social workers in relation to breaching begin to converge, each 'softening' or 'hardening' the other.

Frost *et al.* conclude that one of the challenges for practitioners therefore is to reflect on which practice is based on their 'core' values and which can be modified with the experience of team working. This would require an ability to think critically about their own role and the dynamics of the team. However, the authors illustrate that this can be a challenging task, citing an example of a health based team in which the social worker felt that their 'social model' of health was being subordinated to the dominant 'medical model' in the team.

Inevitably, power relations play their role in this process. Relations within multi-agency teams are not equal but overlaid with issues of the relative status, gender and ethnicity of the professionals within them. A convergence of ideas about practice will therefore not necessarily be equal: the more marginal the status of the practitioner, the less influential their knowledge and values might be. The model of a community of practice does, however, recognise the potential value of 'peripheral' members to group learning, and Frost *et al.* (2005) stress the importance of valuing such members.

4.3 The lead professional

Despite some successful multi-agency work, it has been a frequent complaint from families that contact with many professionals is still required and finding the right information from the right person can be a very frustrating process. The preference for families to have a single point of contact has been identified in several consultations and research studies, particularly in relation to disabled children and young people with complex health needs (Abbott *et al.*, 2005). This idea of a 'key' or 'lead' worker has become more generally enshrined in government policy and, for example, the new youth service in England also proposes to use this 'lead professional' system: 'We want every young person who needs support in a number of overlapping areas to have a nominated lead professional who will be a single point of contact and make sure support is provided in a co-ordinated, convenient and integrated way' (DfES, 2005, p. 9).

The lead professional concept can cut across established professional boundaries. A service introduced in Cornwall for children with complex needs, highlighted the broad range of professionals who have adopted the role. Social workers, health visitors, nurses, teachers and portage workers were all represented among the 43 key workers (Halliday and Asthana, 2004).

Despite the logic of having a single worker to relate to and who will lead families and young people through the maze of professionals and services, the demands this places on the practitioners concerned are numerous. It assumes, for example, that all professionals will have the necessary skills and that they will be able to access the expertise of the rest of their team. In the Cornwall service key workers reported that lack of acknowledgement of the time and resources needed for the role was placing the system under strain. Research with children, young people and parents has shown that its effectiveness is also variable in practice (Abbott *et al.*, 2005). Families were not always clear about what the key worker's role was; sometimes it did cut down on the amount of meetings and appointments and provided helpful advice, but this was by no means universal.

The research by Abbott *et al.* (2005) and that by Halliday and Asthana (2004) both return us to the underlying issue of the balance between professional knowledge and interpersonal skills. A positive view of workers who took time to work directly with the disabled young people re-emphasised that it is about not just the role of the relationship but also its nature. The professionals, when asked which qualities were of most importance to their new lead role, similarly stressed interpersonal skills rather than professional expertise.

In response to proposals for a new youth service, Howard Williamson (2005) posed a different set of questions about lead professionals which may be more relevant to the perspective of young people.

- Does the person have to be a 'professional'? This is contrasted with the idea of a 'trusted adult', which Williamson argues is more in tune with the thinking of young people.

- What choice will be available to young people in being allocated their lead professional and how might they change from one lead professional to another?

- When will they be available? Williamson points to discussions about the value of 24-hour availability and the frustrations that young people have expressed at important practitioners in their lives not being easily available.

Key points

- Inter-professional working has increasingly been seen as the solution to complex work with young people. Research reveals substantial difficulties in practice that can undermine its positive intention.

- It has been suggested that different professionals can work successfully together if they can create a positive learning environment – a community of practice. A challenge remains for individual professionals as to what in their identity can be merged with others and what remains distinct about their values and contribution.

- The role of the 'lead professional' has been significant in new developments. Studies reveal a number of issues that need to be grappled with if the role is to be successful. They also reinforce the underlying importance of relationships and interpersonal skills.

Conclusion

There are a myriad of issues and pressures that currently confront practitioners in a rapidly changing environment and it has only been possible to consider a few of them in any detail. Some long standing competing themes have been identified, together with the challenges of targets, partnerships and professionalism as they relate to the more recent policy context. However, the themes introduced here will echo in the discussions in the following chapters about practice in specific settings and in different types of encounters with young people. Their effects are complex and neither wholly positive nor wholly negative, but their impact on practitioners and the young people they work with needs to be viewed critically and seen within their changing social context. These themes also have an impact on what it means to be a practitioner or a professional. Each practitioner will form an identity, with or without the professional label, having to take account of the demands of changing policy and their own experience, training, values and perspectives on what working with young people is all about.

References

Abbott, D., Watson, D. and Townsley, R. (2005) 'The proof of the pudding: what difference does multi-agency working make to families with disabled children with complex health care needs?', *Child and Family Social Work*, vol. 10, no. 3, pp. 229–38.

Ahmad, Y., Dalrymple, J., Daum, M., Griffith, N., Hockridge, T. and Ryan, E. (2003) *Listening to Children and Young People*, Bristol, University of the West of England.

Bailey, R. and Brake, M. (eds) (1975) *Radical Social Work and Practice*, London, Arnold.

Balloch, S. and Taylor, M. (2001) *Partnership Working: Policy and Practice*, Bristol, Policy Press.

Banks, S. (2004) *Ethics, Accountability and the Social Professions*, Basingstoke, Palgrave.

Beck, U. (2004) *Risk Society: Towards a New Modernity*, London, Sage.

Booton, F. (1985) *Studies in Social Education, Volume 1: 1860–1890*, Hove, Benfield Press.

Bradford, S. (2000) 'Disciplining practices: new ways of making youth workers accountable', *International Journal of Adolescence and Youth*, vol. 9, pp. 45–63.

Cameron, A. and Lart, R. (2003) 'Factors promoting and obstacles hindering joint working: a systematic review of the research evidence', *Journal of Integrated Care*, vol. 11, no. 2, pp. 9–17.

Crimmens, D., Factor, F., Jeffs, T., Pitts, J., Pugh, C., Spence, J. and Turner, P. (2004) *Reaching Socially Excluded Young People: A National Study of Street-Based Youth Work*, Leicester, Joseph Rowntree Foundation/National Youth Agency.

Cripps, C. (2005) 'Voluntary sector: silent partners', *Young People Now*, 2 November, www.ypnmagazine.com/news/index.cfm?fuseaction=full_news&ID=8673 [accessed 07/12/05].

Dalrymple, J. (2005) 'Constructions of child and youth advocacy: emerging issues in advocacy practice', *Children and Society*, vol. 19, no. 1, pp. 3–15.

Devanney, C. and Pugh, C. (2005) Research for *An Everyday Journey: Discovering the Meaning and Value in Youth Work*, unpublished research project, Durham University/ Weston Spirit.

Deverell, K. and Sharma, U. (2000) 'Professionalism in everyday practice. Issues of trust, experience and boundaries' in Malin, N. (ed.) *Professionalism, Boundaries and the Workplace*, London, Routledge.

DfEE (Department for Education and Employment) (2001) *Transforming Youth Work: Developing Youth Work for Young People*, Nottingham, Department for Education and Employment/Connexions.

DfES (Department for Education and Skills) (2002) *Transforming Youth Work: Resourcing Excellent Youth Services*, London, Department for Education and Skills.

DfES (Department for Education and Skills) (2004) *Every Child Matters: Next Steps*, Nottingham, DfES Publications.

DfES (Department for Education and Skills) (2005) *Youth Matters*, Cm 6629, Norwich, The Stationery Office.

Dominelli, L. (2002) 'Anti-oppressive practice in context' in Adams, R., Dominelli, L. and Payne, M. (eds) *Social Work: Themes, Issues and Critical Debates*, Basingstoke, Palgrave/The Open University.

Finlay, L. (2000) 'The challenge of professionalism' in Brechin, A., Brown, H. and Eby, M. (eds) *Critical Practice in Health and Social Care*, London, Sage/The Open University.

Freire, P. (1972) *Pedagogy of the Oppressed*, Harmondsworth, Penguin.

Frost, N., Robinson, M. and Anning, A. (2005) 'Social workers in multidisciplinary teams: issues and dilemmas for professional practice', *Child and Family Social Work*, vol. 10, no. 3, pp. 187–96.

Giddens, A. (1995) *The Consequences of Modernity*, Cambridge, Polity Press.

Gilchrist, R., Jeffs, T. and Spence, J. (eds) (2003) *Architects of Change: Studies in the History of Community and Youth Work*, Leicester, National Youth Agency.

Glaister, A. and Glaister, B. (2005) *Inter-Agency Collaboration: Providing for Children*, Edinburgh, Dunedin Academic Press.

Goodson, I. (2003) *Professional Knowledge, Professional Lives: Studies in Education and Change*, Maidenhead, Open University Press.

Halliday, J. and Asthana, S. (2004) 'The emergent role of the link worker: a study in collaboration', *Journal of Interprofessional Care*, vol. 18, no. 1, pp. 17–28.

Healy, K. and Meagher, G. (2004) 'The reprofessionalization of social work: collaborative approaches for achieving professional recognition', *British Journal of Social Work*, vol. 34, no. 2, pp. 243–60.

Henderson, S., Holland, J., McGrellis, S., Sharpe, S. and Thomson, R. (2007) *Inventing Adulthoods: A Biographical Approach to Youth Transitions*, London, Sage (Set Book).

Home Office (1997) *No More Excuses*: *A New Approach to Tackling Youth Crime in England and Wales*, London, HMSO.

Jeffs, T. and Smith, K. (1996) *Informal Education: Conversation, Democracy and Learning*, Nottingham, Education Now Publishing Co-operative.

Jeffs, T. and Smith, M. (2002) 'Individualisation and youth work', *Youth and Policy*, no. 76, pp. 39–65.

Kehily, M.J. (2007a) 'A cultural perspective' in Kehily, M.J. (ed.) *Understanding Youth: Perspectives, Identities and Practices*, London, Sage/The Open University (Course Book).

Kehily, M.J. (ed.) (2007b) *Understanding Youth: Perspectives, Identities and Practices*, London, Sage/The Open University (Course Book).

Kumrai, R. and Flynn, R. (2006) 'Youth matters: opportunities, inconsistencies and omissions', *Representing Children*, vol. 18, no. 2, pp. 96–110.

Laming, H. (2003) *The Victoria Climbié Inquiry: Report of an Inquiry by Lord Laming*, Norwich, The Stationery Office.

Lymbery, M. (2000) 'The retreat from professionalism: from social worker to care manager' in Malin, N. (ed.) *Professionalism, Boundaries and the Workplace*, London, Routledge.

Malin, N. (ed.) (2000) *Professionalism, Boundaries and the Workplace*, London, Routledge.

McAra, L. (2006) 'Welfare in crisis? Key developments in Scottish youth justice' in Muncie, J. and Goldson, B. (eds) *Comparative Youth Justice*, London, Sage.

Morgan, R. (2004) *Safe from Harm: Children's Views Report*, Newcastle, Commission for Social Care Inspection.

Muncie, J. and Goldson, B. (2006) 'England and Wales: the new correctionalism' in Muncie, J. and Goldson, B. (eds) *Comparative Youth Justice*, London, Sage.

Newman, J. and Nutley, S. (2003) 'Transforming the probation service: "what works" organisational change and professional identity', *Policy and Politics*, vol. 31, no. 4, pp. 547–63.

Osgerby, B. (1998) *Youth in Britain*, Oxford, Blackwell.

Parmar, P. (1988) 'Gender, race and power: the challenge to youth work practice' in Cohen, P. and Bains, H. (eds) *Multi-Racist Britain*, London, Macmillan.

This chapter will address the following core questions:

- What are the main features of practice with young people?
- How does practice change and how can it be improved?
- What is the nature and role of 'relationship' in work with young people?
- How can reflection and reflexivity contribute to improving practice?
- What is critical practice and what does it offer to work with young people?

1 Making sense of practice

What defines 'practice' and distinguishes it from other forms of interaction? You may come into contact with young people in a range of settings and for a variety of reasons (perhaps through family contact, work relationships or voluntary activities), but would you see your involvement as a form of 'practice'? As a parent, for example, I would not describe my interaction with my children as 'practice'. However, as a children and families social worker, the language of practice was very familiar and it felt like a useful shorthand expression for the work we were doing. So when does involvement or interaction become 'practice'? A key distinction may be the context within which the interaction and any associated decision making takes place; more specifically, whether it is a private or a professional context.

Activity 1   Taking decisions

Allow 30 minutes   Look at the two scenarios below. What is different between responding to the situation in a private/informal relationship (for example, as a parent) and doing so professionally (for example, as a residential worker or foster carer)? Note down the key differences in each case.

1   John, who is aged 15, wants to go to a friend's party and stay overnight. He asks the following two people if this is all right:
    –   his father
    –   the manager of the children's home where he is living.

2   Beverley, aged 14, has broken up with her boyfriend. She comes in and bursts into tears. What do you do:
    –   as her best friend
    –   as the male youth worker running the youth club?

Comment

This activity highlights three differences between private and professional decision making. The first, and most obvious, is that for a parent to give permission for their teenage child to stay out overnight is a private matter.

There is not, and could not be, any effective scrutiny of such a decision. Nor should there be. By and large, the assumption is that parents should be left alone to get on with the job of being a parent. Only if their parenting is seen to be seriously problematic, or if the young person's behaviour is provoking concern outside the family, will external agencies, 'the state', intervene. Family life involves private informal negotiation over many issues and it is assumed that their child's welfare will be the parents' central concern.

In contrast, the manager of the children's home, though also concerned with John's welfare, will not have the same discretion about how to respond. For many who work with young people, the law and local and national policies and organisational procedures frame what action can be taken and the factors that ought to be taken into account. So a worker's response is not simply a matter of personal preference.

Second, many who work with young people act within a *system of accountability*. In the past, some abuses of power have gone unchecked and unchallenged, and mistakes have been made, however well intentioned the decisions. Systems of accountability are designed to protect young people when they are outside the presumed safety of their home.

Third, the youth worker in Beverley's story may be concerned about *boundaries* and overstepping the line between giving caring support and comfort, and inappropriate intimacy. A parent or 'best friend' would not necessarily be faced with this problem – their boundaries would be different and differently negotiated.

The idea of practice covers a whole range of interactions and relationships between adults and young people but, as Activity 1 suggests, also provides a useful shorthand expression to distinguish between professional work with young people and the more private roles and relationships of parent or friend. The focus on *professional practice* – that is, on work that takes place in the public rather than the private or domestic arena – includes two related aspects: first, where someone is working as *a professional* (see discussion in Chapter 1, 'Practitioners') and second, where a person is acting *in a professional manner*. These are not necessarily the same thing. So here I will use the term 'practice' to refer both to formal professional work with young people (for example, as a teacher, youth worker, health adviser or counsellor) and to work undertaken with young people in less formal settings or as a volunteer (for example, as coach for a local football team or as a Scout group leader). In the latter examples, the defining issue is the assumption that these are contexts in which the worker would have some notion of and expect to act in *a professional manner*.

Practice: purpose and process

So, what does practice actually involve? At one level, 'practice' is simply a way of referring to all the different tasks undertaken in work with young people, although I have already added to this basic definition by 'locating' it in the public/professional domain. Although practice takes place within a range of settings and within different procedural frameworks, it is likely to include some or all of the following:

- (a formal or informal process of) assessment
- decision making and planning
- intervention/activity
- evaluation
- closure
- recording
- monitoring.

This suggests that work with young people is, at some level, always *purposive*. In formal settings, the agenda may be more explicit, as the discussion in Chapter 1 about targets and outcomes indicated. But less formal contacts between workers and young people are purposive too, perhaps as part of a more gradual process of building rapport.

Practice is also about *process*. The components listed above are not discrete events but form part of a process of engagement and intervention which draws on a range of **knowledge**, **skills** and **values** on the part of the practitioner. This reference to knowledge and skills points to another sense of the word practice, as an activity or set of skills that one can learn to do better: 'practice makes perfect'. Qualifying programmes in teaching, medicine, social work and youth work all provide the opportunity for trainees to rehearse their skills and apply 'college knowledge' to 'real world' situations.

Trying to provide a definitive statement about what practice 'really' is invites argument as different interest groups will want to highlight some aspects and downplay others. But to summarise the main points so far: practice refers to the range of activities and the process involved in working with young people in the public/professional domain. It involves the purposive use of knowledge, skills and values, within an organisational framework, to address the needs and promote the welfare of young people (as individuals and as members of families and communities).

The rest of this section considers knowledge, skills and values in more detail, critically examining the ways in which these components weave together in different forms of practice and discourses of professionalism.

Knowledge, skills and values

1.1 Knowledge

I have suggested that practice involves the purposive use of knowledge, and this incorporates two different (but connected) elements: knowledge *about* (that is, content knowledge) and knowledge *how to* (that is, skills based, process knowledge). The content knowledge that a practitioner needs will, of course, depend on the job. For example, an A level maths teacher will be calling on a different body of information from an adviser on sexual health. Similarly, the kind of 'how to' knowledge that each requires will vary, though there may be a common core of skills that support very different forms of work with young people.

There are many different models of, or approaches towards, practice. Each approach works with different assumptions about the practitioner and the person or group with whom they are working, and is supported by particular ideas about knowledge: how it is produced and how it is applied. This subsection considers some different forms of knowledge creation; in so doing, it addresses some basic epistemological issues. Epistemology is the branch of philosophy concerned with questions about what we know and how we know it, and below we look at some different ways of understanding the links between knowledge and practice.

Approaches to knowledge and practice

Here, I explore in more detail the ways in which ideas about knowledge –
how it is created and how it is applied – inform practice. I start with an
approach that has become dominant within policy and practice and then go
on to offer a critique of this and to pose some alternative ways of thinking
about the knowledge/practice link.

The rise of evidence based practice.   Chapter 1 noted that in recent years
there have been moves to increase the accountability of public services,
with service providers under pressure to demonstrate the effectiveness of
their provision. These moves have been allied to performance indicators,
outcome measures and targets. So how has practice been affected by
increasing and explicit requirements to meet these (often externally set)
outcomes and targets? One response has been the adoption of 'evidence
based practice'.

Evidence based practice (EBP) is an approach that developed within
medicine but has been taken up, with varying degrees of enthusiasm, in
social care and social work (Sheldon and Chilvers, 2000; Macdonald, 2001;
Sheldon, 2001; Bilson, 2005), health care (Cookson, 2005; Dawes *et al.*,
2005) and education (McNamara, 2002). In relation to social care, the
Centre for Evidence-Based Social Services defines it as: 'the conscientious,
explicit and judicious use of current best evidence in making decisions
regarding the welfare of service users and carers' (Research Mindedness,
undated). Essentially, this means that, if research findings indicate that a
particular approach Y is most effective with problem/situation X, then if
problem X is presented, you should respond with approach Y; for example:
'if we know cognitive behavioural therapy to be effective with depression,
and we as practitioners are confronted with a depressed person, then
cognitive therapy should be the method of choice' (Sheppard *et al.*, 2000,
pp. 466–7).

The focus of EBP is on 'what works'; that is, on interventions or strategies
that have been tested according to agreed criteria – ideally using controlled
trials – and been found to be effective in practice. It values a 'scientific' or
'**positivist**' approach (a philosophical approach which believes in
grounding our knowledge of the world in observable evidence) to
knowledge creation and emphasises the rational and considered application
of that knowledge by a rational subject, someone who is not swayed by
their emotions but can identify the 'problem', weigh up the evidence and
then apply it systematically.

Stephen Webb (2002) and Liz Trinder (2000) identify EBP as the product
of a particular time and place, making links to ideas of the 'risk society'
(Beck, 1992). It appears to promise a level of certainty in highly uncertain
times – a set of rational responses to the apparently irrational and risky
world of practice:

The timing of evidence-based practice is not accidental. It has developed within a specific context, particularly the current preoccupations with risk, ambivalence about science and professional expertise, and the concern with effectiveness, proceduralization and the consumer. Much of the initial success of evidence-based practice can be attributed to its ability to both endorse and redefine some of these concerns, drawing them all together within a coherent and tightly bound package ... In response to the emergence of managerialism, the explosion of audit systems and challenges to professionalism, evidence-based practice has offered a professional solution, itself based upon an even more transparent, neutral and rational process, and one which also claims to represent the interests of, and involve, the customer or consumer.

(Trinder, 2000, pp. 12–13)

Focusing on what works is, at one level, difficult to challenge. If there is evidence that some ways of responding to particular problems or situations are likely to be effective, then it would be hard to argue that they should not be promoted. But while EBP has become dominant, it is not the only approach to practice. Indeed, critics have suggested that it offers at best a partial view of practice and that it makes assumptions about the construction and application of knowledge, and about the nature of evidence, that can be challenged.

Criticisms of EBP and alternative approaches. Evidence based practice has a particular view of how knowledge is used in practice which owes much to its roots in medicine. But the diagnosis/treatment model of the practitioner neutrally assessing a situation, choosing the 'best' or 'most effective' response and applying it to the case at hand does not reflect how practitioners actually operate – or at least is not the full story – and ignores the role of tacit or 'practice knowledge' (a point I return to in Section 3 in the discussion of reflective practice). Skilled practitioners make use of a range of sources of evidence, including their own past experience, to make sense of the new situations they encounter on a daily basis. They draw on *practice based evidence* to create their working knowledge.

In addition, although it is centrally concerned with 'what works', EBP takes a rather limited view of what constitutes valid evidence, tending to restrict this to the results gained from particular types of empirical test. However, 'evidence' can come from a variety of sources and there are many ways of producing knowledge. Empiricism, or positivism (introduced above), is only one (albeit often privileged) approach. **Social constructionist** approaches view knowledge as created in dynamic and diverse social contexts, and as reflecting social/power relations. Knowledge in this view is not a neutral, fixed commodity but something that is contested, changeable and, critically, related to issues of power.

Evidence based practice clearly speaks to the needs of certain 'managerially-dominated and procedurally-driven practice environments' (Ruch, 2002, p. 203). It promotes a focus on the more 'rational' procedural or technical aspects of practice, as these are likely to be more amenable to empirical testing. But arguably, it does this at the expense of the affective and social dimensions – how a situation feels to the young person and what it means to them – which form an important part of the 'complex, diverse realities' (Ruch, 2002, p. 203) of day-to-day work with young people. As Kerry Young puts it: 'No longer do we ask why so many young people are struggling with school. We set up "alternative" provision and after-school clubs instead. No longer do we ask why so many (often very) young people are involved in drugs. We pursue harm minimalisation initiatives instead' (Young, 1999, p. 6).

Equally importantly, it ignores the affective dimension of the *practitioner's* experience: by seeing practice as a rational rather than (or as well as) an emotional engagement, it does not consider how their emotional response might shape a worker's interaction with a young person. For many practitioners, these social and emotional dimensions are part of what can be called a 'moral–practical' approach to practice that challenges the 'technical-rational' response of EBP (Hollway, 2001; Taylor and White, 2001; Webb, 2001). Practitioners are not neutral observers: they are part of the process of practice. They have thoughts, feelings and reactions and draw on these in reaching an understanding of a situation. Rather than seeing that as a problem though, a **psychodynamic** approach sees the affective dimensions of interaction – what is going on between the young person and worker – as providing valuable information on which to base practice.

The involvement of the practitioner in the process of practice is also integral to an interpretative approach. An **interpretative**, or dialogic, approach sees knowledge as being created through dialogue between people, and depends on each participant in the conversation being seen as having something to contribute. In this model, each person's understanding is both partial and provisional; knowledge is created through the process of sharing different points of view. This approach to knowledge and understanding involves a commitment to drawing in marginalised voices and creating different socially and collaboratively constructed knowledges. As such, it forms part of an anti-oppressive approach to practice, viewing knowledge as 'a source and means of empowerment' for minority or marginalised groups (Graham, 2001). As hooks (1989, p. 131) puts it: 'Dialogue implies talk between two subjects, not the speech of subject and object. It is a humanizing speech, one that challenges and resists domination'.

The different approaches to knowledge that we have briefly considered here – social constructionist, psychodynamic and interpretative/dialogic – provide a counter to the positivism of EBP and allow for a broader and more complex understanding of how knowledge is generated and what should count as evidence for practice.

Knowledge and professionalism

Consideration of knowledge in practice highlights some of the tensions and contradictions of increasing professionalism: on the one hand, there is a continuing push to 'professionalise' work with young people, with occupational standards, formal qualifications and regulation. But, on the other hand, this increasingly well qualified and 'trained up' workforce is being asked to work in contexts that may devalue the expertise that professional training encouraged them to believe in and achieve. EBP highlights this paradox: it is a way for practitioners to establish their credibility and make claims about the validity of their work, but it can reduce the role of professional judgement and promote routine responses to complex situations and problems, contributing to the process of 'deprofessionalisation' (Malin, 2000) discussed in Chapter 1.

However, this apparent instability perhaps allows for the emergence of a new form of professionalism or 'reprofessionalisation' (see Chapter 1) which takes a different approach to knowledge (Davies, 1998, p. 194; Fook, 2000; Banks, 2004): one which questions whose knowledge is given credibility and status. We will return to this point in Section 2, when we look at the changing nature of professional relationships. But before that, we will continue to explore the different elements of the practice framework set out in Subsection 1.1. Having looked briefly at knowledge and its role in practice, the next element to consider is skills.

1.2 Skills

What is meant by 'skills for practice'? Policy makers (DfES, 2002), practitioners (*An Everyday Journey*, 2004–2006) and young people themselves (Ahmad *et al.*, 2003; National Children's Bureau, 2005) all have ideas about the kind of skills they want to see in practice. And, as the discussion in Chapter 1 illustrated, some skills or attributes do seem to be generally valued, such as listening and the ability to communicate, empathise and engage honestly and respectfully with young people. But rather than compiling lists of skills, my intention here is somewhat broader: to consider briefly the way in which skills for practice are understood in professional discourses.

Within some professional domains, national occupational standards (NOS) have been devised. They provide the 'official' view of the profession and identify key skills required for effective practice. The NOS for youth work (PAULO, 2002), for example, identify that the key aspects of youth work are to:

- build relationships with young people which enable them to explore and make sense of their experiences, and plan and take action

- facilitate young people's learning and their personal and social development

- enable young people to organise and take co-responsibility for activities, events and projects

- work with young people in accordance with the core values of Youth Work

- plan, manage and develop Youth Work

- support and develop effective, efficient and ethical practice in Youth Work.

(PAULO, 2002, p. vi)

With these aspects of practice in mind, the core skills for practice are then framed as:

- communication

- application of number (identified as 'numeracy' in Scotland)

- information technology

- problem solving

- working with others

- improving own learning and performance [not included in the core skills in the national occupational standards for Youth Work in Scotland].

(PAULO, 2002, p. 116)

Other professional bodies or organisations will have similar overarching statements of purpose and associated core skills.

National occupational standards are a way of formalising and standardising practice; they 'bring together the skills, knowledge and values necessary to do the work as *statements of competence*' (Skills for Care, 2006, p. 2, emphasis added). The competence based approach has, however, been criticised on various grounds (Hyland, 1996; Fook, 2000, p. 105; Adams, 2002). The points made by Adams about competence based approaches within social work seem equally relevant to work with young people in other professional contexts:

1   They tend to focus on areas of expertise that are most appropriate in stable, bureaucratic work settings, rather than being directed towards future job requirements.

2   They encourage fragmentation ... of activities which could otherwise be viewed holistically.

3   They are convergent, in that they may bring about a narrowing of ideas consistent with outcome-based activity rather than encouraging divergent thinking and an emphasis on the value of the process of the activity accompanying creative practice.

4   They focus ... on those easily measurable aspects of people's performance.

(Adams, 2002, pp. 253–4)

Adams also suggests that competence based approaches lead to routinised practice by encouraging the acquisition of 'specified techniques rather than developing approaches based on critically reflective practice' (p. 254).

The shift from skills to competences reflects some of the same tensions identified earlier in relation to evidence based practice. On the one hand, a competence framework is a way of ensuring accountability and a proper level of skill within a workforce and, for these reasons, is to be welcomed. But on the other hand, to the extent that it reduces the complexity and creativity of practice to a selected range of core competences to be learned and accredited, it can be seen as another aspect of the process of deprofessionalisation.

Discussion of skills leads to the last component of the framework for practice: values. Young (1999) makes the point that skills are not exercised in an ethical vacuum: workers' values underpin and impact on their practice and, at the same time, work methods and intervention strategies necessarily have particular value positions and principles running through them, even if those values and principles are not easily isolated.

1.3 Values

Work with young people is value laden at many different levels. Framing a purpose for practice, as I did in Subsection 1.1, is a value statement and, while it may not be contentious to state that work with young people should address their needs and promote their welfare, we may all have very different ideas about what that means and how to achieve it. As with the discussion of skills, I do not want just to generate lists of possible values for practice but, rather, to consider briefly where values for practice come from and how and why they matter. To do this, I look briefly at three key value 'domains': personal, professional or organisational, and political.

Personal values derive from a variety of sources; for example, family background or religious teaching. Earlier, I suggested that practice is a form of moral–practical activity, distinguishing this from the application of 'technique', however skilled. From this perspective, personal values are integral to practice: they shape how you understand the job of working with young people (in whatever context), why you do it, how you behave and how you expect others to behave towards you.

Professional values are typically enshrined in formal codes of practice, values or ethics or in statements of principles and link directly to the assumed *purpose* of the work or organisation. The Code of Ethics of the British Association of Social Workers, for example, includes the following statement:

> Social work is committed to five basic values:
>
> - Human dignity and worth
> - Social justice
> - Service to humanity
> - Integrity
> - Competence
>
> (BASW, 2003, p. 3)

Chapter 1 made the point that work with young people in a range of settings – including education, youth work and social work – has been informed by radical values. Such values find expression in the development of anti-oppressive practice (AOP) which is committed to challenging all forms of inequality.

Political values address the broader purpose of work with young people *as an activity in modern society* and are used to frame policy statements and guidance documents; for example, *Transforming Youth Work: Resourcing Excellent Youth Services* (DfES, 2002), the government's specifications for future youth services, includes a statement of values. These values will then have a direct bearing on the way youth work is framed as an activity and the kinds of provision that the government will want to see in place. Values, from this perspective, operate from the top down, in contrast with the 'emergent' values of the personal and professional domains.

Putting values into practice is not always easy and conflicts of values can occur. These may be internal conflicts where different but equally deeply held personal values collide, or external; for example, between young people and workers, or communities of interest and professional value statements. Individuals may find themselves involved in quite complex mediations between competing personal, professional and political values.

For instance, how is it best to support young people from particular faith groups? The statement of values in *Transforming Youth Work* says of youth work that:

- it recognises, respects and is actively responsive to the wider networks of peers, communities and cultures which are important to young people;

- through these networks it seeks to help young people achieve stronger relationships and collective identities – for example, as Black people, women, men, disabled people, gay men or lesbians – and through the promotion of inclusivity, particularly for minority ethnic communities;

(DfES, 2002, p. 20)

A link is made between helping young people to achieve stronger collective identities and increased inclusivity, but inclusion may not be a shared value. Some groups may feel that collective identity is better achieved through the promotion of separatist organisations and will therefore resist attempts to be included in more 'mainstream' provision. For a worker, finding the 'right' balance between the different values in play may be anything but straightforward.

Key points

- Practice refers to the range of activities and the process involved in working with young people in the public/professional domain.

- It involves the purposive use of knowledge, skills and values within an organisational framework to address the needs and promote the welfare of young people as individuals and as members of families and communities.

2 The role and nature of 'relationship' in work with young people

Professional practice involves establishing effective relationships and working in partnership with young people, families and other professionals or agencies. Indeed, the relationship is the medium through which the practitioner works:

In youth work what you see is rarely what you get. On the surface it can appear that not much is going on. We might see young people hill walking, developing their DJ skills, or hanging about talking and stop at that. However, youth work is a lot

> more than activity. It is, at heart, about relationships and
> association – connecting and being with others – and the good
> that can flow from this.
>
> (Smith, 2003, p. 3)

An emphasis on relationship foregrounds the person and personality of the worker and highlights the need for thoughtful 'use of self'. So we will start by looking at what this means and how it affects practice.

2.1 Use of self and the biographical perspective

'Use of self' is again a shorthand term and highlights the relation between the personal and the professional. It refers to the way someone makes intentional use of their own particular knowledge, understanding and experience within a relationship to benefit the person they are working with. This is not the same as thinking that if you have had an apparently similar experience you will therefore understand what someone else is going through. You may do, but then again you may not! Take the experience of starting at secondary school. Most of us will have been through this, but the *meaning* of the experience may vary enormously. Your circumstances and history before secondary transfer, your feelings about the choice of school (if you had any choice) and your own temperament and abilities will influence your understanding. Positive feelings about the move – excitement and anticipation, the prospect of new opportunities and making new friends – may have been balanced or even cancelled out by negative experiences, perhaps of bullying or discrimination as a result of racism, sexism or homophobia. Your own experience may help you relate to someone else, but you would need to check to see if your thoughts and feelings had any resonance for them.

What the idea of 'use of self' conveys is that the individual is, in a sense, a resource for practice: you draw on your own experience, feelings and perceptions to make sense of the world and to frame your understanding of others: 'Where we stand affects what we sense, and our thoughts and feelings affect how we respond to the world around us' (Huntington, 2002, p. 210). This way of understanding the self is central to the psychodynamic and interpretative approaches introduced earlier. It assumes that the identity of the worker – who they are, how they present themselves and how they are seen by others – will have a bearing on the situation. Each of us is 'located' through our race, culture, gender, class, age, physical ability, sexual identity. These 'differences' are particularly critical when they define important differentials in power. Understanding what these aspects of 'difference' mean to us, and the advantages and disadvantages that accrue from them, as well as the potential impact on others, provides the basis from which workers are able to empower themselves and the young people they work with to challenge or change discrimination and oppression. As a practitioner, then, you are not a neutral presence or a blank sheet. You will bring personal, cultural and emotional 'baggage' into each new encounter.

In the companion volume in this series, Rachel Thomson (2007) looks at the way in which a biographical approach can be used to explore experiences of transition in young people's lives. Adopting a similar approach to practitioners' life stories can provide a broader understanding of the meaning of practice for them. Biography plays an important role in shaping one's professional identity and approach to practice.

Activity 2   Becoming/being a teacher

Allow 20 minutes

The following extract comes from a study by Mary Jane Kehily (2002).

One of the things Kehily explored was the link between a teacher's personal biography and their approach towards teaching: the ways in which who the teachers are influence what they do as teachers. In the extract below, two experienced teachers, Miss Green and Mr Carlton, reflect on the personal experiences that have influenced them as teachers. Read the extract and note the connections that the teachers make between their own experience and the way they 'operate' as professionals.

Miss Green had been in teaching for twenty-one years and is head of Religious Studies and Personal and Social Education at Oakwood School. She described her motives for becoming a teacher as 'idealistic', wanting to help young people through pastoral care in the school context, rather than through exam success and academic achievement. She said, 'For me the youngsters who sit in front of me are not just brains, not just sort of heads-on-bodies, they are people'. Miss Green made a direct link between the kind of pupil she was and the kind of pupil she wants to help in the course of her career:

Miss Green: Yeah, I failed at school, I was terrible, but I had a lot of problems from my own background, a lot of emotional problems so I had a lot of emotional garbage which you couldn't get rid of but it had to be dealt with but there was not room for learning because I was such a mess in other respects. Like so many of our kids who come to school, they bring an awful lot of emotional garbage, they bring all the problems and there we are saying, 'Now you must learn this'. It's unrealistic, it's of no – it doesn't mean anything to them so I know what they feel like to some extent.

Miss Green's empathy with pupils like her former self supported her perception that curriculum-based learning seems irrelevant and inappropriate at times. Her use of the term 'emotional garbage' indicates the power of the emotional realm and the felt need to find ways of dealing with pain and hurt in order to move on. The language in which Miss Green compared herself as a pupil with the pupils she teaches now utilised a therapy/counselling discourse which is humanistic and person-centred. Miss Green's teacher identity was interwoven with a pedagogic style that valued pupil centredness, confidence building and relating to pupils as individuals ...

Mr Carlton, a Craft, Design and Technology (CDT) teacher with many years experience at Oakwood, expressed his position in school in terms of a strong working-class regional identity:

Mr Carlton: I'm from here, right, from this part of the world. I grew up in this part of the world, went away and came back and taught here ever since and I've never been to another school – which could be a mistake, but the kids here I've always managed to relate to and I treat them probably the way their parents treat them and I think that's what it comes down to. They know that if I tell them something then I tell them from the heart, not from what other people are telling them. I try to always tell them the truth, even if it hurts, you know, tell them the truth.

[...]

... for both teachers there is an emotional connection between their identity (sense of self) and the pedagogic practices they favour. In the context of the interview, Mr Carlton and Miss Green offer a version of themselves as teachers that reads *what you do* through the lens of *who you are*. From this perspective teacher identity becomes a subjective appropriation of personal narratives and pedagogic styles that become fused in moments of self-definition as, 'this is me, this is what I am about'.

(Kehily, 2002, pp. 173–76)

In this extract, the two teachers discussed how aspects of their personal histories have influenced both their choice of career and their approach to the whole business of 'being a teacher'. In Activity 3, you are asked to think about your own experience and to consider some of the links between who you are and your sense of professional identity; that is, your sense of yourself in a work role, what you do and how you do it.

Activity 3   Personal biography and professional identity

Allow 15 minutes   Looking at your own work history, can you identify links between your biography and your sense of professional identity? You may find the following questions help you to frame your response.

- Can you think of particular events or experiences that influenced your choice of work?
- How have those experiences affected your approach to your work?
- Have they influenced your 'style' or way of working and, if so, how?
- To what extent is your personal identity (through such factors as your class, ethnicity, experience of disability, etc.) reflected in your professional identity?

Comment

There is no right way to answer this question and your response will reflect your understanding of your life experiences, work options, opportunities, and so on. But the sense of personal and professional identity that we are considering here can perhaps be understood in the context of what Anthony Giddens (1991) refers to as the 'reflexive project of self'. This suggests that identity is not fixed and unchanging but is actively created by the individual (though arguably still within certain constraints) to reflect their changing understandings of the kind of person they are – and the kind of person they may want to be.

Use of self, then, is not static but will change with developments in the individual's biography and the story they tell about themselves. At the same time, an analysis of individual careers within youth work/youth services can offer a way of tracking and understanding broader changes in practice. The career can act as both a marker for the history of a given field or area of practice and also, at a more intimate level, as a record of how the individual practitioner has changed and developed.

We need to recognise, therefore, how personal history, as well as organisational structure and expectation, affect the ways in which practitioners work and construct relationships with young people (and vice versa). At the same time, as discussed in Chapter 1, the broader context within which all these relationships are being established is changing, so practitioners are having to make sense of a shifting picture. In the remainder of this section, we will look at two key aspects of change in the nature and role of relationships and explore the implications for practice with young people.

2.2 The changing relationship between experience and expertise

A practitioner should be able to call on a relevant knowledge base, however defined. But practitioners are not the only ones with knowledge, as the growing movement for user involvement in the provision of a range of services demonstrates. The extent to which government policy reflects a willingness to trust young people's expertise about their own situation, however, is open to question. Article 12 of the United Nations Convention on the Rights of the Child (UNCRC) (United Nations, 1989) indicates that the views of children and young people should be taken into account in all matters affecting them, and there are moves to draw young people into a range of forums and decision-making structures; for example, they take part in youth parliaments and school councils, are routinely involved in appointment panels for Connexions staff, and have a significant role in a range of research studies. But such moves co-exist with rather more contradictory views which suggest that young people should be told what to do rather than be consulted: so we see the proliferation of measures such as Dispersal Orders, curfews, street wardens and Anti-Social Behaviour Orders, all designed to keep young people 'in their place'.

Having said that, there are moves to put young people's views more at the centre of policy making and service provision (Barry, 2005). For example, the Department for Education and Skills publication *Youth Matters* proposes that young people should be centrally involved in decisions about services and that they should have much more influence over the facilities and resources that are provided in their locality:

> We need to respond to young people as they are today, with their greater expectation of autonomy and control, not as young people were a decade ago.
>
> [...]
>
> Our first challenge is to put young people themselves in control of the things to do and places to go in their area. We don't want government agencies second guessing them.
>
> (DfES, 2005, pp. 3, 5)

There is recognition here of young people's *agency* and an apparent willingness to accord them a greater degree of autonomy – at least in some areas of their lives. This in turn implies a change in the nature of the relationship between service providers and young people as service users, and a move away from a 'top-down' or 'expert knows best' approach to one based more on mutuality.

The change identified here perhaps reflects a more general (and fundamental) shift in the way relationships between professionals and young people are framed. The notion of 'detraditionalisation' (see Chapter 1) offers a way of understanding the decline of traditional authority and the process by which the role and status of 'the expert' has become increasingly open to challenge in what has been called postmodernity. Drawing on their study 'Youth values: identity, diversity and social change', Rachel Thomson and Janet Holland (2002) identify a change in the way young people understand and relate to different sources of practical and moral authority. They see '(an uneven) shift from traditionally ascribed authority to its negotiation and location in the individual' (p. 11) and note that:

> Traditional authority figures, such as the police and religious leaders received very little automatic respect from young people. They explained that respect must be earned, authority won and merit proven. This **ethic of reciprocity** was particularly apparent in young people's discussion of the purpose and application of school rules and the behaviour of teachers. While young people did not always invest teachers with moral authority, they watched them closely to see if they were worthy of it.
>
> (Thomson and Holland, 2002, p. 107)

This can be seen as a move away from a reliance on 'expertise' to a foregrounding of 'experience', where the young person is the expert on their own situation rather than the passive recipient of the professional's 'higher' knowledge. In terms of the practice that follows such a shift, relationships are based more on negotiation, with the young person setting the terms of engagement. 'Reciprocity' emerges as a defining characteristic of relationships with adults that young people see as legitimate (Thomson and Holland, 2002).

Reciprocity, or mutuality, implies a degree of give and take within the relationship. It involves recognising the separate subjectivity and agency of the other person and calls for a way of working that deals openly with differences of power. These differences may be associated with role and/or with particular aspects of the individual's social identity (such as race, class, sexual identity or disability status). Focusing on power and issues of 'difference' or diversity highlights the importance of working with young people within a broader framework of anti-oppressive practice that is committed to challenging inequalities and promoting empowerment. Mutuality depends on a degree of authenticity on the part of the worker, which recognises the power they hold in relation to the young person and maintains a willingness to promote young people's agency through a relationship of 'negotiated power' (Dominelli, 2004, p. 41).

The increased emphasis on reciprocity focuses attention on *process* and the way in which workers engage with young people. Much of the interaction with young people takes place through conversation and this can be used to promote empowering practice. 'Genuine' dialogue, as noted in Subsection 1.2, involves treating the other with respect and recognising that each person is bringing something useful into the discussion. No individual holds the monopoly on truth: practitioners need to be open to the possibility that their assumptions and views can be challenged, and to work with young people to come to a shared understanding or agreement about the matter under discussion (even if this means an agreement to disagree!).

It would be unwise to overstate the extent of this change. Many young people will no doubt feel that their options for challenging authority are still extremely limited in courts or classrooms! Yet in other situations – for example, within youth work or other settings where young people are voluntarily engaged – such change may be easier to institute. Opportunities for dialogue will still need to be carefully set up if they are to avoid engendering or reinforcing a sense of powerlessness on the part of the young person, but positive outcomes can be achieved when young people are able to exercise agency within a more reciprocal relationship. An example of this can be seen in Voice4Youth (V4Y), a participatory youth project set up as part of the Coalition4Youth in Brighton and Hove.

While Chapter 3, 'Participation', offers a much fuller discussion of the importance of participation, some of the individual, group and communal achievements identified by those involved in the V4Y project are listed in the box below.

In the past year we have ...

- Had fun and made new friends.

- Reached our new member number target.

- Got young people's opinions on concerns that they have about their area.

- Received money from the Scarman Trust.

- Provided people to write articles and edit the Argus Youth page.

- Run a popular dance and DJ event 'Caught on Film'.

- Been to the YMCA's AGM. We got opinions from both adults and children and showed all the people that didn't really know that this group existed!

- Represented our area at the National Youth Council Conference at Swindon.

- Made a video of all the information we received from young people. Showed it at V4Y's premier where many important people in the area attended and took note of the problems.

- Hosted the West Hove Forum. After that night Heather James agreed to take action on the lighting in Stoneham Park and wrote: 'It was clear that there are common concerns across all age groups and that young people are keen to be constructive, to listen and to work with others in the community'.

- Changed the aims of Hove V4Y from a group that didn't just get young people's opinions heard but to one where we actually get things done in the area.

- Filled in an application form to receive money from the Scarman Trust. We planned a website that will give young people the chance to air their views and get them accessed easily by important people. We also planned training for updating websites and teambuilding at Blacklands Farm.

- Helped compile the young people's diary for this year.

- Represented young people at events such as Tomorrow the World.

(Trust for the Study of Adolescence, undated, p. 35)

Many practitioners will welcome this kind of change, and want to promote an ethic of reciprocity, seeing it as an opportunity to develop more empowering and equitable relationships with young people. As one youth worker puts it:

> If I go ice skating with young people they need to help me because I can't skate to save my life. But that's good because, as youth workers, we don't claim to be experts at everything. In fact, sometimes we need the young person's expertise which is good for them as much as for us.
>
> (Quoted in Young, 1999, p. 69)

For others, however, this rebalancing in their relationships with young people may feel destabilising. Again, recent social theory, in particular Beck's (1992) understanding of 'individualisation' (see the discussion in Thomson, 2007), offers a way of thinking about this process. The process of relinquishing authority based on supposed expert knowledge (disembedding) may have liberating aspects: it allows practitioners to rethink their role and perhaps to develop new ways to work with and engage young people. But the disorientation and loss of security that results (disenchantment) may be very uncomfortable. However, Beck's formulation of the process of individualisation suggests that disenchantment can give way to a process of re-embedding and new forms of integration as new practices are developed.

2.3 Establishing boundaries: impersonality and intimacy, formality and informality

The second aspect of change in professional relationships that I want to consider concerns the setting of boundaries. Look back at the scenarios in Activity 1 in Section 1, which addressed the differences between professional and private relationships. It was suggested that a professional relationship has different rules from a private one, particularly with regard to intimacy, and the example highlighted the fact that those working with young people need to be very aware of boundaries (see also A. Taylor, 2003, pp. 21–4). Kehily (2002, p. 170) quotes the example of a feminist teacher 'who had attempted to establish a sisterly bond with young women in her class [and] was regarded as "plain nosy" by these girls'.

Clearly, boundaries may be contentious but responsibility must remain with the practitioner not to misuse the young person's trust. And while workers must continually monitor and review the relationships they establish, the context within which these relationships take place is itself changing. In Section 1, we located professional practice in the public domain, which was differentiated from the private or domestic sphere. But the boundaries between public and private – and with that, the nature of relationship – have been questioned from different perspectives.

Activity 4   Where are the boundaries? A view from practice

Allow 25 minutes   Read the extract below which is taken from an article by Camila Batmanghelidjh in the National Children's Bureau magazine, *Spotlight*. Batmanghelidjh is the founder and chief executive of the charity Kids Company which works with very vulnerable and/or isolated children and young people. As you read, jot down the main points of her argument. Do you agree with the position she puts forward? What, in your view, are the strengths and limitations of this as an approach to professional work with young people?

Working with vulnerable children and young people: the importance of relationships and loving care

Kids Company offers support to exceptionally vulnerable children who refer themselves or their peers. At the children's centre The Arches in 2002–2003 we cared for approximately 500 children who came to us for housing advice, education, food, social, emotional and practical interventions. In 15 schools across London we worked with some 3,500 children using the arts, sports, social work and psychotherapeutic programmes. Despite being recognised as exceptional in our ability to reach extremely disturbed children we relentlessly struggle to keep our resources going. Like many others, Kids Company struggles alongside the children, a witness to their pain and resilience, against a backdrop of social depletion. We endeavour to support them from a point of despair to the possibility of hope and an aspiration for a better future.

As I sit writing applications for funding and creating ever more inventive projects I notice in myself a level of emotional sarcasm which is not usual: Why can't I just write in the funding application that I want to care for some really vulnerable children who need us? Why must I pretend any more or less than this intention?

Institutional Narcissism

The reason I propose is Institutional Narcissism. As care workers we have come to feel ashamed of wanting to care for our clients. The profession has allowed itself to be devalued because it has a poor tradition of defining its Art. Good quality care has a profound aesthetic quality. In the emotional 'middle space' between the care seeker and caregiver there is a reciprocal exchange, which impacts on both and enhances their sense of humanity. With every care exchange, we come face to face with the spiritual dimension of our human expression. Compassion, loving care and the extraordinary power of both elevate us beyond the mundane into the domain of connectedness and personal meaning. We are moved beyond the personal crisis of narcissistic survival.

Sadly, as the care profession fails to define its own boundaries it has been invaded by the value system handed down from the school of 'pretentious management', increasingly becoming an industry with an over importance placed on outcomes and outputs. What can be measured is deemed to be real and valid. A frenzy of targets is let loose on our profession, costing out our every move. Is it really true that the more clients we move along conveyor belts the more quality we are seen to have delivered?

As we march to this sinister tune the agenda setters compliment themselves and marvel at their own achievements. Like Narcissus, a hollow echo reflects back a glory which is loveless.

Denial of loving care

It would be easy to blame government departments and institutions but it may be more helpful to acknowledge that we all have a part to play in perpetuating a society that has as its central crisis the denial of loving care. Vulnerable children present with defences that incapacitate their ability to attach and form pro social relationships. This has an obvious impact on their emotional and social development and their ability to be included in, or include themselves in, mainstream society. Generations of children are born into households where there is a lack of commitment to parenting, or a lack of knowledge and understanding about how to be good enough caregivers.

Emotionally damaged parents abandon their offspring; the children and parents surviving the trauma in a disconnected but parallel world. The lack of connectedness, the severing of loving contact, creates no model for compassion. A narcissistic loneliness pervades in which the strong survive and the weak perish. The children we work with call it 'a dog eat dog world'.

As resources are limited both on our inner city streets and in our services I notice a parallel perversion presenting itself as quality. Our children dress in the latest designer gear. With every outfit an artificial sense of status is created. The 'fashion peacock' is immune from humiliation and attack if he or she has the right label. In a bid to be safe a thirst for material goods drives the senses to present an appearance. Generally, beneath the outfit remains a depleted and emotionally lonely child.

In many ways our services mirror this. The outputs and outcomes are indeed our institutional designer outfits. In a bid to be safe we too list our numbers into an illusion of quality. This process, however, is emotionally vacuous without adequate attention paid to the importance of high quality relationships.

In this narcissistic preoccupation the care contact is compromised and we are unable to create a genuine solution to address the profound disengagement of our clients.

As I keep emphasising the importance of loving in the task of care I can see the cynical grins of so many, particular those who facilitate the numbers game. But this debate is not confined to an imagined polarity – organisation versus loving care. Of course good quality care can only happen within a robust structure. The crisis is created when the structure is mistaken for the task.

(Batmanghelidjh, 2004, pp. 4–6)

Comment

Camila Batmanghelidjh's emphasis on the role of 'loving care' challenges many conventional assumptions about the boundaries around professional helping relationships. The article attacks an organisational and social framework that appears to devalue care and leave children without adequate support. Batmanghelidjh highlights the importance of the ability to both give and receive care and the damage that is done to children who do not have the experience of 'good enough' care. She champions authentic and loving relationships, against the demands of externally derived and imposed 'targets' and outcomes. In the end, her message is simple: care work should be underpinned by love, and workers should not be afraid or ashamed of acknowledging this and working to promote relationships of loving care.

Batmanghelidjh's appeal to 'love' may sound somewhat old-fashioned, but Young, researching the views of youth workers, quotes one practitioner as follows:

> People need to feel connected to each other. Young people will only hear you if they have a level of respect for you and, obviously, if you are open and genuine, but also if they can see that you do actually care about them ... In fact, some youth workers may even talk about a level of love for the young people that they work with – which means having positive regard for them. Viewing them as positive beings and being able to offer them support on their terms.
>
> (Young, 1999, p. 67)

There is a respectable history within both youth work and social work, from 'mainstream' secular and faith perspectives, of practice based on acceptance and unconditional positive regard. So while the language may differ, the basic orientation perhaps remains the same.

But Batmanghelidjh's position leaves some unanswered questions: who has the power to define the nature and terms of the relationship? Is there a shared understanding of 'loving care' and how should it be provided to very vulnerable children? Is it an attitude or are we talking about particular kinds of behaviour; and, if the latter, who decides what is 'OK'? While she does argue that loving care must operate within a 'robust structure', it is harder to see what this would look like – and how boundaries between workers and young people would be understood and managed.

A rather different way of thinking about boundaries – and, in particular, the balance between impersonality and intimacy – is offered by the sociologist Barbara Misztal (2000, 2005) who considers the way different sorts of social relations are managed in conditions of late modernity. In particular, she examines the way public and private relationships are structured along the dimension of formality/informality. Misztal suggests that there are three broad realms of interaction, 'encounters, exchange and pure relationships', and each realm or level of interaction is associated with a particular style. These can be described 'according to their respective levels of impersonality, emotional commitment, disclosure of private emotions, voluntary sharing of private knowledge, warmth in dealing with others, degree of institutionalization and the strategies of their respective actors' (Misztal, 2005, p. 187).

Encounters are the most general and impersonal level of interaction and are characterised by 'civility'. This, understood as 'a style of conduct which provides affirmation of the others' worth, is an interactional practice resting in the universal norm of respect for others' (Misztal, 2005, p. 189). Professional relationships of the sort that we have been considering in this chapter fit most closely with Misztal's description of the second type of interaction, **exchange**, which is managed through the practice of 'sociability': 'Sociability is a style of exchange with reciprocity weaving through it, which is capable of creating a feeling of belonging and providing people with social acceptance and position' (p. 189). Exchange is a form of transaction between people who occupy certain social positions and roles, and is governed by rules and norms which may be codified. The third realm, of 'pure' relationships, includes personal friendships and relationships between partners or lovers and involves a style of interaction based on 'intimacy' – the mutual, voluntary and spontaneous sharing of information and emotion. Misztal suggests that each style is inclusive: so 'pure' relationships are characterised by intimacy but also draw on the practices of civility and sociability; the realm of exchange features sociability but also relies on a more general civility; and in social encounters, civility is 'the sufficient practice' (p. 189).

Batmanghelidjh's position blurs commonly accepted boundaries between public and private ways of relating and brings a degree of intimacy into a public relationship of care that would more usually be found in a private or domestic relationship – Misztal's 'pure' relationship. This is one way of responding to the changes in practice that have been discussed in both this and the previous chapter; in particular, the moves towards a much more regulated, target-driven, outcome led framework that appears to leave little room for the kind of basic 'people work' that practitioners like Batmanghelidjh see as fundamental. But, as I have suggested, it leaves both workers and young people in a rather ambiguous position. Professional relationships have different 'rules' from friendships or other more intimate relationships, and workers – while they may *be friendly* and act in some capacities *like* a friend – are not in the end the same as friends. Working within systems of accountability, practitioners have to maintain a degree of professional distance, which prohibits the level of intimacy found in 'pure' relationships, in Misztal's sense. Locating practice as a form of 'exchange', with its accompanying expectation that interactions should be based on both 'civility' and 'sociability', may provide a way of framing the relationship and securing the boundaries that are needed for safe and effective work.

Key points

- Relationship is the medium through which the practitioner and young person can work together, and it draws on the worker's skilful 'use of self'.

- Some dimensions of the practitioner/service user relationship have changed in conditions of late modernity or postmodernity.

- Effective relationship based work involves reciprocity, civility and sociability, underpinned by an ability to work with 'difference'.

3 Improving practice: reflection, reflexivity and critical practice

In Section 1 we looked at knowledge for and in practice and considered how it is constructed, where it comes from and to whom it belongs. In this section, the emphasis is on how practitioners move from 'knowing about' to 'being able to do', and on the role of **reflection** in developing and improving practice. The ability to explore, reflect on and learn from experience contributes to the development of practice that is more than just a technical or mechanistic application of core competences. It is the key to developing empathy as well as understanding the nature of power in human relationships.

3.1 The reflective practitioner

Drawing on the work of Schön (1983, 1987), the notion of the 'reflective practitioner' has been widely discussed in health, education and social care. At the most straightforward level, reflection means nothing more than 'thinking things through' (Payne, 2002, p. 124); it involves looking back on what you have done and thinking about what you did, how it went and what could have been done differently. Schön calls this process '*reflection-on-action*'. But there is another type of reflection, which Schön calls '*reflection-in-action*': the competent practitioner needs the ability to think 'on their feet', and Schön observed that experienced workers seemed to be able to use learning from previous experiences and apply it to the situation at hand. The knowledge they drew on was not – indeed, sometimes could not be – spelled out. It had been internalised by the practitioner and become part of their tacit knowledge or 'practice wisdom'. Through the process of reflection-in-action, then, practitioners make meaningful links between theory and practice: '*learning through reflection on the here and now ... involves the capacity to draw back in order to reflect on what is happening almost as it happens ... [it] enables learning to take place in a way which allows thought-less action to become thought-ful*' (Yelloly and Henkel, 1995, p. 8).

A further dimension of the reflective process focuses on the dynamics of the interaction between practitioner and service user. Reflection here relates to unconscious process and refers to the way in which the practitioner 'picks up and mirrors, without knowing it, the feeling states of the client [*sic*]' (Froggett, 2002, p. 133). Their behaviour and relationships come to 'reflect' the service user's mode of response. For example, as a social worker, I had very regular contact with a single parent with sole care of a small child with a degenerative illness. She was in inadequate accommodation and her social support was nil. After each visit, I was invariably left with a sense of sadness and overwhelming tiredness. Supervision offered the space to reflect on these feelings and I came to see them as a reflection of the feelings this young woman was projecting. This understanding of reflection, with its emphasis on the power of the unconscious to influence behaviour, has clear links to the psychoanalytic concept of transference.

A common strategy to focus the reflective process is to identify and analyse 'critical incidents'. Critical incidents do not always arrive with a lot of fanfare and may simply be occasions that allow us to think about events in new or different ways. A personal example may illustrate this point. My teenage daughter recently questioned why we had settled on a particular time for her to be home after a night out – and what would convince us to change it. When pushed, I realised that I did not have a convincing answer and that my fixation on a particular time was highly reminiscent of my father's behaviour when I was a teenager. I remembered the 'what time do you call this?' conversations when I stayed up (not necessarily out) beyond a point that he thought reasonable. And here I was, having a similar conversation with my own daughter. Clearly the fear that un-named 'bad things' will immediately happen after the curfew hour – whatever time that is – runs deep! Realising this led to a useful discussion where I was able to state what my concerns were, acknowledge some rather unfocused anxieties about 'safety' and separate out what, if anything, was to do with timing. The upshot was a more flexible arrangement which involves a clear agreement about what information I need about her plans and arrangements for actually getting home safely.

This may be a trivial, everyday incident, but for me, it was quite a pivotal moment in shaping the way my daughter and I manage our relationship. It highlighted some of the tensions between care and control with which I live as the parent of a young adult – in this case, finding a way to balance her need for autonomy with my need to protect her from harm, real or imagined – and provoked me to revisit a range of questions: about the sort of parent I want to be, the kind of boundaries parents should impose, when do trust and flexibility tip over into lack of responsibility; questions that are not always easy to answer or amenable to 'once and for all' solutions.

While in this instance I was starting from a domestic situation, this kind of reflection and the questions it gives rise to would also have resonance for me as a professional, working with young people. The aim of reflection is not to ascertain 'the truth' about a situation or experience, but it can offer an opportunity to make sense of experiences, whether they are positive, negative or just plain puzzling, and to inform practice.

Activity 5   Reflective practice: getting started

Allow 20 minutes   Think of an encounter with a young person that for you has the quality of a 'critical incident'. This could be in the context of a domestic, informal or professional relationship. It could be a situation in which you felt something went well or that left you feeling unhappy, disappointed or angry. Why do you think this incident was significant? The following questions may help you reflect.

- What knowledge did you use?
- What skills did you draw on?
- Did this experience challenge you on a personal or professional level?
- What dilemmas did it raise for you?
- What were your feelings at the time? What are they now?
- What have you learned from this experience?
- What could you do differently next time?

Comment

An exercise like this can seem simple and you may not feel that it threw up any surprises, particularly if you focused on an incident that was in some sense 'successful'. But even situations that go well can generate useful personal and professional learning: perhaps you realised that you had managed a difficult situation more easily than you had thought at the time, or maybe the process of reflection helped to restore your confidence after a period of uncertainty by reminding you that you are able to work and engage effectively with young people.

The reflective practitioner

The learning that comes from reflection is not always either easy or palatable. Focusing on a particular incident may leave you feeling a bit unsettled – perhaps you did not behave as well as you would have liked, or you may recognise attitudes or beliefs at work that you thought you had left behind. Asking practitioners to take reflection seriously involves a recognition of the personal and emotional effort it requires, provision of adequate resources (for example, skilled supervision that can address process as well as managerial/case management agendas) and a supportive organisational culture.

3.2 From reflection to reflexivity

In some quarters – for example, within nursing and on many social work training programmes – the need for reflection in and on practice has almost become an article of faith and the ability to reflect a requirement of competent practice. However, the idea of reflection is not entirely without critics. Maureen Eby (2000, p. 54) notes that, although reflection is intended to improve practice, its use 'to promote self-development can lead to a sense of self-doubt and self-disapproval, since endlessly striving to improve leaves little room for a sense of personal well-being'. Taking this point further, the focus on personal monitoring can become quite oppressive. A Foucauldian critique suggests that, by 'making the individual practitioner visible and inciting them to reveal the truth about themselves' reflective practice operates as 'a form of surveillance that disciplines the activities of professionals' (C. Taylor, 2003, p. 246). So while reflective practice can promote emancipatory and anti-oppressive practice, in this sense it also has the potential to operate as a 'technology of the self'.

A different, but related, criticism concerns the individualism of traditional approaches to reflection: 'The primary focus of reflection is on process issues and how the worker handled their practice' (Taylor and White, 2000, p. 198). While this is certainly worthwhile, as far as it goes, there is a tendency for reflection to remain focused on the individual. The individualism or 'psychologism' of conventional approaches has been challenged on the grounds that it tends to obscure the broader environment of practice. Workers do not operate in a vacuum: practice is located within a social and often highly charged political context. Reflection that fails to acknowledge this risks locking the worker into a culture of self blame. As Eby (2000, p. 54) notes in the following quotation, in which she cites Quinn: 'Reflection places the emphasis for the maintenance and improvement of standards of care on the shoulders of the individual, removing from the organisation the responsibility of providing "adequate staffing levels, effective staff development, and adequate resources".'

The critique of reflection based on its 'psychologism' has encouraged the development of approaches that locate the practitioner explicitly within a broader socio-political and cultural context. This can be seen in the move from 'reflection' to 'reflexivity' that I discuss next.

Reflexivity includes the personal reflection discussed above, which involves reflecting on how your values, beliefs, social identities and experiences impact on your practice. But it moves beyond the individualism of 'simple' reflection to address the situated nature of practice. A key aspect of reflexivity is 'the ability to locate oneself squarely within a situation, to know and take into account the influence of personal interpretations, position and action within a specific context. Expert practitioners are reflexive in that they are self-knowing and responsible actors, rather than detached observers' (Fook, 2000, p. 117). This implies something more than the self awareness required for individual reflection and points to a more fundamental examination of the bases of practice and the kinds of knowledge and assumptions practitioners work with, through a politically aware process of critical thinking. So reflexivity has an epistemological dimension: it involves a process of 'bending back' which allows the practitioner to analyse what they know and how they know it. Like evidence based practice then, reflexivity focuses attention on the nature of knowledge in practice. But unlike EBP, it takes a social constructionist rather than a positivist approach to the process of knowledge creation and includes consideration of the power dynamics that shape that process.

Jan Fook's understanding of reflexivity includes a strong sense of political engagement and a commitment to challenging unequal power relations. Other writers have also made the link between reflexivity and anti-oppressive practice: 'The anti-oppressive principle of reflexivity demands that workers continually consider the ways in which their own social identity and values affect the information they gather. This includes their understanding of the social world as experienced by themselves and those with whom they work' (Burke and Harrison, 2002, p. 229).

The use of terminology in this field can become rather confusing. I have offered one account of 'reflexivity' here, but D'Cruz et al. identify three different approaches to this term, before going on to look at variations such as 'reflectivity' (see, for example, Kondrat, 1999) and 'critical reflection' (see, for example, Issitt, 2004). In some cases these different terms are used apparently interchangeably, although separate definitions or understandings can be teased out (D'Cruz et al., 2006). What reflexivity (as I have used it in this discussion), critical reflection and critical reflectivity all do, albeit in slightly different ways, is to draw attention to the ways in which personal, professional and political factors influence practice.

3.3 Bringing it all together: developing critical practice

Individual reflection and broader notions of reflexivity and critical reflection/reflectivity make a vital link between thought and action, opening up possibilities for change and providing the basis for a way of working that can be described as **critical practice**. Ann Brechin (2000, p. 26) suggests that critical practice involves 'open-minded, reflective appraisal that takes account of different perspectives, experiences and assumptions', and identifies two guiding principles to inform such practice: 'the principle of "respecting others as equals" and the principle of an open and "not-knowing" approach' (p. 31). These principles fit well with the ideas of mutuality and reciprocity that we discussed in Section 2. But as that discussion indicated, more equitable or reciprocal relationships are not always easy to establish. So, any understanding of critical practice will need to address issues of *power* as part of a commitment to emancipatory outcomes for young people.

Although the following statement relates to youth work, it seems to offer an understanding of critical practice that applies equally well in a variety of settings: 'the seeds of critical practice may be found wherever youth workers have managed to create a "special relationship" with young people built on mutual trust and respect, the sharing of power, and purposeful learning' (Bamber and Murphy, 1999, p. 230). Critical practice is about making a difference to the lives of young people (Brechin, 2000). It brings the critical thinking and analysis associated with reflexivity/reflectivity together with action designed to promote more equal and empowering relationships and makes a commitment to 'a process of working towards a preferred, anti-oppressive future' (Bamber and Murphy, 1999, p. 227).

Key points

- The ability to reflect is crucial to any approach to work with young people which aims to achieve some positive change. It is fundamentally about improving practice, and with improved practice, young people will benefit.

- Reflective practice and empathy do not arrive 'ready made'; they need rehearsal, time and a supportive environment within which to grow.

- The move from reflection to reflexivity allows consideration of the personal, the professional and the political factors that shape practice.

- Critical practice brings together critical thinking (individual reflection and broader reflexivity) and action, to promote empowering and equitable relationships and make a difference to the lives of young people.

Conclusion

The aim of this chapter was to develop an understanding of what 'practice' involves, how it operates and how it can be improved, highlighting along the way some of the complexities, uncertainties and challenges of professional work with young people. Practice is a way of referring to the range of activities and the process involved in working with young people in the public/professional domain. It involves the purposive use of knowledge, skills and values, within an organisational framework, to address the needs and promote the welfare of young people (as individuals and as members of families and communities). It is not monolithic and will take different forms in different organisational and professional settings. However, I have suggested that two issues deserve particular consideration as they are integral to good practice, regardless of context: relationship and reflection. Relationship is significant because it is the medium through which practice operates, reflection because the process of enquiry it encourages can provide opportunities for practitioners to deepen their understanding of and improve practice. In particular, critically reflective practice, and the self awareness it promotes, can make a significant contribution to anti-oppressive work with young people. Improving practice and promoting empowering and equitable relationships must always be a key aim for practitioners. Finally, therefore, it is proposed that a framework of critical practice that brings together critical reflection, thinking and action offers a way ahead.

References

Adams, R. (2002) 'Social work processes' in Adams, R., Dominelli, L. and Payne, M. (eds) *Social Work: Themes, Issues and Critical Debates* (2nd edn), Basingstoke, Palgrave.

Ahmad, Y., Dalrymple, J., Daum, M., Griffith, N., Hockridge, T. and Ryan, E. (2003) *Listening to Children and Young People*, Bristol, University of the West of England.

An Everyday Journey: Discovering the Meaning and Value in Youth Work (2004–2006) unpublished research project, Durham University/Weston Spirit.
[Spence, J., Devanney, C., Noonan, K. and Thexton, W. (2007, forthcoming) *Every Day is Different*, report of the research project *An Everyday Journey: Discovering the Meaning and Value in Youth Work*, Leicester, National Youth Agency.]

Bamber, J. and Murphy, H. (1999) 'Youth work: the possibilities for critical practice', *Journal of Youth Studies*, vol. 2, no. 2, pp. 227–42.

Banks, S. (2004) *Ethics, Accountability and the Social Professions*, Basingstoke, Palgrave.

Barry, M. (ed.) (2005) *Youth Policy and Social Inclusion: Critical Debates with Young People*, London, Routledge.

BASW (British Association of Social Workers) (2003) *Code of Ethics for Social Work*, www.basw.co.uk/articles.php?articleId=2 [accessed 22/07/06].

Batmanghelidjh, C. (2004) 'Working with vulnerable children and young people: the importance of relationships and loving care', *Spotlight*, no. 2 (March), London, National Children's Bureau.

Beck, U. (1992) *Risk Society: Towards a New Modernity*, London, Sage.

Bilson, A. (ed.) (2005) *Evidence-Based Practice in Social Work* (2nd edn), Edinburgh, Elsevier/Churchill Livingstone.

Brechin, A. (2000) 'Introducing critical practice' in Brechin, A., Brown, H. and Eby, M. (eds) *Critical Practice in Health and Social Care*, London, Sage/The Open University.

Burke, B. and Harrison, P. (2002) 'Anti-oppressive practice' in Adams, R., Dominelli, L. and Payne, M. (eds) *Social Work: Themes, Issues and Critical Debates* (2nd edn), Basingstoke, Palgrave.

Cookson, R. (2005) 'Evidence-based policy making in health care: what it is and what it isn't', *Journal of Health Services Research and Policy*, vol. 10, no. 2, pp. 118–21.

Davies, C. (1998) 'The cloak of professionalism' in Allott, M. and Robb, M. (eds) *Understanding Health and Social Care: An Introductory Reader*, London, Sage.

Dawes, M., Davies, P., Gray, A., Mant, J., Seers, K. and Snowball, R. (2005) *Evidence-Based Practice: A Primer for Health Care Professionals*, Edinburgh, Elsevier/Churchill Livingstone.

D'Cruz, H., Gillingham, P. and Melendez, S. (2006) 'Reflexivity, its meanings and relevance for social work: a critical review of the literature', *British Journal of Social Work*, Advance Access published online on 20 February 2006, doi:10.1093/bjsw/bcl001.

DfES (Department for Education and Skills) (2002) *Transforming Youth Work: Resourcing Excellent Youth Services*, London, Department for Education and Skills.

DfES (Department for Education and Skills) (2005) *Youth Matters: A Summary*, Nottingham, DfES Publications.

Dominelli, L. (2004) *Social Work: Theory and Practice for a Changing Profession*, Cambridge, and Malden, MA, Polity Press.

Eby, M. (2000) 'Understanding professional development' in Brechin, A., Brown, H. and Eby, M. (eds) *Critical Practice in Health and Social Care*, London, Sage/The Open University.

Fook, J. (2000) 'Deconstructing and reconstructing professional expertise' in Fawcett, B., Featherstone, B., Fook, J. and Rossiter, A. (eds) *Practice and Research in Social Work: Postmodern Feminist Perspectives*, London and New York, Routledge.

Froggett, L. (2002) *Love, Hate and Welfare: Psychosocial Approaches to Policy and Practice*, Bristol, Policy Press.

Giddens, A. (1991) *The Consequences of Modernity*, Cambridge, Polity Press.

Graham, M. (2001) 'Creating spaces: exploring the role of cultural knowledge as a source of empowerment in models of social welfare in Black communities', *British Journal of Social Work*, vol. 32, no. 1, pp. 35–49.

Hollway, W. (2001) 'The psycho-social subject in "evidence-based practice"', *Journal of Social Work Practice*, vol. 15, no. 1, pp. 9–22.

hooks, b. (1989) *Talking Back: Thinking Feminist, Thinking Black*, Cambridge, MA, South End Press.

Huntington, A. (2002) 'Resisting change: what stops us acting for young people?' in Bannister, A. and Huntington, A. (eds) *Communicating with Children and Adolescents: Action for Change*, London, Jessica Kingsley.

Hyland, T. (1996) 'Professionalism, ethics and work-based learning', *British Journal of Educational Studies*, vol. 44, no. 2, pp. 168–80.

Issitt, M. (2004) 'Good practice in open and distance learning – the experience of postgraduate students on the Postgraduate Diploma/MA in Health Promoting Practice', *Research in Progress*, vol. 3, no. 2, pp. 33–8.

Kehily, M.J. (2002) *Sexuality, Gender and Schooling: Shifting Agendas in Social Learning*, London, Routledge.

Kondrat, M.E. (1999) 'Who is the "self" in self-aware: professional self-awareness from a critical theory perspective', *Social Services Review*, vol. 73, no. 4, pp. 451–75.

Macdonald, G. (2001) *Effective Interventions for Child Abuse and Neglect: An Evidence-Based Approach to Planning and Evaluating Interventions*, Chichester, Wiley.

McNamara, O. (ed.) (2002) *Becoming an Evidence-Based Practitioner: A Framework for Teacher-Researchers*, London, RoutledgeFalmer.

Malin, N. (ed.) (2000) *Professionalism, Boundaries and the Workplace*, London, Routledge.

Misztal, B. (2000) *Informality: Social Theory and Contemporary Practice*, London and New York, Routledge.

Misztal, B. (2005) 'The new importance of the relationship between formality and informality', *Feminist Theory*, vol. 6, no. 2, pp. 173–94.

National Children's Bureau (2005) *Consultation with Young People* (unpublished), London, National Children's Bureau.

PAULO (2002) *National Occupational Standards for Youth Work*, Grantham, PAULO.

Payne, M. (2002) 'Social work theories and reflective practice' in Adams, R., Dominelli, L. and Payne, M. (eds) *Social Work: Themes, Issues and Critical Debates* (2nd edn), Basingstoke, Palgrave.

Research Mindedness (undated) *Evidence Based Practice and the Evaluative Agenda*, www.resmind.swap.ac.uk/content/05_in_context/in_context_07.htm [accessed 26/09/06].

Ruch, G. (2002) 'From triangle to spiral: reflective practice in social work education, practice and research', *Social Work Education*, vol. 21, no. 2, pp. 199–216.

Schön, D. (1983) *The Reflective Practitioner*, New York, Basic Books.

Schön, D. (1987) *Educating the Reflective Practitioner: Towards a New Design for Teaching and Learning in the Professions*, New York, The Free Press.

Sheldon, B. (2001) 'The validity of evidence-based practice in social work: a reply to Stephen Webb', *British Journal of Social Work*, vol. 31, no. 5, pp. 801–9.

Sheldon, B. and Chilvers, R. (2000) *Evidence-Based Social Care: A Study of Prospects and Problems*, Lyme Regis, Russell House.

Sheppard, M., Newstead, S., Di Caccavo, A. and Ryan, K. (2000) 'Reflexivity and the development of process knowledge in social work: a classification and empirical study', *British Journal of Social Work*, vol. 30, no. 4, pp. 465–88.

Skills for Care (2006) *A Manager's Guide to Developing Strategic Uses of National Occupational Standards*, www.skillsforcare.org.uk [accessed 22/0706].

Smith, M.K. (2003) 'Inside information' in *Inside Youth Work: Insights into Informal Education from Projects Supported by the Rank Foundation and the Joseph Rank Trust*, www.ymca.ac.uk/rank/publications/index.htm [accessed 05/11/06].

Taylor, A. (2003) *Responding to Adolescents: Helping Relationship Skills for Youth Workers, Mentors and Other Advisers*, Lyme Regis, Russell House.

Taylor, C. (2003) 'Narrative practice: reflective accounts and the textual construction of reality', *Journal of Advanced Nursing*, vol. 42, no. 3, pp. 244–51.

Taylor, C. and White, S. (2000) *Practising Reflexivity in Health and Welfare: Making Knowledge*, Buckingham, and Philadelphia, PA, Open University Press.

Taylor, C. and White, S. (2001) 'Knowledge, truth and reflexivity', *Journal of Social Work*, vol. 1, no. 1, pp. 37–59.

Thomson, R. (2007) 'A biographical perspective' in Kehily, M.J. (ed.) *Understanding Youth: Perspectives, Identities and Practices*, London, Sage/The Open University (Course Book).

Thomson, R. and Holland, J. (2002) 'Young people, social change and the negotiation of moral authority', *Children and Society*, vol. 16, no. 2, pp. 103–15.

Trinder, L. (ed.) (2000) *Evidence-based Practice: A Critical Appraisal*, Oxford, Blackwell Science.

Trust for the Study of Adolescence (undated) *One Year On: Evaluating the Voice 4 Youth Project*, www.tsa.uk.com/training/projects/youthvoice2.html [accessed 22/07/06].

United Nations (1989) *Convention on the Rights of the Child*, Geneva, United Nations.

Webb, S. (2001) 'Some considerations on the validity of EBP in social work', *British Journal of Social Work*, vol. 31, no. 1, pp. 57–79.

Webb, S. (2002) 'Evidence-based practice and decision analysis in social work: an implementation model', *Journal of Social Work*, vol. 2, no. 1, pp. 45–63.

Yelloly, M. and Henkel, M. (1995) *Learning and Teaching in Social Work: Towards Reflective Practice*, London, Jessica Kingsley.

Young, K. (1999) *The Art of Youth Work*, Lyme Regis, Russell House.

Chapter 3

Participation

Heather Montgomery

Introduction

The previous two chapters have focused on the changing relationships between professionals and young people. Key to this change is the issue of participation and the ways in which professionals have moved away from hierarchical ways of working with young people towards more participatory and democratic ideals, empowering young people rather than telling them what to do. Participation is a key word in much contemporary work with young people. Putting the phrase 'young people and participation' into an internet search engine throws up hundreds of sites dealing with policy, practice and examples of participation in action. Yet despite almost universal agreement that participation is a good thing, there is a limited amount of work on the ideas behind it, and the ways in which it can make a positive difference to young people's lives. At its best, participation acknowledges the importance of young people's own agency and views, and as such it provides an important rationale to work with young people. Young people's participation has been promoted in a number of domains such as schools, the health service, child protection or the political arena. It is intended to improve democracy and create new forms of community, to empower young people and make them feel more connected to their communities. It is also seen as a way of making projects more efficient; by finding out what the users really want, waste and irrelevance can be eliminated. Participation has become so central to practitioners working with young people, that it is rarely contested or the notion deconstructed and it is often presented uncritically, as the panacea to many of the problems of working with young people. As Francis Cleaver puts it:

> Participation has ... become an act of faith ... something we believe in and rarely question. This act of faith is based on three main tenets: that participation is intrinsically a 'good thing' (especially for the participants); that a focus on 'getting the techniques right' is the principal way of ensuring the success of such approaches; and that considerations of power and politics on the whole should be avoided as divisive and obstructive.
>
> (Cleaver, 2001, p. 36)

As this quotation implies, participation is seen as the 'gold standard' of practice when working with young people. Projects that focus on young people insist on the importance of participation and claim that young people themselves must be involved in decision-making processes, and all stress the centrality of participation to their organisation or way of working. Yet despite the ubiquity of the participation discourse, its theoretical underpinnings are rarely examined, and the radical concept that lies at the heart of participatory approaches to working with young people is not always clearly understood.

This chapter will address the following core questions:

- What does participation mean?
- Is there a contradiction between participation and protection?
- How can participation improve young people's lives?
- What happens when adults' rights and responsibilities conflict with those of young people?
- Should there ever be limits on young people's participation?

Activity 1   What is participation?

Allow 15 minutes   Read through the following quotations about participation. What are its defining features for the people involved? Does participation mean something different to you? If so, what?

> Participation means it is my right to have the opportunity to be involved in making decisions, planning and reviewing an action that might affect me. Having a voice, having a choice. My voice, my choice.
>
> (Gemma Woolley, winner of the Welsh Participation Consortium's Sound-Bite Competition, quoted in Funky Dragon, 2005)

> The development of an open participatory ethos is of crucial importance to education for citizenship. Schools and early education settings need to function as active learning communities in which participation by all members is encouraged.

> Young people should see that all people in the school are treated with respect, their views sought and taken account of. The way the school is organised and managed, the manner, attitudes and quality of the relationships evident amongst its members, and the ways in which pupils, parents, staff and the wider community interact all provide important indications of what inclusive, participative communities are like in practice
>
> (Learning and Teaching Scotland, Education for Citizenship, 2006)

[Participation means] real engagement, according to age and ability, in all stages and development of a programme, from conceptualization, through operation to evaluation.

(Bartlett, 1999, p. 12)

Young people are particularly adept at realising participation is not all about getting your own way, but a licence to enter negotiations over competing claims. Though some will feel happier about the outcomes of their involvement than others, the value of being heard and taken seriously can be hugely empowering.

(Carnegie UK Trust/Carnegie Young People Initiative, 2005)

Comment

The different comments here have as a common theme the importance of listening to young people, consulting them and including them in decisions that affect their lives. However, whereas the first quotation suggests that participation is a process of individual empowerment, the second suggests that it has a more general purpose; it is a way of turning young people into citizens, making them aware of their responsibilities to others and fostering a sense of community. There is a hint here that participation is a means to an end, a means of producing the sorts of citizens required by the state. In the third quotation participation is seen in its widest sense: it is not just about consultation at the later stages of a project, but getting young people involved at the outset, setting the agenda themselves and being involved in the planning of the project. The fourth quotation recognises that, while participation may not deliver the same results for all young people, and may even prove disappointing for some, its value is in empowering young people and giving them back some control over their lives.

You may have thought of other things that participation means to you; for instance, the right to vote, or to have a youth parliament, being able to change things and make a difference. You may have seen participation as something that young people should achieve on their own, or as something they must negotiate with adults.

There is no one set definition of participation and it is used in different contexts to mean different things. For some people participation is a method of eliciting young people's views; for others, it is an ideal that underpins all their work with young people. Although it is not explicitly defined, it is one of the key components of rights legislation and a common thread that runs through most work with young people. As Judith Ennew writes: 'Just as dignity is the undefined basis and touchstone of human rights, participation is the basis and touchstone of ensuring that children are the subject of those same human rights' (Ennew, 1998, p. xix).

Ennew's comment here is important as it suggests that participation needs to be seen in its widest possible sense, embracing both the public/private and formal/informal divides. As it currently stands, the agenda on participation is very much about the public sphere and about services; about what young people do outside the home and outside their own networks, whether that is participation in schools, young leader projects, or even in the formal political sphere. Participation becomes much more controversial when it infringes on what is understood as the private and the informal, and Section 4 looks in greater detail at young people's rights to control their own fertility and reproduction, and their own bodies. Participation is, thus, not simply a method of working with young people, it is also a way of thinking about young people and about their social relations in the wider society. In a postmodern world, where the boundaries between the public, private and commercial spheres are shifting, participation is a necessarily complex and contested field. Encouraging young people to participate in schools, hospitals, youth groups, and so on, can therefore be seen either as a way of supporting young people's rights in the private sphere, or as a further encroachment of the state, or the agencies of the state, into the private arena where they have no right to be.

Young people work with a 'ladder of participation' looking at different forms of participation

Types of participation

There are various degrees or models of participation, and particular projects will use one of these, or a combination of them, depending on their various circumstances. Participation should be seen as a continuum, from the tokenistic (where young people are brought in at the end of an adult led process and asked to endorse it) to situations in which young people themselves come up with the originating idea and put it into practice without adult intervention. The different types of participation can be spilt into five categories:

- **Young people-initiated and directed**

  Young people have the initial idea and decide how the project is to be carried out. Adults are available but do not take charge.

- **Adult-initiated, shared decisions with young people**

  Adults have the initial idea, but young people are involved in every step of the planning and implementation. Not only are their views considered, but young people are also involved in taking the decisions.

- **Consulted and informed**

  The project is designed and run by adults, but young people are consulted. They have a full understanding of the process and their opinions are taken seriously.

- **Young people-initiated, shared decisions with adults**

  Young people have the ideas, set up projects and come to adults for advice, discussion and support. The adults do not direct, but offer their expertise for young people to consider.

- **Assigned but informed**

  Adults decide on the project and young people volunteer for it. The young people understand the project, they know who decided to involve them, and why. Adults respect young people's views.

(Adapted from Hart, 1992, pp. 40–5)

Actual projects that work with young people usually follow one of these models, although there are often elements of more than one in programmes. The implications of using these models will be explored in the following discussions.

Key points

- Participation is a key word in current policy/practice discourse.
- It means different things in different circumstances, but is based on the idea that young people should be involved in decisions that affect them.
- It can become controversial when the rights and interests of young people appear to be in conflict with the rights, and responsibilities, of adults.

- There are various forms of participation, ranging from the tokenistic, when young people are brought in as 'window dressing', to full participation, when they initiate and run their own projects.

1 How does participation work?

David Green (1999) asserts that there are three key conditions which ensure that young people are included in the decision-making process: cultural attitudes must be such as to encourage participation; political, legal and administrative structures must be in place to ensure rights to participation; and economic and social conditions must enable people to exercise their rights. We will return to the final point in Section 5, but it is clear from this that participation is more than just a set of rules or guidelines on how to involve young people in participation; rather, it is about a culture in which young people are listened to and their opinions are respected, and in which they are actively involved in decision making.

Activity 2	Participation in action
Allow 30 minutes	Below are two examples of projects which encourage participation, the first based in a school in south London and the second in a drugs project in Scotland. As you read through them, make notes on the different ideas about participation that each is bringing to its work. In each case, what do you think are the benefits of a participatory approach? What kind of participation (based on the five categories listed in the Introduction) do you think each project falls into?

Deptford Green Secondary School, London

Characteristics of children/young people involved

- Children aged 11 to 19 years;
- A high proportion of ethnic minority groups and students with English as a second language;
- Area of high deprivation.

Purpose of participation

- Learning and raised achievement;
- Sense of agency/power;
- Emotional literacy.

Ways young people involved

- School council;
- Citizenship GCSE and citizenship in all curriculum subjects;
- Consultations about school and community environment;

- 'Jerry Springer' style assemblies;
- Students help develop school policies.

Example of outputs

- Clocks placed in all classrooms;
- Pupils can wear hats in playground;
- Toilets repainted;
- Trial for students to have clear water bottles in lessons;
- Classrooms redecorated;
- New lighting in a local underpass.

Dumfries and Galloway Youth Strategy Executive Group [YSEG], Dumfries

Characteristics of children/young people involved

- All young people aged 15–24 years;
- Targets under-represented young people such as gay and lesbian young people, young carers, young offenders and those who are unemployed.

Purpose of participation

- To influence policy development through the Executive Committee;
- To discover the needs of young people and relate those needs to policy formulation;
- The personal development of young people involved through improving skills and experience;
- To create a sense of ownership of services in young people;
- To increase awareness of the role of the council;
- The empowerment of young people, irrespective of their disability, 'criminality', etc.

Ways young people involved

- Drug policy for schools (local);
- Millennium Volunteer initiative (national);
- Student Council pilot;
- Involvement in the Development Plan, and the writing of the Annual Report and Rough Guide to Services for Young People;
- The YSEG consult with other young people's groups in the planning, design, and implementation of services/facilities;
- Influencing policy within the local council;
- Funding projects/initiatives;

- In the administration of services such as the Youth Festival and conferences;
- Training events facilitated by the young people of the YSEG;
- Young people evaluate achievement annually in view of the Development Plan and adjust aims and objectives accordingly.

Example of outputs

- Aims and objectives have been tailored to reflect the needs of young people in the area;
- A culture of participation is emerging in the region;
- The council has adopted the recommendations of a document produced in consultation with young people;
- The YSEG has funded and continues to fund various initiatives and projects in the region. They have complete control over the distribution of their £60,500 budget;
- Other organisations have received training from young people on how to treat them, and on the challenges they face;
- Ride 4 Free initiative enabled young people from across the region to access leisure facilities much more easily, and without expense;
- Growth of confidence, self-esteem, communication skills, and experience in young people;
- Young people have developed an understanding and appreciation of the role of the council and the effectiveness of working in an executive group;
- A skate park is in the process of being built following the funding that the YSEG allocated to the project.

(Kirby *et al.*, 2003, pp. 162–3)

Comment

The first example is taken from a secondary school in south London and is more concerned with the everyday aspects of young people's lives. Its aims are to make young people feel more connected to their school and to give them a sense of control and achievement in their daily lives. As a project, it seems to be set up by adults, but is one in which children are fully 'consulted and informed' (and come up with a list of changes themselves). By making small, practical changes, it enables students to feel more in control of their school environment and to see quickly the implementation of those changes for which they have lobbied. In this instance, creating the goals of emotional literacy and a sense of power are achieved through small, concrete, young people inspired changes.

In the second project, the ideals of participation are much broader and on a larger scale. The focus of the project is obviously different, dealing with very marginalised young people who do not constitute an obvious community, such as a school. Therefore the ideals, and outputs, seem less focused. This project relies on young people identifying themselves as one of the target groups and volunteering for the projects, and so it fits into the 'assigned but informed' category. However, this is not to imply that it is less participatory or worse than the Deptford example. Young people are being given a significant role to play in planning and evaluating policy. Their views are being sought and, significantly, young people themselves are educating adults on the challenges that face them. Without more details, it is hard to evaluate claims such as whether a 'culture of participation' is emerging, but young people's voices are being heard.

In both examples, young people are being brought into the decision-making processes on both large and small scales. By making them feel more connected and showing that their decisions and choices do count, initiatives such as these are ensuring that the ideals of participation are being translated into action.

When it works well, participation can make a significant difference to young people's lives and to the adults who work with them. Young people feel that they are being listened to, that their views are respected, and that becoming involved can make a difference. At Cheshire and Warrington Connexions, for example, young people were involved in the design of leaflets advertising the service. They felt that the original leaflets were inappropriate and asked for them to be changed. One of the teenagers involved commented:

> Because we fed our views back about these leaflets – they sent someone down from head office to talk to the group ... and they're actually going to change the leaflets. They're actually going to get rid of these red people [illustrations on leaflets], which is one big move for us.
>
> (Quoted in Kirby *et al.*, 2003, p. 125)

In another example given in the same Department for Education and Skills (DfES) report, teachers spoke of the benefits of a participatory approach:

> Wheatcroft School teachers believe listening and involving children makes classroom teaching more effective. One teacher explained how, because children are used to speaking out and being listened to, they are much more inclined to say when they do not understand something in a lesson.
>
> This increases the knowledge the teacher has of the children's level of understanding, and also informs them of how to improve the learning process.

> 'If they didn't understand something they wouldn't be afraid to say, most children anyway, because they're used to being heard, and that helps us.
>
> That's much more effective. It means we're not just guessing what children want, but the children are getting what they want.' (Teacher)

[...]

Teachers explained that teaching practice is easier and more effective when children are actively working with them rather than being passive and being pushed to learn. Children's peer-support mechanisms have also been successful in reducing class disruption and conflict, which takes the burden off the teacher.

> 'Children are actually solving things themselves. They can go and have a little circle group on their own and try and solve things. When they've had a problem, they've been used to that procedure in my class, and they've said "Can we have a little circle"? It won't be a giggly group or a chance to get out of something; they'll just have a heart-to-heart and a bit of time to discuss it [the issue] and they calm down.' (Teacher)
>
> (Kirby *et al.*, 2003, p. 129)

Participation is often presented as an opportunity for young people, while the needs of practitioners are emphasised less. Quotations such as those above suggest, however, that participation can bring real benefits not only to the young people but to the professionals working with them, and that another reason for encouraging participatory approaches is that they empower the professionals as well as the young people.

Key points

- In order for participation to work it needs a change of culture and attitude, as well as legislation.

- Participation can bring tangible benefits when young people genuinely feel they have an input into the project under discussion, or when they feel they can make a difference.

2 Young people, government policy and participation

The idea of participation has been one of the cornerstones of government policy on young people, especially in the areas of volunteering, which we look at below, and citizenship, which is discussed in more detail in Subsection 2.1. In 2003, the government published *Every Child Matters* (DfES, 2003), a report written in the aftermath of the murder of Victoria

Climbié, an eight-year-old girl from the Ivory Coast who was brought to the UK by her great aunt, abused by her, and finally murdered. The inquiry into her death revealed systemic failings in social services, hospitals and educational services designed to protect children. In response to her death, *Every Child Matters* identified five key outcomes that should be achieved on behalf of all children. These were:

1 being healthy
2 staying safe
3 enjoying and achieving
4 making a positive contribution
5 economic wellbeing.

Subsequently, in 2005, the government published *Youth Matters* (DfES, 2005) which affirmed that the same five outcomes applied equally to young people and were vital to their development (for further discussion of these points, see Robb, 2007a). Interestingly, this report used the term 'empowerment' rather than 'participation', but the idea of involving young people in decisions which affect their future was seen as central to their empowerment. Indeed, the report asked for young people's views and received over 19,000 contributions from them (DfES, 2006, p. 2). The follow-up report, *Youth Matters: Next Steps*, published in 2006, stated:

> We will only achieve lasting and positive change for young people if we place them at the centre of our policies and services. Through reforms of the school and college system and curriculum and qualifications change, we will continue to put young people at the heart of our reform programme, including by legislating for a new, broader curriculum entitlement. In implementing Youth Matters we will do this in three principal ways:
>
> • through a personalised, differentiated approach which responds to the needs of every young person, whilst recognising that group or neighbourhood approaches are also needed
>
> • putting purchasing power in the hands of young people and supporting them to make choices and influence provision
>
> • involving young people in local decisions about what is needed in their communities
>
> ... We believe that empowering young people gives a clear message that they are supported and trusted to make decisions. It gives them the chance to act responsibly and to assume an active role in decision-making and leadership in their communities.
>
> (DfES, 2006, p. 6)

One innovative way that the report proposed to empower young people was through volunteering, and to this end, another report was commissioned setting targets for increasing the numbers of young people involved in voluntary work.

In 2004, the then Home Secretary, David Blunkett, and the Chancellor of the Exchequer, Gordon Brown, set up a commission, headed by Ian Russell, to develop a framework for youth action and engagement. The Russell Commission recognised that young people have a wealth of skills to offer and, most importantly, they have the time, enthusiasm and energy to make a difference. The report from the Commission acknowledged the potential and enthusiasm of young people's voluntary work and countered the idea that young people are apathetic or interested only in themselves. The Commission also acknowledges the importance of participation in voluntary projects, emphasising the benefits of young people initiated projects. It states:

> **The key theme for the Commission is the importance of involving young people themselves in the design and implementation of volunteering activity.** Half of all young volunteers become involved in activities on the advice or recommendation of friends, some of the most successful and inspirational volunteering experiences are those that are led by young people, and young people are uniquely placed to support and mentor their peers on a number of important social issues.
>
> (Russell, 2005, p. 7)

There is, of course, a dilemma in this statement in that, if half of young people who volunteer are becoming involved through a friend, then it can be a signal that young people are already bringing on board other young people very effectively on their own, without the help of the Russell Commission. The whole notion of volunteering as an intrinsic good might also need to be questioned. It is difficult to criticise young people's community work when they are helping older people or working in a local hospital, but volunteering to work, for example, on a political campaign, especially if that involves civil disobedience, such as road protests or animal rights protests, would be seen more negatively by some. Participation in these instances, while it might be empowering and give young people a greater sense of community, does not seem to be what the government is encouraging.

2.1 Participation and citizenship

One of the key areas of participation most obviously championed by the government is the link between participation, citizenship and democracy. In 1997, the Secretary of State for Education and Employment emphasised the

Young people from the Citizenship Foundation meet at the Houses of Parliament in May 2005 to discuss issues of democracy, participation and citizenship

need to teach citizenship and democracy in schools and set up an advisory group to look at this issue and to encourage young people to become involved with, and connected to, their communities and with the wider legal institutions of the UK. The Government Advisory Group on Citizenship, chaired by political scientist Bernard Crick, had, as its terms of reference: 'To provide advice on effective education for citizenship in schools – to include the nature and practices of participation in democracy; the duties, responsibilities and rights of individuals as citizens; and the value to individuals and society of community activity' (quoted in Citizenship Advisory Group, 1998, p. 4).

The aim behind citizenship education is to teach concepts such as community, rights, responsibilities, fairness, rules, laws, respect and tolerance, although much of the teaching of citizenship in schools has concentrated on the formal, democratic institutions of the state and has not focused on young people's roles as consumers, family members or private individuals. It has tended to emphasise public responsibilities rather than private choices.

Activity 3   Should young people have the right to vote?

Allow 15 minutes

At the time of writing, in the UK the legal age at which one can vote is 18, and to stand as an MP it is 21. There has been some debate about lowering the voting age to either 16 or 17 as a way of ensuring that young people take an active part in the democratic process and do not feel disenfranchised. Young people between the ages of 18 and 24 have the lowest turnout of any demographic group. In the 2001 general election only 39 per cent voted, and in the 2002 local government elections only 11 per cent voted. In the devolved assemblies there is similar apathy: in 2003, 16 per cent of young people voted in the elections for the National Assembly for Wales, although 42 per cent voted at the Scottish Parliament elections. In terms of holding office, young people are very rarely represented by their peers. Again at the time of writing, fewer than 1 per cent of MPs in the Parliament elected in 2001 are under 30 years of age, while just 0.1 per cent of councillors on principal local authorities in England and Wales are under 25 (Electoral Commission, 2003).

Given this, what are the arguments for and against lowering the voting age? How much do you think lowering it would encourage young people to participate in the democratic process?

Comment

There is a strong case to be made that young people over the age of 16 should have the right to vote. Young people are also citizens and voting at 16 is the next logical step from citizenship education, which is heavily promoted by the government and now a compulsory subject in secondary schools. The right to vote is a cornerstone of the British political system; however, although young people learn about citizenship from the age of 11, they are not allowed to put what they learn about the political system into action until they reach the age of 18: a gap of seven years, by which time they may become cynical and 'switched off' from formal politics. Another argument is that, if the state deems that 16- and 17-year-olds are competent to leave home, get a full time job, pay taxes, raise children and join the army, then they should be able to vote.

However, there are reasons why the age of voting should not be reduced. These revolve around issues of the extent to which young people are fully competent to make political decisions, how easily they might be influenced and how likely they are to act irresponsibly. When the House of Commons last debated the lowering of the voting age to 16, in December 1999, it was heavily defeated.

Whether the voting age will actually be lowered is highly debatable. More importantly, it is very doubtful that it would make young people feel more connected to the democratic institutions that represent them. It is not just young people who feel disenfranchised and disconnected, but members of all age groups of voters. Turnout is falling in all elections, and attempts to widen participation in the democratic process, such as local elected mayors, have often ended in farce. In 2002, for example, the voters of Hartlepool elected H'Angus the Monkey, the mascot of the town's football team, as mayor, an indication that voting irresponsibly or facetiously is not a preserve of young people, and may in fact be a protest at being involved in processes in which people are not interested.

Having said that, it is sometimes claimed that young people themselves are pushing for the vote to be lowered to 16. Many organisations working with young people, such as Barnardo's, the British Youth Council, the Children's Parliament in Scotland and the Children's Rights Alliance for England (2005), back the campaign, but the extent to which it is young people inspired is debatable. It might be argued that the main thrust behind the campaign comes from a small group of determined young political activists, a vocal minority who do not represent the concerns of many young people. Given that voting behaviour is linked to educational attainment, lowering the voting age may increase the participation of certain groups of better educated young people, but would do nothing for others. On the other hand, citizenship education in schools includes teaching on voting rights and responsibilities, so there may be a new awareness of voting among young people of all abilities, although this remains an under-researched area.

Most studies of young people and their experience of voting suggest that formal political affiliation and voting are not high on most young people's agendas, and that they see participation much more broadly than this. One recent study of children and participation in the political arena argues that:

> For most young people, democracy as they know it is associated with political parties that do not listen, spin and negative campaigning and the pomp and pantomime of Parliament. Politics is regarded as a game in which they are rarely invited to be players – and in which their voices are rarely heard. When asked about their attitudes to democracy, young people express their feelings of abandonment by the political system ...
>
> [...]
>
> ... much of what is offered to young people in the name of 'active citizenship' lacks appeal because it seems to be remote from their everyday experience and disconnected from the levers of power ... rather than witnessing mass apathy amongst young people, what we are seeing is a mass generational migration from old-fashioned forms of participation to newer, more creative forms. There is a need to re-think what we mean by participation.
>
> (Coleman, 2005, p. 2)

Much citizenship education and many understandings of participation are focused on getting young people involved in formal, legal frameworks, which young people seem to be increasingly rejecting. Yet it is clear that young people are engaged in other ways and participate in other areas. Reality TV, for example, and shows such as *Big Brother*, attract more votes from young people than do general elections. As the quotation above argues, it is not necessarily the case that young people are not involved and do not participate, but simply that they do not participate in the ways in which adults think they should. Perhaps the producers of *Big Brother* have been successful in capturing their imaginations in a way that politicians have not.

Away from elections, it is clear that young people do act as responsible, involved citizens. The Citizenship Foundation, which understands citizenship in its broadest context, lists many examples of young people's participation as citizens, making a difference within their communities and publicly participating. In 2000, the Nil By Mouth project in Scotland won an award for their anti-sectarian campaigns in Scotland, which are summarised below.

Young Scots campaign against sectarianism

Sectarian violence is an issue that often goes unheeded in Scotland. But the problem sometimes manifests itself through football.

When Mark Scott died as a result of a sectarian attack when he was returning from a match, school friends Cara Henderson, David Graham and Louise Cumming (all 19) formed Nil By Mouth, a project dedicated to wiping out bigotry in the sport.

The trio wrote their own social charter and have campaigned to highlight the issues surrounding sectarianism in Scotland. Fundraising by charity dinners and a sponsored walk resulted in an advertising campaign to oppose sectarianism in sensitive areas.

They negotiated the involvement of businesses, the council, and charity groups and, crucially of Celtic and Rangers football clubs themselves.

By bringing together both football clubs and the local authority, Nil By Mouth has achieved unprecedented results. 'Both football clubs are now working together in a joint project to eradicate bigotry,' reports David Watt, Celtic's social charter consultant. 'The clubs are working with young people from the city's schools to draw up a youth charter for Glasgow based upon Celtic FC's social charter.'

This project has been recognised as having made significant advances in tackling an enduring and deep-rooted local concern.

(Citizenship Foundation, undated)

Ideally, citizenship and participation ought to cover many of the same areas and be understood as inseparable. There is much more to citizenship than voting in formal, democratic institutions, just as there is more to participation than getting young people's voices heard. What exactly should be taught, and how, are still huge areas of debate for those involved in citizenship education, in the same way that how to encourage young people to participate, and the ways in which it will advantage them, are ongoing discussions in participatory work.

Key points

- The government has attempted to place participation at the centre of its youth policies. The concept has been central to legislation and policy documents.

- Participation has been linked by the government to ideas of citizenship and is envisaged as a way of bringing young people into the democratic process.

- There have been discussions about lowering the voting age to foster among young people a greater commitment to democracy, but these remain controversial.

- Voting rates are falling among several age groups, suggesting that lack of interest in voting is not a youth phenomenon but a failure of politicians to engage with the issues that concern people generally.

- Young people are more likely to be involved with voluntary groups or small-scale citizenship projects than to want to be members of political parties.

3 Key pieces of legislation

Most organisations working with young people base their ideas of participation on the United Nations Convention on the Rights of the Child (UNCRC). The Welsh Assembly, for example, believes that the UNCRC 'should provide the underpinning principles for services for children and young people' (Welsh Assembly, 2002, p. 2). The UNCRC was the culmination of decades of human rights legislation which aimed to give children special protections and rights in addition to those they already had by virtue of being human. It was adopted by the United Nations General Assembly in 1989 and is now the most signed and ratified convention in the history of human rights legislation: at the time of writing, it has been ratified by every country in the world except the USA and Somalia. (Ratification is the process by which international treaties are brought into national law. Upon ratification, a country becomes obliged to review and change its national law to comply with the articles of the Convention. The UK ratified the UNCRC on 16 December 1991.)

The Convention is made up of 54 articles concerning aspects of children's and young people's lives such as their survival, development and education (United Nations, 1989). It defines a child as anyone under the age of 18 and it applies to every person in this age group, wherever they are in the world. However, it makes no special provisions for young people over the age of 18 and does not recognise youth as a category. This has led to 18 being an arbitrary cut-off point at which young people lose certain rights and are no longer entitled to the protection of the Convention.

The rights the UNCRC gives to children and young people can generally be divided into four categories: rights of provision for growth and development, rights of prevention, rights of protection and rights of participation. The first three sets of rights are usually seen as unproblematic; there is widespread agreement that children should be fed, educated and protected from sexual abuse. However, the UK government has lodged reservations against some of the Convention's articles, claiming, for instance, that it cannot abide by the provisions of Article 37 which states that young people under the age of 18 must never be imprisoned alongside adults, as the UK does not have the resources to ensure this. The government's refusal to ban physical punishment also remains controversial. Nevertheless, it is the issue of participation that has proved the most difficult, both conceptually and practically.

The UNCRC does not define participation, although Article 12 is summarised as: 'The child has the right to express his or her opinion freely and to have that opinion taken into account in any matter or procedure affecting the child'. Other articles also affirm a young person's right to freedom of expression (Article 13), to freedom of association (Article 15) and to access appropriate information (Article 17). The overriding principle of all these, however, is stated in the summary of Article 3 which claims that 'all actions concerning the child shall take full account of his or her best interests'. It is often argued that there is an inherent tension in the UNCRC between rights of participation and those of protection: that there are some instances when young people do not know best and that adults should step in to protect them, and that, regardless of a young person's right to express an opinion, there are instances when this right should be superseded in their own interests (Montgomery, 2001).

Activity 4   Challenges to young people's rights

Allow 20 minutes   Read through the article opposite, from the BBC News website, about the 2005 case of Sue Axon, a mother campaigning to overturn a ruling that could allow her daughter to have an abortion without her mother's consent. The current law allows a doctor to claim patient confidentiality and to give out contraception and to perform abortions on young women under the age of 16 if the young women in question are deemed to be able to understand fully their decisions and consent to treatment. There is no need for a doctor to inform a patient's parents of the decision and parental consent is not necessary.

As you read the article, distinguish between the various rights that are being claimed here. Which are the young person's rights to participation? Which are their rights to protection?

Then write brief notes on whose rights you feel are most important in this case, thinking in particular about the idea of the best interests of the young woman, and who is the best judge of this. Try not to discuss the issue of abortion, but concentrate instead on the idea of rights and ideas about participation versus protection.

Parents-know-best view 'outdated'

The view parents know what is best for their children is old fashioned and out of date, the Family Planning Association (FPA) told the High Court.

The FPA's Nathalie Lieven spoke at the case of a Manchester woman Sue Axon, who wants to stop under-16s seeking confidential contraception advice.

[...]

She launched her legal challenge more than a year ago and stressed her two teenage daughters had not sought abortions and that she was bringing the case 'as a matter of principle'.

It emerged on Thursday her 16-year-old daughter, Joy, is expecting a baby.

The divorced, single mother of five from Baguley, said parents need to know if their children seek abortions so they can advise them in times of crisis.

Current guidelines state terminations can take place without parents' consent and doctors should respect girls' privacy.

Lawyers for Health Secretary Patricia Hewitt are defending the guidelines, saying the right of confidentiality enjoyed by under-16s is crucial in reducing teenage pregnancies and improving sexual health.

'Assertion of rights'

Mrs Axon's QC Philip Havers said the public would find the FPA view on the rights of parents 'astonishing'.

But Ms Lieven urged the court to dismiss Mrs Axon's application for judicial review, saying: 'There is no doubt whatsoever that a child has a right to confidentiality.'

She said that a parent's rights 'cannot override a child's rights', and that the best interests of the child 'are paramount'.

'Why then should a child search for help from a doctor in confidence, only to have that overturned by a parents' assertion of rights?,' she said.

'How could it possibly be in the best interests of the child?'

'How can parental rights trump the right of the child, in that situation, to get the help she needs.'

Mr Havers described the FPA submissions as 'astonishing'.

'I would hazard a guess that the vast majority of people in this country would support the proposition that, in the overwhelming majority of cases, the best judges of a child's welfare are his or her parents,' he said.

'I would hazard a guess that the vast majority of people in this country would be astonished to be told that view was out of date and out of step.'

(BBC News, 2005)

Comment

This has proved a very controversial case and there is no right or wrong answer to it. Your own responses will depend on your personal convictions and possibly your own circumstances; for example, whether you are a parent or a practitioner. Nevertheless, there is a clear debate going on here about which rights young people have and which are considered most important by adults. Such cases also emphasise that issues of participation lie at the interface of the public and the private and, as such, are continually negotiated.

Sue Axon and her barrister argue that rights to protection and provision are the most important; she wishes to protect and support her children in a time of crisis, when they cannot be expected to be mature enough to deal with the situation. Her view is that children under the age of 16 are vulnerable and in need of protection, and that their parents, having their best interests at heart, are in the best position to make decisions about their futures. The spokeswoman for the FPA, and the government, on the other hand, argue that young people's right to participate, to make their *own* decisions about their *own* futures, is paramount and that doctors should be able to assess the young person's competence and agree whether or not they are mature enough to make the decision on their own.

What is interesting about the case is that Sue Axon's daughters themselves were never asked their opinions, even though this ruling affected them. There is no evidence that their views were sought, or that they disagreed with their mother, but it is noticeable in a case about participation and about whose rights should be respected – and, indeed, about whether protection should take precedence over participation – that their views might not have been sought.

Finally, the question of best interests is a very fraught one. Most parents probably think that they know their children's best interests and feel that the state should not interfere, but in some cases other professionals do become the arbitrators of the best interests of a young person. What is much rarer is that young people themselves are seen as knowing what is in their best interests. 'True' participation can be extremely threatening (and some would say simply wrong) because it implies giving up adult power and knowledge and letting young people themselves decide their futures. For some people that is the way forward; for others it is an abdication of adult responsibility.

The case was decided in January 2006 in favour of retaining confidentiality, and Mrs Axon was told that neither she, nor any other parent, had an automatic right to know if their child was seeking an abortion.

Sue Axon

The example of parental rights versus young people's rights to confidentiality was, in this instance, played out in the highest court in the land, a long way removed from individual practitioners. Yet the verdict had very serious implications for many people who work with young people. If the verdict had gone against the FPA, thousands of individual doctors, social workers, teachers, school nurses, or youth workers would have had to rethink their relationship with young people in their care. They would have been unable to guarantee confidentiality over issues such as this, and their relationships with young people would have radically altered.

This example also shows up the issue of a private/public split in discussion of participation. Much of the literature on participation has focused on participation as a public good, of young people showing responsibility and taking some part in their community. In this regard, participation is widely seen as something to be promoted. On these more personal issues, however, which also deal with responsibility, participation becomes much more problematic and, if it means upsetting family hierarchies, it becomes a great deal more controversial. The relationship between the formal and informal and the public and private is one that is constantly shifting and subject to continual negotiation, and participation lies at the centre of these debates. Barbara Misztal, in her study of the relationship between formal and informal trust production, focuses on the idea of trust and co-operation, but her analysis is equally appropriate to discussions of participation. She writes:

> [Two, contradictory] trends, one towards the loosening of formal hierarchies and de-conventionalization of organized practices, and the other towards further formalization, will continue to play an important part in the functioning of modern societies. Thus, democratic systems rely on trust generated by familiarity and on trust produced by institutional structures and legal regulations. Being aware of the potential for exclusivity in communities, where mutual trust enhances the definition of strangers as untrustworthy, as well as trying to avoid an illusion that society can be transformed by an act of political will, suggest that only a society that achieves an appropriate balance between institutional-based and interpersonal trust is in the position to create conditions for co-operation and healthy democracy. In order to understand mechanisms of production and decline of trust we need to examine the role of institutions and legal regulations in securing conditions for co-operation as well as the role of informal means of trust production. In other words, a long-term survival of democracy depends upon a just and fair institutional order and upon civic culture, where both cultural dispositions and legal norms foster tolerance and trust, as well as personal and social responsibility for others.
>
> (Misztal, 2005, pp. 190–1)

Despite the UNCRC and its guarantees of rights, many young people have found that the rights it enshrines are not absolute and can be denied to them in certain circumstances. Legislation passed at a national or even international level does have implications for practitioners working on the ground, even when it seems remote or irrelevant. One of the many challenges facing professionals who work with young people is how to integrate the ideals of the pieces of legislation such as the UNCRC in a practical and useful fashion, and there is often a gap between the aspiration and the lived reality. One example of this clash is Article 15 on freedom of association. This sounds a worthy and uncontroversial ideal and yet, for many young people, it is a right they are routinely denied. The banning of young people wearing 'hoodies' in shopping centres, for example, or signs in shops saying 'No more than one schoolchild in at a time', suggest how deeply uncomfortable many adults are with the idea of young people having rights.

A video made in Milton Keynes in 2001 demonstrated how difficult it is for young people to have any meaningful engagement with their rights, and how important participation in decisions that affect them really is. Milton Keynes was a planned city, the building of which started in the 1960s. The city planners thought that young people might want particular places of their own and made provisions for them, but as the following extract from the video suggests, this was done with very little reference to the young people themselves, leaving them feeling disillusioned and disenfranchised.

Marinella [interviewer]:   Are there many places for teenagers to go in Milton Keynes?

[Lee, aged 16]:   Not unless you've got money.

[Lee]:   And not unless you're eighteen. Because, it's mainly pubs, and places like that, especially at night. You know I just, there's still nowhere to go.

[Chrissie, aged 15]:   It's okay when you're quite young because there's like all the little places to go where you can join in little club things, activities now it's a bit boring for us, there's not really anywhere to go.

[Lee]:   When we go up like places up the city the, we're skating and they move us out, and then we say, there's nowhere else to go.

[...]

Lee: Well now someone who started campaigning that we needed somewhere to go, so she says we've got a good idea, they're going to build us a shelter, so this is what they give us. Round seats which you can't properly sit on, and the roof don't give you much protection from rain. We call it the Bosnian bomb shelter.

[...]

Lee: Whenever there's a big group of us, like say on a Friday or Saturday night, then there's like about thirty of us, we're all sitting out here where we are now [outside a parade of shops], but then we always get someone from the shops come out and, sometimes they could be very abusive towards some of us, and occasionally some of us have been banned from the actual shop, for just standing out here so. Sometimes it does begin to be a bit of a problem.

[...]

[Lee]: [The manager has] told us before that, customers have complained, you know been intimidated by us whilst, when coming into the shop, and like we understand that, but we're not, you know being violent or anything we're just literally standing and talking, so.

(Open University, 2003a)

When the adults involved in these young people's lives were interviewed, they came up with very different explanations for what was going on. No one mentioned the young people's rights and that their right to freedom of association was being infringed in these circumstances, and some of them saw these young people hanging out with each other as a problem and a threat to adults.

[Spokeswoman for English partnerships who planned Milton Keynes and its provisions for young people]: We planned the teenage facilities further away from the houses for two reasons. One was actually we thought teenagers would actually prefer to be away from their parents, and do whatever teenagers want to do as a group on their own, not surveyed by everybody. Plus I think a lot of residents aren't always very comfortable with large numbers of teenagers around.

[...]

[Manager of the shopping centre where Lee and his friends like to congregate]: We have had a couple of instances outside the shop, where customers have been intimidated trying to come in, and they've mentioned it to me and I've had to deal with it.

[...]

[Community Police Officer]: I think the general public's consensus is, they hang around in groups, and they're up to no good. That, I don't think is true, I think most of them hang around in groups, because there's nowhere else for them to go, because they want to talk to each other and see what everybody else has been doing, or what they're going to do. Sometimes that entails having a cigarette, and drinking a bit of alcohol. Really, I don't think on the whole the kids are bad, just nowhere to go.

(Open University, 2003a)

Since the ratification of the UNCRC, all the nations of the UK have passed specific legislation protecting and promoting children's and young people's rights. The Children Act 1989, for example, came into force in England and Wales in 1991 and (with some differences) in Northern Ireland in 1996, but does not apply under Scottish Law. It established the principle that children and young people were best off being cared for within their families and that the state should give every support to families. In terms of participation, the Children Act established the principle that children's and young people's own wishes should be taken into account during custody hearings, 'in light of his [sic] age and understanding' and allowed young people to be included in discussions as to where they live after a parental divorce. The Act was further amended by the 2004 Children Act which established Children's Rights Commissioners in Northern Ireland, Scotland and Wales (the next section discusses this further). The Children Act was an attempt to bring the ideals of the UNCRC down to a practical, legislative level and to ensure that children's voices were heard in areas that affected them the most.

Many of the provisions of such Acts are based on children's services, such as primary schools, and are therefore not always relevant to studying young people's lives. The Children Act did, however, represent a significant change in the way in which young people were seen by the courts, and by those working with young people. Nearly all legislation that refers to children and young people now demands some sort of participation by young people themselves and they are given, at least on paper, a great opportunity to participate and have an input into the institutions that affect their lives. Young people are now consulted not only in the family courts but in other areas of their lives. The Standards in Scotland's Schools Act 2000, for example, places a new duty on schools to involve pupils in the preparation of the school development plan, and in decisions concerning the everyday running of their school, and states that: 'an education authority shall have due regard, so far as is reasonably practicable, to the views (if there is a wish to express them) of the child or young person in decisions that significantly affect that child or young person, taking account of the child or young person's age and maturity' (Scottish Parliament, 2000, section 2).

Key points

- The ratification of the United Nations Convention on the Rights of the Child by the UK has had profound consequences for legislation concerning young people. Much of the legislation which has followed it is premised on the understanding that young people should participate in decisions made about them.

- Ensuring young people's rights can prove difficult on occasions when they clash with those of adults, particularly those of parents, to bring up their children as they wish.

- Certain rights, such as the right to confidentiality or to free association, have raised difficult issues about the differences between the public and private aspects of participation.

4 Children's Rights Commissioners

One of the methods of ensuring children's and young people's participation has been the setting up of Children's Rights Commissioners (known in some countries as Children's Ombudsmen) who can examine children's andyoung people's access to services and their quality of life, and ensure that young people are consulted and respected for the choices they make. According to UNICEF, the Children's Rights Commissioner, or Ombudsman, 'must seek greater justice for children both by improving access to existing rights and by promoting the recognition of human rights not yet embodied in legislation, culture or day-to-day practice in children's lives' (UNICEF, 1997, p. 3). Despite the name, a Children's Rights Commissioner's brief usually includes support, not just for children, but for young people up until the age of 21 or 25.

All four nations of the UK now have their own Commissioners, although their brief (and budget) differs substantially. The Commissioners for Scotland, Wales and Northern Ireland have similar powers and remits; they review all laws and policy which affect (or potentially affect) children and young people. They can also instigate public inquiries and subpoena witnesses, although the Scottish Commissioner cannot focus on a case involving an individual child. The English Commissioner has a more limited remit; it is not his or her role to safeguard children's and young people's rights. Instead, the Commissioner must promote the views and interests of young people (although this is a very grey area) and is much less independent of the government. The Commissioner cannot start a public inquiry without the consent of the relevant secretary of state, and can set up an inquiry focusing on an individual child or young person only if the secretary of state decides it has wider implications for children generally.

All these Commissioners have as their basic brief the improvement of young people's lives and the services available to them, and much of the work of Commissioners so far has therefore been focused on the most vulnerable young people, such as those in care or in prison. However, most Commissioners also have a strong commitment to participation; in the case of the Welsh Commissioner in post at the time of writing, part of his interview was conducted by children and young people and they had an important role to play in the interview process.

One of the tensions that several Commissioners have spoken of is that of trying to find the correct balance between protecting young people and taking account of young people's own views and understandings of a situation. An instance of this came before the Norwegian Ombudsman in 2001 when he tried to ban cosmetic surgery on young people under the age of 18. The office of the Norwegian Ombudsman was premised on the basis that young people are competent and can take informed decisions about their own lives. When this decision was reached, many young women of 16 protested, claiming that they knew the risks and were free to do with their bodies what they wanted. The Ombudsman who made this decision, Tronde Waage, discussed the dilemma he faced:

> there was some resistance among girls from sixteen to eighteen when we proposed to higher the age of cosmetic surgery from sixteen to eighteen, and the resistance was about do you not trust us, you don't trust our competence to make a decision about our own lives. And I had to tell them back no, I did not because this industry has an enormous power, and it is defining what is how your body should look like.
>
> (Quoted in Open University, 2003b)

The Ombudsman's dilemma – between respecting young people's competence and protecting what he felt were their best interests – lies at the heart of debates about participation.

It is very early days for the Children's Rights Commissioner for England, but he has already noted that young people are generally not asking for greater participation, and certainly not in the field of formal politics; rather, they are looking for protection, especially from bullying, and asking that adults step in and support and protect them when they face difficulties. He has argued: 'I have had hundreds of in-depth conversations with children since accepting this post and I can tell you that the one thing every child I have met has been affected by, with virtually no exceptions, is bullying' (quoted in Hill and Hinsliff, 2005).

If young people feel unsafe and if they are not having their basic needs met, then ideas about participation or active citizenship become meaningless. It is not that participation should be seen as an additional extra should there be funds and time to explore it; instead, it should involve genuinely listening to young people and taking their concerns on board. These may not be the concerns of the government, nor even of the Children's Rights Commissioners themselves, but if such offices are to be successful, they must be responsive and allow true participation in which young people set the agenda. Otherwise, they will simply be seen as another form of politics, with adults in charge and the tokenistic appearance of one or two highly unrepresentative young people's voices, and young people will end up as apathetic and disconnected to them as they are to other adult political figures.

Key points

- Children's Rights Commissioners have been seen as a way of ensuring that young people can participate and can have a say in decisions made about them.

- There is an intrinsic difficulty in their role in that they are adults promoting young people's interests. At times, they have to step in to protect young people regardless of the wishes of young people.

5 Limits of participation

> [T]he proposition that there are special limits to young people's participation does not stand up to logical critique. How many of us would seriously argue that the efficacy of all sorts of other groups of citizens ought to be somehow limited and only possible in discreet settings, and around pre-determined issues. This is what we often end up doing to young people, who are singled out for special treatment and often treated as 'semi-stakeholders', allowed to participate when it suits organisations and adult decision makers.
>
> (Carnegie UK Trust/Carnegie Young People Initiative, 2005)

In many cases, taking a participatory approach to working with young people has proved highly successful, motivating young people and making them feel involved in their schools and communities, and empowering them to make decisions in their daily lives. It can also help practitioners to deliver services to those young people who most need them. Although organisations such as the Carnegie UK Trust (2005) argue that there should be no limits to participation, in reality barriers certainly still exist and participation remains an ideal for many young people and practitioners alike; projects which encourage young people's full participation remain exceptional rather than normal. Part of the reason for this is lack of funds: many participation projects are funded only in the short term, so that even when they do achieve their goals, their funding is not replaced. Given that the importance of building a culture of participation has been identified as crucial, this will have long term implications for the extent to which participation can ever truly be more than lip service. In other cases, practitioners report that local authorities or health care managers remain unsympathetic to the idea of full participation and are prepared to consult young people only on a tokenistic basis – to endorse their decisions once they have been made – thus giving a project a participatory veneer without properly funding it or implementing participatory approaches.

The differences between young people must also be recognised. Although some organisations claim to work with children and young people between the ages of 0 and 25, clearly there are obvious differences between the needs of toddlers and those of adolescents, and while participation may be an ideal for every young person under the age of 25, the methods needed to ensure their full involvement vary greatly. Similarly, young people at school have very different issues and concerns compared with young people who are homeless and have problems with drug use. Boys and girls also sometimes have different agendas: and Kirby *et al.* (2003) suggest that girls are generally more willing than boys to take part in participatory projects. It is unclear why this should be so, but participation tends to involve emotional literacy and co-operation, skills which boys generally find harder and do less well at than girls (Robb, 2007b). This would suggest that projects which are not involving boys are failing in their attempts to be participatory, and more work still needs to be done to recruit and encourage boys, and in extending ideas about participation in order to include them.

For people who are marginalised or socially excluded, participation seems an impossible dream. Although there are moves to give people a greater say in running their communities, these often do not reach the poorest, who remain excluded due to poverty, lack of transport, fear of crime or racism. Participation cannot overcome these very serious obstacles and simply passing more legislation or encouraging people to participate more is meaningless unless it is backed by adequate resources. Furthermore, directing scant resources only into children's or young people's services does not necessarily improve the lives of the community in general. Thanks to the cut-off points of 18 or 24, young people may find themselves excluded once they reach an arbitrary cut-off age, so that ex-offenders or drug addicts may find good, participatory services that are useful and supportive to them when they are 25, but once they turn 26, they can no longer get help from them and find themselves with less than they had before.

Finally, the idea that participation should be an end in itself needs to be questioned. What does it mean unless it has concrete benefits? Can young people be empowered if they are still living in poor communities with limited educational opportunities? Are participation or empowerment meaningless unless they enable young people to participate *in* something or young people are empowered to *do* something? In an article in *The Times* newspaper, a guest contributor expressed this very clearly when she wrote:

> It is 14 years since I left school but I still come into contact with plenty of school children. At a youth club at one of the council estates in my area I watched as a sea of pubescents were first

frisked at the door for knives and then went on to display a range of anarchy and inarticulacy that made even the supervising adults who had grown up on the estate mutter darkly about the 'youth of today'.

The staff showed me the results of a survey. From a long list of options – 'further education', 'jobs', 'travel' and so on – the children were asked to rank them in order of priority. What preoccupied them most, it turned out, was the category that said 'My rights'. Empowerment is all very well for grown-ups. But do we want our children to be empowered? Do children themselves want it? And if so, I say perhaps it's not up to them.

(Marsh, 2006)

Although a negative view of empowerment, there is an important point here. Rights are meaningless in themselves. If the young people the contributor met had been talking of using their rights to enable them to travel, to get a better job or to improve their environment, then rights have a meaning and a purpose. Having rights for their own sake is not necessarily going to improve young people's lives.

The idealistic answer to these problems is to deal with participation in a holistic manner, and to see it as the thread that runs through all work with vulnerable or marginalised people regardless of their age, and to view it as the catalyst for change, rather than an end in itself. One of the ironies of participatory work with young people is that projects are often focused on the very issues that exclude young people in the first place, so that, for example, youth workers will set up projects to look at racism or homophobia and consult those young people who are most affected by these issues, thereby further reinforcing their separateness and difference. For participation to be truly successful, it must deal with young people as a heterogeneous group, and also as members of a wider community. It must work with the whole community, ensuring that it enables people to feel part of that community without suddenly pushing them out once they reach a particular age. It must also have concrete results which make a difference to young people's lives and opportunities, rather than raising expectations that cannot be fulfilled.

Key points

- When young people are marginalised or socially excluded it is harder for them to participate in a meaningful way.

- Young people are subject to a variety of legislation defining youth in different ways. Not all legislation is applicable to all young people, and legislation does not always recognise the differences between them.

- Participation is a process rather than an end in itself.

Conclusion

Participation has come to occupy a central place in youth work policy and in the planning and implementation of services for young people. As a concept it underpins the vast majority of projects that work with young people, and nearly all projects claim to be participatory. Yet the concept of participation itself is rarely subjected to critical scrutiny. It is assumed to be a good and constructive way of working with young people, encouraging them to contribute more to society and to improve their own lives at the same time. At its best, it can often achieve that, and given that young people are increasingly recognised as experts on their own lives, programmes and policies that do not take their voices into account are likely to fail. Furthermore, encouraging participation undermines the stereotype that young people are apathetic, not interested or involved in their communities and more concerned with ephemera in the media than in serious issues. However, participation is often seen as being most successful when young people's and adults' views coincide and young people participate in the 'right' way.

It can be argued that rioting or civil disobedience are also forms of participation, and may well be the most effective way that disenfranchised or marginalised young people have of getting their voices heard. Participation, in these instances, is a direct challenge to adult authority and, indeed, it is an inherent problem that, if young people were truly to participate, then such challenges would be inevitable. Participation cannot work unless adults are prepared to give up certain power and authority. In some cases, they may well be willing to do so, but there are others in which it is not practical, or safe, for adult workers to relinquish authority. Promoting young people's rights to participation may, in some circumstances, curtail their rights to protection.

Participation is still a relatively new concept, so it is perhaps not surprising that it does not always work or that problems remain with its implementation. Lying at the heart of the debates about the benefits of participation, however, is the question of the relationship between young people and adults and whether or not protection and participation can coincide. In an ideal world they may be able to, but as this chapter has shown, it is not always straightforward, and there are certain circumstances in which one may be more appropriate than the other. The previous two chapters discussed the changing relationships between professionals and young people – participation is a key part of this change. How successful it will be in the long term remains to be seen, but giving young people a voice is a welcome development and one which should allow for a fundamental reassessment of the relationship between practitioners and young people.

References

Bartlett, K. (1999) 'Real engagement by children', *Early Childhood Matters*, no. 91 (the bulletin of the Bernard Van Leer Foundation).

BBC News (2005) *Parents-Know-Best View 'Outdated'*, http://news.bbc.co.uk/1/hi/england/manchester/4425952.stm [accessed 15/05/06].

Carnegie UK Trust/Carnegie Young People Initiative (2005) *Is There a Limit to Young People's Participation?*, press release, 20 October, www.carnegieuktrust.org.uk/cypi/news_and_events/shout_out [accessed 16/12/05].

Children's Rights Alliance for England (2005) *Lowering the Voting Age to 16*, www.crae.org.uk/cms/index.php?option=com_content&task=view&id=30&Itemid=65 [accessed 16/12/05].

Citizenship Advisory Group (1998) *Education for Citizenship and the Teaching of Democracy in School*, London, Qualifications and Curriculum Authority, www.qca.org.uk/downloads/6123_crick_report_1998.pdf [accessed 18/01/06].

Citizenship Foundation (undated) *Young Scots Campaign Against Sectarianism*, www.citizenshipfoundation.org.uk/main/resource.php?s36 [accessed 24/05/06].

Cleaver, F. (2001) 'Institutions, agency and the limitations of participatory approaches to development' in Cooke, B. and Kothari, U. (eds) *Participation: The New Tyranny?*, London, Zed Books.

Coleman, S. with Rowe, C. (2005) *Remixing Citizenship: Democracy and Young People's Use of the Internet*, London, Carnegie UK Trust/Carnegie Young People Initiative.

DfES (Department for Education and Skills) (2003) *Every Child Matters*, Norwich, The Stationery Office.

DfES (Department for Education and Skills) (2005) *Youth Matters*, Norwich, The Stationery Office.

DfES (Department for Education and Skills) (2006) *Youth Matters: Next Steps*, London, Department for Education and Skills.

Electoral Commission (2003) *How Old is Old Enough? The Minimum Age of Voting and Candidacy in UK Elections*, consultation paper, www.votesat16.org.uk/resources/sites/217.206.220.36 3e2c1aed3bcbe8.89092991/Consultation%20Paper%20-%20Full%20version.pdf [accessed 16/12/05].

Ennew, J. (1998) 'Preface' in Johnson, V., Ivan-Smith, E., Gordon, G., Pridmore, P. and Scott, P. (eds) *Stepping Forward: Children and Young People's Participation in the Development Process*, London, Intermediate Technology Publications.

Funky Dragon (2005) *Participation Consortium Sound-Bite Competition Winner*, www.funkydragon.org [accessed 24/05/06].

Green, D.R. (1999) 'Political participation of youth in the United Kingdom' in Riepl, B. and Wintersberger, H. (eds) *Political Participation of Youth below Voting Age*, Vienna, European Centre.

Hart, R. (1992) *Children's Participation: From Tokenism to Citizenship*, Florence, UNICEF International Child Development Centre.

Hill, A. and Hinsliff, G. (2005) 'Children's czar warns of huge leap in bullying', *Observer*, 13 November, http://observer.guardian.co.uk/uk_news/story/0,,1641540,00.html [accessed 23/05/06].

Kirby, P., Lanyon, C., Cronin, K. and Sinclair, R. (2003) *Building a Culture of Participation: Involving Children and Young People in Policy, Service Planning, Delivery and Evaluation*, Research Report, London, Department for Education and Skills.

Learning and Teaching Scotland, Education for Citizenship (2006) *About Education for Citizenship*, www.ltscotland.org.uk/citizenship/about/index.asp [accessed 24/05/06].

Marsh, S. (2006) 'Crippling the life of a teacher is child's play', *The Times*, 23 May, www.timesonline.co.uk/article/0,,1072-2191695,00.html [accessed 23/05/06].

Misztal, B. (2005) 'The new importance of the relationship between formality and informality', *Feminist Theory*, vol. 6, no. 2, pp. 173–94.

Montgomery, H. (2001) 'Intervening in children's lives' in Montgomery, H., Burr, R. and Woodhead, M. (eds) *Changing Childhoods: Local and Global*, Chichester, John Wiley.

Open University (2003a) U212 *Childhood*, Video 4, Band 1, 'Nowhere to go?', Milton Keynes, The Open University.

Open University (2003b) U212 *Childhood*, Audio 8, Band 2, 'Children's Rights Commissioners', Milton Keynes, The Open University.

Robb, M. (2007a) 'Wellbeing' in Kehily, M.J. (ed.) *Understanding Youth: Perspectives, Identities and Practices*, London, Sage/The Open University (Course Book).

Robb, M. (2007b) 'Gender' in Kehily, M.J. (ed.) *Understanding Youth: Perspectives, Identities and Practices*, London, Sage/The Open University (Course Book).

Russell, I.M. (2005) *A National Framework for Youth Action and Engagement*, Report of the Russell Commission, Norwich, HMSO.

Scottish Parliament (2000) *The Standards in Scotland's Schools*, Edinburgh, HMSO, www.opsi.gov.uk/legislation/scotland/acts2000/20000006.htm [accessed 25/05/06].

UNICEF (1997) 'Ombudswork for children', *Innocenti Digest 1*, Florence, UNICEF International Child Development Centre.

United Nations (1989) *Convention on the Rights of the Child*, www.ohchr.org/english/law/crc.htm [accessed 25/08/06].

Welsh Assembly (2002) *Children and Young People's Framework Planning Guidance*, Cardiff, Welsh Assembly Government.

Part 2
Settings

Chapter 4

Neighbourhood

Sheila Henderson

Introduction

> I have often accused youth researchers of being too preoccupied with studying the spectacular, deviant and bizarre. This makes for interesting reading, but distorts the ways in which we understand young people. For we can easily be led into believing the majority are into 'resistance through rituals' or 'new social movements' or 'alternative youth culture'. In contrast, surveys routinely point to the modest and conventional aspirations of most young people. These are the 'ordinary kids', who have only rarely been subject to attention in youth research.
>
> (Williamson, 2004)

This extract is from an opinion piece on the website of *Young People Now*, the only weekly title in the UK aimed at youth workers and other professionals who work with young people. It expresses a sentiment that highlights the differences between academic studies of young people and the everyday reality of young people's lives. I have spent much of my working life as a researcher with young people. I went into this area of research because I was interested in understanding how our identities are shaped as we grow up and how these processes differ for different generations. Dress, style and body language were an important way of expressing identity for me as I grew up and I have always been curious about how this works for other people. As a researcher, I have also had a strong commitment to influencing policy through my research, in the hope that it would have a beneficial impact on young lives. As a 'youth practitioner' of sorts, my own working life has been shaped by the tensions between a number of things: in particular, trends in public perceptions of young people and policy responses to these, and the need to get research funded. The outcome of the interaction between my interests and these different forces at play in my working life has been that much of my research has been into what the commentator above describes as the 'spectacular, deviant and bizarre'. Yet I do not feel that I have helped to 'distort' the way we understand young people, not least because, in the eyes of those involved, the drug cultures and lifestyles that have been the primary focus of my research have often been a pretty ordinary part of life – a far cry from the spectacle conjured by tabloid news coverage.

Previous chapters have introduced you to some of the general changes and continuities, tensions and dilemmas in practice with young people and the role of policy in shaping these. This chapter launches a part of the book which focuses in a more detailed way on settings in which young people and adults come together in particular ways. Our focus in this chapter is on 'neighbourhood'. We will explore neighbourhood settings as a site where professionals work with young people.

The chapter will address the following core questions:

- What is 'neighbourhood' and how can it be defined and understood?
- Why has neighbourhood become a site of practice and a key setting for intervention with young people?
- How do young people's experience of and involvement in their neighbourhoods compare with public understandings of and responses to neighbourhood?
- How can we make sense of policy initiatives on neighbourhood?

We chose to begin this part of the book with the neighbourhoods and communities in which young people grow up because, in a sense, *all* settings for practice – whether education, criminal justice, social welfare or health care – are based in *some* kind of local community, and this makes 'neighbourhood' a more difficult practice setting to define and distinguish from others. At the same time, there is a strong sense in which it is easy to define neighbourhood practice: historically, it has been considered an effective means of making contact, and working on more equal terms, with young people, especially those who may not be reached in more formal settings such as schools and youth clubs.

Work with young people in neighbourhood settings is shaped by competing forces and perceptions similar to those that have shaped my research. In the public mind, young people's role in their communities tends to figure in negative, disruptive terms and it is this perception that tends to shape neighbourhood policy, which in turn funds practice. At the same time, young people are often highly aware of negative adult attitudes towards them and this contributes to a sharply different experience of and purchase on their communities from that of the adult population. Those who work with young people in neighbourhood settings have to find a way of working productively with these competing forces, generational differences, policy imperatives and personal motivations.

This chapter begins with a discussion of ways of defining neighbourhood and community. This is followed by sections on neighbourhood and social policy, what makes neighbourhood practice, and young people in neighbourhoods. The sections provide an incremental way of understanding neighbourhood and the ways in which young people are positioned within them. Neighbourhood provides a site of intervention for work with young people. The changing nature of this work is considered throughout the chapter.

1 Defining neighbourhood and community

In the following activity you are asked to think about the idea of neighbourhood and what it meant to you in the past and means to you now.

Activity 1	Experiencing neighbourhood

Allow 20 minutes

Complete these three interrelated tasks. First, take a moment to think about what the term 'neighbourhood' means to you. Just jot down the first things that come into your mind. Consider the spaces you use in your local area and what you use them for (work, leisure, recreation, caring and voluntary work, for instance), the attachments you feel to this place and the people in it, and how important it is to your sense of self. What kind of place is it? Is it urban or rural? Does it have a small or a large population, good or poor facilities? What other distinguishing features does it have?

On a different sheet of paper, take a few minutes to write down your memory of where you lived as a teenager. It could have been during your early or late teens, depending on what is most memorable for you. Now read the memory and, again, make notes on what it tells you about the spaces you used in your local area and how you used them, the attachments you felt to this place and the people in it, and how important the place was to your sense of self. What kind of place was it?

Finally, compare your notes from both parts of this activity. Organise your thoughts in two columns, one for the present, one for your teenage memory.

Comment

When I did this activity I found some continuity between my two sets of notes: the beach was an important space for me in both, as were friends' houses; I did not (and do not) have a strong sense of belonging to my community and did not (and do not) identify with people in my local area over and above people elsewhere. The strongest continuity is that the place I live in now also happens to be where I had my children and it is near where I grew up.

However, although this suggests little mobility and a strong attachment to the place which has also played an important role in my sense of self, it has not been that simple. I have not always lived here. When I was a teenager I lived by the sea, and the beach was a great resource during the summer, but otherwise I felt the area had nothing to offer me. My friends and I got dressed up on a Saturday to parade in the high street and be seen in the record stores. We hung out in each others' houses and the park. We all felt we had to leave the area in order to get what we wanted from life, and we did. Most of us headed for the big city, hungry for the cosmopolitan lifestyle a working class town by the sea could not provide. Although I have never felt a strong sense of belonging to this area, it has clearly had a role in shaping my identity and my attachment to it has grown over the years.

People in my local neighbourhood often smile and greet each other on the street. Some families have lived here for over a century. Until recently, it was a predominantly white area but this is changing fast. The number and range of local spaces I use now is wider than when I was a teenager: the beach at every opportunity for relaxation, fun and exercise; the local shops, post office, pub, art gallery and theatre; and friends' houses for food and wine, relaxation and conversation. Much of the surrounding area is very beautiful and rural, but I have to drive to get there. In fact, I have to travel to access some important aspects of my life: not just the nearest supermarket and all but the most basic of shops, but my work, my family and a lot of cultural activities. It is hard to get work in this area and I work either from home or in London – where my family and a lot of my friends also live.

Answers to this activity will vary enormously with personal circumstances: our family backgrounds and cultures, class, ethnicity, physical abilities, and so forth. Neighbourhoods across the UK are incredibly diverse: physically, culturally and socially. Some neighbourhoods, like the one I describe above, have a strong sense of community; many people have lived there all their lives and have strong ties with the locality and with others in the area. The ways in which locality shapes our identities and sense of belonging also varies (see Thomson, 2007a, in the companion volume in this series). Physical mobility is often a condition for social mobility in late modern times, disrupting the idea of settled neighbourhoods where families stay over generations. Migration within the UK and globally could mean that we move many times and experience very different neighbourhoods over the life course (see Henderson *et al.*, 2007; and Montgomery, 2007, again in the companion volume in this series). However, doing this activity can also suggest the importance of place and space in shaping our lives as we grow up, and illustrate differences and continuities in these experiences at different stages of our lives.

At an elementary level, neighbourhood can be described as the sphere of the local, the place where you grew up or currently live. It can refer to the few streets that border your house or it may signal a more broadly understood meaning, conjuring up an image of a particular locality such as that estate, that side of town or that part of the city. The term 'neighbourhood' has entered into everyday discourse in the UK: on the one hand associated in popular culture with the 'hood' inhabited by gangs; and on the other, with official or commercial ventures such as local authority neighbourhood offices providing local people with access to housing and benefit advice, or locally based supermarkets. We will consider some of the ways in which neighbourhoods have been researched later in the chapter.

Linked to the idea of neighbourhood is the notion of community. Unlike the term 'neighbourhood', the concept of community has a long history in the social sciences. In anthropology there is a rich body of literature that productively explores the constitution of community and its significance to those who live there. Within anthropological studies community has been characterised in three ways as:

1   common interests between people

2   a common environment and locality

3   a common social system or structure.

The emphasis on commonalities and shared experience indicates that communities tend to be marked by a high level of social coherence. Nigel Rapport and Joanna Overing (2000) describe the anthropological approach to community in the following way:

> Communities have been regarded as empirical things-in-themselves (social organisms), as functioning wholes, and as things apart from other like things. This was in turn the logical basis of 'the community study': the tradition in anthropology of basing research on what could in some sense be treated as a bounded group of people, culturally homogeneous and resident in one locality ... [which would] also serve as a microcosm of a bigger social picture ...
>
> (Rapport and Overing, 2000, pp. 61–2)

Building on anthropological approaches to community, Anthony Cohen (1985) suggests that the notion of community can be seen as a symbolic construct as much as a physical space. Cohen argues that an awareness of community is dependent on people's perception of a boundary, real or imagined, and that this awareness becomes infused with meaning in the social worlds of its members. Members of a symbolic community come to share a body of symbols and a vocabulary of tacitly agreed values. These commonly held ideas give shape and definition to the community and, of course, define the community in relation to others, the people beyond the symbolic boundary who are *not like us*. In societal terms, community represents a space that is broader than family and kinship networks but smaller than ideas of nation or state. As such, it constitutes an important site of continuity for a range of diverse but ultimately linked social relationships.

Yet 'community' remains a difficult term to define. Marjorie Mayo argues that: 'The concept of "community" is notorious for its shiftiness'; and adds: 'It is not just that the term community has been used ambiguously; it has also been contested, fought over, and appropriated for different uses and interests to justify different politics, policies and practices' (Mayo, 1998, p. 104). Mayo cites cultural critic and writer Raymond Williams's view that, despite enormous change and diversity in the way the term 'community' has been used, a common thread is that it is always 'a warmly persuasive word' (p. 105). However, Mayo also argues that the notion can have a more negative aspect, suggesting that 'community' can be a restrictive and even oppressive concept for many women, as in the notion of 'community care' which generally means care by women. Mayo concludes: 'The community can be a prison as well as a source of mutual aid and collective solidarity' (p. 110).

1.1 Community in action

Within the sociological research tradition, Michael Young and Peter Willmott's (1957) study of family and kinship in the East End of London demonstrates the ways in which community works at the level of everyday interaction. Young and Willmott spent three years observing and documenting a working class community in Bethnal Green, an area that, at the time, was renowned for poor quality Victorian housing conditions that were cramped and lacking in modern amenities: the 'classic white slum', as Dick Hebdige (1987) put it. Young and Willmott's study presents a detailed and intimate portrait of family and kinship patterns and their associated community values at a time of rapid social change in the UK:

> Since family life is so embracing in Bethnal Green, one might perhaps expect it would be all-embracing. The attachment to relatives would then be at the expense of attachment to others. But in practice this is not what seems to happen. Far from the family excluding ties to outsiders, it acts as an important means of promoting them. When a person has relatives in the borough, as most people do, each of these relatives is a go-between with other people in the district. His brother's friends are his acquaintances, if not his friends; his grandmother's neighbours so well known as almost to be his own. The kindred are, if we understand their function aright, a bridge between the individual and the community ...
>
> [...]

> In Bethnal Green the person who says he 'knows everyone' is, of course, exaggerating, but pardonably so. He does, with varying degrees of intimacy, know many people outside (but often through) his family, and it is this which makes it, in the view of many informants, a 'friendly place'. Bethnal Green, or at any rate the precinct, is, it appears, a community which has some sense of being one. There is a sense of community, that is a feeling of solidarity between people who occupy the common territory, which springs from the fact that people and their families have lived there a long time.
>
> (Young and Willmott, 1957, pp. 104, 112–13)

Young and Willmott paint a romantic picture of a strong and supportive working class community, characterised by solidarity, common purpose, residential longevity, and being known and knowing others over generations. Young people are depicted as forming a point of continuity with their parents, renewing family ties and relationship networks. Yet Martin Bulmer, commenting on the study, has suggested that what he terms the 'self-help networks' of the old working class communities like Bethnal Green were: 'a realistic response to low incomes, economic adversity and unpredictable economic crisis. In the absence of state support for the relief in the home of illness, old age or unemployment, the "safety net" for most families was the neighbourhood itself' (Bulmer, 1986, pp. 49–50). It did not necessarily follow that this was a happy arrangement; indeed, it could be argued that social cohesion was a product of inequalities, as Philip Abrams maintains:

> Internally, the networks of the traditional neighbourhood were indeed marked by collective attachment, reciprocity and trust. Externally, they were no less plainly marked by constraint, isolation and insecurity. Moreover, the internal characteristics were in large measure a product of the external characteristics, a way of life worked out to permit survival in the face of them.
>
> (Abrams, quoted in Bulmer, 1986, p. 92)

Ethnographic studies of communities have the capacity to capture a real sense of place and the symbolic meanings and significance that people attach to this place. Although Young and Willmott do not comment on the psychological significance of community, it is possible to suggest that locales such as the East End exist as an important source of social recognition for individuals, providing a tangible sense of connection and identity: knowing who you are and where you belong. However, the emphasis on collective identity and shared values may serve to underestimate tensions, power struggles and conflict within the community.

1.2 The breakdown of community and the emergence of neighbourhood?

Concerns with neighbourhood, community and social cohesion have a long history in social policy and sociology. Indeed, it was these issues which were at the core of sociology in the first half of the 20th century. The rampant urbanisation of this period was seen to be producing a social order in which the traditional ties of community – shared space, close kinship links, shared religious and moral values – were being replaced by anonymity, individualism and competition ... Debates about the meaning and conceptual robustness of terms such as 'community' and 'neighbourhood' have continued ever since.

(Forrest and Kearns, 2001, p. 2125)

In the East End: old and new

Late modern social theory suggests that the ideal of community is in decline. Socio-economic changes such as de-industrialisation and globalisation have disrupted many long established work and living patterns. Contemporary Bethnal Greeners are more likely to be a diverse mixture of new migrants, second and third generation migrants, and East Enders with a history of settlement in the area. A recent study from the Institute of Community Studies of 'the new East End' (Dench *et al.*, 2006) reports on the area Young and Willmott researched 50 years earlier, and particularly on relations between the relatively new Bangladeshi community and the poor white population. The flexible economies of developed Western countries increasingly demand an adaptable and mobile workforce. This has led some commentators to suggest that family ties and regional identities are weakening as individuals pursue 'choice' biographies (see Thomson, 2007b, in the companion volume).

The way in which ideas of 'community' and 'neighbourhood' circulate and function within policy discourse exists in dialogue with these economic and social trends. The final years of the twentieth century and the start of the twenty-first saw the concept of 'neighbourhood' enjoying a high profile in public policy (Lupton, 2003, p. 1), replacing 'community' in a policy context that focused on certain areas and populations lacking in the options, choices and resources that the remainder of the population assumed to be normal. These places and the people living in them were seen to be 'disconnected' or 'excluded' from mainstream society and, as such, became a priority for targeted policy initiatives. The decision to call this chapter 'Neighbourhood' rather than 'Community' is a reflection of this turn in terminology.

Key points

- Neighbourhood and community refer to groups with common interests, sharing a common environment and social system.

- Studies of local communities tend to emphasise the importance of social networks and feelings of solidarity among members of the community.

- The term 'neighbourhood' has replaced 'community' in recent policy documents.

2 Neighbourhood and social policy

The Labour government set up the Social Exclusion Unit soon after it came to power in 1997. The Unit analysed the links between poverty and other social problems – such as unemployment, poor skills, crime, poor housing and family breakdown – as a basis for policy development. A plethora of 'joined-up' policy initiatives followed, which emphasised local delivery and stimulating the active participation of local people in their communities. A conceptual link between social exclusion and neighbourhood ran throughout much of the ensuing policy making and implementation, nowhere more so than in neighbourhood renewal policy. A *National Strategy Action Plan* document on neighbourhood renewal, published in early 2001, illustrates the way in which this was central to how the policy problem and its causes were conceived (Social Exclusion Unit, 2001a). In his foreword to the document, the Prime Minister spoke of 'hundreds of neighbourhoods ... scarred by unemployment, educational failure and crime' which had 'become progressively more cut off from the prosperity and opportunities that most of us take for granted' (Social Exclusion Unit, 2001a, p. 5). The problem facing the country in the new millennium, and its causes, were posed in the terms given in the box below.

The problem

1   Over the past twenty years, hundreds of poor neighbourhoods have seen their basic quality of life become increasingly detached from the rest of society. People living just streets apart became separated by a gulf in prosperity and opportunity.

2   These are places where more than two in five people rely on means-tested benefits, where three-quarters of young people fail to get five good GCSEs, and where, across England as a whole, a million homes are empty or hard to fill.

3   Many neighbourhoods have been stuck in a spiral of decline. Areas with high crime and unemployment rates acquired poor reputations, so people, shops and employers left. As people moved out, high turnover and empty homes created more opportunities for crime, vandalism and drug dealing.

4   These neighbourhoods exist right across the country, north and south, rural and urban. They may be cut off on the edge of cities, or close to city centres and wealthy suburbs. They may be high-rise council estates, or streets of private rented or even owner-occupied homes.

Causes

... neighbourhood decline has been fuelled by a combination of factors. These have included economic change and the decline of old industries leading to mass joblessness, skills demands and entrepreneurship of new industries. At the same time, we have seen more family breakdown, the declining popularity of social housing and ever greater concentration of vulnerable people in poor neighbourhoods.

(Social Exclusion Unit, 2001a, p. 7)

Children and young people have been central to the social inclusion agenda. Cross-cutting research conducted by the Social Exclusion Unit (2001b) disclosed a trebling of child poverty for young Britons between 1979 and 1995, with the UK topping the European league for children growing up in workless households. One in four children were likely to have experienced the divorce of their parents by the time they reached 16, one in five were living in lone parent families, and three out of five in every classroom were estimated to have witnessed domestic violence of some kind (see Robb, 2007, in the companion volume). The UK also had some of the highest illiteracy rates in Europe, and recorded exclusions from school quadrupled between 1990 and 1997. Meanwhile, the youth job market virtually collapsed and youth crime doubled between 1980 and 1995. By the mid-1990s, studies were identifying a new class of career criminal involving nearly a third of young men – who were 'perpetual adolescents', never growing out of crime. Jobs, education, good health, family relationships and social life were all harder to achieve for a lot of young Britons than their European counterparts. An expansion in youth markets and culture further marked off young people as a separate group.

As the policy framework developed over time, children and young people within their neighbourhoods became a key issue in government thinking, and policy initiatives were frequently focused at this level. Social exclusion provided a neat explanatory device for policy initiatives that commonly emerged in the following terms:

> Social exclusion happens when people or places suffer from a series of problems such as unemployment, discrimination, poor skills, low incomes, poor housing, high crime, ill health and family breakdown. When such problems combine they can create a vicious cycle.
>
> Social exclusion can happen as a result of problems that face one person in their life. But it can also start from birth. Being born into poverty or to parents with low skills still has a major influence on future life chances.
>
> (Social Exclusion Unit, 2006)

In this policy context, 'neighbourhood' takes on a particular set of meanings: it refers to exceptional neighbourhoods or *poor places* where *poor young people* are lacking in economic, social and physical resources and are more open to risk. Although exceptional, as mentioned in the boxed extract earlier, these neighbourhoods are not limited to the inner cities. The policy solution is viewed in local terms, involving not only sustained delivery at the local level but also the active participation of local people in mutual aid and self help. This development raises many questions concerning social class and the occupation of physical space. For example, is the neighbourhood the preserve of the working class? The middle classes appear to have disappeared to the suburbs, gentrified city spaces and regenerated industrial zones saturated with the signature designs of a chic contemporary lifestyle: loft living, quayside apartments and mill conversions, for example. A possible reading of these changes suggests that poverty and poor neighbourhoods have been reconceptualised as a localised 'problem' associated with people in a particular physical space (or housing estate), rather than a more systemic social problem in which all are implicated.

Building on the idea of neighbourhood as the preserve of the poor, David Byrne (2005) proposes a complementary way of understanding the dynamics of social exclusion. He suggests that a sustained focus on the shortcomings of the locality, as demonstrated in policy documents, overlooks the macropolitics that creates poor neighbourhoods. Byrne indicates that social exclusion has a historical trajectory rooted in socio-economic change:

> There are two crucial elements for any understanding [of] the nature and implication of social exclusion under postindustrial capitalism. The first is a grasp of the actual dynamics of social life today. These dynamics are very different from those of Fordism or from the dynamics of advanced capitalist societies at any time between the 1860s and the 1970s. Throughout that period most people in advanced capitalist societies had better lives than their own parents ... Social mobility seemed to be a real possibility, with much of that mobility derived from the acquisition of better educational qualifications.
>
> [...]
>
> The dynamics of personal mobility are very different now, particularly in inter-generational terms. We now find a situation in which upward educational mobility in terms of acquisition of educational qualifications can be associated with downward social mobility in terms of income ...
>
> [...]
>
> The other crucial generative aspect of social exclusion is exclusion from political power in post-democracy ...
>
> [...]
>
> ... Social exclusion is often equated with permanent unemployment, but the reality is that permanent unemployment is a relatively uncommon condition in contrast with the phenomenon of *chômage d'exclusion*, the cycling from unemployment to poorly paid work ... For the young, there is an additional device on this merry-go-round – experience of 'training'.
>
> (Byrne, 2005, pp. 170, 171, 172)

Rather than poor neighbourhoods existing as a problem of place, lack of skills and resources, Byrne indicates that these localised pockets of poverty and deprivation are the inevitable consequence of post-industrial capitalism. He argues that the distribution of wealth in late modernity places resources with the top 1 per cent of people in the UK, a group he describes as 'the resources superclass' (p. 172). Within this framework,

Byrne is understandably a little cynical about social policy initiatives to address poverty and social exclusion. He suggests that while political investments in the maintenance of the present socio-economic arrangement remain, initiatives to help poor neighbourhoods are misleading and in some ways can also be seen as an exercise in control and regulation.

Key points

- Neighbourhood in policy terms equates with deprived neighbourhoods. This conception of neighbourhood in terms of deprivation equates with neighbourhoods lacking in resources to support 'successful' youth transitions and 'cohesive communities'.

- The potential for a more complex understanding of neighbourhood is absent from policy documents.

- This New Labour policy perspective has, however, increasingly emphasised the need to take young people's experiences and participation on board.

- It also recognises the linked nature of different aspects of young people's lives and emphasises the riskier nature of transitions to adulthood in the deprived neighbourhood.

3 What makes 'neighbourhood' practice?

In this section we focus on interventions with young people in the context of neighbourhood. We consider the shift from 'community' to neighbourhood from a practice perspective and discuss some examples of neighbourhood practice and how it works.

In the 1970s and 1980s the word 'community' began to be attached to a whole range of job titles and roles: examples included community social workers, community education workers and community police officers, as well as, more simply, community workers. Youth work became 'youth and community work'. In these contexts, 'community' carried a number of meanings, some explicit and some implicit, and there was sometimes a tension between meanings.

At its simplest, this use of the label 'community' said something about the *location* of the work, and embodied a shift towards a practice that was more localised and devolved. Thus 'community police officer' might simply indicate that the officer concerned was based 'in the community' (perhaps at a neighbourhood centre, or operating peripatetically, rather than in a remote office) and also that a particular neighbourhood was their 'patch'.

But beyond this, the term 'community' also suggested a certain way of working, or a particular kind of practice. For some professionals, such as community social workers and community educators, for example, it implied a movement towards a more *collective* style of working: working with and alongside existing community groups, rather than simply with individuals. It also suggested a more *collaborative* and participatory form of practice: seeing local people as potential partners rather than those who were 'done to'. Sometimes it entailed working to *develop* the community itself and its capacity to help itself, as in the community development projects of this period. At the more radical 'community action' end of the spectrum, it might involve working alongside community groups to bring about *social and political change*.

For 'youth and community workers' the use of the term 'community' might involve any or all of these elements. Youth workers were encouraged to get out of their youth centres and engage with young people 'where they are', on their home territory. Sometimes this meant not being based in a centre at all, as in 'detached' or 'street' youth work. For many, who saw youth work as a process of emancipatory informal education, working in a 'community' way meant working with young people in ways that were empowering and participatory (see Smith, 1988, for a full discussion of these themes). Thus, practitioners' interpretations of 'community' were often in tension with the deficit model implied in much community policy, which saw neighbourhoods as largely responsible for their own problems and the solution as lying in (re)building a strong sense of community. Yet, it could be argued that both official and practitioner versions drew on similar romantic and idealised notions of what a 'community' should be like.

Many of the explicit and implicit meanings, and many of the tensions between meanings, that were contained in the earlier emphasis on 'community' fed through into the renewed focus on 'neighbourhood' in the 1990s and at the start of the twenty-first century. Then, as now, policy often seemed to be rooted in the same deficit model of poor communities, and in the same vision of 'community' or 'neighbourhood' as both the problem and the solution, though now recast in a neo-liberal framework that has turned away from larger scale state action and systemic change. Then, as now, it can be argued that notions of 'community' or 'neighbourhood' offered the same spaces and possibilities for practitioners to develop practice that is emancipatory and empowering for young people.

As a setting, neighbourhood holds many possibilities for youth workers and professionals working with young people. Building on models of youth and community work in the 1970s and 1980s, there is a recognition that good practice starts from where young people are at in their lives. Working with young people in their own neighbourhood allows for an appreciation and understanding of young people's lives in this way; it is also possible to access 'hard to reach' young people in neighbourhood settings. In the light of this, it can be argued that professionals need to understand the neighbourhood in order to be able to carry out effective neighbourhood work.

It is no coincidence that street-based youth work has grown significantly in recent years; that an influx of new professional partnerships has borrowed from and become involved in this work. The contemporary policy and practice landscape encourages a much wider range of professionals than previously to become involved in this work and there has been a significant shift away from longer term, area based projects towards short term work with particular high risk groups or on particular issues (Crimmens *et al.*, 2004; see also Chapter 6, 'Institutions', in this volume). This has prompted comment from those concerned about the demise of youth work:

> Has youth work ever been so fashionable – or at greater risk? All over the country services which in the past could barely give it the time of day have suddenly discovered that it can reach previously (for them) unreached and unreachable parts of the adolescent population – and help them 'consult' on what they should be doing.
>
> (Davies, 2005, p. 1)

The neighbourhood, then, offers an important site for work with young people that is both participatory and multi-agency, bringing together young people in the locality with public agencies, local authorities and community organisations. However, this idea of neighbourhood practice has historical precedents, as the following activity will demonstrate.

Activity 2   Examples of neighbourhood practice considered

Allow 30 minutes   Read the following descriptions of community projects with young people and make notes on what they tell you about defining this type of work. What kinds of activities are involved? Can you identify particular working methods, or a particular approach? Is 'neighbourhood' about the type of person who carries out the work or the type of young people with whom the work is done, or both? Is it simply about the localities and social settings the work is carried out in? Are there any clues as to what makes it different from other work with young people?

Drama with young people, 'Seagate' 1961

A project involving a group of 10 young people is staging a play by Ionesco in a public hall. The play was attended by 700 people, largely under the age of 21. On the basis of this success, the group went on to perform again at the Seagate drama festival. This project was developed by a lone worker who went to live in Seagate and made contact and 'hung out' with young people in coffee bars and jazz clubs, gaining their trust. He was funded as part of an experimental programme of work mounted by the Youth

Service Development Council to make contact and find ways of working with young people who were not involved in youth organisations.

(Based on Morse, 1965)

The ReachOut bus, West Sussex 1997

A project geared to the needs of young people in rural West Sussex and developed as a result of a partnership between Sussex Rural Community Council and West Sussex Youth Service. ReachOut was a single-decker bus equipped with health and general information leaflets, games, computer, careers advice, and a small kitchen facility and seating area. Staffed by at least two youth workers, it provided a space for young people to 'hang out', have informal contact with youth workers and access information and advice. It also provided structured activities (for example, sessions on the effects of illegal drugs) and a link to local services.

Urban Streetz Smart project, London 2004

A project involving 30 young people, aged between 13 and 18, in staging an urban music event held in the Student Union at City University in London. Half the participants were young offenders and were referred to the project, others were recruited through local youth clubs. The participants were mixed gender and the majority were black. Staff from City University, along with volunteers from thelocal community, a singing coach, a choreographer, Radio 1Xtra DJs and Rampage Crew (a group of musicians/ rappers) all worked with these young aspiring DJs, dancers, singers and event managers. The project was part of a programme of engaging activities aimed at improving relationships between young people and adults resident in the EC1 area of London. It was funded as part of a multi-agency collaboration between the Centre for Career and Skills Development at City University, Islington Youth Offending Service and EC1 New Deal for Communities.

Comment

The range and scope of practice that could be defined as work with young people in their communities is considerable, especially if viewed from a historical perspective. The activities involved vary enormously, but tend to entail engaging with young people's cultural preferences and spaces in some way. This may be viewed as a means of diverting young people from other, less approved-of behaviour. An Ionesco play might not attract many of today's young people but at the time it meshed with a contemporary taste for 'bohemian' culture involving coffee bars and jazz clubs. General approaches and methods of working in this setting also vary: taking up residence in a target neighbourhood would not be an acceptable method for contacting young people and gaining their trust today, but most of the projects involve an element of reaching out to make contact with young people and gaining their trust. The people doing the work differ greatly in terms of motivation, training and professional background and include local volunteers with an interest in contributing to their community, detached youth workers, careers advisers, DJs, probation workers and the police. The kinds of young people the work addresses are by no means uniform, ranging from young white middle class 'bohemians', to inner city minority ethnic youth, to young people in the countryside and young offenders in the inner city. The places and spaces involved, meanwhile, range from the coffee bars and jazz clubs of 1960s Seagate, to the spaces in which young people congregate in rural villages, to the student union of a London university.

These examples begin to illustrate the *diversity* of work conducted with young people in their local communities. They also begin to give a picture of what is unique about this area of work: all the projects addressed young people outside the more formal settings of education and statutory services (criminal justice, social welfare and health care) and engaged with young people's leisure. Even though the Urban Streetz Smart project was led by university staff and used university premises, it was part of a community engagement initiative with non-students and not a student recruitment drive.

This section continues to explore the nature of work with young people in the community in more detail, illustrating not only its diversity but also the continuities involved. It does this by considering the young people with whom this kind of work is conducted, the people who conduct it, their aims and the ways in which they work.

3.1 Which young people in the community?

It has never been assumed that every 'unattached' young person must, by definition, be 'maladjusted', 'a problem', 'anti-social', nor necessarily even 'difficult', and the workers soon confirmed this. There were those young people who had little time or use for an organized youth service because they were fully capable of filling their leisure time in other constructive ways. Then there were those who rejected their local youth clubs because the services were so inadequate that only the maladjusted could have enjoyed or tolerated them ... However, the vast majority of unattached youth contacted ... were in neither category ... they would scorn membership of any kind of organized youth service. But, far from spending their leisure time in any demonstrably constructive fashions, they were manifestly unhappy and frequently delinquent. These were the hard core of the unattached representing the focus of the project.

[...]

> ... their inability to join a youth organization was no more than one expression of a much wider pattern of unstable behaviour. Other expressions of it were to be found in their attitudes towards work, school, leisure, home and family, money values, the opposite sex, and adult authority in general.
>
> (Morse, 1965, pp. 74, 75)

One way of beginning to distinguish work with young people in their communities from other settings is to consider which young people it addresses. The drama project in 1960s Seagate was part of a three-year, experimental project run by the National Association of Youth Clubs and aimed at young people who were 'unattached' to any form of youth organisation. Based on the assumption that 'if properly approached' they could 'be attached and benefit from the attachment' (Morse, 1965, p. 9), the project was all about discovering the 'proper approach', and Mary Morse's report on it – *The Unattached* (1965) – was something of a turning point in youth work in the UK. Morse's account gives an important clue to what is unique about work in neighbourhood settings, in that it addresses those who are not involved with formal leisure service provision. However, her description of the 'unattached' muddies this moment of clarity in that, although the project laid emphasis on work with those exhibiting 'a much wider pattern of unstable behaviour', there was also acknowledgment that not all 'unattached' young people were 'a problem'. The young people the project was most interested in were described as leading 'troubled and restless lives' involving 'a general inability to postpone immediate pleasure for the sake of future gain', 'a pronounced hostility to adults' and a 'craving for adventure' that involved seeking excitement 'through delinquency', rooted in 'emotionally poor home backgrounds' and 'abject social and cultural poverty of the environment' (pp. 73–6). However, the 170 young people involved in the project came from three very different communities with different opportunities and life chances and varied in the degree to which they fitted the problematic definition of 'unattached'.

Urban Streetz Smart project

Does neighbourhood practice engage with young people at leisure outside formal services *universally* or by a narrower focus on 'problem' young people? A return to our three examples of work with young people in the community illustrates how the profile of 'unattached' young people they address varies. They do not match Morse's description of the 'vast majority of unattached youth' (Morse, 1965, p. 74) at all neatly, but arguably entail something of a similar flavour. The young people with whom the Urban Streetz Smart project aimed to work are perhaps the most reminiscent of Morse's description, in that they were growing up in a disadvantaged inner city area with few opportunities and chances, and were 'unattached' to (or, in today's terms, 'socially excluded' from) all formal services other than the criminal justice system. Some projects today are aimed at a much broader target group, including but not confined to those who are 'unattached' to education, work or training. This was also true of the young people with whom the ReachOut bus worked, in that it provided a temporary leisure space for any young people living in the remote rural villages it served. The time and place in which these projects were conducted also had a bearing on the profile of the young people involved: in 1960s Seagate, they were white and largely middle class and 'involved to varying degrees in "an adolescent rebellion"' (Morse, 1965, p. 43); in the rural English village of West Sussex in the 1990s they were largely white and from a range of backgrounds; in inner city London in the first decade of the twenty-first century they were from a range of ethnic and religious backgrounds. All projects involved both young men and young women.

We move on to ask whether considering the people who do this type of work can help us to understand neighbourhood practice.

3.2 Which community workers?

Do the people involved help define and distinguish neighbourhood practice from that in other settings? Is it about a particular type of person? Does it involve a particular profession, attitude to young people or set of skills?

The professionalisation of youth work and other forms of public service is discussed in detail elsewhere in this book (see Chapter 1, 'Practitioners', and Chapter 9, 'Support'). Increasingly, those who work with young people must comply with targets, procedures and formal practices. Yet the personal values and motivations of those attracted to this work may form a point of continuity. If we return to the earlier practice examples, they provide a varied picture of the workers involved, ranging from local volunteers to a range of statutory institutions. The four pioneering project workers with the 'unattached' in the 1960s (two men and two women) differed to some degree in background and experience. Although all were in their twenties, two had some teaching experience (one with additional farming experience), one a little experience in probation and considerable experience in youth club work. Two were university educated and one had few academic qualifications.

Morse described the qualities the National Association of Youth Clubs were seeking in these pioneers of work with the 'unattached' as: 'a capacity to be out on their own; a sympathetic attitude to the unattached, yet one not unduly coloured by previous training and experience; an ability to observe and to record, and also to perceive possible ways of helping; finally, the fresh approach of youth' (Morse, 1965, p. 11).

Although trained youth workers, the other criteria could still be applied to the staff of the ReachOut bus in the 1990s as they reached out to those 'unattached' to youth services by dint of their rural location. However, they are not so applicable when it comes to an example of contemporary, multi-agency, neighbourhood work such as that of the Urban Streetz Smart project. Volunteers within the local community contributed their time, skills, and social networks to the young people who took part, acting as mentors and establishing relationships that had the potential to continue beyond the life of the project. Others were involved as part of their professional role: youth justice workers, careers advisory workers, community police, local authority councillors, urban regeneration workers. For these professionals, this kind of community initiative provides an opportunity to work positively with young people whom they may otherwise meet only in more formal relationships.

These examples suggest an enormous diversity in the kinds of workers who have been, and are, involved in neighbourhood or community based work with young people: from designated 'youth' professionals, through a range of professionals not conventionally associated with youth work, such as the police, to unpaid volunteers. Indeed, the inter-professionalism of neighbourhood work appears to be one of its distinguishing features, both now and in the past, perhaps foreshadowing the more general move towards multi-agency work explored in Chapter 1. Another constant feature seems to be the value placed on local knowledge and understanding, complementing professional and specialist expertise. Finally, another common thread is a more nebulous quality, defined by Morse (1965, p. 11) as a 'sympathetic attitude', which translates into contemporary contexts as an empathy with young people's experience, outlook and culture – that ability to start 'from where they are at in their lives' that was discussed at the beginning of this section, and which seems to be a continuing theme in the long history of community and neighbourhood interventions. The challenges experienced by those working with young people within the community may differ according to their route into this kind of work. Working in informal settings may be difficult for those whose professional identities have been formed in more formal working environments of the health service, education and social services (see Chapter 1). Those who enter the work through a volunteering route may struggle with the boundaries, timeframes and paperwork demanded by funded project work.

3.3 The aims of neighbourhood practice

Activity 3   Articulating aims: reaching young people

Allow 20 minutes   Read the aims of our three practice examples. Compare them and make notes on the differences and any similarities. What do they illustrate about the aims generally of work with young people in the community?

Drama with young people, 'Seagate' 1961

[T]o make contact with unattached young people, to discover their interests and leisure-time activities and, following this, to help in whatever way seems appropriate to provide some of the facilities required.

(Morse, 1965, p. 9)

The ReachOut bus, West Sussex 1997

To plug gaps in service, either as the only form of youth service provision in a village (in which case an attempt may be made to leave some form of centre based provision behind), or as a potential bridge to an existing service.

To increase young people's knowledge of lifestyle issues, particularly drugs, and their ability to solve lifestyle problems.

Urban Streetz Smart project, London 2004

To facilitate mediation between young people and adults; be active in addressing issues surrounding youth crime and antisocial behaviour; and offer access to personal development opportunities and career guidance.

Comment

The Seagate and ReachOut projects both express their aims in terms of addressing a gap in current service provision. The Seagate project was concerned to make contact with the 'unattached' young people who were not involved in youth clubs or other formal services in the area. The ReachOut bus provided a service that was absent in the area. The Urban Streetz Smart project, by contrast, explicitly addresses a crime and antisocial behaviour agenda. In all cases it is possible to suggest that an underlying motivation lies in the assumption that neighbourhood practice can touch young people's lives in positive ways. The projects offer interesting approaches to working with young people: 'starting from where the kids are at', and using informal but sustained work with young people that takes effect over time. In the Seagate and Urban Streetz Smart projects the emphasis is on activity, drawing on the young people's interests to develop and realise a creative project. The ReachOut bus appears to employ the least formal methods, relying on talking, information sharing and building relationships. Getting to know 'unattached' youth can be broken down into three distinct stages: locating groups and individuals, contacting them and gaining their acceptance. Each stage has its own characteristics, but the final one may fairly be said to be the most important and the most difficult.

Key points

- Neighbourhood practice has emerged from youth and community work as a way of working with young people in their locality.

- Neighbourhood practice can include a diverse range of work with different cohorts of young people.

4 Young people in neighbourhoods: lost in translation?

In this final section we discuss how young people's experience of neighbourhood differs from public agenda and policy formulations. It draws on a range of sources to underline the point that young people's perceptions of neighbourhood space may be markedly different from the views of professionals and other adults. The following quotations reflect how young people are seen by others. They are taken from a study entitled *Inventing Adulthoods*:

> The youngsters are usually the dregs of the community. The rest of them, the other ones, the ones in power, don't really like them ;that much but then as they get older they get more powerful and they become the ones who don't like the new younger ones and the new younger ones don't like them, they're too old, it's just a circle.
>
> (20-year-old middle class young man living in a commuter belt area in 2003)

> I'm not saying like everybody's gotta be the perfect person – but they could just try and respect people a little bit more. I mean that's all everybody wants really, is just a little bit more respect off the young people – and to be honest, a bit more respect off the old people as well. Because I mean they go on about how we should respect them, but they never give us any respect.
>
> (17-year-old working class young woman living in an inner city in 2003)

> There is a wider world out there for kids and I think the adults
> need to realise that some of the kids are a lot more grown up
> and more mature than they think they are. You know, and I think
> they need to give the kids a chance really to prove themselves,
> to prove they're not just – you know, they don't just like to go
> and smoke drugs and they don't just like going and getting
> themselves drunk out their face and, you know, don't just like
> going round smashing up people's things. And, you know, that's
> not just – it's not what it's all about really.
>
> (20-year-old working class young woman living in a commuter belt area in 2003)
>
> (London South Bank University, 2006, unpublished data)

As these quotations suggest, young people often feel little sense of
acknowledgement from people older than themselves in their
neighbourhoods, and are highly aware of how they are perceived and can
feel resentful about this. In fact, a Home Office report on crime found that
young people in general are *more* at risk of violent crime, assault and
robbery than older people, and young men are more at risk than young
women (Nicholas *et al.*, 2005). Nevertheless, the perceptions held by
older generations when considering young people's rightful place and
use of space in local communities are highly significant in setting the
agenda for and shaping neighbourhood practice with young people. The
success of New Labour's 'Respect' agenda (www.respect.gov.uk) has, in
large part, depended on and exploited antagonistic relationships between
the generations as they compete for resources and influence in their
local spaces. 'Antisocial behaviour' and its policing are very much
neighbourhood phenomena.

In the late 1990s I was involved in an evaluation of a study of drugs
prevention in rural areas. The following two quotations are from workers in
rural communities who were discussing the pressures and dilemmas of
neighbourhood practice in their area:

> Every now and then you get an explosion. Someone will find
> some drugs or a needle and suddenly there's a big drug problem
> in the village. They want the cavalry. We have to go in and calm
> things down. (Community police officer).

> It can be different incidents which sparks things off. Kids may
> set fire to something, move a public bench from one end of the
> village to another, maybe just sit and share a can on a bench or
> a cigarette. Suddenly, the village has a major problem and
> something has to be done ... We work with young people so it's
> our job. It's like we're the fire brigade. (Youth worker).
>
> (Quoted in Henderson, 1998, pp. 9–10)

The community police officer and the youth worker raise an important aspect of neighbourhood practice: the 'moral panic' (see the companion volume in this series, Kehily, 2007), the perennial impetus for a return of these concerns to the public agenda. The young people in the study of rural drugs prevention felt similarly about this generational divide and even expressed some sympathy for older people:

> I know old people are afraid of us and I can understand why – I would be afraid if I saw a load of young people I didn't know and I had to walk past them! (15 year old female).
>
> (Quoted in Henderson, 1998, p. 10)

One youth worker I spoke with likened herself to an interpreter mediating the cultural and linguistic differences between adults and young people in the same area:

> As workers, we are like interpreters between the two worlds (the adult world and that of young people). It's a skilled job. One of presentation. To each group it's different. To adults it's one way, to young people it's another. Our problem is that it's our job to work with young people. To be really effective, you have to work with both sides. (Youth worker).
>
> (Quoted in Henderson, 1998, pp. 11–12)

Working with young people in a community setting inevitably involves working with the interface between young people's and adults' very different experiences and uses of local space. Although a more holistic approach that recognises the need to 'mediate' between both 'sides' of the interface has been favoured by some practitioners (for example, in the Urban Streetz Smart project), youth and community work has traditionally prioritised young people's experience.

4.1 The neighbourhood from young people's perspective

A literature review published in 2005 argues that young people are, effectively, invisible in the 'fourth environment' (public spaces beyond home and school), beyond the provision of 'token spaces', often inappropriate to their needs (Travlou, 2003, p. 70). In this context, young people create their own 'microgeographies' within their local environment in an attempt to gain spatial autonomy from adults' control and leave territorial markers as symbolic gestures of this distancing (Matthew *et al.*, cited in Travlou, 2003, p. 70). Here the bus stop, the shopping mall and the park feature strongly.

Anoop Nayak's (2003) study of childhood, place and fear of crime in the north east of England supports the view that young people occupy space differently and develop their own understandings of what is happening in

A place to hang out with friends

the locality. Nayak found that young people's perceptions of their neighbourhood may be very different from adult views of the area. Nayak's research recognised that young people generally spend more time on the street than do adults and, as pedestrians, move around their neighbourhoods in ways that give them insights into the dynamics of those neighbourhoods:

> This included knowledge of places where dangerous driving, accidents or car theft were likely to occur. Similarly, their knowledge of drugs (who the dealers were, in what places they operated and who were their respective clients) was equally sensitive. They appeared able to identify 'hot spots' and had developed a complex mental map of 'safe' and 'risky' zones within their neighbourhoods. This enabled them to develop an elaborate local micro-geography through which to navigate and interpret their communities.
>
> (Nayak, 2003)

In this context the idea of local knowledge can take on particular significance for young people and become an important part of day-to-day lives and social experience in the community. Young people in Nayak's study also pointed to the differences between adults and themselves in the labelling of 'gangs'. Young people suggested that, in many cases, the 'gang' was little more than a friendship group in their eyes, though they did recognise that some groups could be threatening. Paul Watt and Kevin Stenson's (1998) study of South Asian, African-Caribbean and white youth in a small town in the south east of England also comments on young people's perceptions of safety and danger in the locality. Their study points to the ways in which ethnic tensions served to divide areas of the town, making them 'safe' or 'risky' for certain youth. In this context the town centre became a contested space for young people, although this was mitigated to some extent by social connections and interracial friendships.

4.2 Developing neighbourhood practice for young people

Activity 4   Neighbourhood and young people in contemporary policy

Allow 20 minutes   This activity asks you to bring together some of the different perspectives outlined in this chapter. Read through the following extract from a National Strategy for Neighbourhood Renewal overview document on *Children and Young People*. This is a document that emerged from a focus on poor communities and social exclusion, but attempts to focus on the needs of young people.

Can you think of one practical strategy that might engage young people in these neighbourhoods? Try to think about the neighbourhood as perceived by young people themselves. Be aware of how an intervention may operate both as a resource and as a form of regulation and control. Who might the workers be? What skills might they need?

What's the Problem?

Young people in deprived neighbourhoods face a wide range of problems. Compared to people of the same age in other areas they are more likely to:

- have difficulties in education and in finding a job
- experience conflict at home
- become homeless
- suffer from health problems, particularly mental health problems
- become involved in crime or drug misuse, and also more likely to be a victim of crime
- experience racism.

On too many indicators the UK is among the worst countries in Europe, and many of the problems have got worse over the last 20 years. This means that young people in these neighbourhoods are more likely to suffer from many of these problems than the generation before them. They face higher unemployment, lower wages, less entitlement to benefits, higher levels of homelessness and lower educational attainment.

Young people also represent a greater proportion of the populations of deprived neighbourhoods

than elsewhere. The problems they experience are summarised below.

- **Education and employment**. Young people in deprived neighbourhoods are more likely to leave school with no qualifications, more likely to have difficulties with literacy and numeracy, more likely to have special educational needs, more likely to be excluded from school and more likely to truant. Moreover, the 16–18 age group in these areas is less likely to be participating in education, training or employment, and from 18 up more likely to be unemployed.

- **Home life**. Young people living in poor areas are more likely than their contemporaries elsewhere to experience conflict at home and more likely to live in workless households. They are also more likely to be young carers, which may limit their opportunities outside the home and puts them at even greater risk of low educational attainment.

- **Access to benefits**. Young people's access to benefits – in particular income support and housing benefit – is restricted by regulations, and can be further impeded by lack of knowledge about entitlements. This is particularly problematic for young people in deprived neighbourhoods, who often experience both the greatest need and the least access to information.

- **Housing and homelessness**. Limited access to benefits can lead to difficulty obtaining housing, which can be exacerbated by limited availability and the low priority given to young people in the allocation of affordable housing. These issues are particularly difficult for young people not living with their family – for example those leaving care – and this contributes to the high rates of homelessness among young people from deprived neighbourhoods.

- **Health**. Young people in deprived neighbourhoods are more likely to suffer from mental health problems, more likely to use drugs, more likely to become pregnant and less likely to have a healthy diet.

- **Crime**. Young people in poor areas are both more likely to be victims of crime and more likely to be offenders.

Racism and the over-representation of people from ethnic minorities in deprived neighbourhoods mean that young people from these backgrounds are disproportionately at risk of exposure to the problems set out here.

(renewal.net, undated, pp. 3–4)

Comment

Reading through the range of difficulties that may be faced by young people in deprived neighbourhoods, you may have been surprised by the needs and levels of disadvantage in these locations. Things that many young people take for granted in other places, such as a good level of health care and educational opportunities, may not be available to young people living in poor neighbourhoods. Alternatively, if you have experience of young people in poor neighbourhoods you may not have been surprised at all. Rather, you may have found the document a recognisable, if somewhat clinical and uncritical, description of the problems associated with growing up in such neighbourhoods. The document points out that young people's difficulties may not be restricted to one area of their life, but may cross the different occupational fields of education, health, work and family life.

Thinking about poor neighbourhoods as a site for intervention and change may lead to a general acknowledgement found in policy documents that socially excluded areas need *more* of everything: more resources, more services, more help from professionals, more facilities and more opportunities. Thinking about the forms of help that it may be appropriate to provide may have led you to suggest increased availability and sustained focus of schemes such as mentoring in schools, family counselling, parenting support, more approachable and accessible health services, information and advice on drugs, and help with curriculum vitae, interview skills and benefit claims. Yet these kinds of targeted interventions can also be understood as problematising and policing the behaviour and values of working class communities (Gilles, 2005).

In much of this chapter we have considered poor neighbourhoods as sites of disadvantage, intervention and change. It would be misleading to suggest, however, that living in a poor neighbourhood is all bad news. The study by Robert MacDonald *et al.* (2005) of growing up in poor neighbourhoods in Teesside in the north east of England acknowledges the ways in which poverty and class inequalities are reproduced in poor neighbourhoods. However, their study also points to the many positive features attributed to the poor neighbourhoods of Teesside, as articulated by young people themselves. Most of their respondents said they preferred living in areas characterised by problems of social exclusion and did not want to move away. In ways not dissimilar to the Bethnal Greeners interviewed by Young and Willmott, most people in the study by MacDonald *et al.* had close family in the area and extensive social networks beyond the family. This feeling of belonging and connectedness led to a desire to stay near to sources of support, both emotional and practical. One young man in the study expressed it in the following way:

> Living here, it's brilliant. We have no problems with anyone. We know all the thugs and the thieves and whatever but everyone's okay ... It's a lot better if you know someone and something goes wrong. If you have problems, you can always call on people. They're always quite loyal in that sense.
>
> (Martin, quoted in MacDonald *et al.*, 2005, p. 878)

Key points

- Neighbourhood practice can be shaped by local agendas and 'moral panics'.

- Neighbourhood practice recognises the different ways in which young people may be disadvantaged and crosses many different occupational fields.

- Young people's experience of poor neighbourhoods may be markedly different from adult perceptions and may include some insights into the dynamics of the neighbourhood.

Conclusion

In this chapter we have discussed ideas of community and neighbourhood and the ways in which neighbourhood has emerged as a site for policy initiatives and work with young people. The chapter has included examples of neighbourhood work and has placed them within the context of socio-economic change, policy perspectives and local agendas. We have also considered young people's experiences of neighbourhood and the ways in which they differ from adult perspectives. Youth work, especially detached and outreach work, has cast itself as the authentic way of working with young people. Informality and anti-professionalism have been key to working with young people 'on their own ground' in the past – as has a sense of providing a 'bottom-up' as opposed to a 'top-down' approach.

Street based youth work has grown significantly in recent years. This has seen a significant shift away from longer term, area based projects towards short term work with particular high risk groups or on particular issues, and a shift in approach from group work to one-to-one case work; an influx of new professional partnerships have borrowed from and become involved in this work (Crimmens *et al.*, 2004).

Finally, it is worth considering what makes neighbourhood work *work*. In an attempt to develop the defining characteristics of youth work, Bernard Davies devised the following questions which can be used as a checklist for good practice: you may want to consider your responses to Activity 4 in relation to them.

- Have young people **chosen** to become involved – is their engagement voluntary?

- Is the practice proactively seeking to tip **balances of power in young people's favour**?

- Are **young people perceived and received as young people** rather than, as a requirement, through the filter of a range of adult-imposed labels?

- Is the practice **starting where young people are starting** – particularly with their expectation that they will be able to relax, meet friends and have fun?

- Is a key focus of the practice on **the young person as an individual**?

- Is the practice respectful of and actively responsive to **young people's peer networks**?

- Is the practice respectful of and actively responsive to **young people's wider community and cultural identities** and, where young people choose, is it seeking to help them strengthen these?

- Is the practice seeking to **go beyond where young people start**, in particular by encouraging them to be outward looking, critical and creative in their responses to their experience and the world around them?

- Is the practice concerned with **how young people feel** as well as with what they know and can do?

(Davies, 2005, p. 7)

References

Bulmer, M. (1986) *Neighbours: The Work of Philip Abrams*, Cambridge, Cambridge University Press.

Byrne, D. (2005) *Social Exclusion*, Maidenhead, Open University Press.

Cohen, A. (1985) *Symbolising Boundaries: Identity and Diversity in British Cultures*, Manchester, Manchester University Press.

Crimmens, D., Factor, F., Jeffs, T., Pitts, J., Pugh, C., Spence, J. and Turner, P. (2004) *Reaching Socially Excluded Young People: A National Study of Street-Based Youth Work*, Leicester, National Youth Agency/Joseph Rowntree Foundation.

Davies, B. (2005) 'Youth work: a manifesto for our times', *Youth and Policy*, vol. 88, no. 1, pp. 1–26.

Dench, G., Gavron, K. and Young, M. (2006) *The New East End: Kinship, Race and Conflict*, London, Profile Books.

Forrest, R. and Kearns, A. (2001) 'Social cohesion, social capital and the neighbourhood', *Urban Studies*, vol. 38, no. 12, pp. 2125–43.

Gilles, V. (2005) 'Raising the "meritocracy": parenting and the individualization of social class', *Sociology*, vol. 39, no. 5, pp. 835–54.

Hebdige, D. (1987) *Subculture: The Meaning of Style*, London, Methuen.

Henderson, S. (1998) *Drugs Prevention in Rural Areas: An Evaluation Report*, Home Office Drugs Prevention Initiative Paper 17, London, Home Office.

Henderson, S., Holland, J., McGrellis, S., Sharpe, S. and Thomson, R. (2007) *Inventing Adulthoods: A Biographical Approach to Youth Transitions*, London, Sage (Set Book).

Kehily, M.J. (ed.) (2007) *Understanding Youth: Perspectives, Identities and Practices*, London, Sage/The Open University (Course Book).

London South Bank University (2006) *Inventing Adulthoods*, www.lsbu.ac.uk/inventingadulthoods/index.shtml [accessed 20/02/06].

Lupton, R. (2003) *Neighbourhood Effects: Can We Measure Them and Does it Matter?*, CASE Paper 73, London, Centre for Analysis of Social Exclusion, London School of Economics.

MacDonald, R., Shildrick, T., Webster, C. and Simpson, D. (2005) 'Growing up in poor neighbourhoods: the significance of class and place in the extended transitions of "socially excluded" young adults', *Sociology*, vol. 39, no. 5, pp. 873–89.

Mayo, M. (1998) 'The shifting concept of community' in Allott, M. and Robb, M. (eds) *Understanding Health and Social Care: An Introductory Reader*, London, Sage/The Open University.

Montgomery, H. (2007) 'Moving' in Kehily, M.J. (ed.) *Understanding Youth: Perspectives, Identities and Practices*, London, Sage/The Open University (Course Book).

Morse, M. (1965) *The Unattached*, London, Penguin.

Nayak, A. (2003) '"Through children's eyes": childhood, place and the fear of crime', *Geoforum*, vol. 34, no. 3, pp. 303–15.

Nicholas, S., Povey, D., Walker, A. and Kershaw, C. (2005) *Crime in England and Wales*, Home Office Statistical Bulletin 2004/2005, London, Home Office, Research, Development and Statistical Directorate.

Rapport, N. and Overing, J. (2000) *Social and Cultural Anthropology: The Key Concepts*, London, Routledge.

renewal.net (undated) *Children and Young People*, Overview, www.renewal.net/Documents/RNET/Overview/Neighbourhood%20Renewal/ Childrenyoungpeople.doc [accessed 01/09/06].

Robb, M. (2007) 'Relating' in Kehily, M.J. (ed.) *Understanding Youth: Perspectives, Identities and Practices*, London, Sage/The Open University (Course Book).

Smith, M.K. (1988) *Developing Youth Work. Informal Education, Mutual Aid and Popular Practice*, Milton Keynes, Open University Press.

Social Exclusion Unit (2001a) *A New Commitment to Neighbourhood Renewal: National Strategy Action Plan*, London, Social Exclusion Unit.

Social Exclusion Unit (2001b) *National Strategy for Neighbourhood Renewal*, Policy Action Team Audit, London, Social Exclusion Unit.

Social Exclusion Unit (2006) *What is Social Exclusion?*, www.socialexclusion.gov.uk/page.asp?id=213 [accessed 21/07/06].

Thomson, R. (2007a) 'Belonging' in Kehily, M.J. (ed.) *Understanding Youth: Perspectives, Identities and Practices*, London, Sage/The Open University (Course Book).

Thomson, R. (2007b) 'A biographical perspective' in Kehily, M.J. (ed.) *Understanding Youth: Perspectives, Identities and Practices*, London, Sage/The Open University (Course Book).

Travlou, P. (2003) *Teenagers and Public Space: Literature Review*, Edinburgh, OPENspace Research Centre.

Watt, P. and Stenson, K. (1998) 'It's a bit dodgy round there: safety, danger, ethnicity and young people's use of public space' in Skelton, T. and Valentine, G. (eds) *Cool Places, Geographies of Youth Culture*, London, Routledge.

Williamson, H. (2004) *Opinion: The Plight of 'Ordinary Kids' in the Media*, www.ypnmagazine.com/news/index.cfm?fuseaction=full_news&ID=4554 [accessed 16/05/06].

Young, M. and Willmott, P. (1957) *Family and Kinship in East London*, London, Routledge.

Chapter 5

Education

Mary Jane Kehily

Introduction

The focus of this chapter is education. In the UK and many other Western countries, education is compulsory for all up to the age of 16, and post-16 routes for many young people include continuing school based education, further education college courses and diverse forms of training. Recent years have been marked by the expansion of higher education for young people: university education is now taken up by almost half of all young people in the post-18 age group. In these circumstances, education can be seen as a key site in which young people come together and learn in the process of becoming adult. This chapter aims to explore education as a setting in which, as in neighbourhoods and institutions, adults and young people interact and create meaning. Education remains influential, commonly having a long term impact on young people's career trajectories and life experiences. The processes of education, however, have been, and continue to be, subject to change.

This chapter traces some of the main changes that have taken place within education since the mid-1970s. Describing and analysing change also brings into focus abiding features of continuity. At a point when the educational experiences of young people have become the subject of media interest and critical debate, it may be timely to ask what is new and what has remained the same in the everyday social worlds of young people in education. In commenting on these themes, I aim to consider some features of educational change that have run concurrently with de-industrialisation, an era of rapid political reform for schools and the education system throughout the UK. The National Curriculum became a statutory requirement for schools from 1988 and was implemented in subsequent years. This was followed by a wave of legislation concerning the organisation and management of schools. These educational reforms had two main effects: an increase in central government control and state intervention in schools, accompanied by a decrease in autonomy at the level of the local education authority. Many of these initiatives have parallel developments in North America, Australia and other European countries.

Specific features of educational change in the UK include a decrease in professional autonomy of teachers following the implementation of the National Curriculum and local management of schools (LMS), making schools responsible for their own budgets, and the expansion of higher education. This period also saw the introduction of appraisal schemes for teachers and the curtailment of initiatives such as anti-racist education and gender and equal opportunity issues, further changing the professional landscape in which teachers lived and worked. The overall effect of these changes made managers and governors of schools more responsible for what goes on on their premises, but at the same time the school was more subject to regulation and monitoring by central government.

In addition to the changes referred to above, which have a direct impact on the running of schools, many urban schools are located in regions that have undergone far-reaching economic change. The Midlands region, for example, has a history of factory employment as well as a former industrial heritage related to the manufacture of cars and skilled craftwork such as jewellery making. More recently, the region has witnessed widespread de-industrialisation, the dismantling of former industries and the emergence of a competitive global economy. Furthermore, in the period since the Second World War, the region has become synonymous with the settlement of diasporic communities from the New Commonwealth countries, as well as large numbers of people from Ireland.

In these 'new times' of global change and development it is the convergence of time and space that has radically transformed English working class culture. The impact of globalisation can be read in different ways. Seen from one perspective, its effects can be cast as a freeing up of traditional class structures and forms of dependency around family, work and community in ways that give subjects increased control over their own destiny (Beck, 1992). Another way of looking suggests that the project of individualisation and the importance of selfhood remain entrenched within class divisions that have a differential impact on educational experiences and life trajectories (Walkerdine et al., 2001). At the local level the very fabric of urban areas in the UK seems to speak of an industrial heritage that can no longer be realised, functioning as neglected symbols of post-industrial alienation.

This chapter will address the following core questions:

- How has education changed in the period since the Second World War and how have these changes had an impact on professionals and young people?
- In what ways do social class, gender and ethnicity affect the educational experience and life trajectories of young people?
- How does schooling shape the identities of teachers and young people?

The chapter is divided into four main sections. The first provides background detail for understanding education in a post-industrial economy. Section 2 focuses on the experiences of teachers and young people in the school system. Matters of pedagogic practice are considered in Section 3, and, finally, Section 4 shifts the emphasis from formal to informal learning by focusing on some alternative sites of learning.

1 Education in a post-industrial economy

Paul Willis's (1977) classic study of working class male counter-culture (conducted in the West Midlands) demonstrated the direct and functional relationship between school and work. For the 'lads', having a 'laff' at school was regarded as preparation for the workplace; the styles of trickery and subversion in which they engaged became the means whereby young men literally 'learned to labour'. Angela McRobbie's (1978) study of working class girls argued that popular cultural forms and the practice of female friendship helped to prepare young women for their future roles as wives and mothers in the domestic sphere. In the post-industrial era, it appears that young people in the present period are hardly 'learning to labour' or preparing for domesticity; their futures in the workplace and the domestic sphere appear less certain and not so clearly defined. The material circumstances of young people's lives pose many big questions for schools, concerning the nature and purpose of education in late modernity and the relationship between school and society in the face of global change. The role of the school and its relationship to the local economy is seemingly less obvious as local industries and long term manual work decline. At the same time, multinational chains in the retail and service sector, together with new forms of 'flexible' employment, have expanded. Observing the scope of economic change prompts many questions. How has economic change impacted on the lives of young women and young men in education? What are the implications for educational professionals? It is against the backdrop of these changes and points of continuity that this chapter aims to make sense of education as a process and a practice that brings young people and professionals together in particular ways.

Activity 1   Changing experiences of education

Allow 20 minutes   Think about the ways in which education has changed since you were at school. Consider things that may have been significant to your school career, such as the school leaving age, your expectations when leaving school, the curriculum, your relationship with teachers, and friendship groups. Did friendship groups fragment or stay together in the post-school years? How similar or different is the school experience for young people today?

Comment

Doing this activity put me in touch with some embarrassing memories of my years in secondary school in the 1970s. School provoked extreme reactions in me. I loved it and loathed it in equal measure. I loved some teachers, but hated others; loved some subjects, but hated others. Everything was either really, really good or really, really bad. I can hear my teenage self whooping and whining as I write this. About midway through my secondary schooling the school leaving age was raised from 15 to 16. Leaving or 'staying on' was much discussed among us girls. My memory of it is that leaving was considered desirable-but-disgraceful while staying on was regarded as dull-but-necessary. Of the three girls I knew who left at the age of 16, one got an office job and became a skinhead, one became pregnant and one got a job in Marks & Spencer (and later also became pregnant and lost her job). I stayed in touch with Chris for a while, after she left school to have her baby. By the end of sixth form, however, all my friends were other sixth formers and we all headed off to university or teacher training college. In looking back, I'm conjuring up a simpler time: paths diverge depending on whether you maintain ties with your school or cut loose. But was it really like that, and how is it now? If I think about it, there were other experiences and other pathways. There was the girl who got into drinking and taking drugs, for instance, and later spent some time in the local psychiatric hospital. I used to see her around the pubs in my home town of Leamington when I was, er, well, drinking and taking drugs. That little spa town was awash with drugs, but that's another story. And, like now, there were contingent factors and critical moments for myself and others when key relationships and circumstances combined to suggest one route over others. I suppose when I think about the experience of being at school I wonder how much has changed. Spending large parts of every day in a classroom, being part of an intense but fragile peer group, the mundane routines of school life punctuated by moments of drama and conflict, appear to be common experiences for young people in the West. This may tell us something about the structure of school as an institution: though subject to educational reforms, in various ways it also remains resistant to change.

When my colleague Heather Montgomery (author of Chapter 3, 'Participation') did this activity her experiences pointed to some marked differences between her schooling and mine. Heather went to a private girls' school in Surrey between 1974 and 1987. She wrote:

> My school was a private girls school which placed equal emphasis on high educational achievement and middle class social values. Along with most of my friends, I attended it from age 4 until 17, moving with the same group through the attached prep school, onto middle school, into the senior school and on into sixth form. It was dull in every sense; I saw the same people every day of my life for 13 years, had no

contact with boys other than painful annual attempts to get us together with the local private boys school for appalling renditions of the *Pirates of Penzance*. It was also mono-cultural and very suburban – no one batted an eyelid when the only non-white girl in the class, an Indian girl called Sunita, was cast as the Christmas pudding in the end-of-term play. No one I knew left school at 16, no one got pregnant, and they would have been expelled if they had done. No one I knew had tried even the mildest illegal drugs – cigarettes and alcohol were the limits of our experimentation.

Very high achievement was expected in public examinations and university was an expectation for everyone. Indeed, at the time, higher education was split between universities and polytechnics and the applications process was separate for both of them. Our school did not keep stocks of polytechnic application forms because to go to one of those was considered a failure. One of the most potent threats during my A-level years was my English teacher telling me that if I didn't buckle down and get on with my analysis of *The Mill on the Floss*, I would end up at Coventry Poly – a fate worse than death. Alongside this was an emphasis on social values and social niceties. We didn't quite learn how to get out of cars without showing our knickers, but we had compulsory elocution lessons. Being caught eating while in our school uniform, even sweets, was an offence punished by detention and we would be suspended if we were caught talking to any boys while in our uniform. I couldn't wait to leave – I knew there was a wider world out there but school had given me very limited opportunities to explore it. Looking back now on my days as a school girl, almost all I remember is interminable boredom. My parents, who had paid vast amounts for me to be bored, of course remember this differently. They feel I had a superb education which imbued me with social and cultural capital (they don't put it like this – they say that I can hold my head up and know exactly how to behave in any social situation) and generally set me up for life.

(Personal communication)

Both sets of memories point to the ways in which social class becomes part of the fabric of educational experience. Heather's middle class route to examination success and university and my working class meanderings between school, friendship groups and the pursuit of pleasure, seemed normal to both of us in our particular milieu. Going to Coventry Poly would have been an acceptable and worthwhile aim for me – in fact, it was just down the road from my home town and some of my friends went there. Not talking to boys or eating while in school uniform would have been a rich and highly laughable source of transgression for myself and my friends. Boredom, however, exists as a point of connection between the two sets of memories. It features in both accounts as a routine part of school life. But is boredom a passive expression of lack of interest? In some ways boredom can be seen as a more active, even aggressive emotion. Boredom, in some cases, may be indicative of a kind of deflected anger: blocked emotions that cannot be expressed in particular contexts. Labelling something as 'boring' may also act as a defence against other feelings, the outcome of conflicting emotions that claim lack of interest to keep other feelings at bay. But boredom can potentially be positive, allowing for something else to arise: other feelings and other interests that can be productive or provoking. Both sets of memories are imbued with feelings, indicating the evocative power of school experiences and their significance to individuals during a formative period in their lives.

At school in the 1970s

1.1 Higher education in new times

We have discussed some of the ways in which schooling has changed in the postwar period. Higher education has also been subject to change. A key change in higher education has been the expansion of the sector, making a university education available to more young people. 'Widening participation' is a national initiative funded by the Higher Education Funding Council for England (HEFCE). It is a strategic aim of HEFCE, and is outlined in the following mission statement:

> Our aim is to promote and provide the opportunity for successful participation in higher education to everyone who can benefit from it. This is vital for social justice and economic competitiveness.

Widening participation addresses the large discrepancies in the take-up of higher education opportunities between different social groups. Under-representation is closely connected with broader issues of equity and social inclusion, so we are concerned with ensuring equality of opportunity for disabled students, mature students, women and men, and all ethnic groups.

(HEFCE, 2006)

Widening participation involves universities in developing a range of initiatives aimed at broadening the appeal of higher education to more young people, particularly those in their localities who, for a variety of biographical and socio-economic reasons, may not consider university as a post-school destination. Widening participation programmes point to some of the ways in which higher education has changed. Many of these changes have been fuelled by a neo-liberal political philosophy which suggests that the future will be decided by the ebb and flow of the market economy. In taking on the logic of the private sphere, neo-liberalism has radically reshaped the public sector. Educational institutions have been restructured, resulting in a battery of changes to the terms and conditions of educational work. The impacts of these changes include intensified workloads for professionals, individualised appraisal schemes, increased competition for fewer resources and the introduction of new managerial practices emphasising productive target setting and individual performance.

Higher education has expanded dramatically since the mid-1970s. A university education no longer signifies exclusivity, privilege and the passage to a professional career. While some universities may like to hold on to a 'golden age' of intellectual endeavour, the sector is permeated by a different ethos. The expansion of higher education and the embracing of neo-liberal ideas create an environment in which young people become customers in the higher education marketplace.

Activity 2   The state we're in: British higher education today

Allow 25 minutes

Read the following extract by Joyce Canaan from a paper entitled 'Recognising the need and possibilities for teaching critical hope in higher education today', written in 2006. Make notes on the ways in which higher education has changed for academics and students. How do these changes affect the way you think about higher education? What is gained and what is lost in the changes?

In the present neo-liberal climate, education generally has been reconfigured as essential to the process of national wealth generation because knowledge is construed as the fuel for the fire of success in a global economic competition in the so-called knowledge economy. In this climate, '[r]aising labour-power quality for national economic competitiveness is deemed to be essential' for our nation's efforts in this competition (Rikowski, 2001: 193). Whilst education has never been free of state control, the degree and quality of that control is being intensified as teachers and lecturers at all levels find that our work is 'being increasingly reconfigured as human capital producers, human capital being the social form assumed by labour-power in capitalist society' (Ibid: 196). Thus education institutions are profoundly 'implicated in the social production of the "human" as capital' and our labour therefore contributes to a project that is anathema to those of us on the left. If education is now generally being reconfigured as the process through which the human capital necessary for national wealth creation in a global economic competition is produced, then HE [higher education] in particular is seen as the necessary linchpin for this wealth creation. As Charles Clarke said in the 2003 White Paper:

> in a world of accelerating change, we all need to understand that our society's principal weapon in ensuring that we master change, rather than surrender to it, is our education system and, principally our Universities (2003, underline in original).

[...]

The system that is so radically re-forming our institutions and our professional identities also is re-forming students' identities. Corridor talk and talk in the THES [*Times Higher Education Supplement*] of students being 'dumbed down', of acting instrumentally, of rising levels of student plagiarism, are indicative of this re-forming. Yet this talk fails to recognise that these qualities students now manifest are symptoms of a more deep-rooted problem in the education system that has produced them. They have undergone testing at 7, 11, 14 and 16 which pitted them in a competition against one other. Their schools were rendered competitors in local and regional markets through league tables and they were pawns in this game that resulted in them being individually stratified long before they entered our classes (Gillborn and Youdell 2000). And this impact has undoubtedly been most profound upon the students that enter the new universities where many of us teach today. For ours are the students who are unlikely to have been amongst those deemed most successful in their prior education. They are most likely to have attended schools not at the top of the league tables where they may not have had great success. As Diane Reay noted of such students, often a 'shadow of academic failure' hangs over such students (2005: 6).

(Canaan, 2006, pp. 2, 3)

Comment

Joyce Canaan presents a powerful narrative of transformation in which education becomes instrumental in political and economic terms. Seeing education as a tool in the neo-liberal armoury of global economic capitalism challenges many of values associated with the pursuit of education, such as knowledge production and intellectual endeavour. The idea of education as a commodity may be a difficult and uncomfortable concept for many people. Reading this account made me realise that my views on what education is and what it is for are a little woolly and old fashioned. Despite working in higher education at a time of dramatic change, living the changes and having many friends who teach in higher education, I labour under the illusion that education is akin to the way in which Samuel Taylor Coleridge, Edgar Allan Poe and Oscar Wilde conceptualised art. Their claim was that art was for 'art's sake'; it was passionate and valuable in and of itself and should be pursued as a beautiful life-enhancing project. I'm not sure whether any of them said that it is good for the soul but that notion can't be far away. Somewhat contradictorily, I also recognise many of the points that Canaan raises concerning student identities. In unguarded moments I can all too easily fall for the 'dumbing down' argument, lament the poor levels of literacy, moan about standards and mourn the loss of scholarship and the enthusiasm of a bygone era. But I also realise that, as Canaan points out, students attending new universities are not part of an elite education system and their identities as students are formed in relation to their experiences of an individualising and inhospitable market led school system.

Key points

- Economic change in the West has had an impact on the domain of education and raised questions about the function of schooling in the late modern period.

- Some aspects of student experience, such as boredom with school routines and the intensity of peer group friendships, remain familiar over time.

- Higher education has changed to accommodate the increased participation of students from a wider cross-section of society.

2 Teachers: being a professional in changing times

This section is concerned with the experiences of teachers and draws on the findings of an earlier study (Kehily, 2002) in which I used a life history approach to interview teachers. I was interested in gaining access to their biographical accounts as former pupils who had made the transition from school to school by taking on the identity of 'teacher'. The study suggests that teachers' biographies and personal experiences play a significant part in shaping and giving meaning to the pedagogic styles they adopt. Approaches to the curriculum and, particularly, the teaching of personal and social issues can be seen to be informed by this dynamic. The following subsections outline two ways of looking at and studying teachers' work and culture: teachers and the labour process, and life history approaches. These ways of looking represent different and divergent routes to developing an understanding of who teachers are and what they do.

2.1 Teachers and the labour process

The conceptualisation of teaching as work has been the subject of much academic research. Early educational analyses placed teachers in relations of constraint as more or less well controlled agents working within the ideological state apparatus of schooling (Althusser, 1971; Sharp and Green, 1975; Bowles and Gintis, 1976). More recent work in the sociology of education views teachers as central to structural and cultural relations that are constitutive of the labour process in schools (Hargreaves and Woods, 1984). Studying teachers from this perspective offers an insight into salient features of teachers' lives in school, such as the sexual division of labour in teaching, notions of career and professionalism and the changing nature of teachers' work.

In contemporary studies of teachers and teaching it is recognised that teachers have an occupational culture of their own which 'gives meaning, support and identity to teachers and their work' (Hargreaves, 1994, p. 165). Andy Hargreaves (1994) suggests that the culture of teachers can be defined as a set of shared values and beliefs: an assumed way of doing things among communities of teachers. Significant to an understanding of teacher cultures is the acknowledgement that the relationship between teachers and their colleagues has an effect on practice. As David Hargreaves (1980) indicates, the occupational culture can be viewed as: 'a medium through which many innovations and reforms must pass; yet in that passage they frequently become shaped, transformed or resisted in many ways that were unintended or unanticipated' (Hargreaves, 1980, p. 126).

In this respect teachers' culture can be seen to mediate educational policy and the curriculum of the school. However, the culture of teachers is by no means coherent. In his 1980 study, David Hargreaves suggests that the occupational culture of teachers is ordered around three themes: status, competence and social relationships. Teachers in the late 1970s, according to Hargreaves, were commonly concerned with broad issues such as their standing in society and matters of respect and remuneration, as well as everyday issues such as coping with pupils and reputations among colleagues. Since the completion of Hargreaves's study, the field of education has been marked by a series of educational reforms which have introduced, among other things, a National Curriculum, local management of schools and appraisal schemes for teachers. An overarching feature of these legislative changes, as mentioned in the introduction to the chapter, is the increase in centralised control and state intervention accompanied by a decrease in autonomy at the level of the local. This shift in relations of power in the domain of education has had many consequences, some of which have been discussed by researchers in terms of 'marketisation' (Epstein and Kenway, 1996; Ball *et al.*, 2002; Ball, 2003). The effects of marketisation on education can be seen in terms of the emergence of new structures and processes in the workplace. In the local context of the school, extended forms of managerialism and a decrease in the professional autonomy of classroom teachers can be seen to produce significant shifts in the nature of teachers' work and identities. The rapidly changing nature and structure of teachers' work has led Mairtin Mac an Ghaill (1992) to comment on the occupational culture of teachers as being in a state of crisis. Mac an Ghaill (1992) postulates that teacher cultures can be located within three main ideologies: Old Collectivists, New Entrepreneurs and the Professionals. In Mac an Ghaill's study, teachers' identification with or against trade unionism, new managerial practices and traditional educational values is utilised as a heuristic device to position individual teachers within analytic categories. Such typologies indicate the presence of different and competing approaches to the practice of teaching that can be seen to reflect a diverse range of political investments and personal identities.

Andy Hargreaves's (1994) study of teachers' work and culture suggests that the changes facing teachers and schools can be located within the context of the transition from modernity to postmodernity. Hargreaves argues that schools can be seen to represent outmoded modernist institutions, failing to keep pace with the contemporary world of flexible economies, globalisation and new patterns of production and consumption. He identifies four broad forms of teacher culture in the contemporary era: individualism, collaboration, contrived collegiality and balkanisation. Balkanisation, in Hargreaves's analysis, refers to the process whereby teachers work in small subgroups around a specific curriculum project. These forms of occupational culture among teachers can be seen as individual and collective responses to educational change and uncertainty as experienced in particular schools.

Studies of teachers' occupational cultures such as those discussed above indicate that the nature of teachers' work, and the ways in which they relate to it, is dynamic and changes over time.

2.2 Life history approaches

A generative approach to the study of teachers' work and culture has been the use of life history and (auto)biographical methods in educational research (Ball and Goodson, 1985; Connell, 1985; Goodson and Walker, 1991; Sikes and Troyna, 1991; Maguire, 2005). This body of literature has focused on the narrative accounts of individual teachers as a way of understanding their relationship to the labour process, pedagogic styles and issues of identity. In these studies, teachers' biographies can be conceptualised as a link between the individual and social structures, capable of providing insights into the interplay between subjectivities and institutional arrangements. As illustrated in Thomson (2007), in the companion volume in this series, biographical methods offer productive possibilities for the analysis of individual accounts and social structures. Personal narratives also elicit particular accounts of individuals' lives, which frequently have the effect of producing a coherent identity seeking to reconcile the past within the context of the present.

Maggie MacLure's (1993a, 1993b) studies of teachers' jobs and lives suggest that the notion of identity becomes an *organising principle* in the complex profile of teachers' biographies. Through identity claims, teachers develop a narrative which constructs the self in relation to others. Such claims frequently involve disclaimers and moral positionings: an articulation of *what kind of teacher you are* also defines and demarcates *what you are not*. In autobiographical accounts teachers 'draw together a wide range of disparate concerns within a single argumentative structure' (MacLure, 1993b, p. 317). In this way the identity of 'teacher' becomes *an argument* which asserts a coherent personal stance in relation to changing or fluid issues such as the curriculum, pedagogic styles, professionalism and lifestyle. MacLure identified two discernible versions of identity among the teachers she interviewed: 'spoiled' identities and 'subversive' identities. Spoiled identities refer to accounts where respondents contrasted the present very unfavourably with a 'golden age' of teaching and learning in the past. In subversive accounts individuals construct the identity of teacher as dull and unadventurous and suggest that they have distanced themselves from such an identity by pursuing other (out-of-school) activities which bespeak the kind of person they want to be. Research into teachers' lives and work indicates that teachers play an active part in mediating, negotiating and shaping school processes. The culture of teachers provides a forum for the construction of teacher identities and pedagogic styles. Moreover, the agency of teachers – their ability to act as autonomous individuals – in relation to their work has a bearing on the ways in which the curriculum is conceptualised and taught, as I go on to demonstrate in the following sections.

Key points

- Teachers' biographies and personal experiences have a bearing on their pedagogic practice.
- Teachers develop personal strategies for teaching and learning that are congruent with their identity or sense of self.

3 Pedagogic practice

The identity of 'teacher' and the hierarchical structure of institutional arrangements inform the learning agenda in significant ways. The position of teachers as instructors/professional educators fosters the deployment of formal teaching methods based on a view of the teacher as holder-of-knowledge and *in control* in the classroom. But teachers also want to be liked by their students and want to build good relationships with them, leading some teachers to develop less formal methods. In a school where I conducted research (Kehily, 2002), attempts to teach using informal methods were not necessarily regarded as successful or welcome from a pupil perspective. Many pupils I spoke with found informal approaches unacceptable and irredeemably sad attempts to generate rapport. Moreover, students were quick to point out the discontinuities with other areas of the curriculum where they were explicitly told what to do and discussion and banter were not encouraged. Bonnie Trudell (1992) suggests that the balancing act between teaching students and being their friend produces 'defensive teaching': forms of pedagogy where teachers make splits between ideals and practice in order to control potentially uncomfortable moments. The recourse to 'defensive teaching' can be understood as an attempt to seek safety and avoid controversy in an area where 'risk' can be seen to engender personal vulnerability, parental complaint and adverse media interest.

3.1 Becoming/being a teacher

The following subsections explore and analyse the experiences of three teachers interviewed during the course of my research. I was interested in the relationship between personal biographies and pedagogic practice in accounts where the interview provided a space for reflections on these themes. The intention was not to evaluate the pedagogic practice of individual teachers but, rather, to focus on the interplay between identities, experiences and approaches to teaching and learning.

Mr Carlton is the Craft, Design and Technology (CDT) teacher discussed in Chapter 2, 'Practice'. Mr Carlton's identification with the pupils is based on his commitment to common bonds of community, class and location. He suggests that this shared experience forges an emotional connection between himself and the pupils which enables him to speak to pupils as a parent would, from 'the heart'. Mr Carlton's pedagogic style is passionately pupil centred: 'In my book the kids come first all the time, every time and it's up to me to see that they get the best out of every situation'. Mr Carlton talked about teaching his subject and getting the best out of pupils as part of the same process:

> If you can't be bothered, you're not going to get anywhere, they're [the kids] the most important thing, they're the raw material that we've got to work with and you've got to work with that raw material and it's something that I've always done, taken a material and made something out of it whether it be a piece of wood or a piece of metal or a piece of a person, you've got to get the kids to work and enjoy the work that they do.

Here, the terms used by Mr Carlton indicated that he locates his teaching activity within the context of industrial processes and manual labour. The analogy of the workplace resists contemporary notions of professionalism and the language of new managerialism pervasive in discussions of teaching as a practice. Rather, Mr Carlton's conceptualisation of teaching forms a point of continuity with his working class identity and regional affiliations to an area renowned for its industrial heritage and large manufacturing base. Mr Carlton further suggests that, because CDT is about 'making things', it is possible to break down barriers between teacher and pupils to some extent. In his classroom, he explains, there is no desk providing a symbolic divide between the two groups; teachers and pupils are involved in the same process of productivity, developing and 'making things' out of 'raw material'. Mr Carlton offers an account of himself as a teacher that makes direct links between his background and experiences and his pedagogic practice. The gendered nature of his experience as a teacher illustrates the difference between 'making things' and *being made* in the encounter between gendered subjectivity and educational experience. For many teachers there is an emotional connection between their identity (sense of self) and the pedagogic practices they pursue.

3.2 The school and social learning

A sense of what is possible and appropriate for schools to achieve in social learning is an important starting point for some teachers. Miss Woods was a senior teacher and Head of House at Oakwood School. She had been teaching for 12 years and had gained experience in four different secondary schools in the region. Miss Woods expressed her concerns in the following way:

> Problems today start with schools being expected to deliver things which the family unit could effectively deliver, er, in a different way because there is constant contact there, they [the pupils] can go back with questions ... a science lesson can do the basics and PSE [Personal and Social Education] can answer questions about things they might see, like the HIV billboards. But I would like to see the family being able to do that. I could never have done it with my parents, I'll be perfectly honest, so

> here's me setting standards and goals and asking parents to take
> on the role knowing full well my parents wouldn't have handled
> it. I hope if I was a parent I would.

Miss Woods uses the language of managerialism in which terms such as
'expectation', 'delivery' and 'effectiveness' become important signifiers
in outlining a social order of who should do what and why. Miss Woods
realises, from her own experience, that the family cannot always take
on responsibility for their children's personal development, but her wish
for this to happen can be seen as a powerfully imagined ideal. Miss Woods
talks about her own sexual learning in the early 1970s as a difficult
and 'painful' time in her life. At her all-girls secondary school,
Miss Woods explained, there was very little formal sex education, but
there was a well developed pupil sexual culture with plenty of informal
learning. Miss Woods describes two hierarchies: the 'in-crowd' of
attractive, streetwise girls who gained credibility through sexual
experience, and the 'other group' of quiet, immature girls who were naive
and inexperienced:

> I was very much *not* a part of the in-crowd, very left out, you
> did feel left out because to be part of it you had to *at least* have
> experienced deep French kissing and it had to be with a certain
> member of the local sixth form, so the quality of who you were
> kissing, all these sorts of things ... the drug scene was very
> prolific and the 'you can sleep with anybody' thing was certainly
> very loudly spoken. People like me would think there was
> something wrong with me – 'My God, what's going on?'

Feeling left out and being out-of-step with the times draws on the contrast
between personal experience and external social relations; the sexual
revolution is turning everybody round but some of us are in the same place.
Miss Woods's reminiscences indicate the importance of sexuality and
sexual practice to peer group status and suggest that girls may codify and
rank sexual encounters in similar ways to boys. Miss Woods discusses
issues of teenage pregnancy and compares her experiences as a pupil with
her experiences as a teacher:

> I remember having one film all about the risk of getting pregnant
> and it was all about this girl who got caught and it was a terribly
> messy experience for everyone, it was awful. She was running
> through a field, running away from the situation. I can still
> remember it ... and that was the only sex education we received
> ... it was very bad to get pregnant if you weren't married, that
> was it. I mean today, for example, last night some girls came to
> the Christmas concert and they brought their babies with them,

now that would never have happened in my day. If a girl was [pregnant], she was expelled from school fullstop, she didn't have any ties with the school afterwards and the school wouldn't have anything to do with her.

The gendered significance of transitions to adulthood is further outlined by Mr Carlton's account of his experiences. Unlike the female respondents, Mr Carlton talked about his youth in strikingly different terms:

Mr Carlton: Not to put too fine a point on it, I was, er, completely and utterly a bastard when I was younger and no female meant anything to me. Now please don't take offence at that (laughs) but I was one of the boys, rugby player, drinking quite a lot, playing the field. And then I met the person I wanted to spend the rest of my life with and her attitudes have rubbed off a lot on me. She made me see that things I was talking about then were not quite right.

MJK: What sort of things?

Mr Carlton: How deep d'you want to go? (laughs) ... My attitude to women was appalling ... she [my partner] always thinks about how what she does affects other people and that's rubbed off on me because before I couldn't give a damn.

Mr Carlton's construction of himself as the rugby-playing, hard-drinking, philandering lad illustrates how the cultural transition into adulthood is a specifically gendered project. His masculine identity is publicly played out and privately appraised in the intimacy of sexual partnership. In his account, 'falling in love' produces a dramatic shift in perspective that encourages reflexivity, especially in the sphere of gender relations. Mr Carlton suggests that his experiences provide a point of identification with the boys in the school:

MJK: What would you do if you came across lads who were like you when you were young?

Mr Carlton: I dread it (laughs). No I don't dread it, no, no, um, I think most lads are like what I was when I was young, or I was like them. It's just a stage of growing up and all I try telling them is there's nothing new, I've done all this. You're not going to shock me by the things that you do because I've done it all and worse 'cos I've got fifteen, twenty years more experience of doing it than you've got. Don't try and pull a fast one ... and once they see that – I bet most of the people you've spoken to who say they can relate to me are boys.

Indeed, many boys I spoke with during my time at Oakwood did speak warmly of Mr Carlton as 'someone you can have a laff with' and 'the best teacher in the school'. The dynamics of this relationship can be seen as a style of camaraderie, structured through power relations, marked by sexism and the privileging of hegemonic forms of masculinity. Certainly the idea that 'laddishness' is a developmental phase for young males would support this view. However, many girls in the school also held Mr Carlton in high esteem and sought him out as someone to confide in in moments of crisis. Mr Carlton did have considerable experience of talking with girls who became pregnant and, in these circumstances, he saw his role as supporting their decision in relation to the pregnancy and talking through the implications with them. It is a measure of his success as a teacher that he was still in touch with many former pupils, girls and boys, whom he had counselled over the years.

Activity 3   Approaches to students

Allow 25 minutes

The concept of 'hidden curriculum' is used by educationalists to refer to all the *unintentional* teaching and learning that takes place within school. This can include the covert messages imparted by teachers and the informal learning that happens among pupils themselves in peer groups and other social encounters. Consider the following dialogue and identify how the hidden curriculum may be working and what this says about the pedagogic style of the teacher.

Miss Green: There's a big gulf between us, they've got a whole world which we are not part of ... to maintain order you have to have a distance. There are two different worlds and maybe that's how it's got to be.

MJK: Do you think that the hidden curriculum might be more effective for students learning about sex than the official curriculum?

Miss Green: Oh I suspect that's the way they get the misinformation or real information, a bit of both I suspect, yes, I'm sure it always will be. It was when I was at school ... I can only say I hope a lot of the accurate information we are able to give them through PSE will filter through to the hidden curriculum and I'm sure it will. It will be made use of in the same way as some of the messages they get from the media will be made use of. Some are going to be conflicting ... but I just hope that the message, the correct information that we're giving them in school is going to be sufficiently helpful to them to make sense of all the other things.

MJK: Do you ever catch glimpses of how the students may be thinking and feeling about sex? Do you ever hear tales or gather pieces of information?

Miss Green: Not unless I actually sit down and talk to a group of youngsters. I was on cover one day and it was girls PE and they couldn't do the lesson so I'd watched a programme about young people and sex and thought 'was this really the case?' So I started talking to these girls and they were very open and quite willing to talk and, yes, only if I do that sort of thing because obviously we don't intrude.

Comment

For Miss Green the world of teachers and the world of pupils cannot be bridged because of the inherent structure of school relations. The discipline and order which teachers must maintain is premised on 'distance' from pupil cultures. The notion of 'two cultures' supports the concept of the 'hidden curriculum' by suggesting that much of what pupils learn in school can be seen as social learning and takes place in informal spaces outside the official curriculum. Miss Green agrees that there is a hidden curriculum in relation to sexual learning, but holds out the hope that Personal and Social Education (PSE) will also have a voice. Here Miss Green suggests that PSE is able to provide accurate information that can be assimilated into pupil perspectives. There is a certain appeal to rationality in Miss Green's support of PSE, promoting the notion that the 'accurate' and 'correct' will triumph over misinformation and will ultimately enable students to make sense of competing messages. In certain moments Miss Green indicated that it is possible to gain access to the pupil world. In this extract Miss Green discovered that a different set of teacher–pupil relationships became possible when the normal school timetable was disrupted. The openness of pupils in this instance challenged, albeit temporarily, the idea of two closely bounded school cultures.

3.3 Teachers as implementers of policy

A consideration of teachers' experiences that traces the connections between their (auto)biographies and subjective investments suggests that the personal plays a part in the development of pedagogic practice. The glimpse into the life histories of the practitioners I interviewed illustrates that their approaches to teaching and learning have been shaped by their past experiences as pupils and as gendered sexual subjects. In many cases respondents provided an account of what kind of pupil they were which was insightful and instructive in understanding their pedagogic style. Teachers' biographies indicate that experience may be translated into pedagogic practice in complex and unexpected ways.

Interviews with teachers also suggest that teacher–pupil relationships provide the context for much personal and social learning and can influence the success of initiatives in this field. Policy approaches to Personal, Social and Health Education emphasise the importance of curriculum documents which strike the 'right' note, encourage certain pedagogic approaches over others and specify criteria for teaching and learning. However, the success of this education depends on a contingency of factors which cannot necessarily be accounted for at the level of policy. Mr Carlton, for example, is unlikely to match the selection criteria drawn up in a person specification for the post of sex educator. Rather, his profile as rugby-playing, heavy-drinking lad would place him beyond the bounds of desirability for the teaching of a subject that requires sensitivity and understanding, especially in relation to issues of gender politics. However, the success of Mr Carlton's approach to sex education and PSE generally indicates that other factors may be in play in the development of 'good practice'. Mr Carlton's identifications as local, working class, speaker of the regional dialect and part of the community give him a grounding which facilitates the development of positive and mutually affirming pupil–teacher relationships. In many ways, Mr Carlton's approach to teaching is reminiscent of informal education and youth work discussed in Chapter 4, 'Neighbourhood'. Like informal youth work strategies for engaging young people, Mr Carlton also stresses the importance of relationship building, establishing a rapport with students and starting from where they are at. In Oakwood School, the qualities, characteristics and identities valued by the student population become important to the success of pedagogic practice as a whole. In this context there is an engagement between the local culture of the school and Mr Carlton's organic approach to teaching and learning that makes him popular with students and successful as a teacher. This points to the importance of place and context-specific relationships to policy initiatives and pedagogic strategies and the difficulties involved in specifying a formula for 'success'. There appears to be a need for good practice to emerge organically from the context of the institution and, crucially, to provide points of connection with the values and priorities of young people on the receiving end of policy in that locality.

3.4 Young people's experience of school

Earlier in the chapter you were asked to think about your own experiences of school and how schools may have changed. If we think about young people's experience of school at a general level there are many points of continuity. Many young people experience school life as rigid and controlling, they hate certain teachers and like others and may form intense and sometimes difficult peer group relations. But how have the changes in education had an impact on the day-to-day experience of being a student in school? Diane Reay (2004) suggests that the marketisation of education has created a greater gap between schools premised on geographical location and social class. This has an impact on access to resources and, crucially, the ability of the school to demonstrate effectiveness in league tables and other modes of assessment. Reflecting an increased polarisation between rich and poor at a societal level, schools, especially in inner city areas, have acquired powerful reputations as either middle class with good educational standards or working class with poor educational standards. Processes of demonisation and pathologisation operate to construct inner city schools as dangerous and dirty places for the 'lumpen proletariat', the 'losers in the educational game' (Reay, 2004, p. 1018). Reay's study based in 19 secondary schools in London indicates that young people are acutely aware of these class based constructions and their place within them. They refer to local schools in terms of waste and excrement as 'rubbish', 'crap' and 'full of tramps'. Reay documents the ways in which young people attending these schools develop strategies to cope with the experience of attending an inner London 'sink' school and, in some cases, attempt to recuperate the negative associations into a more positive account.

In a study that focused on children's and young people's experiences of home and school, conducted in the UK in the late 1990s, Pam Alldred *et al.* (2002) paid attention to the views of young people themselves. They identified certain features of school life that young people felt strongly about:

> in our research, the children and young people characterised school as involving formal rules and timetables, and general constraints upon feelings and behaviour. The inability to eat when you wanted, or lose your temper or generally be 'loud', were often used as illustrations of the constraints involved. It was these regimented aspects of school life as part of the group 'pupils' that featured large ... rather than education and learning ...
>
> 'Bad' teachers were described as those who took the regulation and control of children too far; who would not listen to them, shouted at them, and ordered them around peremptorily. They might also be too 'nosey' about children's lives outside the classroom ...
>
> (Alldred *et al.*, 2002, p. 126)

Students in the study saw school as a place to hang out with friends. Inevitably, friendship groups were shaped in relation to the structure of the school organisation and students were involved in the constant negotiation of school rules and routines. However, the regimented nature of school life did not mean that students necessarily felt safe. Many pupils in the study spoke of the fear of threats and bullying by peers and teachers, while some students reported that they had actually been bullied in school.

A further study of student cultures (Kehily and Pattman, 2006), in which I was involved, focused on young people's experience of school; we were interested in charting the journey from pre-sixth form to sixth form as articulated by students themselves. Our study was based in four schools in Milton Keynes: three in the state sector and one private, fee-paying school. In keeping with earlier qualitative studies of student cultures, young people in our study spoke of a differentiated world of competing groups and social practices (Willis, 1977; Pollard, 1984; Connell, 1985; Nilan, 1992). In interviews with Year 10, students positioned themselves on a social hierarchy: the most popular being a combination of smokers, and sporty, physically attractive, 'hard', loud and rebellious people; and the least popular 'boffs' (boffins) or quiet and conscientious workers who were usually viewed as 'uncool' and deferential to school authority. These constructions of peer popularity were gendered, with physical attractiveness a common criterion of popularity for girls and sporting ability for boys.

Sixth formers we interviewed indicated that these categories were enduring. They were highly critical of the popular students, all of whom were said to have left by sixth form. They referred to them as 'wasters' and 'yobs', terms that resonate with the notion of an 'underclass' of undeserving poor whose actions render them unteachable and unemployable. Sixth formers suggested that the 'wasters' were essentially inauthentic, using smoking and 'style' to create a tough and bad image. Some of the sixth formers seemed to delight in constructing them as failures and losers, often emphasising how much smoking had wasted the popular boys physically. One boy, Gary, had this to say:

> The ones that used to piss around and that. They can't afford to go to the bars and clubs, they have to sit outside the front of the shop drinking from cans ... and they've stopped growing since like Year 9 cos they smoke anyway, they're scrawny little things and you think, 'Pathetic!'

By reconstructing the formerly popular boys as weak and scrawny, it seemed sixth form boys, like Gary, were seeking retribution through the articulation of a revenge narrative that made them feel more comfortable about the past. The sharp binary invoked by sixth formers between popular 'dropouts' and less popular achievers indicates that the two groups exist in opposition to each other as bounded categories that cannot be breached. We suggest that the invocation of this binary opposition is important to the ways in which sixth formers make sense of their educational experience. While it may be the case that some sixth formers had a 'popular' crowd past and that some dropouts may have been academic achievers, the significance of the binary lies in its explanatory power. For sixth formers it produces a narrative of cause and effect that presents them as agentic, superior and successful. It also provides individuals with a way of coming to terms with the pain of the past, to shake off the 'boffin' tag and the anxieties associated with being 'uncool'. Identifying as weak and boffish entails occupying what Wetherell (1998) calls a 'troubled subject position' and very few sixth form boys actually 'admitted' being boffs in their earlier years. Rather, they presented themselves as taking a 'middle' position, lying somewhere between the boffs and the popular ones. In individual interviews, however, a few sixth form boys recalled being small, weak or 'boffish'. Imran, a South Asian boy, recalled how he was teased by the popular boys because of both his small stature and his ethnicity:

> They all used to congregate round the back of the gym and like, have a fag. But we'd all have to walk past them to get to our next lesson ... all of them lot just leaning against the wall and chatting in their group ... we'd all have to look at them, and we had no ... choice, we'd all have to look at them.

His response was to go to the gym to make himself bigger:

> When I received it [racism] I knew that I couldn't change the colour of my skin ... so it made me unhappy about who I was ... so the only thing I thought I could change was my size.

Imran's response points to the dialogue between ethnicity and masculinities in school and the ways in which masculinity is, literally and metaphorically, a 'pumped up' concept that young men make considerable efforts to grow into (Back, 1994; Nayak and Kehily, 1996; Connolly, 1998; Frosh *et al.*, 2002). By working hard, both mentally and physically, Imran felt the tables had turned. The rebels who bullied him were now working in low paid jobs with no future while he was destined to go on to university. He was also bigger and fitter than them now, as he had been working out in the gym while they were smoking round the back of it. Like many other sixth formers we interviewed, Imran associated leaving school with going to university, a move characterised not in terms of further commitment to study but more as a release from and reward for the hard work they had put in at school while the rebels messed around and taunted them. The reward was freedom and hedonism. Imran said:

> I'm planning on going to uni this, what, this coming September ... so I mean, from the stories I've heard from all my friends at university ... it's like, out drinking every night and stuff ... and I'm kind of like, looking forward to like, the independence and stuff, and like, mm, like, meeting new people and making new friends and stuff.

The emphasis on academic achievement, going to university and broadening horizons beyond the immediate locale can be seen as an expression of the individualisation thesis in which postmodern identities are forged by the loosening up of regional affiliations to family and community. However, the sixth former's path from school to university can also be viewed as a point of continuity with the past; a clear exercise of *choice* commonly taken by middle class kids and their parents that has been theorised in terms of the reproduction of class relations (Willis, 1977; Ball *et al.*, 2002).

In contrast to their fantasies about university life, the sixth formers emphasised, often in quite patronising ways, how insular and limited the lives of the school dropouts were. The formerly popular boys were mocked for working in warehouses, on building sites or being unemployed, while the ex-popular girls were ridiculed, mainly by the girls, for doing hairdressing or courses in childcare, or becoming pregnant. Sixth formers we interviewed at the private school identified as autonomous individuals with bright futures, in opposition to state school pupils. State school pupils were constructed as non-academic, rough, obsessed with image, prone to peer pressure, fixated with groups and antisocial, especially towards them. As with the sixth formers in state schools, they frequently associated their 'Others' with smoking and drug taking, while maintaining that the 'few' sixth formers who smoked tobacco or cannabis did so not to impress others or be bad, but because they *chose to* as individuals. Middle class students' emphasis on individuality and choice is drawn on as a point of distinction between themselves and working class kids. Through notions of physicality, academic success and the promise of a bright future, sixth formers engage in discursive manoeuvres that pathologise the behaviour of working class kids. Walkerdine *et al.* (2001, p. 209) suggest that working class and middle class students become 'each other's Other' in the making of modern neo-liberal subjects. Our interviews illustrate some of the ways in which this is an active process in which middle class students claim a strong sense of agency, in opposition to what they perceive as the destructive, herd-like behaviour of working class students.

Key points

- Learning can be enhanced when teachers and students share a value system.

- Teachers can be unreliable and unpredictable mediators of education policy.

- Social class, gender and ethnicity have an impact on the teaching and learning process and can be interwoven into educational experience in complex ways.

4 Alternative sites for learning: the YWCA and Milton Keynes Christian Foundation

The traditional assumption that education takes place in educational sites such as schools, colleges and universities is increasingly challenged in the late modern period. De-industrialisation, the emergence of new flexible economies and the breakdown of the notion of 'a job for life' point to the emergence of a different status for education in young people's lives. Rather than being the pathway to a career, education now occupies a seemingly more central place as a life-long pursuit. Contemporary educational discourse suggests that individuals have a responsibility to carry on learning throughout the life course, to constantly update their skills and knowledge base in order to maintain their position in the contemporary labour market. In secondary schools in the UK every pupil is required to keep a Record of Achievement portfolio (as discussed in the companion volume, Kehily, 2007), documenting the successful completion of courses, periods of study and training. Post-school, the curriculum vitae takes on the responsibility of individualising achievement and profiling the person in ever more particular ways. However, there is growing recognition that education can happen outside the educational arena in spaces other than the mainstream. Many alternative sites of learning exist as interventions designed to meet the needs of a local population. Such initiatives tend to be promoted and run by charities in partnership with local authorities and other well-established local organisations.

Earlier in the chapter, Miss Woods indicated that when she was at school in the 1970s, becoming pregnant signalled the end of your educational career. She noted with some surprise that girls she teaches today do not appear to carry the stigma of single motherhood and commonly come back to school for social visits with their babies. However, there was no suggestion that these young women could return to school to complete their education. Some schools in the UK are creating an environment in which young mothers can return to school, while other initiatives aim to support young mothers in alternative educational sites in the community. The Young Women's Christian Association (YWCA), a leading charity in the UK, hosts 'Young Mums to Be' courses at centres across the country. The courses provide a traditional educational curriculum adapted to the needs of young mothers. Women are taught in small classes and emphasis is placed on support and encouragement. The YWCA (2006) report that the majority of young women on the courses complete their GCSEs and subsequently take jobs or move on to further and higher education.

Like the YWCA, Milton Keynes Christian Foundation runs programmes to support young women (aged 15–18) who are pregnant or have a young child. The Foundation has been established for 20 years and provides a range of courses and community initiatives to support young people. It operates with the following principles:

- A belief that all people and all things have an essential value and potential

- A commitment to deliver the highest possible standards, so as to challenge low self-esteem, raise expectations and enable our trainees and residents to take significant steps forward in their lives

- A focus on Groups on the Margins, Regeneration, Environmental Concern and Economic Justice and on the interconnectedness of these themes

- A belief in the importance of partnership working with people and with organisations, which hold similar values and with whom we share common concerns

(Milton Keynes Christian Foundation, 2006)

The Milton Keynes Christian Foundation project to help young people prepare for parenthood is called 'Foundation for Parents' and is funded by the Learning and Skills Council and the European Social Fund. Unlike the YWCA project, the emphasis is not on formal educational qualifications. Rather, the Foundation for Parents course offers a range of activities and training sessions such as parenting classes, relaxation classes, literacy and numeracy classes, and support with curriculum vitae and job applications. The focus is on practical learning and skills development that prepare young people for parenthood in direct ways. Young people attending the course report feeling supported and safe. Chloe is 17 and expecting her first child. When her parents found out she was pregnant they asked her to leave home. At the same time, her boyfriend broke up with her. Describing this period as a 'rubbish' time in her life, she moved into a mother and baby unit run by Milton Keynes Council. Through staff at the unit she found out about and began attending Foundation for Parents. She speaks of the course in the following way:

All different ones [professionals] come to Foundation for Parents. Baby massaging people came in and we've had Indian head massage and Bollywood dancing, art and craft where you can make your first baby's picture frame ... It's given me so much more confidence ... I think all the girls there feel that kind of confidence ...

And it makes you feel much more knowledgeable ... Going to the Foundation for Parents is the best thing I think I could have

Milton Keynes Foundation for Parents: an alternative site for learning

done. And I think that's easily – that's better than my GCSE grades, going there and learning absolutely everything that you can learn about – everything from labour to breastfeeding to child development.

(Thomson and Kehily, 2006)

Activity 4   Learning for life: young motherhood

Allow 20 minutes   What are your responses to the two initiatives for young mothers, described above, run by the YWCA and the Milton Keynes Christian Foundation? Make notes on the differences between the two projects. What do you consider to be an appropriate education for young mothers-to-be, and why?

Comment

Chloe's comments indicate that, far from signalling the end of education, pregnancy for her has heralded the start of a whole new learning process that she has eagerly embraced. Chloe suggests that the course she attended at the Milton Keynes Christian Foundation has given her the knowledge and confidence to embark on her new role as a mother, and values this form of learning more highly than her GCSE qualifications. The education of young mothers is a sensitive and controversial subject that commonly touches on a moral agenda shaped by ideas on teenage sex, single parenthood and public resources. Intertwined with this moral agenda is a clearly discernable class dynamic. As Walkerdine *et al.* (2001) point out, teenage pregnancy is largely a working class affair. Of the 20,000 under 18-year-olds who become mothers every year, the majority are more likely to be working class and disaffected from school. For middle class girls, however, pregnancy is usually regarded as a disruption to the educative process and a barrier to educational success. Indeed, the goal of a professional career 'acts as a contraceptive for middle-class girls' (Walkerdine *et al.*, 2001, p. 194).

Key points

- For some young people, important learning may take place outside of formal education.

- Informal education can engage young people in positive ways, especially when it reflects their interests and life experiences.

Conclusion

In this chapter we have focused on developing an understanding of the ways in which education has had an impact on the lives of professionals and young people. Many examples of professional practice and student experience are included in order to illustrate this. Socio-economic changes in late modernity have shaped the domain of education in particular ways. The chapter has engaged with these changes in order to make sense of educational experience in the present. Social class, gender and ethnicity have an impact on the educational experience and life trajectories of young people, as illustrated in many of the examples throughout the chapter. Finally, the chapter has considered the ways in which the identities of teachers and students may be shaped by the educational process.

References

Alldred, P., David, M. and Edwards, R. (2002) 'Minding the gap: children and young people negotiating relations between home and school' in Edwards, R. (ed.) *Children, Home and School: Regulation, Autonomy or Connection?*, London, RoutledgeFalmer.

Althusser, L. (1971) 'Ideology and ideological state apparatuses' in Althusser, L., *Lenin and Philosophy and Other Essays*, London, New Left Books.

Back, L. (1994) 'The "White Negro" revisited' in Cornwall, A. and Lindisfarne, N. (eds) *Dislocating Masculinity*, London, Routledge.

Ball, S. (2003) *Class Strategies and the Education Market: The Middle Classes and Social Advantage*, London, Routledge.

Ball, S., Davies, J., David, M. and Reay, D. (2002) 'Classification and judgement: social class and the "cognitive structures" of choice in higher education', *British Journal of Sociology of Education*, vol. 23, no. 1, pp. 51–72.

Ball, S.J. and Goodson, I. (1985) *Teachers' Lives and Careers*, London, Falmer.

Beck, U. (1992) *Risk Society: Towards a New Modernity*, London, Sage.

Bowles, S. and Gintis, H. (1976) *Schooling in Capitalist America*, London, Routledge and Kegan Paul.

Canaan, J.E. (2006) 'Recognising the need and possibilities for teaching critical hope in higher education today', unpublished paper, Birmingham, University of Central England.

Clarke, C. (2003) *Statement to Commons by Education and Skills Secretary Charles Clarke, 22.01.03*, www.dfes.gov.uk/hegateway/strategy/hestrategy/word/Statement%20to%20Parliament%20Charles%20Clarke.doc [accessed 06/11/06].

Connell, R.W. (1985) *Teachers' Work*, Sydney, George Allen & Unwin.

Connolly, P. (1998) *Racism, Gender Identities and Young Children: Social Relations in a Multi-Ethnic, Inner City Primary School*, London, Routledge.

Epstein, D. and Kenway, J. (eds) (1996) *Discourse*, vol. 17, no. 3, Special Issue.

Frosh, S., Phoenix, A. and Pattman, R. (2002) *Young Masculinities*, Basingstoke, Palgrave.

Gillborn, D. and Youdell, D. (2000) *Rationing Education: Policy, Practice, Reform and Equity*, Buckingham, Open University Press.

Goodson, I.F. and Walker, R. (eds) (1991) *Biography, Identity and Schooling: Episodes in Educational Research*, London, Falmer.

Hargreaves, A. (1994) *Changing Teachers, Changing Times: Teachers' Work and Culture in the Postmodern Age*, New York, Teachers' College Press.

Hargreaves, A. and Woods, P. (eds) (1984) *Classrooms and Staffrooms: the Sociology of Teachers and Teaching*, Milton Keynes, Open University Press.

Hargreaves, D. (1980) 'The occupational culture of teachers' in Woods, P. (ed.) *Teacher Strategies: Explorations in the Sociology of the School*, London, Croom Helm.

HEFCE (Higher Education Funding Council for England) (2006) *Widening Participation*, www.hefce.ac.uk/widen [accessed 03/07/06].

Kehily, M.J. (2002) *Sexuality, Gender and Schooling: Shifting Agendas in Social Learning*, London, RoutledgeFalmer.

Kehily, M.J. (ed.) (2007) *Understanding Youth: Perspectives, Identities and Practices*, London, Sage/The Open University (Course Book).

Kehily, M.J. and Pattman, R. (2006) 'Middle class struggle? Identity-work and leisure among sixth formers in the United Kingdom', *British Journal of Sociology of Education*, vol. 27, no. 1, pp. 37–52.

Mac an Ghaill, M. (1992) 'Teachers' work: curriculum restructuring, culture, power and comprehensive schooling', *British Journal of Sociology of Education*, vol. 13, no. 2, pp. 177–99.

MacLure, M. (1993a) 'Mundane autobiography: some thoughts on self-talk in research contexts', *British Journal of Sociology of Education*, vol. 14, no. 4, pp. 373–84.

MacLure, M. (1993b) 'Arguing for your self: identity as an organising principle in teachers' jobs and lives', *British Educational Research Journal*, vol. 19, no. 4, pp. 311–22.

Maguire, M. (2005) 'Textures of class in the context of schooling: the perceptions of a "class crossing" teacher', *Sociology*, vol. 39, no. 3, pp. 427–43.

McRobbie, A. (1978) 'Working class girls and the culture of femininity' in Centre for Contemporary Cultural Studies, *Women Take Issue*, London, Hutchinson.

Milton Keynes Christian Foundation (2006) *Annual Review 2004*, www.mkchristianfoundation.co.uk/pdf/april04.pdf [accessed 26/10/06].

Nayak, A. and Kehily, M.J. (1996) 'Playing it straight: masculinities, homophobia and schooling', *Journal of Gender Studies*, vol. 5, no. 2, pp. 211–30.

Nilan, P. (1992) 'Kazzies, DBTs and tryhards: categorizations of style in adolescent girls' talk', *British Journal of Sociology of Education*, vol. 13, no. 2, pp. 201–14.

Pollard, A. (1984) 'Goodies, jokers and gangs' in Hammersley, M. and Woods, P. (eds) *Life in School: The Sociology of Pupil Culture*, Milton Keynes, Open University Press.

Reay, D. (2004) '"Mostly roughs and toughs": social class, race and representation in inner city schooling', *Sociology*, vol. 38, no. 5, pp. 1005–23.

Reay, D. (2005) 'Who goes where in higher education: an issue of class, ethnicity and increasing concern', paper given at April 2005 Social Diversity and Difference Seminar 2, Pre-entry, Birmingham University.

Rikowski, G. (2001) 'Fuel for the living fire: labour-power!' in Dinerstein, A. and Neary, M. (eds) *The Labour Debate: An Investigation into the Theory and Reality of Capitalist Work*, Aldershot, England and Brookfield, VT, Ashgate Publishing.

Sharp, R. and Green, A. (1975) *Education and Social Control*, London, Routledge and Kegan Paul.

Sikes, P. and Troyna, B. (1991) 'True stories: a case study in the use of life history in initial teacher education', *Educational Review*, vol. 43, no. 1, pp. 3–15.

Thomson, R. (2007) 'A biographical perspective' in Kehily, M.J. (ed.) *Understanding Youth: Perspectives, Identities and Practices*, London, Sage/The Open University (Course Book).

Thomson, R. and Kehily, M.J. (2006) Fieldnotes, *The Making of Modern Motherhoods*, unpublished research project, Milton Keynes, The Open University.

Trudell, B. (1992) 'Inside a ninth grade sexuality classroom, the process of knowledge construction' in Sears, J. (ed.) *Sexuality and the Curriculum*, New York, Teachers' College Press.

Walkerdine, V., Lucey, H. and Melody, J. (2001) *Growing up Girl: Psychosocial Explorations of Gender and Class*, Basingstoke, Macmillan.

Wetherell, M. (1998) 'Positioning and interpretive repertoires: conversation analysis and post-structuralism in dialogue', *Discourse and Society*, vol. 9, no. 3, pp. 387–412.

Willis, P. (1977) *Learning to Labour: How Working Class Kids Get Working Class Jobs*, Farnborough, Saxon House.

YWCA England and Wales (2006) www.ywca-gb.org.uk [accessed 03/07/06].

Chapter 6

Institutions

Helen Evans

Introduction

> Residential care has played a significant role in the care and protection of young people.
>
> (EUROARRCC, 1998)

This quotation is taken from a report produced by the European Association for Research into Residential Childcare (EUROARRCC). The report draws on research undertaken in Finland, Spain, Ireland and Scotland, which has attempted to identify aspects of safe caring in residential establishments across Europe. This chapter will interrogate the EUROARRCC assertion by seeking to investigate the nature of the 'significant' role played by residential care and by exploring changing approaches to the provision of such care. For the most part, the focus of this examination will be residential care as it has been provided in Ireland, with links made to England, Scotland and Wales when and if they occur.

The need for discrete residential provision for young people emerged as a political imperative in the British Isles, as in many parts of the Western world, in the middle of the nineteenth century and was bolstered by what Christine Griffin (1997, p. 18) calls the 'coalescence' of a number of trends in social thought and social organisation. First, the effects of the Industrial Revolution gave rise to the need in capitalist organisations for a youthful, cheap and passive workforce, and to the population shift from rural to urban areas which aroused concern among reformers about the living conditions of the young. Second, the 'discovery' of adolescence by Granville Stanley Hall (1904) and the developing **'cult of heterosexual masculinity'** (a belief in the dominance of men, both intellectually and physically, and a rejection of homosexuality as 'unmanly') created a specific social category which required attention. Hall, an early psychologist, was one of the first to identify adolescence as a distinct biological phase with concomitant physiological needs and urges (Kehily, 2007). As Griffin explains: 'The emerging ideology of adolescence marked out a biologically determined norm of youthful behaviour and appearance which was white/Anglo, middle class, heterosexual and male ... Women, girls and the feminine were associated with weakness and fragility, and men and masculinity with virility and strength' (Griffin, 1997, p. 18). Such a source of potential energy had to be contained and harnessed or controlled. However, Hall's thesis, underpinned as it was by the growing respectability of social scientific thinking and methodology which had begun to emerge in the nineteenth century, also fed into the reforming impetus known as 'Victorian philanthropy'.

Until the 1850s, young people who were deemed to have transgressed social norms were treated as adults and sent to prison. Those who were perceived to be in need of 'care' were sent to the workhouse. The definition of 'care' was, as we shall see, a limited one, but the move towards separate provision for young people did represent a recognition that young people's needs were of a different order from those of adults.

Thus, the latter half of the nineteenth century witnessed the erection of structures, both legislative and physical, to address the newfound problem of 'youth', especially male youth. In Section 1 of this chapter we will consider how approaches to the residential care and custody of young people have changed, and attempt to understand why these changes have evolved. In Sections 2 and 3 we will explore the provision of care at the macro and the micro levels. At the macro level, we will take a historical perspective and trace changes in approaches to residential care over time. By adopting this perspective we will be able to see how ideas about the residential care of children and young people have changed. We will draw on the ideas of Foucault with regard to developments in social and political organisation, and on Goffman's analysis of institutions. At the micro level, we will be looking at the experience of individuals and groups of young people who are or have been in residential care. As you read, you may wish to reflect back on what you have learned in the first part of this book about what it means to be a 'practitioner', what influences ideas about practice, and the extent to which some young people are able to participate in decisions affecting their lives.

This chapter will address the following core questions:

- What are the antecedents of residential care as it is provided in the twenty-first century?
- How do staff approach work with young people in residential settings?
- What ideas inform their approach?
- How do the structures of and dynamics within residential care affect young people?
- What impact does a period in residential care have on the individual's biography and self concept?

1 Learning from the past

The ensuing story of residential care and custody is illustrated by the biography of one institution which typifies the evolution of residential services for older children and young people and which demonstrates the complexities of the care/custody and welfare/justice discourses. This story is about Glenmona Resource Centre and is set in Northern Ireland. We have opted to use this institution to illustrate the dynamics at work in institutions generally and the structural factors which impact on them. Although this example is located in Northern Ireland, it has been influenced by legislative and ideological factors that are, and have been, at play in the rest of the UK and in Ireland. It offers a way into understanding how institutions operate, why they have evolved in the way they have and their impact on the lives of young people and on those who work in them. We hope you will find that the issues highlighted by this case study are pertinent to similar settings with which you are familiar or which you have read about. At the very least, the case study should provide a concrete focus for thinking about institutions as an interface between practitioners and young people and about the theories which are introduced.

The box below gives the legislative context by explaining the political development of Northern Ireland as an entity within the UK.

From 1801 to 1920, Ireland was ruled as part of the UK. In 1920, as a result of a long campaign waged for Home Rule, Ireland was divided into two political entities – Northern Ireland and Eire (now formally referred to as the Republic of Ireland). The former continued to be part of the UK, although it had its own government, while the Republic broke away entirely from the UK and set up its own administrative procedures. In practice, this meant that Irish agencies and services established prior to 1921 were British in origin and structure. Although separate Acts were usually passed for Scotland and Ireland, the substantive focus of the law was in keeping with that in England and Wales. For Glenmona, the specific implication of the division of the island of Ireland was that, after 1921, it was no longer part of a network of facilities across Ireland and was now subject to different influences from those which affected comparable facilities in the Republic of Ireland. In 1921, a provincial parliament was established in Northern Ireland. From then until 1972, legislation on most issues was made in the form of Acts of the Northern Ireland Parliament. Since 1972, Northern Ireland has, for the most part, been ruled directly from Westminster with legislation adapted and implemented in the form of 'Orders' rather than 'Acts'; for example, the Children Act 1989 was enacted as the Children (NI) Order 1995.

1.1 The case study

Glenmona Resource Centre is an agency which operates five residential childcare units on a campus-style site on the outskirts of Belfast. The units accommodate thirty-six young people, male and female, ranging in age from 10 to 18 years. The young people are referred to Glenmona by social services agencies from across Northern Ireland, usually because other forms of care (family care, foster care, children's homes) have not worked for them. As a specialist regional facility, it provides for young people who display challenging behaviours which reflect the varying degrees of physical, emotional and sexual abuse or neglect they have experienced prior to their admission to the Centre. Most of the young people are from the greater Belfast area, but for some the local community may be 70–100 miles away. On average, they spend 18 months to two years in Glenmona. Some have been in youth custody or are on the brink of coming to the attention of the criminal justice authorities, and some may be on Probation or Supervision Orders. The director of the Centre at the time of writing, Liam Dumigan, avers that the service provided there is premised on the reality that almost all these young people have serious educational, social, relationship and identity problems. Liam Dumigan is something of an authority on the subject of residential care for young people because he has worked at the Centre for 30 years and has been involved in the implementation of many of the recent changes.

Glenmona offers a concrete illustration of the impact of institutions on young people's lives because it epitomises the evolution in thinking around the institutional care of young people, the rationale for it and the ongoing debate about whether there should be discrete accommodation for those deemed to be in need of care and those deemed to require control. The latter will be a recurring theme for this chapter.

Glenmona began life in 1873 under a different name: St Patrick's Industrial School, the first of its kind in Ireland. Between the 1850s and 1870s, a network of industrial and reformatory schools was established across Britain and Ireland to provide care and accommodation for young people (initially only young men). Industrial schools were to provide for those who were considered to be neglected, known as 'waifs and strays'. Previously, such young people had been accommodated in workhouses. Reformatory schools were intended for the training and reformation of older children who had committed offences. In these latter institutions, 'care' was tempered with punishment. Indeed, Una Convery, who has undertaken research into the use and nature of custody in the youth justice system in Northern Ireland, states that both types of institution 'assumed a penal role' (Convery, 2002, p. 52). However, the legislation which led to the establishment of industrial schools and reformatories did represent a recognition, for the first time on the part of the state, that children constituted a special and vulnerable group and that it had a duty to provide for them. In particular, there was a humanitarian concern to reduce the large numbers of children in prisons. However, the legal distinction between those who were in need of care and those who required control was always difficult to apply in practice. Thus, by the middle of the twentieth century, industrial and reformatory schools were amalgamated, signifying a merging of criminal and welfare concerns, with an increased emphasis on the welfare of children regardless of the reason underlying their having come to the attention of the authorities.

The new institutions were called 'training schools' and they remained a feature of the residential care system until the 1990s. They maintained many of the vestiges of the industrial and reformatory schools, occupying the same premises and, in Ireland, continuing to be run for the most part by religious orders. They resembled, in appearance and ethos, the large asylums which were established in the late nineteenth and early twentieth centuries for psychiatric patients and people with learning difficulties, and the sanatoria and fever hospitals which had been set up for those with contagious illnesses. Like these other establishments, they tended to accommodate large numbers of people (in 1978 there were 190 boys in St Patrick's, looked after by between 16 and 20 staff); to be secluded and more or less cut off from the rest of society; and to be run on regimental lines. Convery (2002, pp. 33–6) claims that the involvement of religious orders in the running of training schools masked their repressive nature. The locations of St Patrick's and some other training schools are identified in the map overleaf.

1.2 Characteristics of an institution

The concept of a *total institution* was developed by Erving Goffman (1961). This work has provided a useful framework for an examination of various settings in which people interact and where there is a power imbalance. Goffman identified four key features which characterise an institution, acknowledging that they will be evident to a greater or lesser extent, depending on how restrictive the regime is. These features are:

- Batch living: this refers to the block treatment of residents, with no opportunity for personal choice regarding clothes, food or personal space.

- Binary management: this refers to the social distance between staff and residents; they eat separately (possibly from quite different menus) and pursue leisure activities separately, with the staff supervising rather than participating. Power is exerted through this separation of worlds.

- The inmate role: the resident is stripped of their former identity and becomes, essentially, depersonalised. Everyday life is organisation centred rather than user centred.

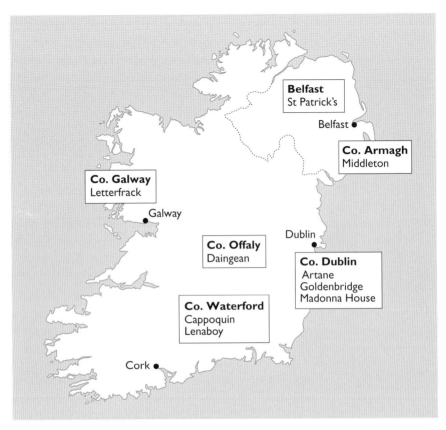

The island of Ireland since 1921, showing the location of St Patrick's and some other training schools

- The institutional perspective: over a period of time the institution completely takes over and becomes the only frame of reference for the individual, who cannot see beyond the institution and more or less succumbs to its demands. The rigidity of routine and lack of power are accepted. This feature describes the process of becoming institutionalised and may apply as aptly to workers in a large organisation as it does to patients in a psychiatric hospital.

Although somewhat dated, Goffman's paradigm is extremely useful for examining settings in which people are cared for. Some are clearly 'total' closed institutions. Others may be more 'open' but are almost inevitably characterised by some of the hallmarks of institutionalisation.

Over the years, the service which St Patrick's Training School offered evolved in response to ideological and legislative change but, until the late 1980s, the school was still run on institutional lines, with all the vestiges of batch living: collective clothing, dormitory sleeping, services provided on site (doctor, nurse, shop, church); that is, effective separation from the local community. It was a total institution in the sense that dependence was encouraged. James Atherton (1989) has noted that residential settings were closed systems because 'the overall dynamic of getting the establishment to run smoothly is one of homeostasis, partly between the system as a whole and its environment, and partly between the parts of the system' (in Craig *et al.*, 1998, p. 10).

This tendency was clearly evident in institutions such as St Patrick's where the management and staff belonged to a religious order, with all the uniformity which that implies, and consequently lived on site.

Activity 1 The institutional experience

Allow 15 minutes

Try applying Goffman's framework to what you have read about Glenmona in its earlier incarnation: St Patrick's Training School. Do you think that the characteristics delineated above would have been evident? In particular, how do you think the binary system would have operated in practice?

Comment

You might have considered that catering and caring for as many as 200 boys would demand a high level of routine with regard to meal times, bed times and laundry management. Such a system does not seem to leave much scope for emotional care or the meeting of individual needs. You may have reflected on the fact that it would be difficult to run a residential home for young people without clear rules and systems to ensure that a group of people can live relatively harmoniously together. However, there is some evidence to suggest that the power wielded by the caregivers in these large institutions, where the binary system kept those in receipt of care in a subservient position, was excessive. This dynamic impacted on staff as well as residents and it was not uncommon for caregivers in this context to become institutionalised in the role of authority figure.

1.3 The welfare/justice dilemma

Letterfrack, Co. Galway is typical of Irish training schools. It closed down in 1974

Throughout the twentieth century, a debate rumbled on about the extent to which training schools (and their forebears) should have, as their primary function, the application of justice – in the form of punishment and retribution – or the provision of welfare, for those whose disadvantaged circumstances had brought them to the attention of the authorities. Increasingly, other forms of care were used – for example, smaller children's homes and fostering – but training schools remained as the ultimate sanction for those who did not comply. There had been an attempt in the 1960s to reinforce the welfare model, but this proved difficult in practice because the admissions system was administered by the courts. Young people were committed to training schools by court orders rather than referred by social services agencies. The regime of using the courts to control and corral young people who were troublesome had begun in the nineteenth century and proved difficult to moderate. Policy makers and practitioners continued to be exercised by the tensions between the welfare orientation of childcare policy and the need to provide controls for young people who broke the law. For St Patrick's, radical change only came with the 1995 Children Order, the Northern Irish version of the 1989 Children Act. This piece of legislation was directly informed by the Black Report of 1979, which had criticised training schools on the grounds that they failed to separate children who were committed for care purposes and those convicted of offences; that they kept children for too long (the semi-indeterminate nature of some Training School Orders meant that children with no criminal record were kept longer than serious offenders); that they failed to ensure that young people had adequate contact with their families and communities; and that they were too large and paid inadequate attention to individual needs (Northern Ireland, Children and Young Persons Review Group *et al.*, 1979).

The Black Report, in fact, recommended that training schools should have no role in providing for children in need of care and protection. Consequently, training school managers devised a range of strategies to counteract the Black Report's criticisms. These strategies included, for example:

- a reduction in the number of young people accommodated

- the introduction of more targeted assessment to inform care programmes

- inter-agency work, maintaining links between the young person and their family/community.

The result was that, under the Children (NI) Order, St Patrick's and other training schools in Northern Ireland became part of the residential care system under the aegis of the Department of Health and Social Services (NI). This represented a major departure for the institution, in practice requiring St Patrick's to de-register as a training school and to re-register as a children's home. This change was phased in over four years. By 2000, St Patrick's had relinquished its juvenile justice function and its name; it became Glenmona Resource Centre, catering solely for young people deemed to be at risk. In future, admission was to be planned and negotiated with the referring social services agency. Young people would no longer be placed as the result of a court order and Glenmona would not have statutory power to detain them.

The reasons why young people are referred to Glenmona have also changed. Whereas in the past many young people were sent to St Patrick's for trivial reasons – perhaps for non school attendance or petty crime – Glenmona is now attracting very isolated young people who are the victims of long term care and/or fostering breakdown, who do not have a supportive family or community network to return to, and who are, or potentially could be, in serious trouble with the law. John Muncie (1998, p. 198) contends that, as a result of the Children Act 1989, 'the way in which the "deprived" and the "delinquent" were dealt with was finally to be separated'. In essence, what this has meant for Glenmona is that the young people who use the service are not labelled delinquent because they have not been processed through the criminal justice system but are, nevertheless, presenting with very complex difficulties.

The implications of the Children (NI) Order for facilities such as Glenmona are set out in the table below. The elements listed in the table are also central to the Children Act 1989.

Implications of the Children (NI) Order for residential care

Principles of the order	Effects
Parental responsibility	There was an ideological shift from a presumption that 'if you can't look after your children the state will' to 'if you are having a problem looking after your children the state will support you'
Compulsory intervention to be minimised	A court should make an order affecting parental responsibility only when to do so would be better than making no order at all; that is, the young person would be at risk of *significant harm*
Flexibility	A wider range of orders was to be available; for example: Residence Order, Contact Order, Emergency Protection Order, Child Assessment Order
The welfare principle	The child's/young person's welfare was to be *paramount*

Although the behaviour of the young people Glenmona now caters for has been disruptive and, at times, offending, they are placed there by social services agencies with the expectation that they will be cared for, not punished. Perhaps this is not so different from the aspiration of those who set up the first reformatory in 1858. It could be argued, however, that the new arrangements represent a significant development from the very punitive and restrictive institutions which were established in the nineteenth and twentieth centuries to deal with youth offending, and express a very different attitude to young people and to the idea of 'reform'.

The transmutation from St Patrick's Training School to Glenmona Resource Centre may be characterised by a number of factors: the withdrawal of theChristian Brothers; the transfer of function from a training school, with a juvenile justice remit, to a voluntary residential home; a dramatic reduction in the number of places available; and an increase in the number of female staff: in 1995 there were six women on the staff, in 2005 there were 28 – that is, 50 per cent of the staff complement. This latter development is, perhaps, an indication of the move from a relatively authoritarian regime to one which is characterised by an official acknowledgment that social work practice should be the underpinning framework for intervention, with individual programmes of supervision drawn up for each young person, focusing on personal needs, behaviour and community/family circumstances.

1.4 *Plus ça change?*

The literature on residential care sometimes gives the impression that the care/justice distinction had just been invented in the 1990s. However, Convery (2002, p. 38) asserts that, in spite of legislative change, the institutions at the end of the twentieth century were not significantly different, in terms of function and remit, from those at the beginning of that century. The way in which she profiles the residents of these establishments is set out in the table below.

Profile of young people in institutions

1900	1999
High recidivism rate	High recidivism rate
Majority of residents previously in workhouses	93% of residents formerly in children's homes
Majority illiterate	Almost one-third had physical/learning disabilities

(Adapted from Convery, 2002, p. 38)

Activity 2   Change? Or more of the same?

Allow 15 minutes   What differences can you deduce between the early custodial function of St Patrick's Training School and the more recent Children (NI) Order requirements of residential care?

The following mission statements may give you some insight into the intentions of the management and staff with regard to the young people resident there. Focus on key changes and continuities both before and after the Children (NI) Order.

St Patrick's Training School

Mission statement
St Patrick's accommodates and cares for young people committed by the courts, on remand or convicted of offences. We wish to nurture and respect young people's spiritual needs and to imbue in them values and principles which will enable them to avoid re-offending and which will prepare them for living in the community. We provide care in a way which respects their rights and dignities, and we deliver service in accordance with explicit

standards, consistent with the requirements of NIO [the Northern Ireland Office] and DHSS [Department of Health and Social Services, NI], monitored to ensure that the quality of service is maintained.

Slemish House (one of the units in Glenmona Resource Centre)

Mission statement

Slemish House Voluntary Children's Home exists to make available to children placed in care high quality services which promote their health, education, personal safety and spiritual well being. The service provided shall strive to enhance the self worth of each child and uphold his/her right to privacy, independence and continuity of care, by providing openness, sharing and the participation of child, parents, those with parental responsibility and relevant others in partnership with the placing agency.

Comment

You may have noted a more pronounced emphasis, in the Glenmona statement, on respecting young people's rights, involving parents and promoting parental responsibility. A welfare orientation seems to be prioritised whereas the theme of reform is stronger in the first statement.

In the next section we will look more closely at how the structure and focus of residential care has been influenced by the political environment and the needs of society at large.

Key points

- The antecedents of residential care for young people may be traced back to the nineteenth century.

- The provision of residential care has been influenced by discourses which seek to privilege *either* the importance of welfare *or* the prerogative for justice.

- Within a residential setting, rules and routines are established to facilitate the smooth running of the facility. This may lead to institutionalisation – acquiescence to the needs of the organisation over and above the needs of the individual – which impacts on staff as well as on residents.

- The provision of residential care for young people continues to be influenced by an ideological concern with justice and the need to contain, although young people's rights and integrity are now formally acknowledged.

- A major change in the twentieth century was the reduction in the number of young people 'sent away', with an extension of the social work service and the promotion of foster care. These changes occurred in response to a growing recognition of children's developmental needs and to the critique of large institutions, led by Goffman. Residential centres now tend to be smaller and more needs led.

2 Forms of surveillance

Residential care is often perceived as society's response to a social problem. Young people who are referred to public care are constructed as either *having* a problem or *being* a problem. However, as we saw in the previous section, the practice of removing young people (and children) from their home environment for the purpose of having them looked after in a residential (some would say 'institutional') setting is a relatively recent one.

2.1 The shift from punishment to reform

The ideas of Michel Foucault, the French theorist, are useful in attempting to understand how this practice has developed and what its social function is. In his classic work *Discipline and Punish* (1979), Foucault contends that, at the beginning of the nineteenth century, attitudes to punishment for crimes were changing in the Western world (namely, across Europe and the USA). Specifically, he notes the 'disappearance of torture as a public spectacle [and its replacement by] ... the essentially corrective character of the penalty' (Foucault, 1979, pp. 7–8).

Why did this change occur? Foucault has noted that the economic and social changes associated with industrialisation and new forms of political organisation – 'the great transformation of the years 1760–1840' (1979, p. 15) – necessitated more systematic control over the individual, which resulted in a move from punishment, which chastised the body, to reform, which touched the soul. The new social and economic system required citizens who could make a constructive contribution to the capitalist project. Therefore, the possibilities for training and reforming the young were to be harnessed. Punishment alone could not produce benefits for society: what was needed was deterrence and reform. Foucault identified the development of a 'new morality concerning the act of punishing' (p. 12) which employed 'a whole army of technicians ... warders, doctors, chaplains, psychiatrists, psychologists, educationalists ...' (p. 11). His central thesis was that changes in approaches to punishment were not merely 'qualititative' ('less cruelty, less pain, more kindness, more respect, more "humanity"'), but that the 'objective' of punishment had changed (p. 16). What is this 'objective'? It is increased state control of the individual, what some have called 'governmentality' and Foucault describes as 'surveillance'. Chapter 7 explores these concepts further in relation to risk taking.

Jose Harris, meanwhile, in her analysis of British society in the period 1870–1914, notes a growing public spiritedness towards the end of the nineteenth century, but asserts that it operated 'within a legal and cultural framework prescribed by a moral and intellectual elite' (Harris, 1994, p. 253). Both Foucault and Harris offer a critique which can help us understand why it was considered necessary and beneficial to provide residential care on a grand scale with a view to educating, not simply punishing, the young. Thus, the genesis of the story of residential care for young people may be located in the reforming instinct which gained momentum in the mid-nineteenth century and resulted in the establishment of large institutions to accommodate young people, segregated from adults. Roger Bullock *et al.* (1993) have interpreted the increase in the number of children accommodated in large institutions at this time as a response to 'a desire to offer children a total experience encompassing every aspect of their life and capable of enhancing their spiritual well-being as well as their physical and psychological health' (in Craig *et al.*, 1998, p. 9).

2.2 A different way of caring

Two important physical characteristics which industrial and reformatory schools shared were that they tended to be geographically isolated and were capable of accommodating large numbers. In the 1930s, there were 5,000 children in reformatory and industrial schools in Ireland, with one school in Dublin catering for as many as 800 boys. Since the total population of the country stood at only three and a half million, these figures represent a significant trend towards the committal of young people into care or custody. These included many young people who would nowadays be in children's homes, or placed with a family in foster care. The trend towards containment of children in the nineteenth century was symptomatic of an increasing trend towards corralling the young if they gave any trouble – what Foucault has termed the 'carceral': the 'task' was 'to produce bodies that were both docile and capable' (Foucault, 1979, p. 294). The widespread use of custody as an appropriate way of dealing with young people, and the ideology underpinning this practice, pertained until well into the twentieth century. The EUROARRCC research has highlighted the fact that: 'These institutions remained virtually unaltered until the 1970's' (Craig *et al.*, 1998, p. 18).

Activity 3   The importance of size and structure

Allow 20 minutes Taking into consideration the two factors identified above, geographical location and size:

1   Do you think that these institutions can be described as residential care establishments?

2   What sort of ideology (set of ideas) about young people would have underpinned such establishments and the legislation which created them?

3   How different is that ideology from the one which prevails today?

Comment

1   You may have likened these early attempts at residential care for young people to 'warehouses'. They were characterised by lack of contact with families, and institutionalised and heavily routinised systems for the provision of care. The term 'care', as we use it here, gained prominence in the twentieth century. There is little evidence that 'care' was an espoused objective of residential establishments for young people in the nineteenth century. Their purpose was 'reform' and 'rehabilitation', perhaps 'rescue' in some cases. Derek Fraser (2003, p. 114), in line with Harris (1994), asserts that the rise of such institutions was a pragmatic response to a relatively new problem. He argues that reformatory/industrial schools were essentially utilitarian in purpose: the most efficient way of dealing with the problem of young people who were out of control. It is probably fair to surmise that, by the mid-twentieth century, a more holistic view of care was beginning to seep into the social psyche, thanks to the popularisation of psychotherapeutic analysis. However, even in the 1950s the focus was very much on treatment, reform and control. The only 'needs' that were catered for were shelter and hunger, both in the most cost-efficient way possible. The remote geographical location of many of these institutions ensured that the residents were not exposed to external influences or stimulation. Margery Fry (1951, p. 127) described reformatories and industrial schools as grim places, which trusted largely to a discipline based on fear, facilitated by the isolated location in which many were sited.

2   Although it was acknowledged that separate provision for young people should be made, the study of young people's needs was in its infancy and attention to primary needs, which could be provided for on a large scale, seemed to be sufficient. As noted in Section 1, the idea of adolescence as a phase of human development with specific developmental needs, arising from physiological changes, was very new. A clue to the thinking which influenced the residential care legislation is the use of the term 'school' to describe these establishments. State education provided universally was not introduced in Britain until 1870. Therefore it is interesting that almost 20 years earlier there had been a recognition that education could resolve some of society's ills and that it would assist individual

reformation. But the objective was to tame and to train, not to care for. Young people were minors in law and were expected to be passive subjects of adult decisions. The dominant ideology dictated that young people could be controlled through segregation and isolation; institutional care was a device aimed at moulding them into good citizens.

3   It could be argued that, politically, the protection of society is pre-eminent. Muncie (1997, p. 140) states that: 'Custody is a political decision'. However, policy makers are also concerned to equip young people in residential care with the educational and vocational skills to enable them to be economically independent. This is an aspect of practice which was to the forefront in training schools. In addition, there is now more emphasis on catering for the range of needs with which young people present, and ensuring that their rights are not infringed.

2.3 Progress?

A clear ideological continuity may be noted in the attempt to make separate provision for those in need of care and those subject to criminal litigation. This has been a recurring theme over the last 150 years, with the pendulum weighted in the direction of welfare initiatives for some decades and then swinging towards an emphasis on the imperative for justice. Pete Alcock and Phil Harris (1982, p. 95) have noted the 'muddled reasoning' which prevailed well into the twentieth century, pointing out that there has not been a straightforward progression towards enlightened intervention but, rather, that the authorities have tended to vacillate between measures which emphasise punishment and those which emphasise treatment. In the 1980s, under the New Right, the 'rhetoric of treatment and rehabilitation' was openly replaced by 'the rhetoric of punishment and retribution' (Muncie, 1998, p. 192). The apparently regressive approach of the 1980s may be understood in Foucauldian terms as a response to the need for economic growth and regeneration in post-recession Britain. It was believed that this could be abetted by 'short sharp shock' regimes introduced in detention centres (Muncie, 1998, p. 192). Muncie concludes that 'the study of youth justice tells us more about the political "need" for order than it does about the nature of youth offending itself' (p. 209).

Although we may be accustomed to the ideological preoccupations identified – the desire to educate and reform, and the balancing of the welfare/justice dichotomy – it is important to remember that they were just emerging in the nineteenth century. In the intervening 150 years there has been a shift from the 'traditional medical treatment model', which was predicated on an imperative to cure individual 'badness', to a more integrated programme of intervention involving home, peer group, school and the wider society (Gilligan, 1991, pp. 197–8). Nikolas Rose, drawing on Foucault's ideas, alerts us to the influence of what he calls the **'psy disciplines'** – the human and social sciences, especially those with a 'psy' prefix – on the 'reform of human capacities in relation to certain objectives' (Rose, 1999, pp. viii, xiii). He claims that 'psy expertise has developed in symbiosis with a culture of liberal reform' (p. viii). This idea is developed along a different tangent by Barbara Misztal (2001, p. 374), a sociologist interested in political theory, who points out that 'the long-term survival of democracy depends upon a just and fair institutional order'. Whereas in medieval societies the deterrent effect of sanctions may have been sufficient to maintain order, 'the growing division of labour, globalization and the development of new means of communication [have resulted in] the declining efficiency of prohibitively costly monitoring and surveillance systems' (Misztal, 2001, p. 376). Consequently, the function of institutions for young people today is to instil self control rather than impose external control, what Rose (1999, p. 3) calls 'governance of the self'. Behaviour modification systems, anger management training and therapeutic crisis intervention are strategies commonly used in residential settings, with the aim of encouraging young people to take responsibility for their actions and to reflect on the consequences. Disciplinary action is intended to be educative rather than retributive and staff are trained to use techniques which seek to understand, not merely to correct.

However, such grand theorising does not detract from the fact that working with young people, some of whom are offenders, within a childcare environment, is challenging and complex. Angus Skinner, Chief Inspector of Social Work Services at the Scottish Office, has proposed that the purpose of residential care is to 'provide good quality care, support, education and opportunities for development to young people and children' (quoted in Craig et al., 1998, p. 8).

The next section looks at how this may be achieved.

Key points

- Residential care in the twenty-first century may be construed as more benign and more young person centred.

- Foucault, Rose and Misztal help us to see that institutional responses to the 'problems' which young people present have evolved as a result of fundamental economic, social and political changes.

- Current approaches to residential care employ subtle and sophisticated methods of social control.

3 Approaching work with young people in a residential setting

A review of the history of residential care reveals at least two common and recurring themes: a desire to rehabilitate and a concern to provide 'care' (physical and emotional). So, has anything changed? In fact, some very tangible differences may be discerned. For example, residential units are now much smaller (reflecting, to some extent, the decrease in the number of young people in care) and units are less isolated geographically. The EUROARRCC research notes that: 'substantial actual improvement in the basic quality of life of young people has been made in terms of the location and style of buildings and the size of living groups' (Craig *et al.*, 1998, p. xii).

It is intended that smaller units will make for a more 'home-like', less institutionalised atmosphere, while the fact that units are less isolated should enable more contact with families and communities. In the industrial and reformatory schools, visits from family were logistically difficult and actively discouraged. Maintaining contact with family and community is now seen as a priority. So the philosophy which underpins residential care today articulates a sincere attempt to learn from the lessons of the past. But a third dynamic poses a challenge for the care givers. The residents of the industrial and reformatory schools were aged from four years upwards, with the younger children perhaps being more malleable and easier to contain. By the time a child had been in one of these institutions for six years, they had become so institutionalised that they were, on the whole, easily managed. However, Glenmona Resource Centre admits young people between the ages of 14 and 17. The fact that older young people are the focus of attention means that many of those being cared for have extensive experience of care, often having been subject to a pattern of unsuccessful and disrupted previous placements, and consequently present with 'a range of complex social, emotional, educational and behavioural problems' (Craig *et al.*, 1998, p. 82). The implication for practice is that residential care 'may offer the last possibility of meeting the rights and needs of ... children ... whose behaviour ... is most challenging' (Craig *et al.*, 1998, pp. 14–15). This view is corroborated by Liam Dumigan who describes Glenmona as the 'end of the line' for many of the residents there.

Another manager, Mandy Moorehead, has come into residential care by a more circuitous route than Liam Dumigan, having worked in the community as a social worker before being employed in 2003, by the local social services agency, to set up a six-bed Intensive Support Unit. These units are being established across Northern Ireland (there is one at Glenmona) in response to *Children Matter* – a review of residential childcare services in Northern Ireland (Social Services Inspectorate, 1998)

– to cater for 12–16-year-old 'severely damaged' young people in an attempt to prevent them entering the criminal justice system. The home that Mandy Moorehead manages is called Cherrygrove and it differs from Glenmona in that it is purpose built and bereft of history or associations with earlier models of practice. Mandy Moorehead has made a determined effort to establish a living environment which meets the needs of the individuals who reside there, rather than the needs of the organisation. While managing 'significant levels of risk', she and her staff are assisted by the design of the physical environment which 'makes it easy to supervise'. With a fairly small group to look after, it is not difficult to cater for individual food tastes, and meals are not always eaten communally or at set times. Few cupboards are kept locked and each young person has their own room. Mandy Moorehead states that 'most of what we do is subtle'. The emphasis is on therapeutic intervention (drawing on the expert knowledge of what Rose, 1999, calls the 'psy disciplines': see Subsection 2.3) and high staff ratios facilitate direct work with each young person, based on individual programmes of care and the resilience model (see Chapter 8, 'Safeguarding').

The EUROARRCC research emphasises that: 'The relationship between staff and the young people they care for is crucial. In many ways, this is the heart of residential childcare' (Craig *et al.*, 1998, p. 66). The importance of relationships underpins Mandy Moorehead's and Liam Dumigan's approaches to the management of their respective units, although the extent to which institutional care can meet the emotional needs of vulnerable young people has been questioned by Camila Batmanghelidjh (2004) who believes that the organisational structure is often privileged to the detriment of relationship building (see Chapter 2, 'Practice'). The experience of one 17-year-old young woman, who spent three years in care (more than two of them in Cherrygrove), seems to support Batmanghelidjh's position. She asserts that good communication can moderate the malign influence of organisational structures but cautions as follows:

> residential social workers ... make life changing decisions for you and on you but very rarely with you! This does need to change, all young people need to have some sort of say and control in their lives ... which is why communication is so vital ... young people within the care system yearn to live as normal a life as possible but ... there are so many restrictions put on your life that it feels physically impossible to try and live a normal life ... so I feel it's important that social workers try as best they can to try and make it easier for the young person and be as sensitive as possible.
>
> (Quoted from a speech given in 2006 to trainee social workers, Armagh)

The EUROARRCC research supports her view. Its findings indicated that young people were expert in making 'balanced and sensible assessments of the care they received' (Craig *et al.*, 1998, p. 74). In enabling them to meet this responsibility, the key worker system is crucial. Other research has established that successful outcomes, including an improvement in the young person's self esteem, can best be achieved through this model of working (Gibbs and Sinclair, 1998). Note that in the reformatory schools the 'relationship' with young people was not important. There was no key worker system and no opportunity for young people to air their views. Goffman's binary system was firmly in place. Liam Dumigan comments that: 'The problems haven't changed but the structures have – there are now more staff, there is more space and more time'. The high ratio of staff to young people (11 staff/8 young people in each of the units in Glenmona) facilitates the development of relationships and enables staff to tune into individual young people. However, Batmanghelidjh's (2004) comments about the pre-eminence of structures is borne out by the experience of one young man who spent time in Glenmona and whom I will call Gary. His story is recounted in the box below. It is very much his version of events and is offered as his perspective.

Gary's story

Gary was taken into foster care when he was five years old. This placement broke down and he was placed in a residential home when he was eight. One Friday evening when he was 10 he threw a tantrum and assaulted a member of staff. His memory of that evening is that he was taken by the police and deposited in Glenmona. He says that he had never heard of Glenmona and does not recall any admissions procedure. He spent the next three to four years in Glenmona but he was constantly running away because he did not like his key worker and clashed with her on a daily basis. He did undergo anger management training, but feels that it didn't help. His impulse to act up and to kick out resulted in his being punished regularly and he was eventually removed to a Youth Justice Centre where, once again, he was subject to disciplinary action, usually being 'locked up' and denied privileges such as videos and outings. Gary is now 16 years old and lives in a hostel. With hindsight he can see that staff wanted to help; however, he insists that 'places like Glenmona should not exist'.

Gary repeatedly returns to the foster home where he spent his early childhood. In this more informal, unstructured setting he finds carers who are prepared to persevere and who are not bound by shift patterns. However, the emotional demands placed on them and their family by a troubled young man are considerable.

Activity 4   Institutional caring

Allow 15 minutes   Both Liam Dumigan and Mandy Moorehead, as managers and carers, are motivated by an interest in improving the life chances of young people who have been placed in residential care. Spend a few moments reflecting on Gary's story and then note down what the challenges and dilemmas are for practitioners working in residential settings.

Comment

Caring for young people in a residential setting is at once unpredictable and routine. One member of staff has commented that 'staff have to be prepared to get stuck in and put up with all sorts ... methods of physical control are sometimes needed'. Liam Dumigan is emphatic in stating that it is not helpful for an organisation to be doctrinaire about a model of intervention. Rather, he recommends the importance of relationship building with each individual young person and he encourages staff to develop their own practice in the key worker relationship, giving them scope to respond to the individual needs of each young person. Gay Graham (1994), in her work entitled 'Residential childcare: an analysis of activities and tasks and the implications for the organisational design of residential childcare units', has identified 'four dimensions of complexity in residential care work ... interdependence, heterogeneity, unpredictability and unanalysability' (quoted in Craig et al., 1998, p. 76) (note: unanalysability refers to that which is difficult or even impossible to analyse).

Include Youth, a voluntary organisation based in Northern Ireland, which promotes best practice with young people at risk of social exclusion, has noted that: 'Worker consistency and continuity is critical for young people who experience chaotic and disjointed lifestyles, many of whom may have had multiple placements throughout the care system' (Include Youth, 2005, p. 9). However, as we have seen, those in receipt of care do not always experience it as an empowering, supportive environment. Gary experienced the system as restrictive and bucked against it. The rationale for Intensive Support Units is the provision of residential care which mimics foster care in its capacity, within existing structures, to respond flexibly. Voice of Young People in Care (VOYPIC), a Northern Irish organisation with counterparts in the other countries in the UK and in the Republic of Ireland, commends Cherrygrove for its staff's commitment to young people with challenging behaviour, expressed by the fact that young people are always welcomed back and feel reassured that staff will not give up on them (interview, 08/02/06).

In Glenmona, staff are assisted to develop their thinking about the childcare task by being encouraged to undertake training and to be reflective and critical of the structures and practice which they see around them. The development of a professionalised and skilled workforce is facilitated by a senior practitioner who observes and reports on practice development, sharing their observations with staff internally and working with an external consultant who brings a fresh, objective view. The organisation relies on the professional competence of staff, and professional autonomy is reinforced and supported at every level. Delegation of responsibility is evidenced by the approach to health and safety, which is of primary importance in residential care but which is subject to the principle of subsidiarity – every member of staff who has contact with the young people has responsibility for health and safety.

3.1 A person centred environment

The primary function of residential care is the provision of care in a safe environment. This aspiration was enshrined in the Care Standards Act 2000 which emanated from the recommendations of the Waterhouse Report (Waterhouse *et al.*, 2000) on the long term physical and sexual abuse of young people in residential homes in north Wales in the 1970s. Current practice acknowledges that the resolution of emotional or social problems can be attended to only when physical needs are adequately met. And such needs tend to be met in an inclusive environment which, as far as possible, avoids a 'them' and 'us' structure. There is a concerted effort, in today's residential establishments, to erode the binary system and learn from the lessons of the past.

Residential care in the twenty-first century is underpinned by the following principles:

- the importance of identity – choice of decor in bedrooms, for example
- the importance of personal space – a move away from use of dormitories to individual bedrooms
- the person being cared for should be treated with dignity and respect
- individual views and preferences are valued.

Activity 5   Characteristics of the environment

Allow 20 minutes

1   Consider how the inclusive environment mentioned above might be created, bearing in mind Goffman's explanation of the binary system.

2   Residential establishments often put great store in trying to create a 'homely' environment for young people in care. How might such an environment be created? Consider physical and social characteristics.

3   How realistic is the attempt to create such an environment? Is a replication of 'home' the best structure to aspire to? What are the difficulties? What kind of home is being replicated?

Comment

1   You might have considered the importance of the sharing of tasks, a flexible workforce prepared to cross boundaries and involve young people in the maintenance of their environment. Possibly the most important factor is the provision of opportunity for young people to exert some influence over their environment, even if only with regard to colour schemes. Liam Dumigan asserts that 'it is essential for the residents to have some sense of ownership of the place in which they live'. Mandy Moorehead, acknowledging that organisations could do more to involve young people, states that 'good therapeutic work starts with the basics'; for example, sharing meal times, facilitating individual food preferences, and being around and available when young people come in from school, college or work. However, best practice is constrained by employment structures – notably the fact that staff have a life outside the residential centre, spending leisure time away from it – and organisational accountability.

2   I identified the following characteristics, but this is by no means an exhaustive list.

Physical characteristics	Social characteristics
Individual bedrooms with choice of décor and bedding	Opportunities to participate in sports and to pursue hobbies
Access to kitchen and food store	Non segregated education
External play area/garden	Group activities with staff; for example, eating together, going out on trips, attendance at religious services
Comfortable living area	
Limit to number of occupants (no more than 10)	
Choice of clothing	

As Sarah Craig *et al.* (1998, p. 54) have stated: 'The architectural challenge is to create an environment which has a normal, domestic appearance, but which gives sufficient space and privacy for a group of unrelated young people and staff'.

3   There is often an attempt to conform to Western middle class norms with regard to family life, but this may be alienating for some young people who seek to escape the confines of family life (which they may have found abusive or oppressive) and to live more autonomously as individuals without the emotional expectations of family life. Some groups of people live communally without attempting to emulate the family model. However, this model is favoured in residential care because some of the people in the group are in receipt of care, although it has been proved to be difficult to emulate family life within a residential framework. Matthew Colton found a marked contrast between residential staff and foster carers in their 'caretaker roles'. He notes that, while:

> the foster parent role is characterised by *social child care* (e.g., playing any sort of formal or informal game with children or amusing them in other ways; watching TV with children; sitting

down to talk with children and taking an interest in their everyday affairs and activities, etc.) ... staff roles seem to involve an emphasis on supervisory and, though to a lesser degree, administrative duties.

(Colton, 1988, pp. 34–5)

VOYPIC has found that creating a home from home may not be desirable because many young people whom they represent have indicated a preference for residential care rather than foster care (interview, 08/02/06).

3.2 Rights

In order to ensure that the relationship between care workers and young people is positive, nurturing and beneficial, current thinking suggests that the organisation must have clear policies and support systems in respect of three aspects of residential care provision: the exercise of rights by those being cared for; their involvement in decision making; and the involvement of their parents or guardians in their care and plans for their future. Angus Skinner has developed a set of principles to be used as a framework to evaluate the quality of care provided. The residential care sector in Scotland is required to work to these standards, placing the young person at the centre of any evaluation of effectiveness. They are given below.

Young people should expect

- Their rights to be respected

- Their parents' rights to be respected, and wherever possible, their parents' involvement as partners in the care provided

- To be treated with respect and dignity, to be treated as individuals with their own unique relationships, experiences, strengths, needs and futures

- To participate in the decisions that affect them, and those that affect the running of the home or school

- To feel safe and secure in the home or school

- To have privacy, and dignity; with special regard paid to this when they need personal care

- To have a 'special person' to relate to during the time they live in the home or [residential] school; and to be able to talk to that person in confidence

- To be protected from harm, including self-harm

- To have appropriate limits set for their behaviour

- To be well looked after physically; to be comfortable and well fed

- Their health to be given individual attention

- To be actively encouraged in their formal education, and, as they get older, in further education, vocational training or employment

- To have new, varied and positive experiences

- To learn how to look after themselves in a practical way, and to be assisted to develop the common skills required of adults

- To have the opportunity to work on emotional issues when they need to

- To be admitted to the home or [residential] school in a planned and sensitive way

- To move on to well-planned situations

- To be fully and carefully prepared for any moves out of the home or school, whether back to their own home, to some other form of care, or to independent living

(Quoted in Craig *et al.*, 1998)

Young people in care are in a vulnerable position and have, consequently, been the subject of considerable interest on the part of organisations which seek to promote human rights. Historically young people's rights have not been at the fore in residential care. Although this was also true of society at large, the potential for abuse in residential settings has been exploited and this has been partially attributed to the denigration of young people's rights. A determined effort has therefore been made to affirm these rights, to inform young people of them and to encourage young people to exercise them. For example, Glenmona presents young people, on admission, with an easy-to-read pamphlet on their rights and how they apply in everyday situations. Of course, such a strategy is dependent on the young person having the literacy skills to interpret the pamphlet, but the key worker's role is to advocate on the young person's behalf, enabling them to express concerns or misgivings. In acknowledgement of the need for young people to have advocacy vehicles and support systems, organisations such as the Irish Association of Young People in Care (IAYPIC) have been established, with a brief to 'give a voice to what young people in care are saying, to promote the rights of children in care, to provide information, advice and support to young people and to promote the participation of young people' (Carty, 2003, p. 2).

Organisations and individual carers are faced with the challenge of setting safe boundaries for young people while promoting their rights. Staff have to balance the requirement to manage behaviour which is often difficult with the requirement to ensure the smooth running of establishments catering for eight to ten young people with diverse needs. Such organisations are characterised by a regular turnover of staff and residents; a division of labour between care staff and domestic staff; 'batch living', which is an inevitable consequence of a large number of people residing together; and staff shift patterns. Management of such complexity requires clearly set out rules and routines. One way of ensuring that rules are complied with is the use of a behaviour modification system. Punitive forms of behaviour modification were used in reformatories; more sophisticated versions are used today, particularly in custodial settings (Convery, 2002, p. 37).

An example of one such system is the 'progressive regime' in operation in Rathgael Juvenile Justice Centre in Northern Ireland. Like all behaviour modification systems, this 'regime' operates on the basis of privileges and incentives earned by co-operating with staff and by behaving compliantly, and is in keeping with Foucault's (1979) assertion that the 'prisoner' is to be observed, retrained and rendered obedient, liable for punishment or reward according to their observed behaviour. There are four levels of privilege, the highest of which is platinum. This level is achieved when the resident is fully co-operating with staff, working to their 'training plan', achieving change and requiring little or no supervision. One privilege at this level is an 11.00 pm bedtime, when the resident is also allowed to remain unsupervised in the living area of the unit from 10.15 to 11 pm. Removal of this privilege results in a 10.00 pm bedtime.

Activity 6 Balancing rights with behaviour management

Allow 15 minutes

What problems might imposition of a 10.00 pm bedtime cause for staff? How does such a regime differ from ways of managing young people's behaviour in a domestic environment? Is the power balance equivalent to that between a young person and their parent? Is there more or less potential for conflict or confrontation in an institutional setting? Are staff likely to respond to confrontation in a formulaic way? Are such regimes conducive to conflict?

Comment

Such a systematic approach to the tagging of behaviour and the issuing of related penalties or privileges does seem to be very instrumental, leaving little room for staff to manoeuvre. A recent investigation of custody for young people calls for 'more creative' ways to deal with difficult behaviours (McKeaveney, 2005, p. 33). But the implementation of more creative strategies will require additional resourcing. Staff may be disinclined to engage in lengthy negotiations or take the time to get to the bottom of a conflict at the end of a shift when they are tired and keen to get home to their families.

It is difficult to invoke a rights based framework if staff are not adequately respected and valued. Michael Donnellan (interview, 24/03/05), formerly director of a secure youth justice facility in Dublin, believes that effective management of such a unit is predicated on an acknowledgement of the equal right of young people and staff to feel safe and to be cared for.

3.3 Participation

A significant effort is invested by practitioners and organisations in preparing young people for each stage of the residential care experience, but those young people who were consulted by the EUROARRCC researchers believed that they could be more effectively involved in the decision-making process (Craig *et al.*, 1998, pp. 66–7). Most respondents felt that staff were in control of this: 'The staff ... do listen to us. But at the end of the day, [they] are the bosses' (Craig *et al.*, 1998, p. 54). The young woman quoted earlier in this section appreciated the fact that, in Cherrygrove, 'the staff are aware of how much control they have'. She also spoke of *her* need, as a young person in care, to feel in control.

Michèle Clarke has noted that consultation with young people is a 'new departure for residential child care, and presents real challenges for management, staff and children alike ... to reflect the individuality of each child living in a residential centre, children should be involved in decisions that affect their daily lives, and their medium and long-term plans' (quoted in Carty, 2003, p. 11). This view is corroborated by the EUROARRCC Report which asserts that: 'Professionals who take decisions about [young people], without their clear and express involvement and that of their family, are unlikely to be effective' (Craig *et al.*, 1998, p. 52).

Consider, for a moment, how different this approach is to the one which was characteristic of the forerunners of Glenmona where the institutional perspective pertained and young people were not expected to question or complain. Nevertheless, the more child centred approach which permeates all aspects of childcare and education today is more difficult to implement in residential care because it is provided within a system which is procedural and outcome driven. Consequently, organisations such as VOYPIC, IAYPIC and Who Cares Scotland have been established to address systemic shortcomings.

There is also, currently, an emphasis on the centrality of parental rights and responsibilities with regard to their children. An example of the concrete expression of the meaning of 'partnership with parents' is given below. It is taken from a Republic of Ireland departmental guidance document:

> The young person, parents and significant others are involved in drawing up the care plan and receive copies of the care plan.
>
> [...]
>
> Visits from family and friends are encouraged and facilitated in private, unless safety and security are compromised, or otherwise directed by the courts.
>
> A young person's individual log should contain a complete record of all contacts between family and young person and all appointments and/or efforts made to establish contact. A record of non-contact with parents or guardians will be maintained.
>
> Where a review meeting has established that contact is prohibited, this should be clearly explained to the young person concerned ...
>
> (Department of Education and Science, 2004, pp. 13–14)

In practice, application of such directives is problematic. Although Liam Dumigan is fully supportive of attempts to maintain family links and contact with the young person's local community, he also avers that, since the 1970s, there are more young people coming into the system who do not have a caring family to return to.

3.4 Care or custody?

In the first two sections of this chapter we traced the development of a movement which began with the introduction of residential services for children and young people, and has now reached a point where the rights of young people in care are foregrounded and there is considerable investment in staff and physical resources. We have used Foucault's ideas to analyse how certain approaches have gained supremacy and influenced practice. Another useful way of thinking about such developments is Anthony Giddens's theory of structuration. Giddens (1991) argues that structure and agency may be conflated; that is, that structures are formed and amended by individuals, their actions and interactions. Although social structures emerge out of social interactions, they gain power and autonomy in their own right, independent of any individual. Thus, approaches to residential care have been influenced by individuals and groups, but have gained a momentum of their own; specific ways of working have become institutionalised (that is, seen as the only way to do things or provide care) and have taken decades to change and be superseded by new approaches.

This theoretical approach may help explain the over-representation of young people from care backgrounds in custody. In 2004 there were 392 residential childcare places available in 52 residential establishments across Northern Ireland (Criminal Justice Inspection NI, 2004, p. 14). Fifteen per cent of these young people were accommodated at the two Regional Care Centres, of which Glenmona is one, and five per cent were in secure accommodation. Although 42.9 per cent of all admissions were girls, there was just one girl in Glenmona, and the Juvenile Justice Centre at Rathgael and the Young Offenders' Centre at Hydebank (both in or near Belfast) do not cater for girls. Consequently, girls as young as 15 may be detained on a wing of a high security adult prison, a practice which harks back to the era before industrial schools when young people were sent to prison.

In 2004 it was estimated that, in Northern Ireland, 70 per cent of 10–13-year-olds detained in custody had been in the looked after system, and 25 per cent were admitted directly from residential care (Criminal Justice Inspection NI, 2004, p. 14). The point we are seeking to make is that, in spite of valid and sincere attempts to improve the quality of care which children and young people receive when being looked after by the state, there is still a reliance on institutional-type custody for a minority. This situation has prevailed in spite of the recommendation from the Criminal Justice Review, reporting in March 2000, that 'children aged 10–13 ... who are found guilty of criminal offences should not be held in juvenile justice centres, and that their accommodation needs should be provided for by the care system' (McKeaveney, 2005, p. 1). Include Youth has questioned whether non custodial and therapeutic interventions would be a more appropriate way of dealing with troubled young people, but the legacy of the industrial school is difficult to erode.

Drawing on the Criminal Justice Inspection NI (2004) report mentioned above, Include Youth maintains that there is a 'leakage' of care experienced children and young people into the youth justice system, and into custody in particular, and explains this 'drip feed' by reference to two enduring patterns. First is the fact that the 12 per cent of looked after children who reside in residential establishments 'present the looked after system with the greatest challenges as they frequently have complex social, behavioural, psychological and educational needs' (Kilkelly et al., 2002, p. 189). Second is the fact that young people in care sometimes find themselves charged with relatively serious offences for behaviour which would not necessarily attract the attention of the law in a domestic setting. There is some evidence to suggest that inexperienced staff in residential homes, particularly bank staff working at weekends, are inclined to call in the police rather than resolve a situation internally. One young person has been quoted as follows: 'I was 13 when I first went into custody, and have been in four times since. Three of these was directly from the children's home – all incidents because of my reaction to being restrained' (Include Youth, 2005, p. 5).

Key points

- Relationship building is an important way of working with young people in care.
- The physical environment in which care takes place is significant.
- Current models of good practice in residential care attempt to redress the mistakes and abuses of the past by making it possible for young people to play a central role in the design and delivery of services, enabling them to exercise their rights and providing opportunities for parents or guardians to participate in the care of their young people.
- There are pragmatic difficulties involved in implementing best practice in residential care and custody.

Conclusion

Residential care has developed and evolved in response to social change and political imperatives. It is therefore essentially a cultural product, expressed in ideological discourses and legislative initiatives. The notion of accommodating young people in centres separate from adults is a relatively new one and, consequently, strategies for working in such establishments are still being evolved. However, the many scandals associated with residential care, which have been widely publicised, have led to a formalised determination, in both the UK and the Republic of Ireland, to improve the service which is provided in an effort to realise the potential of young people who are deemed to require care in a residential setting.

Practice in residential care – as in all social work/social care contexts – is inherently political and the caring function is subject to scrutiny and evaluation because it involves the use of power. The many organisations, policies and research reports alluded to this in chapter convey the message that poor quality care will not be tolerated, and it seems, on many fronts, that the provision of residential care has evolved and improved since it was introduced to Ireland and the UK in the mid-nineteenth century. Units are now smaller and more comfortable, discipline is less severe, and systems and organisations have been set up to protect the rights of young people. However, young people in care are still subject to surveillance – monitoring, analysis and assessment – to a greater extent than those who have managed to avoid the care system. Residential facilities for young people still also manifest the vestiges of institutionalisation – albeit at the softer end of Goffman's spectrum – because collective living demands a systematic approach to house-keeping and care giving. We will close this chapter with a quote from the young woman who was first mentioned in Section 3 and who, incidentally, hopes to train as a social worker:

> Residential care is difficult, what with the turn-over of kids and the lack of privacy and security. But it can work if there's time to build relationships, space for people to be themselves, and if staff can acknowledge mistakes.
>
> (Quoted from a speech given in 2006 to trainee social workers, Armagh)

References

Alcock, P. and Harris, P. (1982) *Welfare, Law and Order*, London, Macmillan.

Atherton, J.S. (1989) *Interpreting Residential Life: Values of Practice*, London, Routledge.

Batmanghelidjh, C. (2004) 'Working with vulnerable children and young people: the importance of relationships and loving care', *Spotlight*, no. 2 (March), London, National Children's Bureau.

Bullock, R., Little, M. and Millham, S. (1993) *Residential Care for Children: A Review of the Research*, London, HMSO.

Carty, C. (2003) *Here 2B Heard: Irish Association of Young People in Care Strategic Plan 2004–2009*, Dublin, Irish Association of Young People in Care (IAYPIC).

Colton, M. (1988) 'Foster and residential care practices compared', *British Journal of Social Work*, vol. 18, pp. 25–42.

Convery, U. (2002) 'The use and nature of custody for children in the Northern Ireland criminal justice system', unpublished doctoral thesis, University of Ulster.

Craig, S., Donnellan, M., Graham, G. and Warren, A. (1998) *Learn to Listen: The Irish Report of a European Study on Residential Childcare*, Dublin, Centre for Social and Educational Research, Dublin Institute of Technology.

Criminal Justice Inspection NI (2004) *Inspection of the Juvenile Justice Centre (NI)*, Belfast, Northern Ireland Office.

Department of Education and Science (2004) *Standards and Criteria for Children's Detention Schools*, Dublin, Department of Education and Science.

Donnellan, Michael, interview, 24/03/05.

Dumigan, Liam, interview, 8/02/05.

EUROARRCC (European Association for Research into Residential Childcare) (1998) *'Care to Listen?' 'Haluatko Kuunnella?' '¿Nos Esforzamos Por Escuchar?'*, Glasgow, Centre for Residential Child Care.

Foucault, M. (1979) *Discipline and Punish: The Birth of the Prison*, London, Penguin.

Fraser, D. (2003) *The Evolution of the British Welfare State: A History of Social Policy Since the Industrial Revolution*, Basingstoke, Palgrave Macmillan.

Fry, M. (1951) *Arms of the Law*, London, Gollancz/Howard League for Penal Reform.

'Gary', interview, 24/03/06.

Gibbs, I. and Sinclair, I. (1998) 'Treatment and outcomes in children's homes', *Child and Family Social Work*, vol. 4, no. 1, pp. 1–8.

Giddens, A. (1991) *Modernity and Self-Identity: Self and Society in the Late Modern Age*, Cambridge, Polity Press.

Gilligan, R. (1991) *Irish Child Care Services*, Dublin, Institute of Public Administration.

Goffman, E. (1961) *Asylums*, London, Penguin.

Graham, G. (1994) 'Residential childcare: an analysis of activities and tasks and the implications for the organisational design of residential childcare units', M.Litt thesis, Dublin, Trinity College.

Griffin, C. (1997) 'Representations of the young' in Roche, J. and Tucker, S. (eds) *Youth in Society: Contemporary Theory, Policy and Practice*, London, Sage.

Hall, G.S. (1904) *Adolescence: Its Psychology, and its Relations to Anthropology, Sex, Crime, Religion and Education* (2 vols), New York, Appleton.

Harris, J. (1994) *Private Lives, Public Spirit: Britain 1870–1914*, London, Penguin.

Include Youth (2005) Paper submitted to the UN Committee on the Rights of the Child for its General Day of Discussion on 'Children without Parental Care'.

Kehily, M.J. (2007) 'A cultural perspective' in Kehily, M.J. (ed.) *Understanding Youth: Perspectives, Identities and Practices*, London, Sage/The Open University (Course Book).

Kilkelly, U., Moore, L. and Convery, U. (2002) *In Our Care: Promoting the Rights of Children in Custody*, Belfast, Northern Ireland Human Rights Commission.

McKeaveney, P. (2005) *Review of 10–13 Year Olds Entering Custody*, Belfast, Youth Justice Agency.

Misztal, B. (2001) 'Trust and cooperation: the democratic public sphere', *Journal of Sociology*, vol. 37, no. 4, pp. 371–86.

Moorehead, Mandy, interview, 13/03/06.

Muncie, J. (1997) 'Shifting sands: care, community and custody in youth justice discourse' in Roche, J. and Tucker, S. (eds) *Youth in Society: Contemporary Theory, Policy and Practice*, London, Sage.

Muncie, J. (1998) 'Give 'em what they deserve: the young offender and youth justice policy' in Langan, M. (ed.) *Welfare: Needs, Rights and Risks*, London, Routledge/ The Open University.

Northern Ireland, Children and Young Persons Review Group *et al.* (1979) *Legislation and Services for Children and Young People in Northern Ireland: Report of the Children and Young Persons Review Group* (The Black Report), Belfast, HMSO.

Rose, N. (1999) *Governing the Soul* (2nd edn), London, Free Association Books.

Social Services Inspectorate (1998) *Children Matter: A Review of Residential Child Care Services in Northern Ireland*, Belfast, Department of Health and Social Services.

VOYPIC (Voice of Young People in Care), interview with Alicia Toal, 08/02/06.

Waterhouse, R., Clough, M. and le Fleming, M. (2000) *Lost in Care: Report of the Tribunal of Inquiry into the Abuse of Children in Care in the Former County Council Areas of Gwynedd and Clwyd Since 1974* (The Waterhouse Report), London, The Stationery Office.

Part 3
Encounters

Chapter 7

Risk

Claire Smith, Wendy Stainton Rogers and Stan Tucker

Introduction

This chapter is about risk and young people, focusing on young people whose risk taking and exposure to risk raise concern: about their own safety and wellbeing and that of others. The first section examines risk as a concept, and some of the theoretical frameworks that help us gain insight into the risks associated with being young. There then follow three sections looking at different aspects of risk and the ways in which each of these can be addressed. Section 2 discusses ways of tackling the risks that young people pose, Section 3 explores approaches to diverting young people away from risk, and Section 4 looks at initiatives working with young people to overcome risk.

The chapter will address the following core questions:

- Does the categorisation of young people's lives into various 'at risk' groupings help us to understand better their everyday experience?
- What are the advantages and drawbacks of viewing young people's experience through this lens?
- How can those working with young people be encouraged to see them as a heterogeneous group with diverse needs and aspirations?

1 Putting risk in context

Risk is a much debated and highly contentious concept. It is also a very powerful one, since concerns about risk lead to calls 'to do something about it'. *What* to do depends on your definition of what 'risk' means. For young people in the West, the transition to adulthood was once inextricably linked to the movement from school to work. In the period following the Second World War, manufacturing employment was seen to offer viable, if restricted, opportunities for young people, especially young men. Though monotonous, work was seen as providing the material benefits of regular pay, stability, security and a 'job for life'. The decline in manufacturing jobs in Western countries has in part been supplemented by an expanding service sector economy and the urban regeneration of old industrial quarters. Although this shift has seen an increase in youth participation in the labour market, it is characterised by more casual forms of labour, marked especially by part time working hours, fixed term contracts, more 'flexible' patterns of employment and pay scales that barely rise above the minimum wage (see Thomson, 2007b, in the companion volume in this series).

At structural and cultural levels, then, the 'pathways' open to young people, as they make the transition to adulthood and the world of work, are rapidly changing yet increasingly individualised. In the post-industrial period, transitions to adulthood continue to be marked by opportunity, risk, uncertainty and labour market insecurity. Late modern theorists suggest that the notion of 'risk' characterises the contemporary period (Beck, 1992; see also the discussion by Thomson, 2007a, in the companion volume). However, rather than leading to the collapse of social class distinctions, it is possible to argue that the risk-infused sensibility of the age appears to *strengthen*, rather than abolish inequality in late modernity. It is within these new times that young men and young women are attempting to rewrite their identities and labour biographies and in so doing are found to be pursuing multiple, fragmented or unaccomplished transitions: the increasingly individualised biographies include complex, fractured and 'insecure transitions' (MacDonald, 1999, p. 171) mediating across school, work and local–global networks.

Most people will agree that risk is about taking a chance where there is a real possibility of something bad happening. Yet 'nothing ventured, nothing gained' is also common wisdom: if you don't take risks then you miss out on opportunities. Whereas other terms – such as 'hazard', 'threat' and 'danger' – always carry a negative meaning, risk taking is much more ambiguous: except, that is, risk taking by the young. Youth plus risk taking always seems to add up to a bad thing! That is, if you are an adult. Young people rarely think about their lives in terms of risk. Rather, risk-taking behaviour among young people may be spoken about as forms of pleasure seeking, having fun, being adventurous. In this chapter we will examine the notion of risk in young people's lives and how it is conceptualised, and look at some of the consequences.

Activity 1   Young people and risk

Allow 30 minutes   Below are three extracts from websites, each one about young people and risk. The first is from AVERT, an international HIV and AIDS charity based in the UK, with the aim of averting HIV and AIDS worldwide; the second is from Youth at Risk, a charity dedicated to young people whose reality has become crime, exclusion from school, unemployment, drug and alcohol abuse and other self harm; and the third is an edited article from Reuters on a report from the Financial Services Authority (FSA).

Read these extracts and then note two or three ways in which they are saying the same thing and at least one way in which they have something different to say.

When you have done that, make some notes about how and why young people are seen to pose risks to themselves and to others.

Risk A: HIV infection

Young people are often particularly vulnerable to sexually-transmitted HIV, and to HIV infection as a result of drug-use. Young people (15–24 years old) account for half of all new HIV infections worldwide – more than 6,000 become infected with HIV every day (UNAIDS, 2004). More than a third of all people living with HIV or AIDS are under the age of 25, and almost two-thirds of them are women. In many parts of the world, young people in this age-group are at particularly high risk of HIV infection from unprotected sex, sex between men and IV [intravenous] drug-use because of the very high prevalence rates often found amongst people who engage in these behaviours. Young people are also often especially vulnerable to exploitation that may increase their susceptibility to infection. Even if they are not currently engaging in risk behaviours, as they become older, young people may soon be exposed to situations that put them at risk. Indeed, globally, most young people become sexually active in their teens. The fact that they are – or soon will be – at risk of HIV infection makes young people a crucial target for AIDS education.

(AVERT, 2006)

Risk B: Becoming 'beyond hope'

Youth at Risk gets to the very heart of youth disaffection by working with the most difficult and damaged young people – as well as those who may be heading that way – to turn their lives around.

The alarming rise in youth crime, truancy, unemployment and apathy affects us all. Youth at Risk recognises the enormous cost of recurring anti-social behaviour, both to young people as well as to their communities.

Those who vandalise, commit burglaries and muggings, are excluded from school or on benefits often feel alienated.

Their families, the police and their schools find it extremely difficult to deal with them. The young people themselves believe they are 'beyond hope'.

(Youth at Risk, 2006)

Risk C: Money problems

Lack of financial understanding is identified by policymakers as a key reason why people, especially the young, are not saving enough for their old age at a time when citizens are expected to enjoy longer lifespans ... Among its findings, the FSA survey found that 70 percent of respondents had not taken any steps to cope with a drop in income, although 28 percent of respondents had experienced such a drop in the past three years.

[...]

Lack of knowledge is particularly acute among young people, who now face an increasingly complex financial world, potentially heavy student loans as well as the attractions of products like credit cards that did not exist for earlier generations.

[...]

This combination of pressures means that the cost of not having the necessary skills to make sound financial decisions is becoming increasingly significant ... The FSA will target schools and workplaces to boost financial education. While dramatic improvements are unlikely over the next few years, the FSA expects to see a steady rate of progress.

(Reuters, 2006)

Comment

There are a fair number of commonalities between these extracts. Even though they are about very different kinds of risk, all three portray the young as vulnerable, mainly because they are seen to be lacking – in experience, understanding, knowledge, 'the necessary skills', and so on. They also identify risky behaviour as harmful to the young people concerned. Do notice, though, that the extracts also, in different ways, raise concerns about the risks young people can pose to others. This can be directly, for example, by the impact of their antisocial behaviour; or it can be more indirect, by becoming a financial burden on others, for instance. Not surprisingly, then, another common theme is that all use 'risk' as a justification for intervention. In Extracts A and C this is mainly seen in terms of a need to educate the young; in B a specific programme of action is being promoted, targeted at those young people who 'believe they are "beyond hope"'.

The differences are much more subtle. These depictions consider risk in young people's lives at different levels. Extract A takes a global perspective, Extract C a national perspective and Extract B a more localised viewpoint. This determines the level at which intervention is being justified: global, national or local. There is also a difference in standpoint: universal (where intervention is directed to all young people) or targeted (just at those whose risk taking is seen as causing serious harm).

So what does this tell us about the way in which adults typically construe the riskiness of the young? Certainly they are identified as a particularly vulnerable group, more prone to taking risks than adults. In popular imagination, risk taking is almost a defining characteristic of youth. Youth is seen as a time of being feckless and careless – a danger to yourself and to others. The young are defined by their lack: their lack of care in what they do, lack of concern for others and lack of self control and self discipline. It is hardly surprising, then, that the adult world finds their risk taking disturbing – even threatening – and hence seeks to prevent, reduce or curtail it.

1.1 The problematisation of young people's riskiness

This leads us into consideration of the concept of '**problematisation**' – an ugly but useful word that refers to the way in which young people's behaviour is presented as inevitably and inherently problematic. In other words, the dominant representation of young people means that whatever they do, they are positioned, in the eyes of the adult world, as 'being a problem'.

This concept can be seen at work in media coverage of young people. Kirk Astroth (1993) suggests that this has a historical trajectory, citing the cover of a 1954 issue of the US magazine, *Newsweek*, which was headlined: 'Let's face it: our teenagers are out of control'. The article within the magazine lamented, he notes, a 'national teenage problem – a problem that is apparently getting worse' (cited in Astroth, 1993). The same problematising agenda is evident today in the way in which young people are represented. The following extract provides an example.

> **The trials of living with the feral youths of Salford**
>
> Gang-related violence in British cities has made people wary ... of the young.
>
> [...]
>
> Derek, 64 [says] ...
>
> 'I was never as bad as these kids. I see them driving up and down the street at night. You can't see their faces. They're coming out with shooters and knives and they're terrorising people. They can't hold their ale or they're high as kites. They've no respect for you if you're over 25. That's why people my age are scared to go out.'
>
> [...]

> 'Breaking the law means nothing to these kids. Even prisons aren't a deterrent, and don't get me started on the police. A man can be kicked to death in the street and the thugs can't be identified because they're too young? ...'
>
> (Butt, 2005, p. 8)

The newspaper report articulates a range of dominant discourses which present the young as 'troubled', 'feral', 'disaffected' and 'delinquent'. Particular groups of young people seem to be identified as 'in need of intervention' and this approach has become the rationale of policy making and service provision. Judgements are made about the actions of those working with young people in terms of the contribution that is made to fostering and sustaining interventions that address young people's 'difficult', 'unruly' and 'disruptive' behaviour.

The problematising approach of such reports can be used to declare groups of young people to be 'at risk' and 'out of control'. Thus, specific forms of risk-taking behaviour are constructed through problematising discourses. These in turn justify adopting a range of regulatory strategies to control the apparent risks. An example is the way in which groups of young people congregating in public places make others feel uncomfortable and wary of what they may be up to. This 'threat' then becomes the justification for calling on the police or security guards to 'move them on'. A similar, more everyday example is the notice put up in shops that limits the number of under-16s who can enter at the same time.

Media images and stories frequently portray young people as 'problems'

Writing about plans to introduce juvenile curfews in the late 1990s, Tony Jeffs and Mark Smith argued that such measures were 'discriminatory and fundamentally wrong' because they 'criminalise perfectly legal and acceptable behaviour' on the grounds of age:

> Walking the street, standing in public places talking to friends, moving quietly and peaceably from one place to another, going to a late night movie are all harmless activities which should never be criminalised – whatever the time of day. To select young people and criminalise them for doing what the rest of the population can freely do is doubly discriminatory. Youth curfews

identify young people as an enemy within, a dangerous other, therefore curfews must be seen as morally repugnant and divisive.

(Jeffs and Smith, 1996, p. 12)

Not only is the problematising of young people unfair, but it may also hinder the impact of strategies that seek to support communities and promote social inclusion. So, for example, Dawn Stephen and Peter Squires, critiquing recent UK government approaches to 'risky' youth, argue that an approach based on an institutionalised mistrust of youth 'serves to further marginalise young people, and their families, most in need of inclusion and support' (Stephen and Squires, 2004, p. 366).

To claim that the young are *positioned* as 'problematic' through the operation of problematising discourses is not to deny that some young people sometimes behave badly and can seriously intimidate others, including other young people. What *is* being claimed, though, is that in many subtle ways the *same* behaviour is often judged very differently if enacted by a young person as opposed to an adult. It is not that young people are (or ever were) 'little angels'. Rather, it is a question of why we *expect* the young to be a problem. Why are all sorts of exclusions and controls set up to manage their behaviour that are not applied to adults behaving equally badly?

Activity 2   Looking for examples of problematisation

Allow 60 minutes

Over the next week or so, try to identify occasions when young people are not only treated or seen differently from adults, but are treated as 'problems' by definition.

Comment

One area that you might have identified is leisure and sport, where facilities are provided for adults for their own benefit: to enjoy themselves or keep fit. Similar facilities for young people are intended more to 'keep them off the streets'. Many facilities explicitly exclude those aged under 21, even though they are legally adults.

1.2 Governmentality and risk taking

As we have already noted, the apparent 'riskiness' of young people's behaviour makes them targets for control. The French theorist Michel Foucault proposed that governments seek to regulate any behaviour of their citizens considered disruptive: according to him, they 'supervise the individual, to neutralize his dangerous state of mind, to alter his criminal tendencies, and to continue when this change has been achieved' (Foucault, 1977, p. 18).

Foucault was particularly interested in exploring forms of **governmentality** (strategies used to regulate and control). Some he identifies are 'the prohibition of entering certain areas', imposing 'obligatory medical treatment' and interventions designed to make 'behaviour changes'. You may recall the discussion in Chapter 6, 'Institutions', of Foucault's ideas in relation to young people in institutions.

Crucially, Foucault draws attention to the fact that, in any society, certain groups have the power to define what actions mean and what they signify, and the responses they promote or prohibit. In our context, this is about defining which actions constitute risky behaviour and which do not. A good example here is the way in which some substances (such as ecstasy and marijuana) are determined to be 'risky' and hence classified as illegal drugs, while others (alcohol, aspirin and tobacco) are 'risky' enough to be controlled (with age limits for purchase) but not enough to be made illegal. Those who have the power to define meanings, Foucault warned, gain considerable power over people's lives – and, in some circumstances, their deaths.

Yet power over the risk agenda is not as closed as it might at first appear. Foucault also pointed out that individuals and groups have the ability to resist dominant discourses in order to assert their own visions and ideas. Challenges to dominant discourses can arise out of 'innumerable points of confrontation, focuses of instability, each of which has its own risks of conflict, of struggles, and of an at least temporary inversion of the power relations' (Foucault, 1977, p. 27). From this perspective it is possible to see just why some groups of young people raise the hackles of politicians and those whose job it is to care for and educate young people – given that the young have a whole armoury of strategies for resistance. Indeed, it can be argued that the young are problematised *because* they are so good at rebelling against adult power.

1.3 The moralisation of risk

A number of theorists have argued that one of the features of **neo-liberalism**, a political philosophy that rejects direct government intervention in the economy and which appears to be achieving global dominance, is an emphasis on new and more indirect forms of regulation and control over the lives of individuals. One way in which this is manifested, they claim, is through greater regulation of risk taking. Radical economists, for example, claim that our society is becoming one where 'the active management of responsible choice in risk-taking is the core of neo-liberal governance' (Ericson *et al.*, 2000, p. 553) and in which 'the ideal liberal citizen' is one who 'possesses remarkable qualities of self-discipline' (Ruhl, 1999, p. 109; see also the discussion by Robb, 2007b, in the companion volume in this series).

According to this analysis, one of the ways in which neo-liberalism promotes itself is by a *moralisation* of risk taking: making the taking of risks blameworthy. A good example is in relation to the risks people are seen to take with their health:

> Risk [is] ... a tool for blaming those who fail in the face of choice ...
>
> [...]
>
> ... people are blamed if they become ill and cannot demonstrate that, not only did they avoid risky behaviours and situations, but they also did everything in their power to be healthy so as to overcome the risks intrinsic to a lack of action.
>
> (Galvin, 2002, p. 120)

Blaming someone is very powerful. Not only is it a means of attributing responsibility to the risk taker: the blameworthy person becomes *responsible* for the harm that befalls them. According to Stephen and Squires: '"Dangerous" young people and families, through the moralistic rhetoric of "responsibilisation" ... become firmly subject to that great "epistemological fallacy" (Furlong & Cartmel 1997) of late modernity in that they are encouraged to formulate individual solutions for problems that remain, largely, of a structural nature' (Stephen and Squires, 2004, p. 352). Blaming also warrants highly invasive forms of intervention, on the argument that risk takers cannot be trusted and must be managed 'for their own good' as well as to protect the law-abiding and responsible others.

1.4 Risky circumstances

Blaming people for the harms that befall them has other consequences. Not only does it warrant intervening in their lives, it also deflects attention away from alternative explanations for the harm. As theorists such as Ulrich Beck (1992) point out, some young people face an 'abundance of risks' that arise not from their own actions but from their circumstances. Young people born and raised on disadvantaged estates face a variety of increased risks compared with those growing up in the leafy suburbs: much greater risks of violent attack and of being unemployed, for instance. And, although it goes on in the most elite public schools, not only are the risks of getting drawn into drug taking and drug dealing greater, but, more crucially, so are the risks of getting caught and then of being convicted and imprisoned.

Young people who have grown up in the care of a local authority are far more at risk of being homeless than those who have grown up within a family. Young people who are disabled or who have debilitating conditions such as ME (Myalgic Encephalopathy) can easily become cut off from their friendship networks and wider communities (Tucker and Tatum, 2000), putting them at risk of social isolation and the concomitant problems that can bring. Young mothers supporting themselves and their child(ren) on a very low income face risks to their health (including their mental health), to their education and to their life opportunities (Osler and Vincent, 2003).

In risk terms, the stakes are heavily loaded against some young people and can have an additive effect where one set of risks, such as mental health problems, makes them more vulnerable to others, such as social isolation, which in turn can lead to yet others, such as homelessness. We will explore some of these risks further in the remainder of this chapter.

Key points

- 'Risk' characterises the late modern period. It is a highly contested concept that provides a justification for taking action. How risk is defined determines what action is possible and what is not.
- Young people's behaviour tends to be understood through a problematising discourse which portrays them as particularly vulnerable to risk, to be harmed by it and therefore 'in need' of being controlled.
- It is argued that current policy towards young people is informed by neo-liberalism which views 'riskiness' as an individual quality.
- Some young people face an 'abundance of risk'. They will require extra support and services if they are to achieve a good quality of life.

2 Tackling the risks posed by young people

This section examines how current government policy seeks to deal with the way in which young people's behaviour exposes others to risk.

Activity 3	Young people as 'the enemy'
Allow 20 minutes	Read the extract below and consider the issues raised – both for young people and for the communities in which they live – by the curfew that has been imposed on local young people. What questions do you have after reading it?

> The young people in and around Hillhouse were confused about why adults made complaints to the police about them when they were simply hanging about with friends. Fear of young people is such that contact between the generations appears to be declining. Rather than talk to young people who hang about the street, today adults often assume that young people would attack

them verbally or physically. Rather than taking some responsibility for the behaviour of these young people, by assuming the worst many adults are handing this responsibility to the police. In the minds of these adults, it is likely that the curfew will have confirmed their worst fears about these young people, who will remain strangers to them.

(Waiton, 2001, p. 149)

Comment

This is a powerful piece of writing in that it depicts a disintegrating community where there is little in the way of dialogue between young people and adults, and even less in the way of personal and collective responsibility being taken for what is going on. The young people are clearly puzzled and a 'fear of young people' helps to create a gap between generations. There is no sense of community cohesion or conversation between the young people and the adults.

One response might be that the curfew may have accomplished its aim – removing young people from the streets – but at what cost? Is this a price worth paying? Is the risk posed by the young being appropriately addressed? Isn't there a better alternative that builds on a community's strengths rather than exposes its weaknesses and makes them worse?

2.1 How real is the threat?

The threat posed by some young people's behaviour has preoccupied government in recent times. Images of youthful disorderly behaviour and unrest grab the headlines and create a sense of political and public unease (see the discussion in Robb, 2007a, in the companion volume in this series). Dangerous streets and playgrounds, 'no-go' housing estates and disorderly town centres are seen as places that require greater levels of surveillance, control and regulation. Antisocial and disorderly behaviour within such locations is viewed as a public risk in that environments are created where other members of the public feel threatened and intimidated. For many, 'fear of crime' has increased to the point where it imprisons them in their homes, and the young are seen to be ever more 'out of control'.

This section will argue, however, that policy responses to threats of this kind are complex in the way in which they link together matters of social concern, parental responsibility and the need to control the behaviour of the young by restricting their activities. At the same time, as John Springhall (1998, p. 8) argues, the media have also been highly influential in shaping the public perception of risk via 'exaggerated reports about the "effects" on their children's behaviour of "sensational" and violent amusements'. A number of theorists (such as Waiton, 2001; Hendrick, 2003) argue that there has not been any real increase in such behaviour but simply greater media coverage of it, coupled with changed perceptions of what constitutes misbehaviour.

Indeed, it has been argued that contemporary 'moral panics' about youthful delinquency, increased fear about public safety and, in particular, the failure of parents to control their children adequately, can be traced back to the murder of two-year-old James Bulger by two boys in 1993 (Hendrick, 2003). Harry Hendrick argues that following this tragedy a discourse focused on promoting children's welfare was replaced by one based on a concern for 'justice' and a desire for retribution and punishment. This shift, Hendrick claims, led to a call for increased levels of state intervention in the lives of young people and families seen to pose a threat to social order. He maintains that 'under the influence of such a "moral panic" Labour first inherited a climate of opinion that demonised "troublesome" young people, and then it set about consolidating this age prejudice' (Hendrick, 2003, p. 225). Since then, media reports of gang violence, unsocial activity and disorderly behaviour have helped to reinforce and sustain the retributive justice discourse.

From the perspective of government policy making, what has happened in the public domain can be directly linked to a range of family, cultural and social factors. It is claimed that contributory influences to antisocial activity include underachievement at school, family dysfunction, mental health problems and drug and alcohol abuse. Other factors extend to the unemployment of parents, growing up in poverty, social exclusion and inadequate community facilities. By citing such influences a conceptual link between vulnerability, risk and antisocial behaviour is forged. However, this form of analysis has a long history, in the sense that delinquent activity has frequently been linked to deprived families and cultural backgrounds. At the same time, from this perspective elements of any 'solution' also need to address personality 'deficiencies' as well as 'inadequate parental discipline' (Griffin, 1993, p. 104).

2.2 Intervention based on the retributive justice model

One of the most significant policy innovations to have been shaped by ideas of risk has been the establishment of Anti-Social Behaviour Orders (ASBOs), Parenting Orders and the 'sweeping' of shopping malls for truanting children (normally involving the police and social services). A clear connection is being made between what young people do on the streets and their family and community networks. For example, ASBOs were first introduced under the 1998 Crime and Disorder Act in England and Wales and later adopted in Scotland and Northern Ireland. As civil orders requested by local authorities, the police or landlords, and made in court, ASBOs are statutory measures that can be employed to protect the public and they prohibit the offender from committing specified antisocial acts or from entering a particular area. They are effective for a minimum of two years.

Since their inception ASBOs have generated a great deal of argument both for and against their use with young people. On the positive side, they do seem to 'work'. Residents in areas affected by what is viewed as 'yobbish' and antisocial behaviour have reported improvements in their neighbourhood when ASBOs have been issued to young people, and it is this perception that has tended to dominate media coverage of their use. Arguments against them include concerns that young people's rights to anonymity are undermined if they are 'named and shamed' (Monahan, 2005), that they demonise young people, unnecessarily bringing more teenagers into the criminal justice system (Bradley, undated), and that they stigmatise families (Monahan, 2005). It is also argued that ASBOs could be counterproductive, acting more like a 'badge of honour' among teenagers.

In addition to ASBOs, the government has also introduced curfews for young people (see again Activity 3), which aim to stop those under the age of 16 years being out after 9 pm unless accompanied by an adult. Again, these have generated much discussion, usually centring on young people's rights and the appropriateness of excluding particular groups of young people from certain public spaces. On the other hand, it could be argued that the use of curfews can effectively reduce the risk of young people becoming involved in crime. As Waiton (2001, p. 31) noted with regard to a curfew introduced in Hamilton, this aimed 'to prevent crime happening by monitoring the behaviour of the young people who hung about the streets. It also aimed to protect children and young people from the "many dangers that they face when out at night"', thus juxtaposing crime with personal safety issues.

Dispersal Orders and Fixed Penalty Notices have been introduced as part of the Anti-Social Behaviour Act (2003 in England and Wales, 2004 in Scotland and Northern Ireland). Under this legislation police can disperse groups of two or more young people who are perceived to be a threat or intimidating, and any within the group who are aged 16 or under can be escorted home. Again, these policy developments have generated much debate surrounding their impact. The National Youth Agency (undated) has argued that Dispersal Orders generate even more negative perceptions towards young people, classing them as troublemakers and worsening relations between young people and authority figures. Fixed Penalty Notices were introduced as a rapid response for dealing with low level disorder (for example, being drunk and disorderly through binge drinking; throwing fireworks) outside of the courtroom. Penalties depend on the type of offence and the age of the person involved; for example, Fixed Penalty Notices can now be given to 16- and 17-years-olds causing disorderly behaviour through alcohol misuse. A number of theorists in this field are highly critical of intervention of this kind. For instance, Bob Coles *et al.* (2000, p. 25) argue that 'keeping children and young people in the home or continually moving them on is not a reasonable policy response to their needs'.

Curfews put maintaining public order above the harm that they do to young people's social lives and friendship networks, especially for those living on impoverished housing estates or in other deprived areas. These young people are unlikely to have any space at home in which to 'hang out', or parents who will ferry them about if they want to go out, as many middle class youngsters do. Reporting research that examined a range of disadvantaged housing estates, Coles *et al.* (2000, p. 25) comment that 'although some activities were often available within walking distance or on main bus routes, many young people did not have the financial resources required to take them off the estate'. Stephen and Squires (2004, p. 366) criticise a range of recent Community Safety initiatives undertaken by the UK government on the grounds that they represent a 'civilianisation' of crime prevention that can absolve the authorities from their responsibilities to uphold the rights of young people and their families, such as the right to a fair trial. They report the sense of injustice felt by many young people on the receiving end of measures such as Community Safety Orders:

> The main frustration expressed related directly to the notion of 'anti-social behaviour' itself and the sense that the young people had been 'picked on' for behaviour rooted in mental health or special educational needs problems; behaviour they perceived as minor when compared with the types and extent of crime in their neighbourhoods, which the research participants did not see being tackled anywhere near so forcefully.
>
> (Stephen and Squires, 2004, p. 366)

They report one young person as saying:

> I thought it was bullshit 'cause we didn't do half the things that goes on in this estate. Yes, I was worried that we'd be evicted, but it seemed completely over the top for a couple of things when you see what others're doing ... but with me, they'd be straight in on my case. No it ain't fair is it, but that's just the way the world is.
>
> (Quoted in Stephen and Squires, 2004, p. 360)

Less punitive approaches include providing extra services and support to young people with few financial or social resources. And, as we shall see in the next section, preventative forms of intervention are used to divert 'at risk' young people away from becoming embroiled in antisocial and criminal behaviour.

Some further welfare focused interventions have been introduced to sit alongside ASBOs. For example, under the Criminal Justice Act 2003, Individual Support Orders (ISOs) were introduced to ensure that children and young people issued with ASBOs are given professional help; for example, counselling to tackle alcohol abuse, or drug rehabilitation for drug abusers.

Key points

- Although it is a common assumption that young people's misbehaviour is becoming more extreme, theorists argue that this is a 'moral panic': more a matter of increased media coverage and a growing 'law and order' political agenda.

- Policy on how to manage misbehaviour appears to be shifting. Whereas young troublemakers were once mainly seen as 'deprived' and hence in need of welfare measures, now they are seen more as 'depraved' and hence in need of regulation, punishment and retribution. This is evident in a range of new measures, including ASBOs, Dispersal Orders and curfews.

- Critics argue that these prioritise public order to the detriment of young people's friendship and community networks, their opportunities and their quality of life. They are thus likely to increase alienation and exacerbate rather than alleviate many of the factors leading to 'delinquency'.

- Welfare services are still available, but are not given high priority.

3 Diverting young people away from risk

Diversionary intervention works on the principle that it is better to resolve problems when they are minor than to wait until they get really serious: a 'nip it in the bud' approach. It is targeted at young people who are identified as 'risk prone': in Youth at Risk's terminology (see Activity 1), not so much 'the most difficult and damaged' as 'those who may be heading that way' (quite possibly because they are involved with the 'difficult and damaged'). The idea is that intervention can divert the young person: away from a life of crime, for example. The risk *potential* is identified by observing behaviour that is seen as:

- already heading towards becoming dangerous, for the young person and/or others

- arising from circumstances, relationships or activities that have the potential to push the young person across the line into illegality and/or unacceptability

- sufficiently concerning at a societal, service or community level to justify some form of early formal or informal intervention.

The next activity is designed to help you reflect on the factors that might lead to young people heading towards such a state of affairs.

Activity 4   What makes people risk prone?

Allow 20 minutes

What kind of personal, social and economic factors do you think may contribute to young people becoming a danger to themselves and others in this way? What leads some young people into antisocial behaviour and criminal activity? List three or four different factors that you think are important and write short notes for each on why you think so. When you have done that, reflect on how some of these factors might combine to increase the likelihood of young people becoming the focus of public attention and early intervention.

Comment

Clearly this is a contentious area. You may agree with those who argue that behaving badly is the outcome of social forces and situations, such as being raised in a 'bad neighbourhood' or 'getting in with the wrong crowd' (for this argument see, for example, Shaw and McKay, 1969). On the other hand, you may consider criminality to have a psychological basis – in personality, for instance. In this case you may see some young people as having an innate and biologically driven propensity to become involved in delinquent activity (see, for instance, Mednick *et al.*, 1987; Caspi *et al.*, 2002).

Probably, though, you identified a range of factors. Research by David Farrington (1996) lists a series of connected categories that focus on 'backgrounds', 'circumstances' and 'attitudes'. Included in these are matters concerned with:

- *personality:* including impulse, 'hyperactivity' and 'restlessness' and an inability to understand the outcomes of offending behaviour

- *intelligence and attainment:* including poor school performance, a failure to comprehend the feelings of potential victims and a low level of intelligence

- *parental supervision, discipline and conflict:* including poor quality and inconsistent parenting, parental disharmony, separation and divorce

- *socio-economic status:* including families living on low incomes and benefits, unemployment and poor quality housing

- *delinquent friends and community influences:* including peer group relationships, impoverished housing estates, a lack of youth facilities and environmental factors.

(Adapted from Farrington, 1996, p. 2)

The important point about this list is not whether you agree or disagree with the content, but the way in which the factors listed might be used to justify intervening in the lives of young people. The young people concerned may not, in fact, have done anything wrong – merely 'hung out' with those who have.

3.1 Approaches based on the 'vulnerability' model

As an example of the discussion above, if the view is taken that a particular housing estate in an inner city area is a 'breeding ground' for young people who 'go wrong' (informed, say, by socio-economic and community factors), then this provides legitimacy for 'doing something about it'. For instance, the police might mount truancy patrols; youth workers could become involved in street level work; and a programme of diversionary activities may be offered by a local or national youth charity. The primary intention of all these approaches would be to prevent young people becoming involved in risky activity that could lead to antisocial behaviour and criminality. Intervention here is justified by the assumption that certain individual and groups of young people are 'vulnerable'. For Simon Bradford, the link to the idea of vulnerability is central to the way in which young people are declared to be 'at risk':

> By identifying their 'at risk' status (that is, their vulnerability), early *diversionary* or *preventative* intervention is thought possible. Rather than privileging characteristics which are thought to reside *in* individuals, the concept of 'risk' concentrates attention on abstract factors which constitute an individual as being 'at risk' ... almost anything can be plausibly incorporated.
>
> (Bradford, 2004, p. 250)

Bradford raises an interesting point in terms of the way in which it becomes possible to extend the concept of risk by concentrating on a young person's vulnerability. Emphasis is placed on 'abstract' factors that seem to shift the focus away from the individual through the identification of 'new sites for expert intervention in the social and material worlds' (Bradford, 2004, p. 250). With this form of analysis, nothing is 'off limits', in the sense that a great deal of the things young people do and say have the potential to place them at some level of risk, particularly when viewed through a problematising discourse.

The important point to focus on here is the way in which the concept of 'risk' arises out of processes of social construction that are influential in permitting different forms and levels of intervention. Problematising discourses are, in effect, extended to include those who have the potential to become 'at risk' at some time in the future. In turn, the seriousness of

Young people living on poor estates are often seen as particularly 'at risk'

particular activities can be assessed and managed more effectively. Attention is given to the categorisation and ranking of certain forms of behaviour and activity according to their potential to generate deviance, dysfunction and disruption.

The influence of this kind of policy and practice agenda can be seen in a range of interventions. For instance, the link between risk and prevention features significantly in debates about the need to safeguard children and young people from abusive situations and relationships. Indeed, Sir William Utting, in reviewing safeguarding structures and processes for 'children looked after', spoke about the need for 'proactive' interventions to keep children and young people safe (Utting, 1997). A useful example of this can be seen in the way in which Personal, Social and Health Education (PSHE) within schools is now being used as 'an essential part of preparing children and young people to protect themselves from harm and abuse and is especially important for vulnerable children with disabilities' (Joint Chief Inspectors' Report, 2005, p. 20). In essence, the approach is underpinned by the idea that young people, if provided with good quality information (and the opportunity to explore the information in a supportive climate) on issues concerned with sex education, bullying, self harm, personal safety or drug awareness, are more likely to avoid situations that place them at risk (see Chapter 8, 'Safeguarding'). Diversionary programmes have received significant levels of funding from central government. One such programme, The Neighbourhood Support Fund (DfES, 2004), has been effective in meeting the needs of marginalised young people. It is claimed that, through the financial investment (some £60 million over a three-year period) provided, the Fund has allowed community based work to be carried out with over 50,000 young people in the 13–19 age group:

> Of those involved, 25% had been excluded from school and 16% long term non-attenders. 55% had low levels of educational attainment and 13% special educational needs. 25% were identified as young offenders or at risk of offending. The programme also engaged young people with drug and alcohol and mental health problems ...
>
> (DfES, 2004, p. 4)

It is important to note that the aims of the programme, and the associated outcomes of the work, reflect wider government ambitions for marginalised and at risk young people. Opportunities were provided to young people to help them re-engage in educational activities, develop 'soft skills' concerned with, for example, anger management, confidence building and personal responsibility, and become involved with training.

Such an initiative, then, has to be painted into a much bigger picture and reflects the demand for government to respond to the needs of a significant number of young people (estimated at over 160,000) who opt out of education, training and employment once they leave school – these young people are referred to as the 'NEET' (Not in Education, Employment or Training) group (Social Exclusion Unit, 1999a). Indeed, a claim is made by the DfES that the Neighbourhood Support Fund enabled 68 per cent of participants to go on to 'further learning or employment – a significant contribution to the Connexions target of reducing "NEET" numbers by 10%' (DfES, 2004, p. 4).

What becomes evident in examining the approaches outlined above is the shift in policy strategy that has occurred. The important point to bear in mind is that there has been a move away from offering 'universal' services and towards an approach based on targeting services at the vulnerable (see Chapters 1, 'Practitioners', and 9, 'Support'). Increasingly, work with young people is set within boundaries that:

- categorise what are viewed as areas of activity that can increase the likelihood of longer term risk

- determine how significant levels of financial and human resource are to be invested to prevent the escalation of exposure to risk

- define the skills (both 'soft' and 'hard') and personal attributes that young people need to acquire, or increase, to avoid risk – and it is the promotion of appropriate skills and attributes that is the central function of a programme of intervention.

The management of risk, then, has become an important function for government. In turn this kind of work is used to respond to a wider concern about the way in which some young people in society are seen to be at risk of experiencing social exclusion. Such a form of exclusion might be the product of a variety of factors, including a lack of education, employment and training, economic hardship, inappropriate lifestyles, drug and alcohol abuse or involvement in crime. To understand social exclusion from this perspective is to comprehend how cumulative forms of disadvantage come together to shape individual and collective behaviour and place some young people 'at risk'. More effective management of the environments that young people experience is seen to be important. In turn, different forms of intervention (sometimes carried out through inter-agency activity) are required to counter personal and collective vulnerability, marginalisation, discrimination and dysfunction. The theme of 'joined-up' government policy making and service development has dominated discussion as a way of reducing young people's exposure to risk (see Chapter 1).

3.2 Alternative approaches

So far the discussion has focused on how risk management has increasingly been used to support early interventions in the lives of young people. Yet at the same time there are important questions to ask about the different forms of discourse that are currently used to inform work within this area. Does the categorisation of young people's lives into various 'at risk' groupings help us to understand better the nature of their day-to-day experience? Is there a risk of stereotyping the lives of young people through such approaches? Is there a danger that those working with young people will see them as a homogeneous group and fail to respond to their individual needs and aspirations? The fact remains that much of the discourse underpinning the need for early forms of intervention to reduce risk remains preoccupied with a deficit agenda that advocates various forms of 'treatment'. It is important, therefore, that an attempt is made to see the lives of young people who are potentially 'at risk' from different perspectives.

One such perspective shifts from the focus on young people's vulnerability (usually predicated on the 'failure' of their family and/or community) to one which concentrates instead on their resourcefulness and resilience and how their families and communities can promote these qualities (see, for instance, Little and Mount, 1999). An example is a programme called Communities that Care. Gordon Jack, in discussing the ideas that underpinned the programme, outlines how work with young people considered to be at risk can take on a very different focus: 'It involves assisting communities to assess their own strengths and weaknesses, in a systematic and standardised way, and to use existing research evidence to develop effective strategies to reduce risk and enhance the prevention of harm to children' (Jack, 2001, p. 191).

A variety of strategies is employed to work with the young, including education, youth work and family support. Yet what marks this approach out as potentially different is that it is underpinned by a clear focus on the need to pursue *community* development strategies that will empower and potentially change the lives of young people. Young people and their families become important stakeholders when it comes to assessing the nature of risk (based on research evidence) and the strategies that need to be introduced to counter it. When this strategy is followed, the assessment of risk takes on a very different form, in that it is based on the particular threats and troubles facing a specific community.

To move away from problematising perspectives and towards a position where the voices of young people are heard as equal participants in the risk assessment process, it is necessary to create a different kind of working environment:

> In order to be considered successful many of the more innovative recent policy interventions *presuppose* an ability to engage with children and to enlist their participation and consent ... We need ... to think about the conditions under which

> children's deliberative participation can occur, and about the efforts of translation involved in mediating between children's and adults' frames of meaning.
>
> (Sparks *et al.*, 2000, p. 205)

The participation of young people in assessing risk, then, needs to assume both a practical and a symbolic significance. Indeed, the passing of the Human Rights Act 1998 has helped to foster a situation where the voices of young people assume an increased level of importance. To pursue the kind of interventions that Richard Sparks *et al.* advocate, there is a need to move away from viewing young people as 'lacking' and 'incompetent' to a position where power imbalances between professionals and young people are acknowledged and, as far as possible, countered in order to promote the best interests of the young.

Activity 5   Emphasising the positive

Allow 20 minutes

Reflect for a few minutes on the arguments made in this section. Consider how diversionary work with young people can move away from problematising them and thus emphasising their vulnerabilities. Draw up a list of the key principles that will underpin policies and professional practice that build on the strengths of young people, their families and their communities.

Comment

The list below, adapted from original work undertaken by the Department of Health (DoH, 1999, p. 10), includes a range of principles that might potentially inform risk assessment practice in work with young people. See how they compare with the principles that you produced.

Diversionary intervention with young people needs to be:

- young person focused
- rooted in the development of the young person
- ecological in approach in that it takes account of personal, social, cultural, family and community circumstances
- based on partnership
- underpinned by equality of opportunity
- based on strengths as well as difficulties
- informed by multi-agency approaches
- seen as a continuing process, not as a single event
- grounded in evidence based knowledge.

If adopted, these kinds of principles can radically change the nature of work undertaken with young people. They make it possible to move away from a preoccupation with what is 'wrong' with youth and, instead, to look for their strengths and build on them. Often young people are disaffected because they lack control over their lives and feel powerless. Instead of trying to rack up the level of control the adult world imposes, it can be much more effective to share responsibility in ways that enable young people to be active participants in projects, rather than have them imposed on them (see Chapter 3, 'Participation').

Key points

- Diversionary intervention is a 'nip it in the bud' approach, targeted at young people heading for trouble.
- Historically, intervention strategies have worked on a model of vulnerability. They sought to identify risk factors and then find ways to reduce their impact: for instance, through education.
- Such strategies are inherently paternalistic and inevitably stigmatising.
- Alternative strategies are being developed that build on the strengths of young people, their families and communities. Such intervention seeks to engage young people as active participants, both in the analysis of risk and in planning ways to flourish in spite of it.

4 Working with young people to overcome risks

This section looks at ways to reduce the risks to which some young people are exposed: either by circumstances beyond their control, or by their own actions (and often a combination of both). Building on the principles developed in the previous section, the focus here is on:

- directly involving young people in understanding the nature of those risks
- creating conditions where they can be active participants in developing strategies to tackle them.

In essence, this section is about how particular kinds of initiatives can be used to empower the young to be more responsible in the management of their risks, life chances, needs and aspirations. The empowerment and engagement of young people in decision making, it will be argued, is likely to lead to an increased level of personal responsibility and the possibility of more desirable outcomes for some young people whose lives are heavily influenced by the kinds of risks that they take, or are considering taking.

This section will briefly look at the management of risk for two particular groups of young people: those who are homeless and young mothers. These two groups of young people have been chosen not only because the challenges they face are different, but also to show how community based policy initiatives can be used to achieve different kinds of outcomes. The initiatives selected are based on the assumption that young people have the potential to significantly change their own lives if they are given the right kind of support.

4.1 Homelessness

Homelessness can include sleeping rough on the streets, living in bed and breakfast accommodation or hostels, or lodging temporarily with family or friends. According to a report on *Rough Sleeping* produced by the Social Exclusion Unit (1998), a quarter of the street homeless are aged between 18 and 25 (Coles, 2004). Many of these young people are those who have been 'looked after' and care leavers. Approximately 129,000 children run away from home every year and end up on the streets (Schopen, 2005).

Living on the streets exposes young people to many risks, including taking and dealing drugs, sexual and physical abuse, sexual exploitation and prostitution. As Kurt Johnson *et al.* (2005, p. 232) highlight: 'substance use, depression, delinquency, and physical and sexual abuse have all been linked to characteristics of social networks. Runaways who report smaller, more transient networks are more likely to be exposed to or engage in high-risk behaviours'.

A report by Barnardo's (2005) highlights the fact that 'young people in the UK are more at risk of homelessness than in any other part of Europe, one fifth of all young people experience homelessness at some point in their lives and a quarter of these have been in care'. Running away from home can lead to a downward spiral of self destruction for a young person, for as Johnson *et al.* (2005, p. 232) state: 'running away and living on the streets profoundly affects adolescent social development. It weakens ties to supervising adults at home and at school, weakens or severs ties to school and neighbourhood friends, and establishes unconventional ties in the street culture'. Accordingly, various initiatives have sought to identify the reasons why young people feel the need to run away, and thereby attempt to help those concerned overcome these issues, or at least indicate that there are alternatives.

Young people living on the streets need a wide range of support services. These must be accessible (in terms of both local availability and the receptiveness of staff) and operate in ways that are valued by the young

Young people are more at risk of homelessness
in the UK than anywhere else in Europe

people who use them. Two examples of schemes that have had a positive impact on young people facing homelessness are the Safe in the City scheme and the Safe Moves project.

Safe in the City

The Peabody Trust and Centre Point established the London based Safe in the City charity in 1998. It aimed to address the causes of youth homelessness in order to find ways to prevent it. The scheme was originally funded for a six-year period via the Single Regeneration Budget, which provides resources to support local regeneration initiatives in England. By the end of the scheme, it was estimated that Safe in the City would have worked with 1,200 young people in reducing their chances of becoming homeless (Havell, 2001).

The work of the scheme was underpinned by a multi-agency approach which attempted to tackle the problems that can lead to a young person becoming homeless before crisis point is reached. Participants were supported through individualised and tailor-made programmes of activity. Effective programme management was based on the principle of responding to each individual young person's own needs and not treating them as a homogeneous group. An evaluation of the scheme focused on the fact that:

> key issues affecting a young person's outlook on life – family problems, low self-confidence and self-worth, entrenched world views – were tackled first through one-to-one support and family work if a young person was willing. Once outlooks had shifted, subsequent interventions could then help to facilitate change in other areas, for example education and employment.

> (Dickens and Woodfield, 2004, p. 4)

Young people, for their part, reported that the scheme had had a positive impact on their confidence, self esteem, motivation and emotional health. An example of this fact was presented by Cathy Havell in her conference report to the Safe in the City charity in which she stressed that 'what had worked for him [a homeless young person] was not a roof but a plan – and crucially, that it was his own plan, and not one imposed on him by well meaning professionals' (Havell, 2001, p. 12). For Havell, the key to the success of this kind of initiative depends on young people being given the opportunity to directly influence policy and practice (Havell, 2001, p. 12). In addition, the management of a young person's future needs to be left under their individual control whenever possible.

Safe Moves

The second example focuses on an initiative promoted by the Minister for Homelessness, Jeff Rooker, in 2004. Initially established as an 18-month pilot scheme launched collaboratively by the Foyer Federation and Connexions in 2002, Safe Moves aimed to identify young people aged between 13 and 19 who were at risk of becoming homeless and help them to avoid this.

Intervention measures included life skills training, family/inter-generational mediation and support, peer mentoring and help to move into supported accommodation if required (Quilgars et al., 2004). The scheme also assisted young people to access education, training and employment where appropriate. According to the evaluation report: 'In two fifths of cases, Safe Moves was helping to maintain, or had helped maintain, a young person in the parental home. A small number of young people had also returned to the parental home or had been helped to move to a more secure setting' (Quilgars et al., 2004, p. x). Again, a central feature of the initiative was to place young people themselves at the centre of any risk reduction strategy development. The scheme operated at two levels – resolution of the first order of risk (that is, being ejected from home) and then exploring other opportunities for improving the young person's life chances. There also existed an element of peer support and guidance where young people were empowered to work together to understand their collective and personal circumstances.

The policy responses cited here are centrally concerned with countering the risk of homelessness through a variety of preventative, educational, mediating and empowering strategies. Through increasing a person's positive perception of him- or herself, making them more confident and aware of choices available, young people facing such a risk can be supported in taking greater control of their lives.

4.2 Young mothers

Becoming a mother at the age of 14 was nothing unusual historically and remains commonplace in many parts of the world, though this is changing as young women's educational expectations change. In contemporary Britain it is, however, generally seen as a risk – to the young woman's education and life opportunities and also to a wider society in which early motherhood is seen as one of a range of indicators of bad outcomes for children. Young mothers themselves generally see it as less of a problem, attributing the difficulties they face more to the lack of resources, support and services (such as education) geared to their circumstances than to motherhood in itself (Phoenix, 1991; The Prince's Trust, 2001). These failures do pose risks to young mothers:

> Education, employment and training is not going to be an option for young mums until the groundwork for surviving in the world is done prior to dropping them into it. Juggling home/work and family is a major task for most people, just imagine doing it alone, with no support and without the weapons needed for survival!
>
> (Lesley Barnett, teenage pregnancy reintegration officer, Wolverhampton, quoted in YWCA, undated)

According to the Social Exclusion Unit's *Report on Teenage Pregnancy* (1999b), there were 90,000 teenage conceptions in the UK in 1997, which was twice the rate in Germany, three times the rate in France and six times that of Holland. The problem lies in the fact that most young women who become mothers in their teenage years are generally already suffering deprivation. According to Coles (2004, p. 94): 'those who became pregnant were shown to be spatially clustered in areas of social housing, deprivation and poverty and high levels of parental unemployment'. Quite often it can be a case of 'history repeating itself', as teenage mothers are, in many instances, children of teenage parents themselves.

In response to the prevailing situation, the government aims to reduce the number of teenage conceptions by half by 2010 (Social Exclusion Unit, 1999b) and, in support of this, several policy initiatives have been introduced. Crucially, it is also important to note that such initiatives are in a significant sense guided by the need to reduce the 'benefits bills'.

Sure Start Plus

Teenage parenthood is seen as a risk to a young woman's life opportunities

In 1999 the Teenage Pregnancy Strategy was launched, and as part of this Sure Start Plus was introduced in England in April 2001 to provide advice, guidance and support on a one-to-one basis to pregnant young women and young mothers. Working in collaboration with other government initiatives such as Connexions, Health Action Zones and Supported Housing, the key aims were to improve the levels of health experienced by teenage mothers and their children and to decrease the risk of young mothers becoming socially excluded and raising their children in poverty.

Sure Start Plus Pilot Programme

Sure Start Plus advisers give:

- Personal, confidential advice and support to pregnant teenagers
- Specially tailored support to young parents to help with: healthcare during and after pregnancy, parenting skills and support, practical housing and benefit assistance, access to education, training, work and childcare
- Group and one-to-one sessions
- Advice on contraception for teenage mothers and fathers

The various projects running in Sure Start Plus areas offer practical help such as support with breast-feeding, cooking on a budget, managing money, relationship advice, confidence building and help to stop smoking during and after pregnancy.

(Teenage Pregnancy Unit, undated)

The evidence from the national evaluation of Sure Start Plus indicates that the programme is having a positive effect on teenage mothers, improving their physical and emotional wellbeing and personal relationships, and giving them a more positive outlook for the future, which, in turn, will benefit the life chances of their children.

The evaluation concludes that Sure Start Plus projects have 'increased support for emotional issues, improved the young woman's family relationships including reducing the incidence of domestic violence; improved accommodation situations; and increased educational participation for those aged under 16 years' (Teenage Pregnancy Unit, undated). Here, government funding has been specifically used to promote community based work, much of it situated in deprived areas. The young women and their children were helped to access health, social care and educational resources, with the emphasis on self help as well as mutual support and providing opportunities for young women to meet.

Key points

- Good practice in working with young people to overcome risks uses a partnership approach, directly involving the users of services in its planning and delivery.

- Good practice takes a holistic approach, rather than dealing with different risks in isolation, which draws on the support of families and communities.

- Such intervention can be used to tackle a diversity of risky circumstances.

Conclusion

Risk is a complex topic and ideas about what constitutes risk in the lives of young people are influenced by a variety of social, personal, political and economic factors. In a very real sense risk can be viewed as a 'contested concept'; that is, a concept that is seen in different ways by different people and for different reasons. For example, it could be argued that new categories of risk are invented to permit a greater level of surveillance over the lives of young people.

If this is the case, then a rights based agenda for working with young people has the potential to challenge expert views and preoccupations. By involving young people in risk assessment activities, power relations are significantly changed. In providing a legal framework that encourages rights based work, the exploration of their views is formally sanctioned.

Yet as Helen Roberts (2003) argues, we also have to consider both the 'risks and benefits' associated with encouraging the participation of young people in risk assessment processes. In particular, she points to the major risk of developing consultation activities that are eventually seen to be largely 'cosmetic', for such activities 'may well be seen as a disbenefit, drawing on one of the few resources over which children and young people exercise some direct control – namely, their time' (Roberts, 2003, p. 32).

A key point to emerge from the discussion is the way in which risk is assessed. It is reasonable to argue that governments attempt to assert control over the risk agenda when they feel under pressure from the media or public opinion. On such occasions quick, strong and decisive action is viewed as necessary to prevent situations running out of control. In these circumstances the actions of young people are viewed as risky and problematic in that they are seen as a threat to public order. Such debates tend to focus on socio-political concerns about the need to better control the actions and activities of the young. Specifically though, as Jock Young (1999) argues, such a risk agenda has been underpinned by government concerns to produce 'correct' forms of both behaviour and speech in the public domain. In effect, in these instances the concern is to police 'moral boundaries' that are seen to be under threat.

Yet it is also clear that young people frequently make conscious choices to engage in risk-taking activity because of their personal or collective inclinations and circumstances. In this they are no different from adults, though they may well lack the resources that adults have to carry it off. A 13-year-old may decide to have a child for much the same reasons as a 30-year-old, the difference being that she is much less likely to have the income to make motherhood anything but a struggle, and the resources (such as a network of other mothers to share childcare) to support her.

Thus helping young people to understand better the risks they take is not enough; it has to be accompanied by support systems and resources. The difference is that, when young people are given encouragement to take part in choosing what these are and how they will be delivered, they are far more likely to use them and gain benefit from them. What is being advocated here is a different approach to risk assessment and service delivery that places young people at the centre of the process. Public and political responses to risk that are seen as harsh and punitive are likely to be greeted with hostility and resentment on the part of young people. Risk analysis that 'problematises' and stereotypes is likely to fail to respond to the real needs of particular individuals and groups. Risk-taking behaviour that leaves young people exposed and isolated is likely to foster a sense of resentment and increase the chances of alienation and exclusion.

References

Astroth, K.A. (1993) 'Are youth at risk?', *Journal of Extension*, vol. 31, no. 3.

AVERT (2006) *HIV, Aids Education and Young People*, www.avert.org/aidsyoun.htm [accessed 18/04/06].

Barnardo's (2005) *Poverty Wrecks Futures*, www.barnardos.org.uk [accessed 28/11/05].

Beck, U. (1992) *Risk Society: Towards a New Modernity*, London, Sage.

Bradford, S. (2004) 'Management of growing up' in Roche, J., Tucker, S., Thomson, R. and Flynn, R. (eds) *Youth in Society: Contemporary Theory, Policy and Practice*, (2nd edn), London, Sage/The Open University.

Bradley, T. (undated) *Policy Briefing – Anti Social Behaviour*, www.homeless.org.uk [accessed 28/11/05].

Butt, R. (2005) 'The trials of living with the feral youths of Salford', *Guardian*, 21 May, p. 8.

Caspi, A., McClay, J., Moffitt, T.E., Mill, J., Martin, J., Craig, I.W., Taylor, A. and Poulton, R. (2002) 'Role of genotype in the cycle of violence in maltreated children', *Science*, vol. 297, pp. 851–4.

Coles, B. (2004) 'Welfare services for young people: better connections?' in Roche, J., Tucker, S., Thomson, R. and Flynn, R. (eds) *Youth in Society: Contemporary Theory, Policy and Practice* (2nd edn), London, Sage/The Open University.

Coles, B., England, J. and Rugg, J. (2000) 'Spaced out? Young people on social housing estates: social exclusion and multi agency work', *Journal of Youth Studies*, vol. 3, no. 1, pp. 21–33.

DfES (Department for Education and Skills) (2004) *Transforming Lives, Re-Engaging Young People through Community-Based Projects*, London, Department for Education and Skills.

Dickens, S. and Woodfield, K. (2004) *Evaluating An Innovative Scheme for Preventing Youth Homelessness*, York, Joseph Rowntree Foundation.

DoH (Department of Health) (1999) *Framework for the Assessment of Children in Need and their Families*, London, Department of Health.

Ericson, R., Barry, D. and Doyle, A. (2000) 'The moral hazards of neo-liberalism: lessons from the private insurance industry', *Economy and Society*, vol. 29, no. 4, pp. 532–58.

Farrington, D. (1996) *Understanding and Preventing Youth Crime*, York, Joseph Rowntree Foundation.

Foucault, M. (1977) *Discipline and Punish: The Birth of the Prison*, London, Penguin.

Furlong, A. and Cartmel, A. (1997) *Young People and Social Change: Individualization and Risk in Late Modernity*, Buckingham, Open University Press.

Galvin, R. (2002) 'Disturbing notions of chronic illness and individual responsibility: towards a genealogy of morals', *Health*, vol. 6, no. 2, pp. 107–37.

Griffin, C. (1993) *Representations of Youth: The Study of Youth and Adolescence in Britain and America*, Cambridge, Polity Press.

Havell, C. (2001) 'From the margins to the mainstream: social inclusion and preventing homelessness', *Social Inclusion: Is It the Only Way to Prevent Homelessness?*, Safe in the City Conference Report, London, Safe in the City.

Hendrick, H. (2003) *Child Welfare: Historical Dimensions, Contemporary Debate*, Bristol, Policy Press.

Jack, G. (2001) 'An ecological perspective on child abuse' in Foley, P., Roche, J. and Tucker, S. (eds) *Children in Society: Contemporary Theory, Policy and Practice*, Basingstoke, Palgrave.

Jeffs, T. and Smith, M.K. (1996) '"Getting the dirtbags off the streets" – curfews and other solutions to juvenile crime', *Youth and Policy*, no. 52, pp. 1–14.

Johnson, K.D., Whitbeck, L.B. and Hoyt, D. (2005) 'Predictors of social network composition among homeless and runaway adolescents', *Journal of Adolescence*, vol. 28, no. 2, pp. 231–48.

Joint Chief Inspectors' Report (2005) *Safeguarding Children: The Second Joint Chief Inspectors' Report on Arrangements to Safeguard Children*, Newcastle, Commission for Social Care Inspection.

Little, M. and Mount, K. (1999) *Prevention and Early Interventions with Children in Need*, Aldershot, Ashgate.

MacDonald, R. (1999) 'Insecure transitions: the case of Teesside' in Vail, J., Wheelock, J. and Hill, M. (eds) *Insecure Times: Living with Insecurity in Contemporary Society*, London, Routledge.

Mednick, S., Moffitt, T. and Stark, S. (1987) *The Causes of Crime: New Biological Approaches*, New York, Cambridge University Press.

Monahan, J. (2005) 'Who are you calling a yob?', *Guardian*, 21 June.

National Youth Agency (undated) *NYA Response to Home Affairs Committee Inquiry into Anti-Social Behaviour*, www.nya.org.uk/Templates/internal.asp?NodeID=90783&ParentNodeID=88951 [accessed 15/06/05].

Osler, A. and Vincent, K. (2003) *Girls and Exclusion: Rethinking the Agenda*, London, RoutledgeFalmer.

Phoenix, A. (1991) *Young Mothers?*, Cambridge, Polity Press.

Quilgars, D., Jones, A., Pleace, N. with Sanderson, D. (2004) *The Safe Moves Initiative: An Evaluation*, York, The University of York, Centre for Housing Policy.

Reuters (2006) 28 March, http://reuters.co.uk [accessed 18/04/06].

Robb, M. (2007a) 'Gender' in Kehily, M.J. (ed.) *Understanding Youth: Perspectives, Identities and Practices*, London, Sage/The Open University (Course Book).

Robb, M. (2007b) 'Wellbeing' in Kehily, M.J. (ed.) *Understanding Youth: Perspectives, Identities and Practices*, London, Sage/The Open University (Course Book).

Roberts, H. (2003) 'Children's participation in policy matters' in Hallett, C. and Prout, A. (eds) *Hearing the Voices of Children: Social Policy for a New Century*, London, RoutledgeFalmer.

Ruhl, L. (1999) 'Liberal governance and prenatal care: risk and regulation in pregnancy', *Economy and Society*, vol. 28, no. 1, pp. 95–117.

Schopen, F. (2005) 'Young runaways', *Children Now*, 1–7 June, p. 19.

Shaw, C. and McKay, H. (1969) *Juvenile Delinquency and Urban Areas*, Chicago, IL, University of Chicago Press.

Social Exclusion Unit (1998) *Rough Sleeping*, Cm 4008, London, The Stationery Office.

Social Exclusion Unit (1999a) *Bridging the Gap: New Opportunities for 16–18 Year Olds Not in Education, Training or Employment*, Cm 4342, London, The Stationery Office.

Social Exclusion Unit (1999b) *Report on Teenage Pregnancy*, London, The Stationery Office.

Sparks, R., Girling, E. and Smith, M. (2000) 'Children talking about justice and punishment', *International Journal of Children's Rights*, vol. 8, no. 3, pp. 191–209.

Springhall, J. (1998) *Youth, Popular Culture and Moral Panics: Penny Gaffs to Gangsta Rap 1830–1996*, Basingstoke, Macmillan.

Stephen, D.E. and Squires, P. (2004) '"They're still children and entitled to be children": problematising the institutionalised mistrust of marginalised youth in Britain', *Journal of Youth Studies*, vol. 7, no. 3, pp. 351–69.

Teenage Pregnancy Unit (undated) *Sure Start Plus Pilot Programme – Background*, www.dfes.gov.uk/teenagepregnancy/dsp_content.cfm?pageid=73 [accessed 17/07/06].

The Prince's Trust (2001) *It's Like That*, London, The Prince's Trust.

Thomson, R. (2007a) 'A biographical perspective' in Kehily, M.J. (ed.) *Understanding Youth: Perspectives, Identities and Practices*, London, Sage/The Open University (Course Book).

Thomson, R. (2007b) 'Working' in Kehily, M.J. (ed.) *Understanding Youth: Perspectives, Identities and Practices*, London, Sage/The Open University (Course Book).

Tucker, S. and Tatum, C. (2000) *Speaking Up: An Examination of the Experiences of Children and Young People with ME*, Milton Keynes, Association of Young People with ME.

Chapter 8

Safeguarding

Andy Rixon and Danielle Turney

Introduction

The previous chapter argued in some detail that 'risk' is a complex and contested concept: one that is socially constructed. The discussion of teenage mothers and homeless young people illustrated how constructions of young people as 'at risk' and 'risky' are significant for public policy and the way in which young people are responded to. That chapter paid particular attention to the way some young people are perceived to represent a risk to others or society at large. In this chapter, we shift the focus and concentrate on young people who are defined as being 'vulnerable' or 'at risk' from 'harm'. The following activity illustrates how these labels are different but can sometimes coincide or overlap.

Activity 1	Whose risk? An example

Allow 10 minutes

Carl is 14 years old. Consider the following comments from different people in Carl's life. Note the different ways in which he might be viewed in terms of being 'at risk' (to himself or others?) or 'vulnerable'.

Neighbour: At around 10 pm I saw Carl with a big group of lads outside the shops. They were talking noisily and shouting abusive comments at passers by. Then a bin got set on fire so I called the police.

Youth worker: Carl comes to the club occasionally. I know Carl is very unhappy at home; he has told me about numerous arguments and how his dad always swears at him, calling him names and threatening him.

Teacher: When he is in school, which is not very often, Carl can be very challenging and a suspension is being considered. We are also aware though that Carl has been subject to some bullying which started, it seems, because of the poor state of his clothes.

Comment

This is a simple illustration of how young people can attract a variety of labels which will affect the degree to which they are seen as in need of 'protection' or 'safeguarding' (terminology we will return to). In the first instance, Carl may well have been viewed as primarily a risk to others – an instigator of 'antisocial' behaviour. However, is it possible that a neighbour or a police officer would also see this as behaviour that was putting himself at risk, or even that Carl is at risk due to lack of parental supervision? The youth worker is more likely to be concerned about Carl's home circumstances and to place him more squarely 'at risk'. At school perhaps Carl will be seen as a vulnerable young man through poor school attendance and bullying, although simultaneously as a difficult and disruptive pupil who can pose a risk to others.

The comments above gave no information about Carl's background, but we could have thought about how this might affect the framing of this scenario. Previous chapters have stressed how factors such as ethnicity, social class and gender also influence the way in which young people are responded to.

These labels are particularly important in relation to older young people. Homeless young people can easily be labelled as a risk to themselves or others, and may have run away from situations – of neglect, domestic violence, or sexual abuse – where they would also have been identified as experiencing harm and as being 'at risk' from some of the adults in their lives. While questioning where these boundaries are drawn, it is not our intention to contribute to the 'problematising' discourse identified in the previous chapter. The focus here is less on the risks young people may choose to take and more on the situations in which they are experiencing harm from others, and where a 'safeguarding' or 'protection' response from practitioners is required.

Although emphasising a different area of concern about young people, we would again argue that the language used to describe these situations is significant. The first section of this chapter will discuss the way in which this language has shifted over time and explore the extent to which different discourses signal changes in the focus of work with young people, reflecting different ways of understanding 'abuse' or 'harm'. At the same time, though, we stress that, whatever the debate over language and terminology, substantial research now exists on the potentially damaging and long lasting effects of experiences of abuse and violence. So, in the first section we will also consider some of this evidence.

We will be discussing a system and a way of working which is designed to protect young people. Yet it has often been noted that, despite intending to be 'child and young person centred' and to operate in their 'best interests', this focus is easily lost. The degree to which young people are at risk and in need of protective services is defined mainly by the practitioners and other adults in their lives. How, then, do young people experience this system? And is it working in their best interests?

The second section will look in more detail at issues arising from ways in which young people seek help, and how, for example, questions of confidentiality impact on the way they use professionals and systems of protection. How services to protect children and young people are constructed depends, in part, on how our notion of childhood itself is constructed. The relevance of these different perspectives on childhood, and the ambiguities they create for young people, will also be explored in the second section.

If 'young person centredness' can easily be lost in practice, what approaches to intervention can help maintain this focus and develop positive ways of working with young people? Section 3 explores some key issues, concentrating particularly on strategies to promote empowerment and resilience. Throughout, the chapter will consider some of the complex issues for practitioners: the changing environment in which they are working and the impact on them of this area of practice.

This chapter will address the following core questions:

- What are the changing discourses around concepts such as 'harm', 'protection' and 'safeguarding'?

- What is the impact on young people of experiences of violence, neglect and abuse?

- How do young people experience the system designed to safeguard them, and what lessons can be learned for practice from their perspectives?

- How can safeguarding responses be young person centred and focused on strengths in a young person's life, rather than on problems or 'negatives'?

- What are some of the tensions and dilemmas in safeguarding work for practitioners from a range of agencies, and for young people themselves?

1 Protecting and safeguarding

At heart, the discussion and debates in this chapter are about intervening in the lives of vulnerable young people defined as being 'at risk', in order to protect them from abuse or harm. In line with the earlier suggestion that our understanding of 'risk' is socially constructed, we would argue that the meanings of 'harm' and 'abuse' are also historically and culturally situated and therefore open to debate. The definition of abuse can reflect 'the concerns of the definers' (Corby, 2000, p. 40) and the influences of values and theoretical perspectives (Lawrence, 2004), and can be a 'phenomenon where moral reasoning and moral judgements are central' (Parton *et al.*, 1997, p. 67).

1.1 Changing discourses

For Nigel Parton, a key writer on protection issues in relation to children and young people, the professional systems responsible for protecting children and young people have become preoccupied with assessing, monitoring and managing risk without acknowledging the central problem of how to define what is being assessed. At one level, therefore, the labels 'abuse', 'protection', 'safeguarding' or 'in need' are secondary as they sidestep this crucial issue: 'the words may change but they may only act to obfuscate an already shrouded and complex sphere of professional, personal, and social life' (Parton *et al.*, 1997, p. 245).

Nevertheless, changing language can be a reflection of real changes in perspective on how concerns about harm to children and young people should be addressed. The choice of 'safeguarding' for the title of this chapter is an example of a word current at the time of writing, but which will undoubtedly be overtaken at some stage by another that implies a different emphasis on the topic. In the following discussion you will see that these shifts are more a product of debates about younger children than about young people, but their key features are relevant to all those under the age of 18. That they have focused more on children also gives rise to some of the dilemmas experienced by young people and practitioners, to which we will return later in the chapter.

Ideas about harm in relation to children have changed through history, but even since the 1960s the discourse has moved from the 'battered babies' syndrome described by Henry Kempe (Kempe *et al.*, 1962), through 'child abuse' and 'child protection', to the position outlined in the Green Paper *Every Child Matters* (DfES, 2003) and formalised in the Children Act 2004: of 'safeguarding and promoting the welfare' of children. Each term operates within a particular discursive field. Parton *et al.* (1997) suggest, for example, that the move from the term 'child abuse' to 'child protection' in the 1980s represents a shift from a medico-social to a socio-legal discourse; that is, a shift from a medicalised understanding towards a more overtly 'forensic' model which emphasises the quality of the evidence that could be presented in court to support an allegation of abuse.

In another shift, during the 1990s, significant attempts were made to move from an emphasis on 'child protection', and its concerns with those 'at risk of significant harm', towards more supportive interventions for children 'in need', in order to reduce what was seen as an excessive number of investigations into allegations of abuse. Research from a number of

Department of Health (DoH) studies (summarised in *Child Protection: Messages from Research*: DoH, 1995) had highlighted that many families were drawn into the child protection 'net' through these investigations, but that if 'abuse' was not substantiated, professional attention tended to move to the next investigation rather than to a full assessment of need and the provision of appropriate support (DoH, 1995). *Messages from Research* also stressed the importance of placing issues of concern in context and proposed that child abuse could be seen on a continuum: a key question then being where on this the threshold should be placed that would trigger the use of child protection procedures. According to one commentator (Garrett, 2003), this reference to the idea of a continuum is significant as it represents the first 'official' acceptance that abuse is socially constructed.

Arguably, this increased focus on investigations resulted from a number of child death inquiries and the procedures and professional anxieties following them. As Gordon Jack argued, changes in emphasis and terminology have often been shaped by high profile inquiries (typically, into the deaths of younger children), with not entirely positive consequences: 'By basing the existing system on the most extreme cases ... the pattern of responses developed has often proved to be inappropriate for the vast majority of cases in which children's lives are not at risk but their health and development are, nevertheless, being undermined' (Jack, 2001, p. 186).

However, it was again the recommendations of an inquiry into the death of a young child – eight-year-old Victoria Climbié – at the hands of her 'carers' that gave momentum to a further set of changes, structural as well as terminological, in the way risk and harm to children and young people were addressed and their 'safeguarding' ensured (Laming, 2003).

The term 'safeguarding' is not new. It appeared first in the Children Act 1989 and then in other guidance documents and reports, but its meaning appeared to evolve as it assumed a higher profile usage. The renewed emphasis on safeguarding signalled an intent for a more proactive, preventative approach to protection within the broad context of child welfare. This change was emphasised by the government in the Green Paper published in response to the Climbié inquiry: 'child protection cannot be separated from policies to improve children's lives as a whole. We need to focus both on the universal services which every child uses, and on more targeted services for those with additional needs' (DfES, 2003, p. 5).

This broader commitment to 'improve children's lives as a whole' was reflected in the five key outcomes for children and young people identified in *Every Child Matters*, with 'staying safe' becoming one of the priorities, along with 'being healthy', 'enjoying and achieving', 'making a positive contribution to society' and 'achieving economic well-being' (DfES, 2003, p. 14). All new developments in England were to be seen in the context of these priorities, including the proposals for a new youth service (DfES, 2005).

The idea that safeguarding would involve a more proactive and preventative approach to protection is explored in the next activity.

Activity 2   Extending the scope of protection

Allow 15 minutes

Read the following extract from *Every Child Matters*. Note what you think it illustrates about the approach to protecting children and young people, and how the government intends this to work in practice.

Early intervention and effective protection

Victoria Climbié came into contact with several agencies, none of which acted on the warning signs. No one built up the full picture of her interactions with different services. Children with problems such as special educational needs, or behavioural disorders, or suffering from neglect, can also find that services often come too late. This Green Paper sets out the long term vision for how we intend to intervene earlier. It focuses on:

- **improving information sharing** between agencies, ensuring all local authorities have a list of children in their area, a list of services they have had contact with, and the contact details of relevant professionals

- **establishing a common assessment framework.** The Government will move towards a common assessment framework across services for all children. The aim is for core information to follow the child between services to reduce duplication

- **identifying lead professionals** to take the lead on each case where children are known to more than one specialist agency

- **integrating professionals** through multi-disciplinary teams responsible for identifying children at risk, and working with the child and family to ensure services are tailored to their needs

- **co-locating services** in and around schools, Sure Start Children's Centres and primary care settings

- **ensuring effective child protection** procedures are in place across all organisations.

(DfES, 2003, p. 51)

Comment

A key idea here is that effective protection is seen as a broad concept: child protection procedures are just one among a range of other elements. The emphasis is clearly on early intervention and not providing help 'too late'. You might have made a link to the discussion in Chapter 1, 'Practitioners', that solutions to problems are increasingly sought in the integration of different disciplines and the use of 'lead' professionals. Many of the other proposals are designed to enable this strategy, so this extract also makes clear the importance of information sharing and the creation of a new assessment framework 'common' to all disciplines, the flow of information across agencies mirroring the proposed breaking down of boundaries between professional groups.

Careful tracking of children and young people, recording where any concerns have been raised, and the importance of sharing this information among agencies, has become a key element of safeguarding. A proposed new information-sharing index for all children and young people in England will indicate those who have professional involvement or have had a (common) assessment.

This emphasis on placing protection in a much broader context is not just a feature of policy for England. *Keeping Us Safe: Report of the Safeguarding Vulnerable Children Review* (Thomas, 2006), commissioned by the Welsh Assembly, comments: 'Safeguarding goes much wider than the responsibilities of parents and the professional activities of teachers, social workers, health professionals and the police. It involves a wide spectrum of activity in all walks of life' (Thomas, 2006, p. 23). The end result has been a significant widening of the concept of protection. For Parton (2006), although the Climbié inquiry gave these developments their impetus, they in fact represent the coming together of many strands of existing government thinking – particularly the view that, increasingly, early intervention is an effective solution to a whole range of problems, not just abuse but also social exclusion and its consequences:

> The combination of wanting to introduce changes which would broaden the scope of prevention while trying to reduce the chances of a child dying in the tragic circumstances experienced by Victoria Climbié meant that the role of the state would become broader, more interventionist and regulatory, all at the same time.
>
> (Parton, 2006, p. 139)

This new emphasis on early intervention allows for the different perspectives on risk discussed earlier to be brought together. It can encompass young people who are at risk from others (of abuse) as well as those who are seen as a risk *to* others (via their 'antisocial' activity). The strategy has been to seek evidence of causal factors in order to attempt to counteract them at an earlier 'preventative' stage. Despite the fact that this has proven difficult to achieve, this 'risk and protection focussed prevention paradigm' (France and Utting, 2005, p. 80) has been highly influential, not just in UK policy but also in Australia and Europe, drawing heavily on research evidence from programmes in the USA.

This broader approach to safeguarding has many potential positives. It can, for example, enable issues which may be of particular concern to young people (such as bullying) to be raised in the same forum as child protection. But at the same time, this shift towards early intervention may also have potentially negative consequences. Paul Michael Garrett (2003), in his analysis of the modernisation of social care, points to the potential civil liberties and human rights implications of preventative intervention and information sharing. He argues that, although these strategies can be interpreted as a positive way of ensuring vulnerable young people do not fall through the net, they can also produce a substantial increase in 'surveillance' – a central element of 'virtual control' in the modern state (Garrett, 2003, p. 133). Chapter 7, 'Risk', discussed Michel Foucault's idea of 'governmentality' as applied to young people and this can be seen to have relevance here too as policies are applied to prevent 'potential' risks to young people as well as the risks that they themselves might pose.

This preventative focus on risk factors does acknowledge the links between the features of social exclusion and specific social problems; for example, research that shows the impact of poverty on physical abuse, neglect and failure to thrive (Bradshaw, 2001). However, Jack (2004), a long standing advocate of an ecological approach, while welcoming this development, argues that the child protection system remains too focused on the individual. A true ecological perspective would recognise the major role played by poverty and inequality in contributing to child abuse, and the importance of social support at a community level. He also stresses the need to address even broader social and cultural attitudes (for example, power relationships and those that sanction physical punishment) in addressing the problem.

1.2 The impact of abuse and harm

Debates about what constitutes abuse or harm should not deflect attention from the very real and difficult experiences of some young people. An increasing number of outcome studies have demonstrated the damaging effects that experiences such as living in situations of neglect, domestic violence or sexual abuse, or living with a parent with mental health difficulties or alcohol related problems, can have on young people's health and development.

In attempting a brief overview of the impact of abuse and harm, it needs to be recognised that research studies are also beset by the definitional and terminological issues we have touched on earlier (including introducing other labels such as 'maltreatment'). Their measurement of the impact of these experiences on young people is also influenced by different perspectives – for example, on development and adolescence – which are themselves subject to debate (Kehily, 2007). Generalisations from research studies should also not obscure the fact that each young person's experience and reaction is unique.

In a broad overview of studies of abuse and neglect, Pat Cawson (2002) identifies links with a wide range of concerns, including mental and physical health problems, suicide and self harm, personal and social problems, poor self esteem, lower educational achievement, increased likelihood of bullying and the development of antisocial and criminal behaviour. Cawson (2002) also reports on a survey for the National Society for the Prevention of Cruelty to Children (NSPCC) of maltreatment in the family among a national random sample of 2,869 young people aged 18–24. The survey reveals complex interrelationships, in both causes and consequences of abuse, among personal factors, family relationships and environmental stress. One-third of those reporting maltreatment reported effects ranging from 'short term' to 'lasting and harmful' (Cawson, 2002, p. 73). These self-reported effects reinforced the broader research findings of personal, social and psychological problems. In addition, the research noted some marked differences across the group, with women and those in lower socio-economic groups reporting a much higher level of harmful effects.

In a summary of the impact of chronic neglect on children's development, Karen Tanner and Danielle Turney (2003, p. 27) stress the evidence of 'pervasive and persistent damage' to health, education, emotional and behavioural development, family and social relationships, and social presentation and self-care skills. Highly critical and punitive parenting is also closely associated with poor outcomes (Gibbons *et al.*, 1995), and the negative effects of domestic violence are also now well documented (Hester *et al.*, 2000). For example, Marianne Hester *et al.* cite a Swedish research study illustrating the impact on a 15–16 age group:

> According to these young people, they had all tended to adopt passive responses to the violence when they were younger, whereas when they were older they were able to react differently, either by staying away or running away from home, or by using drugs and/or alcohol. At other times they had dealt with the violence by denying it, lying about it or by creating another fantasised reality for themselves in which there was no violence ... Unlike younger children, none of the young people reported having physical signs of their distress, such as headache or sleep disturbances, but some did appear to have eating disorders and mood swings, and some had made suicide attempts.
>
> (Weinehall, cited in Hester *et al.*, 2000, p. 51)

This extract reinforces the fact that although young people may be able to remove themselves from situations of harm, this can make them vulnerable to harm of a different sort. Some studies have demonstrated that high proportions of homeless 16–25-year-olds left home because of domestic violence (Hester and Radford, 1996), reinforcing our earlier discussion of the link between 'at risk' and 'risky' behaviour: 'I caught my mum and dad arguing. My dad hit my mum and I went and tried to talk to him but he hit me instead. I swore at him and then he told me to leave because I was disrespecting him' (quoted in Rees and Siakeu, 2004, p. 8).

Hedy Cleaver *et al.* (2003), following a child development model, also stress the importance of identifying the features of harmful experiences that are specific to young people. In a review of the impact of parental mental illness, they identify the main problems for those over the age of 15 as problem alcohol use, drug use, domestic violence, increased risks of school exclusion and poor performance, problems with sexual relationships, self blame and guilt, accidents, social isolation and increased aggression. Examples from young people themselves illustrate these findings: 'Dad drinks and hits mum. I took an overdose last week – I want to die. I can't talk to mum because it would only add to her problems. It's all my fault' (Cindy, aged 15, ChildLine, quoted in Cleaver *et al.*, 2003, p. 96).

The survey reported on by Cawson (2002) found that levels of maltreatment for disabled children and young people were as high and usually higher than for the sample as a whole. This confirms growing evidence in the UK and the USA (Westcott and Jones, 1999; Kennedy, 2000) that disabled young people are at higher risk of abuse and neglect. Contributory factors include communication issues, stress on carers, the higher degree of institutional care and invasive treatments. The extent to which disability itself is a vulnerability 'factor' is discussed later in this chapter; however, there is clearly an interrelationship with discriminatory societal attitudes. Margaret Kennedy identifies another feature of these attitudes as the constant pressure to become 'normal' which is 'detrimental to positive self-identity, confidence and self-esteem' (Kennedy, 2000, p. 94).

1.3 The practice context

The first two chapters of this book suggested some themes for a changing social context for work with young people. The broad changes are characterised by social mobility, globalisation and a society in which traditional forms of authority are in decline, emphasising the importance of individually negotiated relationships. Harry Ferguson (2004), in his analysis of child protection and modernity, suggests that these changes have a substantial impact on practitioners as they experience a heightened sense of risk, danger and complexity and an increasing expectation of speed of response.

In analysing two child death inquiries 30 years apart, Parton (2004) illustrates how some of these complexities are affecting the context for practice in this area. Although these two inquiries – about Maria Colwell (in 1973) and Victoria Climbié (in 2003) – were concerned with young children, the changing landscape they reveal is equally applicable to work with young people. Compared with the earlier inquiry, that of Victoria Climbié was marked by features of constant movement and little involvement of the local community. The international mobility of Victoria and her family was matched by the workers involved; Parton points out that, at the time, in one London borough all the duty social workers had received their training abroad, all were on temporary contracts, and 50 per cent of their workload was related to another consequence of mobility: that of unaccompanied minors.

Although the management and sharing of information is a theme common to both inquiries, again there is evidence of increasing complexity, which had evolved, in part, in response to problems identified in the succession of inquiry reports over this 30-year period:

> The growth of managerialization, audit, procedural guidance and new systems of information technology and information management all seem to have contributed to an increasing complexity in the nature of the work as far as frontline professionals are concerned. While introduced with all the best intentions, it is not self-evident in the Victoria Climbié report that their impacts have been positive. In trying to manage and order uncertainty, it seems that new uncertainties and complexities have been created.
>
> (Parton, 2004, pp. 89–90)

For many practitioners, shifting priorities or broader perceptions of protection are mediated by their sense of, at best, static resources. There also seems to be plenty of evidence that the nature of the work and its shifting context takes a toll on those involved. Gibbs (2001) reviews the difficulties in both Australia and the UK of maintaining front-line child protection workers and considers the role of stress, anxiety and living with a culture of blame. A study of 'burn-out' characteristics of front-line workers discovered that all showed a high degree of emotional exhaustion (Stevens and Higgins, 2002). Janet Stanley and Chris Goddard (2002) focus specifically on how issues of violence have rarely been the subject of inquiries and stress the importance of the impact of antagonism and violence. Although these factors may be more acute in statutory services, the context also affects the range of voluntary organisations involved in safeguarding work.

Key points

- There is substantial evidence for the long term negative impact of abuse and harm on young people.
- A historical perspective suggests that changing language about child abuse and protection reflects changing constructions of the problem and its potential solutions.

- More recently, the idea of safeguarding has placed protection concerns about children and young people in a much broader framework which also emphasises much earlier intervention to tackle both 'at risk' and 'risky' behaviours.

- There has been an accompanying development in mechanisms for sharing information and monitoring and tracking children and young people.

- Taking a historical perspective also reveals that practitioners experience the safeguarding task as increasingly complex.

2   Young people's perspectives

> If they, like, have clothes that they had for quite a while and they've grown out of it, and be, like, sort of too short for them and all, then people call them tramps and smelly and all that.
>
> (Cally, aged 14, quoted in Ridge, 2002, p. 68)

This quotation is taken from research by Tess Ridge (2002) into young people's perspectives on poverty and social exclusion. She argues that policies that are being created and pursued in the best interests of children and young people are not necessarily informed by their lived experience. The young people in her study had very clear views on the impact of poverty on their lives. Lack of money reduced opportunities for involvement in social activities, school trips and transport. A particularly serious issue for them was clothes: lack of money meant lack of the 'right' clothes, which in turn led to concerns about being different and the increased fear of being bullied as a result. In Activity 1 we considered how Carl might be defined by the adults he is in contact with and the priorities of different forms of risk. Yet Carl's perception of what is most harmful to him may fit more with the views of these young people.

As we will illustrate below, there has long been evidence of a gap between what policies and procedures define as harm, and therefore prioritise, and what young people see as harmful or of most concern to them. In the previous section we considered how abuse and harm have been defined, but Mary MacLeod points out that there are other perspectives to take into consideration: 'Central to the debate about how abuse should be defined is a recognition that naming happens from a number of points of view – one of which ought to be the child's' (MacLeod, 2000, p. 132). Given, as we will see, that young people tend not to report concerns, particularly about abuse, to professionals, this raises the issue of whether the system, supposedly designed to help and safeguard them, is effective in practice. Whether and how this can be the case is the topic for this section. To what extent can young people have 'agency' in formal and adult oriented procedures and processes? What can be learned from the way in which they decide whether and how to seek help? What particularly is the role of confidentiality in this process?

2.1 Harm and help seeking

Evidence from research with young people at home and in care (Hallett *et al.*, 2003), school surveys (Balding 1998, 2002) and helplines (for example, MacCleod, 1999) has clearly demonstrated that although young people are concerned about issues such as physical and sexual abuse, which are often the primary focus of professionals, they are also concerned about a broad range of issues relating to school, friends and family. In a summary of research in this area, Brid Featherstone and Helen Evans (2004, p. 15) note that key anxieties for children and young people centred on problems with friends, bullying, tensions with and between parents, illness or death of people close to them, problems with schoolwork and personal appearance. They also identify mismatches between what adults believed were the biggest problems young people had to face (for example, drugs) and the views of young people (who more commonly mentioned physical and mental health, suicide, self harm, eating disorders and smoking).

The majority of young people will seek help with problems from their families and other formal or informal networks, with peer relationships being increasingly significant as they get older. However, a substantial minority do not. In a study by Christine Hallett *et al.* (2003), 40 per cent of boys and 24 per cent of girls (aged 13–14) said they would tell 'nobody', with young people also reporting a variety of avoidance and displacement activities to address their problems, ranging from listening to music to aggression and self harm. Perhaps most worryingly, the more extreme activities (for example, running away) were most common in a sample of young people in residential care; that is, those who may have already experienced most harm or disruption (Hallett *et al.*, 2003). Although this group was more likely to talk to key workers or social workers, 33 per cent of girls and 57 per cent of boys still said they would not tell anyone about their problems.

It is likely that levels of help seeking are even lower in relation to specific forms of maltreatment. The NSPCC prevalence study (Cawson, 2002) found that only a quarter of people who had experienced sexual abuse as a child told anyone at the time. Featherstone and Evans (2004) suggest that the issue of telling, and who young people tell, cannot be separated from the social, psychological and familial context, which includes factors such as the extent to which various forms of abuse receive publicity and young people's experience of wider social norms.

Various models have been proposed for identifying the different stages or thought processes young people might go through before seeking help

(Murray, 2005). An exploration of these stages reveals some implications for those wishing to provide services to help and safeguard young people.

Cathy Murray (2005), in a research study of young people in Scottish schools, found that, in order to recognise that something is a problem, young people may also need validation from adults – 'problem legitimization' – a point which seems particularly pertinent to the discussion of who defines 'harm': 'In common with other relatively powerless members of society young people might well be expected to play less of a part in defining what problems are legitimate, and, in consequence, problems for which society would expect them to seek help' (Murray, 2005, p. 483). For example, her findings suggested that although young people did feel that bullying was taken seriously by adults, particularly in schools where there were clear policies, problems in personal relationships with friends were frequently not, either by professionals or by parents: 'she [mother] doesn't say even "well, you could go and apologise" or whatever. She just says "oh it'll sort itself out". She doesn't give any advice. She just says "everything will work out in the end"' (quoted in Murray, 2005, p. 484).

This quotation illustrates another significant factor emphasised by Murray, which is the previous experience of help seeking. Not surprisingly, an unhelpful response would result in that pathway not being used again: 'Well first of all I told the teacher ... and then they told me to go to my guidance teacher. So I went to my guidance teacher and he said he couldn't do anything, *so that was that*' (quoted in Murray, 2005, p. 486). This implies the need for practitioners to be encouraging, sensitive to the young person's agendas and non judgemental in their responses. These conclusions are common to other studies that reinforce the importance of relationships and trust. Given that we know the added feelings of stigma and shame that can surround some concerns, it is likely that young people will need to have had positive experiences of help seeking if they are to turn to a professional worker to disclose serious concerns.

Both the concerns of young people and the pattern of help seeking have dimensions of gender and ethnicity to which practitioners also need to be sensitive. In Murray's (2005) research in Scottish schools, one-third of girls reported that they would prefer support, whether formal or informal, to come from another female. The high volume of calls to a Muslim Youth Helpline suggests that the expectation of culturally sensitive assistance may also promote help seeking (Leason, 2006). Statistics of calls to the helpline showed that the topics of concern to young Muslims were largely the same as those of all young people discussed above, but that they also had a cultural and faith dimension.

2.2 Confidentiality

Another clear finding from these research studies was that young people were concerned that seeking help would begin a process that would rapidly get out of control. This raises the issue of confidentiality and the extent to which young people can discuss problems without the information automatically being passed on to others: 'The question arising for young people seeking to influence their own lives is how to access the services designed to protect them while themselves maintaining control of the process' (Dalrymple, 2001, p. 151).

Murray (2005), in the study discussed above, suggests the need for clarity about the rules of confidentiality (for example, in this case with teachers in schools). Jane Dalrymple (1999, 2001, 2005) has illustrated in her work on advocacy that it is possible to negotiate clear guidance around confidentiality with young people, including an understanding that there will be limits: 'Young people themselves, although rarely involved in defining confidentiality and negotiating policies, also acknowledge the need for confidences to be breached in defined circumstances' (Dalrymple, 2001, p. 156). MacLeod (1999), writing about ChildLine, has argued in

Confidential helplines may enable young people to work in a way that suits them

favour of fully confidential services such as helplines. She believes that they have enabled young people to work in a way that is more suited to them; for example, in a more 'haphazard' way or with 'quick and fast bursts of contact' (p. 150), rather than at a pace dictated by adults.

Confidentiality is not straightforward for most of those who work directly with young people. The need to pass information on is stressed in procedures and there would usually be sanctions for workers who were talking to a young person about abuse without passing that information on. It has also become accepted as a fundamental plank of good practice that there are reasons for acting, and breaking confidentiality, even if this was not the wish of the young person concerned. The arguments here have been that the secrecy that frequently surrounds abuse needs to be broken rather than mirrored by professionals and that children and young people may not fully understand the long term consequences of remaining in an abusive situation. Practitioners also need to consider whether the information they receive has consequences for other children or young people in the family. Enabling young people to have more control over the process of disclosure can therefore create difficult practice dilemmas.

Activity 3   The dilemmas of confidentiality

Allow 15 minutes

Donna (aged 15) attends an after school club. She has a very good relationship with Tess, one of the workers. The last few times Donna has attended she has seemed worried about something but, although the worker has asked her if she wants to tell her about it, has not said why. One evening she is very upset and suddenly reveals that life at home is miserable because of the violence of her father towards her mother. She herself has been slapped in the past when she tried to intervene. Donna hints that there is something else, more serious, but can't say what it is. After recovering herself, Donna thanks Tess for being a good friend and asks her to promise that she will not tell anyone. Donna says she will do something about it, but isn't ready yet to handle the 'fallout'.

In the light of the preceding discussion of confidentiality, what issues and dilemmas might a scenario like this raise for the worker involved?

Comment

This may be a familiar scenario for many of those who work with young people and there are, of course, many practice issues, some touched on above. For example, are the ground rules for confidentiality and the child protection procedures clear in the club? However, even if the worker is clear about whether the procedures require this information to be passed on, they may still experience a common dilemma. Tess may be balancing, on the one hand, her knowledge of the effects of living with violence, and concerns about the potential for other forms of abuse or abuse of other children in the family, with, on the other hand, the impact on the trusting relationship she has with Donna, which she has spent time carefully building up. Passing this information on could feel like a breach of trust. Might more time and another opportunity to talk enable Donna to reveal more of her concerns, and empower her to take action? There may indeed be serious 'fallout' which it might be reasonable for Donna to think through. Tess would, however, also have to 'contain' the knowledge of continuing harm and abuse that Donna is experiencing without being able to act.

This dilemma has been described as the confidentiality 'trap' (Wattam, 1999) where practitioners can feel a professional (and partly moral) obligation to pass information on, but also a moral (and perhaps partly professional) duty to honour a request for confidentiality. In reality, many skilled practitioners are working with confidentiality in the difficult terrain between these two positions, with the specific nature of the problem unspoken, highlighting the need for good guidance and training.

Chapter 3, 'Participation', considered this issue of confidentiality and protection using the example of abortion and young women under the age of 16. This highlighted some of the complexities and contradictions in law and in practice. It was interesting to note that the government representative in that instance argued in favour of confidentiality as being essential to the success of their teenage pregnancy campaign. Government policy has also advocated consultation with young people and their active participation in service delivery. In the government's own consultation exercise with young people for *Every Child Matters* (DfES, 2003), 24 per cent responded that it was 'never' acceptable for information to be shared without consent. However, as discussed in Subsection 1.1 above in relation to the plans for 'effective protection', information sharing between agencies is increasingly encouraged. Not only is effective safeguarding seen to depend on inter-agency working, but the situation is further complicated by the fact that the degree to which different agencies can keep information confidential can vary.

There has been a growth in confidential services which can often be managed more easily by voluntary organisations. However, the conflicts we have been discussing can still be challenging for agencies to manage, as illustrated in the box overleaf.

Example of NSPCC Young People's Centres

The NSPCC is an agency with statutory responsibility to investigate concerns about harm to children and young people, but which has also recognised the problem of young people tending not to report their concerns. The NSPCC decided to develop Young People's Centres on the grounds that:

- The child protection system is failing to meet the needs of a large number of children and young people, in particular children who are disabled, Black children and children in [and] out of home care

- A significant number of children and young people tell no one of their abuse

- Current child care policy and practice is over-influenced by the criminal justice system

                    (Salford Centre for Social Work Research, 2004, p. 3)

One strand of the work has been to try to develop a more child and young person centred approach to protection where 'children and young people are viewed as consumers of services enabling them to have some choice and control' (Salford Centre for Social Work Research, 2004, p. 3). Young people can discuss their concerns anonymously and their ideas are seen as central to the running of the Centres. There are still limits to confidentiality, but at a higher threshold negotiated with other agencies in the child protection system. The level of this threshold has varied as the agency has worked to reconcile this with their statutory duties to report all child protection concerns:

The challenge of providing a safe, private place for young people to build trust whilst also seeking to keep them safe from themselves and/or others is one we have had to grapple with a lot.

                            (Time Out Young People's Centre, 2005)

Evaluation of the Centres from the young people's perspective highlighted areas for change, but was generally positive about the opportunities for confidential discussions.

The NSPCC subsequently took on the management of ChildLine and will have to find ways of working with a fully confidential service.

In considering whether other strategies are available in terms of both confidentiality and flexibility within the child protection system, a European perspective may be helpful. Rachel Hetherington and Andrew Cooper (2001) consider a number of European models, some of which allow for more mediation. These models include 'negotiative spaces' in which potential solutions can be discussed with young people and their families in the context of a 'conditional' confidentiality in which prosecution or referral to the legal domain can be avoided if progress is made towards certain objectives:

> what we have seen elsewhere are approaches that understand the 'interests of the child' differently and that ... many European countries give more power to children over the process of interventions. The interests of the child are seen in some European countries in a less individualistic light as being closely bound up with the community and the family; in others, there is an emphasis on the importance and appropriateness of the child exercising some control over, or significantly influencing the outcome of, the process of being helped or protected.
>
> (Hetherington and Cooper, 2001, p. 104)

2.3 Age, status and transitions

In the Introduction to this chapter we suggested that services for young people are constructed partly in relation to how childhood itself is constructed. The key strands are often categorised as, on the one hand, an idealisation of childhood and a view of children as innocents who need to be protected by adults, and, on the other, a construction of children and young people as social 'agents', able to participate actively in decisions that affect their lives (Prout, 2003). This latter view would support a different configuration of services, allowing for a greater understanding of how young people see the world rather than relying exclusively on adult perceptions of it. This could potentially support the involvement of young people in the operation of protective systems, as we discussed above.

These ideas about how childhood is constructed are complicated further when considering the specific place of young people. Young people cannot be contained within the idea of an innocent childhood, yet having left that phase they are not seen as having adult status either:

> In Britain as elsewhere in the West today, many young people in their mid-teenage years, whilst not admitted to an unequivocal adult status, are nonetheless seen as having left childhood behind them. These young people are thus between childhood (with

powerlessness) and adulthood (with agency), and here the notion of 'youth' serves to define a third, intermediate social and cultural category.

(Hall and Montgomery, 2000, p. 13)

Older young people can have an ambiguous position within services for support and protection which can seem to be geared primarily for children. This may be a result of allowing young people the sort of agency that we have been discussing above. But it can also be a result of attitudes and pressures, which may mean that they do not get the level of safeguarding they should. This point was illustrated in one study of working with young people with complex needs: 'I think the fact that he is 16 next April ... sadly as young people get older there is a tendency to think "there's no hope of change now, let's concentrate on the younger end"' (quoted in Worrall-Davies *et al.*, 2004, p. 183).

This ambiguous status between childhood and adulthood raises some serious dilemmas for practitioners, as Activity 4 illustrates.

Activity 4   Between childhood and adulthood

Allow 15 minutes

Read the following extract, which is based on a real-life example. How was Peter categorised by the agencies involved? What does the example reveal about the difficulties faced by practitioners when trying to balance a young person's apparent desire for independence with concerns about their welfare?

> Peter was a 17-year-old with a number of difficult family related problems. He also had diabetes requiring the use of insulin. At the age of 15 he began to frequently go missing from home and started a pattern of repeated crisis admissions to hospital as a result of not taking his insulin appropriately. He was aware that he would become seriously unwell if he did not take insulin but continued with this pattern over the next two years. Eventually, family problems led to Peter moving, at the age of 16, to supported accommodation with the assistance of social services.

> Shortly before his seventeenth birthday, Peter was transferred to adult services for the management of his diabetes. He was keen to manage his situation as independently as possible. At the same time, his supported lodgings arrangement broke down and, being treated as homeless by the housing department, he moved to independent accommodation.

> Shortly after his seventeenth birthday he was discharged from hospital after another crisis admission. He died shortly afterwards.

Comment

In this case, it seemed that Peter came to be seen as an adult, and certainly as a young man very capable of expressing his views and exercising 'agency'. Adult services would want to actively promote the self management of his diabetes. From this perspective, Peter could be seen to be making informed choices about his life even though the result of these choices was tragic. There was, however, evidence of a long history of not managing his condition that had resulted in the frequent admissions to hospital. From a children's services point of view, he could be seen as an extremely vulnerable young man (and technically not an adult), who was exhibiting essentially self-harming behaviour. The family difficulties may also have meant that he had few sources of informal support. From this second perspective, Peter could perhaps have been the subject of a fuller assessment and a plan that would have attempted to follow him up more supportively on discharge. Peter was, in practice, classified as a non compliant adult rather than as a child 'in need' or a child in need of 'protection'. Of course, even the best plan may still not have affected the outcome, but this example illustrates how such cases present practitioners with complex and challenging decisions.

Attitudes and practice towards young people over the age of 15 involved in prostitution illustrate another aspect of work with this age group. In this difficult area of work for practitioners, usual practice had arguably involved a reluctant acceptance that, once over the age of consent, there was little that could be done for these young people and they were beyond the practical application of the child protection procedures. A number of agencies involved in this area of work argued for a change of attitude and approach to these young people, wanting to reframe 'prostitution' as 'sexual exploitation' (for example, Barnardo's, 1998). Subsequent government guidance stressed the need for 16- and 17-year-olds still to be considered as children who should be safeguarded, and that cases of sexual exploitation should *always* trigger the child protection procedures (DoH, 2000a, 2000b). A review of the policy after one year demonstrated that change was slow: 'For under 16s there is always an inter-agency planning meeting, but for 16/17 year olds we consider if a planning meeting is necessary' (DoH, 2002, p. 17).

One key point in Peter's story is that the transition between services for children and those for adults can be problematic. The meaning of 'transitions' for young people is contested and the ways in which young people move to independent adulthood are varied, complex and changing (Kehily, 2007). Often procedures and the structure of service provision have a clear cut-off point at the age of 18 without the flexibility to meet the varying needs of those crossing this boundary. The following are three other examples of how this boundary can create difficulties.

Sexual exploitation, not prostitution

This 'transitional' period has been identified as particularly problematic in services for disabled young people. As Bob Hudson (2006) comments, if borderlines are imprecise between childhood and adulthood generally, then this is all the more so for disabled young people, and their transitions are 'characterised by discontinuity' (p. 49) rather than continuity. Hudson's interviews with young people, parents and professionals reveal that, although planning for this transition has been addressed by government through law and policy, inter-organisational problems continue to complicate the move from one service to the other.

A similar issue can be found in the mental health services and was illustrated in the research discussed in Chapter 1, with a child and adolescent mental health service (CAMHS), by Richards and Vostanis (2004). The researchers discuss a gap in service provision as neither the CAMHS team nor adult services were well equipped to deal with the 16–19 age group. The practitioners were clear that these young people had distinct needs, represented by the view of an educational psychologist that they were 'in a period of transition, so issues around identity in all its forms, be that sexual, be that cultural or whatever ... young people's services have to be receptive to that' (quoted in Richards and Vostanis, 2004, p. 119). However, again structural, financial and inter-disciplinary boundaries made addressing these needs difficult.

Heather Montgomery (2007) explored the many issues facing unaccompanied asylum seekers moving to the UK, revealing a very uneven level of response both legally and in terms of service provision. This was despite the recognition that their experiences – for example, of isolation and racism – were likely to make them even more vulnerable. Those aged 16 and 17 in particular have often been placed in unsuitable bed and breakfast accommodation with little support. The problem has been exacerbated by the ending of certain entitlements at 18, which can occur during the delays in awaiting the outcome of the asylum determination process. Research by the Scottish Refugee Council (Hopkins and Hill, 2006, p. 54) stresses that 'the children's need to be recognised as children is paramount'. The Separated in Europe Programme recommends that access to services for these young people should be maintained even if they become adults during the course of the process (Save the Children, in Hopkins and Hill, 2006, p. 88).

Key points

- Young people make limited use of the formal system which is designed to offer them a protective service.

- Research into young people's perceptions of social exclusion, concerns about harm, and help seeking behaviour can give practitioners insights into ways of responding in a manner that is more focused on the needs of young people.

- Confidentiality can be a major issue for some young people and, although problematic for practitioners, creative ways of managing this may help ensure that more young people seek advice and assistance.

- The way that the child protection system works is influenced by the way in which 'childhood', 'youth' and 'adulthood' are framed. Older young people can be in a particularly ambivalent position within systems usually designed to end at the age of 18.

3 Approaches to positive practice

As this chapter has shown, working to safeguard young people raises a number of practical and moral dilemmas for practitioners, not the least of which is how a system designed to protect young people from harm can sometimes operate in ways that are perceived as alienating and disempowering. But are there ways in which practitioners can work that are more empowering, young person centred and focused on strengths as well as problems? While recognising that the following discussion cannot be exhaustive, we have chosen in this section to explore some approaches which try to take account of these perspectives and which can contribute to the development of positive practice with young people.

3.1 Empowerment and advocacy

The previous section highlighted issues for practice in relation to listening to and understanding young people's own perceptions of risk and harm, and drew out some potential lessons for practitioners in relation to young people's help seeking behaviour. There will be constraints on practitioners in the extent to which they can effect any change in how procedures operate, but there may be ways in which young people can be empowered and encouraged to have more agency within these systems. Continuing the themes of empowerment and confidentiality, Dalrymple (2001) proposes that confidential advocacy services can be part of the solution. The principle of participation and of the use of advocacy has been increasingly encouraged and adopted by practitioners. However, Dalrymple argues that the style of advocacy is influenced by the same constructions of 'childhood', 'youth' and 'adulthood' that we explored in the previous section. If the protectionist perspective on the welfare of young people is dominant, then advocacy tends to be undertaken in a passive way: 'advocating *on behalf of*' young people within an adult oriented system, 'rather than *enabling* them' to express their own views (Dalrymple, 2001, p. 149).

Dalrymple's example focuses on the care system where young people not only have less power than adults, but can become dependent on professionals as they are unable to influence the processes and systems to which they are subject. The potential effects of this in terms of increasing vulnerability have been reinforced in reports on abuse in residential care (Utting, 1997; Waterhouse, 2000). So although professionals have attempted to ensure that young people are consulted and involved in all relevant meetings, the system remains a very adult oriented one in which the professionals have the power to make decisions; for example, about what is confidential and what is not. Some practitioners may be constrained both by the different roles they need to fulfil in relation to young people in care and by limits on confidentiality set out by their agencies. Independent advocacy services (again with clear confidentiality policies) may be an important contribution to ensuring better protection for young people. These principles of advocacy may be even more relevant in ensuring a voice for black or disabled young people who are often the most marginalised within existing systems.

3.2 Individual work

Cawson (2002), in reporting on the extensive survey of maltreatment within the family discussed earlier, goes on to identify that, although many interventions need to be directed at the family context, another significant area is the help required by young people themselves. Indeed MacLeod (2000, p. 140) states that, in her view, the clearest message from calls to ChildLine was that 'what is good for the family cannot necessarily be assumed to be good for the child'. This does not lessen the importance of work that includes the family, but highlights the need to assess and respond to the individual needs of young people too. In addition to finding strategies to access initial help, callers to ChildLine wanted emotional support and help in coming to terms with their experiences. The idea of the central importance of 'the relationship' – discussed in Chapter 2, 'Practice', and echoed in other chapters – is equally relevant here as young people valued practitioners who were able to provide this sort of support, were available and were seen as trustworthy.

There is good evidence that, for some forms of abuse, specific psychological treatments are valuable in improving outcomes (Jones and Ramchandani, 1999). However, the lack of availability of therapeutic services has often been identified, and the survey discussed by Cawson reinforces this: 'For [the] respondents as children being maltreated, the unavailability of professional help at the time is a staggering indictment of our services' (Cawson, 2002, p. 77). Cawson also found that such help was needed not just at the time of the original experience, but also later when young people were leaving home for the first time:

> the survey results do show that much more attention should be given to making help accessible to children and young people at the time they are experiencing maltreatment, and later when they are coming to terms with it. Many of the 18–24 year olds interviewed in this research were leaving home and becoming independent for the first time. For maltreated children, it may well be the process of leaving home which first enables them to put their childhood experience into perspective, and perhaps to realise that their childhood was not like that of their friends, or not one they would wish to perpetuate for their own children. Help to come to terms with their experience at this time of their lives may be crucial in avoiding longer term health and social problems.
>
> (Cawson, 2002, p. 76)

3.3 Promoting resilience and challenging vulnerability

Increasingly, practitioners working with those who have experienced harm have been encouraged to use a theoretical framework for their interventions, which looks at adverse and protective factors and categorises the individual experiences of children and young people along an axis of vulnerability and resilience.

Resilience has been defined as 'a dynamic process encompassing positive adaptation within the context of significant adversity' (Luthar in Gilligan, 2004, p. 93). It is clear that young people can experience seemingly similar harmful events and yet be affected in very different ways, some exhibiting major health and social difficulties while others appear relatively unaffected. What factors enable some to be more 'resilient' than others? Through longitudinal studies in particular, researchers, rather than just focusing on risk and adversity, have sought to identify these key factors and influences. 'Internal' and 'external' factors have been identified, operating at the individual, family and broader environmental levels of the system in which a young person lives. The box below includes some examples.

Examples of sources of resilience and vulnerability

Sources of resilience
- Good attachment experience
- Affectionate ties with alternative caregivers
- Intelligence
- Internalised positive set of values
- Positive self concept
- Capacity to make and sustain friendships
- Involvement in sibling care
- Social maturity and sense of responsibility
- Experience of overcoming stressful situations
- Good school experience

Sources of vulnerability
- Lack of problem solving skills
- Established pattern of conduct disorder
- Poor self esteem
- Significant poverty
- Experience of separation and loss
- Social isolation
- Parental domestic violence

(Adapted from Daniel *et al.*, 1999)

This is a developmental model rooted in attachment theory. From this perspective, secure attachments with key adults provide a 'secure base' from which a young person can develop emotionally and socially. Robbie Gilligan, who has written extensively on resilience in practice, argues that, for young people without such a base, a '"scaffolding" of social support, based on work, social, educational, recreational and professional helping relationships is probably the best practical alternative' (Gilligan, 2004, p. 95). He suggests that a major task for practitioners is to help construct this scaffold which may provide 'an important buffer' against adverse life experiences (p. 95).

A resilience framework provides the opportunity for positive practice because it encourages practitioners to identify strengths as well as vulnerabilities, and protective as well as risk factors. Practitioners can look for and attempt to enhance strengths in young people: influencing one element in a young person's life can produce a positive ripple effect (Daniel *et al.*, 1999). This approach emphasises that schools in particular have a crucial role to play as they have a wide range of opportunities to boost resilience by improving self esteem and fostering talents and interests (Daniel *et al.*, 1999). It also enables quite practical strategies for assessment and intervention (Daniel and Wassell, 2002). It is a framework that can be drawn on by any of the wide range of practitioners involved in a young person's life, fitting with a multi-professional approach to safeguarding and 'promoting' wellbeing. Gilligan argues that resilience could be the main 'guiding principle' in work with young people who have suffered harm, in particular those who are looked after away from home: 'Resilience – the capacity to transcend adversity – may be seen as the essential quality which care planning and provision should seek to stimulate as a key outcome of the care offered' (Gilligan, 1997, p. 14).

In our example of Carl, whom we discussed at the start of the chapter, it would be easy for all those who have contact with him to identify the problematic aspects of his behaviour and potential sources of adversity; for example, poor school experience, possible history of emotional abuse or neglect, subject to bullying, etc. The challenge for the youth worker and teacher would be to assess if there are other, potentially positive, factors in Carl and his life that could be strengthened or developed.

Activity 5   Promoting resilience: Carl revisited

Allow 15 minutes

Go back to Activity 1 and remind yourself about Carl. You may also want to re-read the box earlier in this subsection, which highlights some resilience and vulnerability factors. Now read the additional information about Carl given below.

What internal or external factors can you identify which might point to Carl's degree of resilience? How could the professionals responsible for Carl intervene using a resilience framework?

> Not long after the incident described in Activity 1, Carl's relationship with his Dad finally broke down and he was 'accommodated' (that is, he moved into local authority care). Carl (now aged 15) has been living with his current foster carers for six months after two previous placements lasted only a few weeks each. He had been in care before when he was five and again when he was nine because of concerns about physical abuse, neglect, and parental conflict.

He has had little contact with his parents (who describe him as being 'out of control') or siblings, although regularly sees one of his uncles, to whom he has always been close.

Carl's sudden changes of carer have been due to his 'difficult' behaviour although he now appears to have 'calmed down' a bit and is well liked in his current placement. After being excluded from his previous school, Carl is attending school regularly and, after a disruptive beginning, is starting to do better socially and academically.

Comment

This framework would suggest that Carl has clearly had a number of experiences which have increased his vulnerability in terms of early experiences and disruptions to attachments both at home and in subsequent placements. There are internal (for example, intelligence) and external (for example, current good school experience, positive relationships with carers) factors that could be seen as sources of resilience which would provide a positive base to build on for practitioners. The framework could also guide practitioners to consider family factors; for instance, to see whether sibling relationships could be rebuilt. This is obviously a superficial picture and in reality would require careful assessment: the uncle is potentially a significant figure, but someone needs to explore what this relationship actually means to Carl. A more detailed understanding of Carl's life may also reveal other opportunities for intervention (for example, fostering his interests or talents).

What counts as adversity, and is therefore significant in terms of resilience, could be seen as another example of a social construction. For example, whether or not 'being disabled' is an adverse factor may depend on whether societal attitudes are positive or negative. Similarly, the emphasis placed on gender as a factor will vary depending on the value placed on girl and boy children. Much of the research on this framework has been done in Europe and North America, and a cross-cultural perspective reinforces this question of how universal these factors are and the extent to which they are context specific:

Specifying internal and external risk and protective factors must not overlook the extent to which expectations of children and of the ways they are treated are culturally defined. Arguably these cultural expectations will powerfully modify whether a particular type of personality or a particular set of experiences count as risk factors.

(Montgomery *et al.*, 2003, p. 29)

It can also modify the point of intervention. Although our current framework in the UK is an ecological one, the emphasis is still on the 'separate, individualised, developing child' (Montgomery *et al.*, 2003, p. 30) and so the site of intervention is more likely to be the individual than the community. In his analysis of the idea of wellbeing in relation to young people, Martin Robb (2007), in the companion volume in this series, stresses that, while the resilience model is a positive one, the degree to which individual or social factors are emphasised may vary. There can be a danger, therefore, of focusing on individual change rather then challenging the bigger cultural and societal factors; for example, attitudes and expectations around disability and gender.

Michael Ungar (2004) suggests that the current framework takes a positivist approach; that is, it seeks predictable relationships between risk and protective factors that are 'generalisable'. That some young people do appear to cope well in spite of many adversities is self-evident, but the identification of resilience factors can suffer from the same criticisms levelled at the search for risk factors. Ungar argues that the interrelationship between individual and broader social and environmental factors is poorly understood and often lacks empirical evidence. Cawson makes a similar point, noting that, although research has identified some important factors, on an individual level the situation is very complex; she concludes that 'we have much to learn about the best approaches to providing help and about enabling and supporting children's resilience' (Cawson, 2002, p. 73). Arguing for a constructionist perspective on resilience, Ungar contends that the individual's experience of resilience is much more diverse and complex and can be understood only through individual narratives rather than through broad generalisations. This can be important in directing the interventions of practitioners. He cites examples of young people who have a sense of agency and confidence – seen as elements of resilience – but express it in highly antisocial ways. This is not to argue in favour of such responses, but to highlight the need for practitioners not to make assumptions about the young person's perspective.

Gilligan (2004) suggests that the work of practitioners to identify and develop strengths can be aided by reflective practice (a concept discussed in more detail in Chapter 2). Reflecting on where their own sources of strength lie may in turn help identify sources of strength in young people with whom they are working. However, he also goes on to question the viability of achieving this in front-line practice, with its frequent problems of morale and recruitment. This is a reminder that positive, empowering, young person centred practice also needs to be enabled and promoted by the organisations in which practitioners work.

Key points

- There are potential strategies for the empowerment of young people, such as encouraging the use of advocacy.
- Research with young people who have experienced abuse or neglect suggests that individual work can be important both at the time and subsequently, at points of transition in their lives. However, therapeutic or relationship based work is not always readily available.
- Resilience provides one framework for practitioners, which can be positive and young person focused.
- The mechanisms of resilience are not fully understood and need to be seen in a broader cultural context. It can also be crucial to understand the individual young person's perception in order to find the best strategy for intervention.

Conclusion

The current conception of 'safeguarding' encourages practitioners to look beyond narrow definitions of 'protection' and place the needs of young people in a broader context, helping to ensure that they achieve in all areas of their lives. Policies are directed increasingly towards earlier preventative interventions and closer working between all those responsible for the welfare of young people. Although this may have positive outcomes, there are also significant consequences attached to moving in this direction – not least in terms of the substantial growth in monitoring and surveillance of young people that will result.

Practitioners need to ensure that they understand relevant procedural frameworks for dealing with concerns about harm or abuse, and respond accordingly. But the encounter between young person and practitioner in relation to an issue of risk is sensitive and often complex. It is not just a case of operating procedures, but demands skills of communication and sensitivity in an emotive and stressful area of work. These encounters can also highlight some problems and contradictions. Aspects of the ways in which systems operate do not always fit with the perspectives of young people and ideas of agency and participation. They can also result in an uncertain response for young people aged 16 and 17, while adult services starting at the age of 18 might not meet their needs.

Policy makers and practitioners need to consider whether the protection system and subsequent interventions can take on board some of these problems to ensure they respond more specifically to the needs of young people. This is not to suggest that the views of young people should always be adopted without question: decision making will always be complex in this area of work. But the research we have discussed in this chapter provides some ideas about how young people can be enabled to seek help in the first place and be empowered to engage with the decisions about how they will best be safeguarded.

References

Balding, J. (1998) *Young People in 1997*, Exeter, Schools Health Education Unit.

Balding, J. (2002) *Young People in 2001*, Exeter, Schools Health Education Unit.

Barnardo's (1998) *Whose Daughter Next? Children Abused Through Prostitution*, Ilford, Barnardo's.

Bradshaw, J. (ed.) (2001) *Poverty: The Outcomes for Children*, London, Family Policy Studies Centre.

Cawson, P. (2002) *Child Maltreatment in the Family: The Experience of a National Sample of Young People*, London, NSPCC.

Cleaver, H., Unell, I. and Aldgate, J. (2003) *Children's Needs – Parenting Capacity: The Impact of Parental Mental Illness, Problem Alcohol and Drug Use, and Domestic Violence on Children's Development*, London, The Stationery Office.

Corby, B. (2000) *Child Abuse: Towards a Knowledge Base*, Buckingham, Open University Press.

Dalrymple, J. (1999) 'What is confidentiality? Developing practice relating to young people', *Practice*, vol. 11, pp. 27–38.

Dalrymple, J. (2001) 'Safeguarding young people through confidential advocacy services', *Child and Family Social Work*, vol. 6, pp. 149–160.

Dalrymple, J. (2005) 'Constructions of child and youth advocacy: emerging issues in advocacy practice', *Children and Society*, vol. 19, no. 1, pp. 3–15.

Daniel, B. and Wassell, S. (2002) *Adolescence: Assessing and Promoting Resilience in Vulnerable Children (3)*, London, Jessica Kingsley.

Daniel, B., Wassell, S. and Gilligan, R. (1999) *Child Development for Child Care and Protection Workers*, London, Jessica Kingsley.

DfES (Department for Education and Skills) (2003) *Every Child Matters*, Norwich, The Stationery Office.

DfES (Department for Education and Skills) (2005) *Youth Matters*, London, The Stationery Office.

DoH (Department of Health) (1995) *Child Protection: Messages from Research*, London, HMSO.

DoH (Department of Health) (2000a) *Framework for the Assessment of Children in Need and their Families*, London, HMSO.

DoH (Department of Health) (2000b) *Safeguarding Children Involved in Prostitution*, London, HMSO.

DoH (Department of Health) (2002) *Safeguarding Children Involved in Prostitution: A Guidance Review*, London, HMSO.

Featherstone, B. and Evans, H. (2004) *Children Experiencing Maltreatment: Who Do They Turn To?*, London, NSPCC.

Ferguson, H. (2004) *Protecting Children in Time: Child Abuse, Child Protection, and the Consequences of Modernity*, Basingstoke, Palgrave Macmillan.

France, A. and Utting, D. (2005) 'The paradigm of "risk and protection-focussed prevention" and its impact on services for children and families', *Children and Society*, vol. 19, no. 2, pp. 77–90.

Garrett, P.M. (2003) *Remaking Social Work with Children and Families: A Critical Discussion of the Modernisation of Social Care*, London, Routledge.

Gibbons, J., Gallagher, B., Bell, C. and Gordon, D. (1995) *Development After Physical Abuse in Early Childhood: A Follow Up Study of Children on Protection Registers*, London, HMSO.

Gibbs, J. (2001) 'Maintaining front-line workers in child protection: a case for refocusing supervision', *Child Abuse Review*, vol. 10, pp. 323–35.

Gilligan, R. (1997) 'Beyond permanence? The importance of resilience in child placement practice and planning', *Adoption and Fostering*, vol. 21, no. 1, pp. 12–20.

Gilligan, R. (2004) 'Promoting resilience in child and family social work: issues for social work practice, education and policy', *Social Work Education*, vol. 23, no. 1, pp. 93–104.

Hall, T. and Montgomery, H. (2000) 'Home and away: "childhood", "youth" and young people', *Anthropology Today*, vol. 16, no. 3, pp. 13–15.

Hallett, C., Murray, C. and Punch, S. (2003) 'Young people and welfare: negotiating pathways' in Hallett, C. and Prout, A. (eds) *Hearing The Voices of Children: Social Policy for a New Century*, London, RoutledgeFalmer.

Hester, M., Pearson, C. and Harwin, N. (2000) *Making An Impact: Children and Domestic Violence. A Reader*, London, Jessica Kingsley.

Hester, M. and Radford, L. (1996) *Domestic Violence and Child Contact Arrangements in England and Denmark*, Bristol, Policy Press.

Hetherington, R. and Cooper, A. (2001) 'Child protection: lessons from abroad' in Cull, L. and Roche, J. (eds) *The Law and Social Work: Contemporary Issues for Practice*, Basingstoke, Palgrave/The Open University.

Hopkins, P. and Hill, M. (2006) *This is a Good Place to Live and Think about the Future: The Needs and Experiences of Unaccompanied Asylum-Seeking Children in Scotland*, Glasgow, Scottish Refugee Council.

Hudson, B. (2006) 'Making and missing connections: learning disability services and the transition from adolescence to adulthood', *Disability and Society*, vol. 21, no. 1, pp. 47–60.

Jack, G. (2001) 'An ecological perspective on child abuse' in Foley, P., Roche, J. and Tucker, S. (eds) *Children in Society: Contemporary Theory, Policy and Practice*, Basingstoke, Palgrave/The Open University.

Jack, G. (2004) 'Child protection at the community level', *Child Abuse Review*, vol. 13, pp. 368–83.

Jones, D. and Ramchandani, P. (1999) *Child Sexual Abuse: Informing Practice from Research*, Abingdon, Radcliffe Medical Press.

Kehily, M.J. (ed.) (2007) *Understanding Youth: Perspectives, Identities and Practices*, London, Sage/The Open University (Course Book).

Kempe, C.H., Silverman, F.N., Steel, B.F., Droegmueller, W. and Silver, H.K. (1962) 'The battered child syndrome', *Journal of the American Medical Association*, vol. 181, pp. 17–24.

Kennedy, M. (2000) 'The abuse of disabled children' in Baldwin, N. (ed.) *Protecting Children, Promoting their Rights*, London, Whiting & Birch.

Laming, H. (2003) *The Victoria Climbié Inquiry: Report of an Inquiry by Lord Laming*, Norwich, The Stationery Office.

Lawrence, A. (2004) *Principles of Child Protection: Management and Practice*, Maidenhead, Open University Press.

Leason, K. (2006) 'Listen up', *Community Care*, 9 February,
www.communitycare.co.uk/Articles/2006/02/09/52739/Listen+up.html?key=LEASON
[accessed 15/11/06].

MacCleod, M. (1999) '"Don't just do it": children's access to help and protection'
in Parton, N. and Wattam, C. (eds) *Child Sexual Abuse: Responding to the Experiences
of Children*, Chichester, Wiley.

MacCleod, M. (2000) 'What do children need by way of protection? Who is to decide?'
in Baldwin N. (ed.) *Protecting Children, Promoting their Rights*, London,
Whiting & Birch.

Montgomery, H. (2007) 'Moving' in Kehily, M.J. (ed.) *Understanding Youth: Perspectives,
Identities and Practices*, London, Sage/The Open University (Course Book).

Montgomery, H., Burr, R. and Woodhead, M. (2003) 'Adversity and resilience'
in Montgomery, H., Burr, R. and Woodhead, M. (eds) *Changing Childhoods:
Local and Global*, Chichester, John Wiley/The Open University.

Murray, C. (2005) 'Young people's help seeking: an alternative model', *Childhood*, vol. 12,
no. 4, pp. 479–94.

Parton, N. (2004) 'From Maria Colwell to Victoria Climbié: reflections on public inquiries
into child abuse a generation apart', *Child Abuse Review*, vol. 13, pp. 88–94.

Parton, N. (2006) *Safeguarding Childhood: Early Intervention and Surveillance in a Late
Modern Society*, Basingstoke, Palgrave Macmillan.

Parton, N., Thorpe, D. and Wattam, C. (1997) *Child Protection, Risk, and the Moral Order*,
Basingstoke, Macmillan.

Prout, A. (2003) 'Participation, policy and the changing conditions of childhood'
in Hallett, C. and Prout, A. (eds) *Hearing the Voices of Children: Social Policy for a
New Century*, London, RoutledgeFalmer.

Rees, G. and Siakeu, J. (2004) *Thrown Away: The Experiences of Children Forced to Leave
Home*, London, The Children's Society.

Richards, M. and Vostanis, P. (2004) 'Interprofessional perspectives on transitional mental
health services for young people aged 16–19 years', *Journal of Interprofessional Care*,
vol. 18, no. 2, pp. 115–28.

Ridge, T. (2002) *Childhood Poverty and Social Exclusion: From a Child's Perspective*,
Bristol, Policy Press.

Robb, M. (2007) 'Wellbeing' in Kehily, M.J. (ed.) *Understanding Youth: Perspectives,
Identities and Practices*, London, Sage/The Open University (Course Book).

Salford Centre for Social Work Research (2004) *A National Evaluation of the NSPCC's
Young People's Centres by Young People*, Salford, University of Salford.

Stanley, J. and Goddard, C. (2002) *In The Firing Line: Violence and Power in Child
Protection Work*, Chichester, Wiley.

Stevens, M. and Higgins, D. (2002) 'The influence of risk and protective factors on burnout
experienced by those who work with maltreated children', *Child Abuse Review*, vol. 11,
pp. 313–31.

Tanner, K. and Turney, D. (2003) 'What do we know about child neglect? A critical review
of the literature and its application to social work practice', *Child and Family Social
Work*, vol. 8, pp. 25–34.

Thomas, G. (2006) *Keeping Us Safe: Report of the Safeguarding Vulnerable Children
Review*, Cardiff, National Assembly for Wales.

Time Out Young People's Centre (2005) *Annual Report 2004/2005*, London, NSPCC.

Ungar, M. (2004) 'A constructionist discourse on resilience: multiple contexts, multiple realities amongst at-risk children and youth', *Youth and Society*, vol. 35, no. 3, pp. 341–65.

Utting, W. (1997) *People Like Us: The Report of the Review of Safeguards for Children Living Away from Home*, London, Department of Health.

Waterhouse, R. (2000) *Lost in Care: Report of the Tribunal of the Inquiry into the Abuse of Children in Care in the Former County Council Areas of Gwynedd and Clwyd Since 1974*, London, HMSO.

Wattam, C. (1999) 'Confidentiality and the social organisation of telling' in Parton, N. and Wattam, C. (eds) *Child Sexual Abuse: Responding to the Experiences of Children*, Chichester, Wiley.

Westcott, H. and Jones, D. (1999) 'The abuse of disabled children', *Journal of Child Psychology and Psychiatry*, vol. 40, pp. 497–506.

Worrall-Davies, A., Kiernan, K., Anderton, N. and Cottrell, D. (2004) 'Working with young people with complex needs: practitioners' views', *Child and Adolescent Mental Health*, vol. 9, no. 4, pp. 180–6.

Chapter 9

Support

Jean Spence

Introduction

This final chapter of the book explores those encounters between practitioners and young people whose aim is to provide 'support' in various ways. The chapter suggests that work with young people is shaped by a combination of professional values and purposes, the needs of young people themselves and the imperatives of policy. Any tensions that arise in the relationship between these interests must be managed by workers in their practice. Although the orientation in the field is towards the immediacy of interventions in young people's lives, workers must be consistently aware of the wider policy context in which organisational and strategic decisions are made. Policy initiatives are imposed largely through targeted funding and systems of accountability and these affect the priorities of practice, but workers interpret policy through the lens of their professional knowledge and their understanding of the young people who come into their sphere of influence. The demands of policy and the interests of young people as understood through the discipline of a profession cannot always be easily reconciled.

The discussion draws on data from a range of historical and contemporary sources, and intends to be relevant to a range of practice settings that offer support to young people; for example, in education, health, advice and counselling services. It uses youth work as the primary focus because the principle of voluntary engagement which characterises the informal approach of youth work means that young people are afforded a degree of power in the process of engagement. In so far as youth workers must negotiate with young people in order to maintain their involvement, the process of reconciling policy imperatives with the immediate demands of practice relationships can be more acute than in other professional contexts. This becomes even more difficult if the demands of policy are tightly defined and controlled.

Data from a research project funded by the Big Lottery and entitled *An Everyday Journey: Discovering the Meaning and Value in Youth Work* (referred to as *EJ*) has been used to illustrate the chapter (*An Everyday Journey*, 2004–2006). This project, undertaken in partnership between the youth organisation Weston Spirit and Durham University, conducted focus group discussions with youth workers and young people in five locations, and undertook participant observation and interviews with workers and young people in 15 different youth organisations across the UK between 2004 and 2006. The data used in this chapter was gathered by Carol Devanney, Carol Pugh and Wayne Thexton, and the project has been managed by Kylie Noonan and Jayne Wilson of Weston Spirit. The research material was gathered in order to explore how youth workers and young people understand the everyday practice experience of youth work. It is presented here with the intention of communicating the issues and complexities of supportive practice from the perspective of those involved.

Section 1 of this chapter explores the practice contexts in which the notion of 'support' for young people has played a key part. Section 2 analyses the links between approaches to support and the discourse of transitions, while Section 3 places that discourse in a historical perspective. Section 4 considers an alternative model which emphasises youth as a time of 'being', and Section 5 discusses the importance of empowerment in more radical strains of youth work. Section 6 examines the impact of increased targeting of services, and, lastly, Section 7 looks at workers' needs for support.

The chapter will address the following core questions:

- What does 'support' mean in the context of work with young people?
- What models of support have been important in the history of youth work and to what extent do they influence current practice?
- What kinds of alternative models of support have been developed by those working with young people?
- How has recent youth policy influenced the ways in which services offer support to young people?

1 Support in context

In professional work with young people across a range of services, the idea of support is intrinsic. Being commonly understood, it seldom provokes critical interrogation. Support is one of the key concepts used by workers to describe and give meaning to their interventions. It might be part of a whole approach, as in Connexions, and designed as a 'Youth Support Service' (DfEE, 2000a); it might be a framework for practice, as in generic youth work where it underpins informal education; or it might be one aspect of practice, such as in school teaching, where support is complementary to formal, curriculum based education. Sometimes the idea of support is used in conjunction with another descriptor to further define the nature or content of the support offered, as in 'advice and support' (Holman, 2000, p. 79) or 'support and guidance' (DfEE, 2000a).

In whatever context it is used and however it is described, a 'supportive' approach necessarily uses *relational* methods to *help* others. This can be conceptualised using an architectural or building metaphor, which can be used to open up some important questions about the qualities of the supportive relationship in work with young people. For example, does the building represent young people themselves or the wider society? Who is responsible for designing the building and identifying where the support structures are necessary? Who has financed the building and how important are they? Are structures designed for support sometimes put in place when they are not necessary?

One important question relates to the deficiency of any building which lacks support. Support is *compensatory* in relation to a building's weakness. Whether a building is a metaphor for 'young people' or a 'society' in which young people are an essential part, the idea of support must inevitably refer to something which otherwise might not be stable or in shape. The inference is that young people need support to be kept in shape, or that society needs support with reference to young people in order to maintain social stability. Notably, the policy document *Transforming Youth Work* indicated that the first priority for youth work in the context of the new Connexions service was to keep young people in 'good shape' (DfEE, 2001, p. 13).

Less obviously, support is not only compensatory, but also creative. Used imaginatively, it might facilitate the extension and development of a basic structure, adding height or ornament. With appropriate support mechanisms, either young people might be enabled to achieve a potential which might not be immediately obvious, or the relationship between young people and their society can achieve a constructive, developmental dynamism. Workers who use the terms 'facilitate and support' (National Youth Agency, 2001, p. 1) to explain their practice, or who refer to 'support and empowerment' (for example, Melrose, 2001, p. 210), are thinking in these more creative terms. In *Transforming Youth Work*, the government seemed to embrace such aspirations in the determination to develop 'participative and democratic models' designed to give young people 'a voice' in shaping organisational and political decision making (DfEE, 2001 p. 15).

Different types of support in buildings serve different functions. In work with young people the nature of the support that can be offered depends on the definition of the help needed and the particular character of the responding service.

Activity 1   Different kinds of support

Allow 20 minutes   Think about one of the professions that work with young people, perhaps the one with which you are most familiar, and reflect on these questions:

- What kind of support does this profession offer to young people, their families and their local communities?

- Is the approach predominantly compensatory or empowering?

- Where are the boundaries of the profession and where does it overlap with other services?

Comment

Counsellors, for example, concentrate on intensive, one-to-one support in response to a particular individual set of problems, while youth workers offer informal educational support to groups of young people with the purpose of encouraging them to engage constructively with their local circumstances. But professional boundaries are not absolute. Youth workers sometimes offer one-to-one support and basic counselling in order to help a young person participate effectively in a group, and aspects of the work of counsellors might be characterised as educational. Thus, boundaries blur and overlap, but it can be argued that practitioners who understand their core professional priorities, exercise their core skills appropriately and acknowledge the complementary features of other services will be most effective in their interventions.

There is therefore a good case for disciplinary clarity within each profession and for co-operation and networking between discrete areas of practice. Boundaries can be a place of negotiation and possible mutual development in a comprehensive set of support services relating to young people and their social worlds. At their most effective, such services would work separately and together to prevent or solve problems on the one hand and to extend scope on the other.

The Connexions service was introduced to exploit the possibilities of networks and boundaries. It was initially intended that youth workers would co-operate with (or become) Connexions Personal Advisers (PAs), identifying the different needs of individual young people and signposting them to appropriate support within a network of co-operating agencies. Connexions has not flourished as intended, but its basic principles remain intact in policy. The Green Paper *Youth Matters* (DfES, 2005), following on the principles of the agenda of *Every Child Matters* (DfES, 2003), outlines the intention to 'give Local Authorities working through children's trusts the necessary responsibility, resources, authority and incentives to lead the way towards a more responsive and integrated service for teenagers', which is designed to:

> enable integrated planning and commissioning of the full range of services for teenagers from universal activities through to more specialist and targeted support. This will lead to an integrated youth support service, focused on and structured around young people's needs and involving a wide range of providers, including voluntary and community organisations.
>
> (DfES, 2005, pp. 9–10)

In a network of services, connected by the principle of targeted support, practitioners need to be clear about the possibilities and limits of their own professional contribution, that which can be made by other professionals and the creative possibilities of working in the interface.

The model that has been adopted by policy makers seems simple and logical; however, the practice has proved to be complex. Part of this complexity relates to practical matters. For instance, in the Connexions design, adequate account was not taken of the differences in the legislative framework under which specific services operate (Coles, 2005). Another part relates to values and meanings. For example, there is an incongruence between the brokerage role ascribed to PAs in Connexions and the self-defined identities and practice knowledge of youth workers (Crimmens *et al.*, 2004; Holmes, 2004; Wylie, 2004). The differences in the meaning of support in this context are significant. Connexions as a 'support service' was designed to be universally applicable, but its main focus was dealing with individual problems. This does not correspond with the developmental notion of support incorporated within the informal educational philosophy of youth workers who were supposed to work closely with Connexions.

People are not fixed and passive like buildings. They actively interpret and create their own definitions of the support that they need, can use or offer. The assumptions and expectations inscribed within policy documents can be accepted, reframed or resisted by young people, members of local communities and professional workers. Moreover, this happens in a fluid context in which different interest groups communicate and negotiate and in which there is no necessary agreement between parties about the nature of youth in society as it is or ought to be.

Key points

- Support is one of the key concepts used by practitioners and services to give meaning to their encounters with young people.
- Support for young people may be either compensatory or empowering.
- The boundaries between different support services may be quite fluid.
- Young people and practitioners actively interpret and create their own definitions of support.

2 Support and transition

Support is perceived as integral to work with young people because 'youth' is experienced as a time of change. The process of change is replete with energy and opportunity, but also beset with danger for individuals and society. In recent years, theory and practice relevant to this time of change have been dominated by the discourse of transition (Wallace and Cross, 1990; Coles, 1995; Furlong and Cartmel, 1997; Johnston et al., 2000; MacDonald et al., 2005; see also Thomson, 2007a, in the companion volume in this series).

Transition is not a new concept (for example, Eisenstadt, 1956), but it has specific resonances in relation to the socio-economic conditions of post-industrial societies and the political management of age. As discussed in Chapter 7, 'Risk', changes in the economy and the complications of achieving the requisite skills and attitudes required for satisfactory adjustment to the labour market mean that unqualified and inexperienced young people have found it increasingly difficult to access well paid work (see also Thomson, 2007b). For these young people, the terrain between dependent childhood and independent adulthood has become especially hazardous, for themselves and for the wider society. There is much anxiety about education and training for work, about social order and cohesion and about the maintenance of participatory democracy with reference to young people who are identified as belonging to socially excluded families and communities, who are defined as disaffected and who seem to have little or no stake in wider social norms and values (MacDonald, 1997; Measor and Squires, 2000; MacDonald and Marsh, 2005). Governments have therefore systematically sought to manage the transitions of those negatively labelled as 'Status Zero' (Williamson, 2002) or NEET (Not in Education, Employment or Training) (DfEE, 2000a, 2000b; DfES, 2005) through institutionally based interventions underpinned by support and control.

Although the idea of transition includes the notion that youth can be a universally problematic life stage, policy makers working within the discourse of transitions have been concerned mainly with specific deficiencies, targeting issues and areas which are associated with disaffection and exclusion among young people, and focusing attention on those individual young people identified as most 'at risk' to themselves and others. Support offered in these terms is compensatory, concentrating on weakness, vulnerablility and deviance. It is the ameliorative end of a continuum, which, at its other end, is punitive (DfES, 2005). Where supportive interventions are unsuccessful, methods of discipline and control, such as Anti-Social Behaviour Orders (ASBOs), are used to restrain the young in order to support communities and protect them from the problems particular young people create (Pitts, 2003; Thomas, 2005; see also the discussion in Chapter 7).

Political strategy deriving from the question of youth transitions has impacted on professional practice in a number of ways. First, it has involved some refocusing of pre-existing services in relation to specific issues associated with 'risk' (for young people as individuals and for society in relation to young people as a group). Second, in order to minimise risks it has demanded improved and formalised co-operation between those professions traditionally representing 'support' such as youth work, and those representing 'control' such as the police. Third, it has informed the creation of new initiatives of which Connexions has been the most ambitious, but including time-limited and targeted schemes such as the Youth Inclusion Projects (YIPs) and Positive Futures (Youth Justice Board, 2006).

The use of the concept of 'support' in policy has become explicit, moving beyond the implicit meanings understood within practice. Policy initiatives now require publicly funded organisations to support young people with reference to clearly defined areas of transitional risk. This highlights areas of special concern where workers must collaborate across professional disciplines. So, for instance, identifying sexually transmitted infection as a high risk for young people leads to the creation of special projects which might involve workers from different disciplines such as health, social work and youth work, or who might have special subject interests such as sexual identity. Workers must find a way to work collaboratively, to construct partnerships with linked services and to encourage young people to use and participate in schemes focusing on special issues. This means that the framework of practice has become increasingly complex and professional, and organisational relationships increasingly important (see Chapter 1, 'Practitioners').

2.1 Practitioner responses

Workers are sometimes receptive and sometimes resistant to social policy directives, but they always act as agents, engaging with policy not only according to the possibilities and limits of the everyday realities of the practice situation, but also through the medium of their own personal and professional knowledge, values, politics and ethics (see the discussion of challenges from professionals in Chapter 1). The impact of each new initiative depends on the extent of co-operation among practitioners 'on the ground'. Practitioners such as youth workers who are in place already, who are asked to work alongside new professionals, or to develop new professional skills as in the case of PAs, as well as those who train, advise and manage workers, are themselves decision makers. They carry with them their understanding of their specialism and their own intellectual and experiential knowledge and history (Holmes, 2004; Wylie, 2004). As one worker, asked about the purposes of youth work as part of the *Everyday Journey* project, declared:

> For me, on a personal level, not taking into account the principles of youth work set by policy, it's working with young people where they're at, giving them the information and support they need, require or want, request. But they're determining what they need in order to progress.
>
> (*EJ* Workers' Focus Group d, 2005)

This worker explicitly sets policy purposes to one side in order to identify what he considers to be the heart of supportive work, which for him is to be responsive to the needs of young people. His personal interpretation of the meaning of his work is as important as the principles set by policy.

Sometimes workers adopt policy language but within a stance which is implicitly oppositional:

> Mark: Transitional relationships in a lot of ways is what we try and teach those young people. What point are we trying to take them from, or what point are they at, to what point they might end up going – whether that's positive or negative ... What I don't want to do is stick to the statutory stuff because I think that's part and parcel of, sorry, of the rules and regs we have to adhere under, I don't think that's the bulk of our relationship with the young people. So it's taking them through that transitional stage.
>
> (*EJ* Workers' Focus Group d, 2005)

At other times workers understand their practice in direct opposition to policy:

> Civil servants don't understand the job that we do, they're not youth workers, they don't tend to be, they don't want to know.

They're looking for cost benefit, cost benefit analysis, they're looking at the quick fix, they're looking at short term and they're looking at what election time is coming up. What can I stand by? And that's what they do and they don't understand the process of evaluation, and they don't understand it's a long process, you can't sustain billions or millions of numbers doing what you do. It's small, focus based youth work, it takes quite a long time. But they don't understand that, they want to see results.

(*EJ* Workers' Focus Group a, 2005)

'Support' is thus contested terrain in practice. The abstract idea of 'supporting young people through transition' is filtered through a complex set of professional discourses in the processes of practice. These discourses are informed by ideas about the relevance of youth transitions and about the nature of the relationships that need to be built in order to have support accepted by the recipient.

Key points

- Recent youth policy has targeted needs arising from changes in the transition to adulthood, especially in the absence of traditional transition routes to work for working class young people.

- Services have focused increasingly on areas of 'risk', which has involved bringing together 'support' services with those representing 'control'.

- New initiatives have been created which require collaboration across professional boundaries.

- Practitioners have responded to these initiatives in a variety of ways.

3 Historical models of support and transition

It is useful to consider the relationship between supportive approaches and the idea of transition from a historical perspective, because that can help delineate the core principles which workers have inherited and which implicitly inform their decisions and perspectives in practice.

Since the Industrial Revolution, when the institutions of family and work were separated, youth has been identified as both a vulnerable life stage and a transitional period of potential disorder (Gillis, 1981). However, at different historical moments, particular aspects of social and pathological models have been emphasised, with implications for the type of working relationship pursued with young people.

3.1 The social structural model

In the nineteenth century, philanthropic social workers generally attempted to offer support to the poor, but they were particularly keen to help young people make a successful adjustment to appropriate gender and class roles. The maintenance of stability within the working classes gained a high priority in establishment politics, and voluntary youth social work concentrated almost entirely on 'working' girls and boys (Stanley, 1985 [1890]; Freeman, 1904; Russell and Rigby, 1908). As Edward Johns Urwick argued in his influential text, *Studies of Boy Life in Our Cities* (1904, p. vii): 'it is on this class that the comfort, the security, the possible efficiency of all others ultimately rest'.

In the nineteenth century, 'youth work' was directed almost entirely at working class young people

Middle class men and women set about helping poor young people by offering the means to rise beyond the circumstances of their parents via the establishment of cross-class relationships of trust. These relationships were crucial because the presentation of an alternative set of values could be perceived as a challenge, threatening the cultural practices that were deemed necessary for survival in the everyday world which the poor inhabited. There are many instances reported of refusal of help and of conflict between workers and young people's families when the sympathy of workers failed to extend to empathy, or where families perceived disrespect, patronage and superiority in social work attitudes (for example, Spence, 2001a, pp. 82–3). It was essential that some element of reciprocity be achieved in order for the material help offered to be accepted in the first instance and for negotiation to take place around different class and cultural values.

The practice relationships achieved in these circumstances came to be described by workers sometimes as friendship and at other times as familial. In discussing the pioneers of the boys' clubs, W.M. Eager identified friendship as crucial to their approach:

> By giving friendship, and winning it, they discovered the quality of working-boys and so potentially of the working-classes. Without self-consciousness or self-seeking they made themselves friends of boys who had no claim on them except that they were deprived of privileges to which boys had a right, and of opportunities without which they could not grow to sound manhood. Friendship threw the first bridge across the gulf of class consciousness, with its contemporary assumption of innate inferiority and its consequent tolerance of gross inequity.
>
> (Eager, 1953, pp. 12–13)

Lily Montagu, who developed the West Central Jewish Girls' Club in the 1890s, described her relationship with the club members both in terms of friendship and in terms of motherhood. In her last letter to club members, discovered after her death in 1963, she addressed her words to her 'dear friends', emphasised the importance of a 'high ideal of friendship' and of its benefits to the happiness of club life, and signed herself, 'Your affectionate friend and club mother' (quoted in Levy, undated, p. 70).

Friendship implied a more equitable and less patronising approach to the helping relationship. It avoided the implication that working class parents were deficient, while foregrounding the personal commitment of the worker to the young person. Friendship was increasingly favoured as paid professional work replaced the voluntary ethic and the class composition and motivations of the workforce changed during the twentieth century (Spence, 2001b). Although the language of friendship was designed to transcend class difference, it never completely erased the compensatory assumptions of this model. The immediate intention was to offer personalised help to individuals who were responsive, but the wider purpose was for social order stability and cohesion in a fundamentally unequal society. Some doubt must be cast on the possibility of authenticity in friendships conceived in relationships of class inequality.

3.2 The life course model

During the early twentieth century another set of concerns provoked a different interpretation of support, and a different type of practice relationship. These emphasised the 'essential' characteristics of 'youth' and the pathological condition of adolescence. The burgeoning voluntary youth movements of the period, of which Scouting was the most successful representative, played to an idealised and romantic vision of the nature of youth. Class orientated organisations, including the Boys' Clubs, had also incorporated some of these views. Even the social scientist Urwick, despite his principal desire 'to draw attention to the influences for good or evil which their environment contains' (Urwick, 1904, p. ix), referred to what he defined as 'the natural instincts of boyhood' (p. xii) which he believed were being distorted by working class conditions.

Within such a paradigm, problems associated with youth could be explained partly by the disturbing effects of adolescence and partly by the lack of opportunity or guidance to develop the best aspects of personal character. Interventions framed in this mode began to draw the outlines of a new profession of youth work, distinct from social work, and were conceived of mainly in romantic, masculine terms. On the grounds of a universal experience of youth, they offered collective provision which would seek to play to the best character of 'the boy' in order to lead him to an upright and idealised version of independent and responsible 'manhood'. In so doing, they intended to minimise the possibility of him succumbing to the physical, psychological and emotional traumas of adolescence, diverting his sexual energies through alternative challenging, group based activity (see Robb, 2007, in the companion volume in this series).

Youth was a life moment to be captured and shaped. Workers were to support young people by emphasising the positive attributes of youth, providing opportunities to play and learn in conditions which enhanced the virtues required for democratic citizenship. Workers adopted positions of leadership rather than friendship, but leaders were exhorted to retain an empathetic as well as a sympathetic regard for 'the boy'. Sometimes, like Baden-Powell of the Scouts, a leader might become a 'boy-man' himself, an authoritative 'older brother' (Jeal, 1989, p. 498) winning the loyalty and affection of his young followers. This model was increasingly applied to work with young women, who were to be shaped to be fit companions for men and mothers for their children. It emphasised the virtues of the cross-generational rather than the cross-class helping relationship. Workers performed as adult rather than class role models.

3.3 Contemporary impact

Ideas about the nature of adolescence remained powerful within the discourses of practice until the last quarter of the twentieth century. When the relative numbers of young people in the population began to decline and the numbers of young unemployed increased, youth once again became problematic in what could be argued were class terms. By the 1980s, young people were no longer perceived primarily as a pathological group experiencing physical and psychological 'storm and stress', but as a group with a difficult relationship to the labour market. Indeed, Jeffs and Smith (1998/9) argued that the changed conditions call into question the whole idea of youth as a special life stage. Nevertheless, both historical models remain extant in practice.

Activity 2   The continuing impact of historical models

Allow 30 minutes   Consider the following extracts from a discussion among youth workers. Can you trace the principal features of the two historical models of transition in them?

Susan: It's important that we're supporting them so that they can get accreditation. So that they can turn around when they're 17 or 18 and say 'No I'm not useless, because I did this, this and this. And I've got all of this to show what I've done. And yeah I didn't do well at school but that just wasn't my environment.' So I think that's important and we're doing our best to move things in that direction. The project is run by a youth management committee with support from the council and we're looking at trying to give them a bit of back up with all the skills and the work they carry out. I mean a lot of the ones that will be going on to college and things like that they know how to use it, they know how to write an application form of what they've done, they know how to use that information. But then we also have lots of young people involved in the management of the centre that really don't. And they don't. And if we're even filling in forms with them and we're helping them to do something and 'why have you left that section blank?' 'Well I haven't done that.' 'Well you did this and this and that.' And its like, 'Oh, right. Does that count?' And they have no concept of how valuable that is and that is an experience they can use ...

Claire: It's about supporting them and encouraging them to take positive steps from being a child, like early ages of being a young person, to young adulthood because that's quite important, because you've got a big influence on that stage of their life.

Louise: Positive role-modelling I guess is another one. I think that is sometimes forgotten. Because it's so essential, because it's what Claire's saying, it is such an influential part to play in somebody's life.

(*EJ* Workers' Focus Group d, 2005)

Comment

These contemporary examples suggest that workers are incorporating both models into their practice. You might notice the type of work undertaken 'with support from the council' and that 'positive role-modelling' is considered to be essential but 'sometimes forgotten'. This reflects the current formal bias towards the social model of transition where the worker gives objective advice. The workers are more reflective about their personal influence on the young people when thinking about the more diffuse practice of role modelling. Thinking about the quality of self as a feature of practice demands a self consciousness about relationships which goes beyond 'advice and support'.

In contemporary practice, workers can no longer talk innocently about familial or friendship relationships. Yet they know that interpersonal dynamics are often crucial to the success of their interventions with young people. In another part of the discussion cited above, but not quoted there, Claire talked rather self-consciously about the importance of 'love' in her work:

> It's giving them that sort of – love's probably the wrong word to use these days, right, because it's taken far too much out of context – but they do get that to an extent. One of the main things folk need, and it isn't just young folk it's everybody, they need that certain extent of love and somebody that's really caring for them.
>
> (*EJ* Workers' Focus Group d, 2005)

Such sentiments imply a particular type of commitment, and a personal ethic of service motivates many practitioners in their work with young people. Because it is personal, those who hold to it are consistently confronted with the question of their identities and purposes as workers. To assume the right to help and support others raises important questions about the terms in which such help is offered. Self doubt and questioning operate in a different dimension from the formal policy inspired language of practice which stresses evidence based interventions underpinned by objective information and seeks to systematise relationships with reference to particular specialisms and issues.

Relationship building is difficult territory in view of the possibility of workers exploiting and abusing positions of trust with young people. The maintenance of professional distance has become important to the creation of safe spaces in practice, and a self consciousness of risk and danger pervades the relational dimensions of the work:

> The young woman said that she thought youth workers were not like teachers because they were more like friends. The manager said at this point that they are not actually friends and that youth workers have to be careful as there could be a chance that their role is misinterpreted by being looked at in this way. He said

that they were friendly but not friends. The young woman thought about this and then agreed that this was what she really meant by what she had said!

(*EJ* Research notes, Location 3, 2006)

Yet the need to use the interpersonal in order to offer support which is humanised has not gone away. How young people are to be won over, how well workers can know and communicate with them, and how interclass and interpersonal relations are to be lived in the organisation and the locality remain areas of concern for the type of support that might be offered by any organisation.

Given the stress on objective professionalism, the role of worker-as-leader has re-emerged as a less taxing approach. The 'boy-man' model is no longer appropriate in organisations concerned with risk and in a world concerned with social transitions. Instead, the emphasis is on the need for responsibility and the transmission of skills.

The role of leader encourages workers to develop specific practice skills which can be used to train, challenge and influence young people while minimising the inter-subjective emotions. Practice relationships can be pursued through the medium of the skill. The worker becomes an instructor and the young person a trainee or apprentice. Support here is concerned with task completion.

Different workers and young people will find different styles of working and of relationship appropriate to their needs and interests. Practice organisations draw from their own historical traditions and adapt to the realities of contemporary conditions. Mostly, and mainly because of limits on public expenditure and the orientation of policy towards solving social problems, the attention of workers is directed towards social difficulties associated with youth transitions. Sometimes young people want or demand very little from practitioners other than the provision of resources and activities. However, in so far as they build interpersonal relationships with young people, practitioners can develop a humanistic approach which changes the nature of support from the compensatory towards the creative.

Key points

- The relationship between support and transition has been conceived of in different ways at different periods in the history of youth work.

- The social structural model aimed to support working class young people in adjusting to gender and class roles, and used models of friendship and familial relationships to describe the relationship between young people and professionals.

- The life course model saw youth as a universal experience to be shaped and directed, and emphasised the role of the professional as leader and role model.

- Contemporary work with young people incorporates elements of both models, though workers tend to be more reflective and questioning about their roles and relationships with young people.

4 A third way? Being

Although compensatory transitional models are dominant in policy, in a variety of professional arrangements and in multi-agency support for young people, there is a third position, which focuses on the creative potential of youth as a time of 'being' as well as 'becoming':

Danny: It's that they're welcome, we just provide a little bit of breathing space for them to be, begin thinking about, or not thinking about, or just however they want to be, with whatever might be going on for them at the time. We just provide that little extra space that they can begin to sort of move through whatever it is that they want to do, or get the support for.

(*EJ* Workers' Focus Group a, 2004)

This is not exclusive to, but it is more common within, youth work than in other services. The long term popularity of youth provision, including clubs and specialist facilities offered as a youth dominated space, a place to be in the present, is related to the fact that in itself it does not respond to any supposed deficiency in young people or in their family and community life. It does identify young people as a particular social group with needs and interests related to their age and social structural position, but any deficiency is located in the body politic vis-à-vis services and attitudes towards youth.

The principles of support from this perspective are that, first, it should be *collective*: understanding that young people inhabit a distinctive social world as a group; and second, that it should be offered on the basis of universal access in order to provide the conditions wherein young people can participate voluntarily and on their own terms *as individuals*. Such an approach has been characteristic of open access leisure provision for young people, and became dominant in the youth service as it expanded following the 1960 Albemarle Report (Ministry of Education, 1960). Youth issues and the problems of transition were never far from the agenda, and the collective ideal was inevitably distorted by the dominance of white, able-bodied masculinity; but universally accessible provision recognised the principle that youth could be enjoyed for its own sake, that such provision contributed to minimising social disorder associated with youth, and that young people could exercise choice about participation and seek support in their own time and on their own terms.

Perhaps accidentally, but reflecting the mood of the 1960s, such principles also created the conditions in which the idea could flourish of encouraging young people to *create* change, to transcend their problematic condition as a group subject to the instabilities of change. The thinking of those who stress the importance of social or informal educational approaches to work with young people is informed by the experience of such practice (Davies and Gibson, 1967; Smith, 1988; Jeffs and Smith, 2006). Working with young people to encourage them to identify and critically engage with the conditions of their own present lives, invariably politicises practice in circumstances where resources are distributed unequally and this has been especially relevant with reference to the ideal of universalism.

Questions of equality and power which characterised the politics of practice in the 1970s and 1980s took as a given the right to universally accessible provision and encouraged young people to argue for equal access to youth facilities and resources across educational and welfare services, understanding this as part of a wider political campaign for social equality (Carpenter and Young, 1986; Parmar, 1988; Spence, 1996). The following is an extract from a worker's report about an experimental project working with girls defined as 'at risk' in the 1980s. The Asian youth worker was working with Asian young women in a school setting:

> Mr. Timmins came in at one point to see me, and Nasim covered her comments up. This has often happened in my groups – conversation stops completely when we've been discussing racism experienced from white people, when a white person comes into the room. Or hostile comments start to flow within the group, in whispers, when a white teacher walks into the room, and we're at the other end of the room. Or the teachers are patronizing to the girls and put them down, when they don't realize that I'm with them. They apologize when they *do* recognize me, or when the girls point me out.
>
> (Jamdagni, 1980, p. 110)

This extract raises important questions about the relationship between the worker and the young people in this context, and about the kind of support she could offer to the Asian young women if there was a conflict between them and a white teacher. It also raises the question as to whether black and minority ethnic workers should retain an objective professionalism in the face of racism from fellow (white) professionals.

Working with the realities of inequality and difference in the here and now of young people's lives has sometimes segmented workers into competing interest groups within and between professional disciplines. When the relationships constructed between practitioners, young people and their families and community members are based on common identities and common personal–political interests, professional boundaries can become blurred and professional identity can all too easily become subsumed in personal identity.

Ironically, and possibly in response to the weakening of objectivity in professionalism which foregrounded identity as the main principle of support, arguments for the empowerment of subordinate and minority groups of young people through professional interventions paved the way for politicians to argue for whole services to be targeted at those experiencing social inequality as 'excluded' groups and to remove the political agenda of practitioners through insistence on the centrality of the objective, technical features of professionalism. It is in this way, for example, that a feminist inspired movement promoting informal educational work with girls and young women, and female empowerment, could eventually be transformed into a problem orientated approach to young women's sexuality and pregnancy (Spence, 1996; Greene, 2003/4), and that informal education could be transformed into compensatory approaches to those failing in the formal educational setting.

In so far as politicians claim to be addressing in their policy initiatives questions that practitioners have suggested are important, so the meanings of the terminology as used in the context of practice become destabilised.

Activity 3   Empowerment and policy

Allow 20 minutes   Read the extract below from the 2005 Green Paper *Youth Matters*, and think about the limits and possibilities of the model of 'empowerment' that it offers.

Empowering young people: things to do and places to go

All young people should have the opportunity to take part in a wide range of positive activities in their leisure time. We want more young people to take part in these activities by empowering them to shape what is on offer. We want to put them in control of the things to do and places to go in their area and give them greater choice over the activities in which they participate. We need to focus particularly on young people who are disadvantaged or who are not currently participating in positive activities.

We therefore propose to put buying power directly in the hands of young people themselves by

* supporting Local Authorities to develop and pilot 'opportunity cards'. Cards would give young people discounts ... to spend on their choice of sports and other constructive activities from a range of accredited providers. The Government would

contribute a subsidy to top up the cards of disadvantaged 13–16 year olds. This subsidy would be withheld from young people whose behaviour is unacceptable and the card suspended or withdrawn;

- making an 'opportunity fund' available in each Local Authority to be spent at young people's discretion on projects to improve things to do and places to go in their area.

(DfES, 2005, p. 25)

Comment

It can be argued that in this document 'empowerment' refers to consumer choice in a free market of 'things to do and places to go'. This can be seen as displacing to the commercial sector or as commercialising the open access practice which has traditionally responded to youth as a time of 'being.'

'Sports and other constructive activities' have historically been integral to those professional approaches which seek to offer young people opportunities and experiences which not only divert and challenge them, but which feed their dreams and take them beyond the mundane. Sports and activities have also been used as a medium for the development of practice relationships, as tools through which workers can pursue conversation, develop trust and identify problems and issues in the lives of young people. Supporting young people in identifying appropriate activities, organising these and evaluating and discussing them afterwards are all features of participative educational processes used by teachers, youth workers and social workers (Spence, 2001c). Some would argue that it is unlikely that these methods will be encouraged in a commercialised setting.

If those 'who are disadvantaged or who are not currently participating in positive activities' require special attention, then the conception of organised activities is of compensation and deficit. This perception is reinforced by the threat of withdrawal of the opportunity card for those whose behaviour is unsatisfactory. Referral to the supportive and punitive public services which concentrate on 'problems' is the fall-back position for those who lose their cards in this way.

It can be argued that the realignment of practice language in policy documents is pushing into a subordinate and sometimes oppositional position the conceptual understanding of youth as a creative time of 'being' and any collective approach to youth which accompanies this. The universal right of access to public resources, where young people might find support to develop creative and critical understanding located in personal and social identity, appears to have been squeezed out of policy

Sport has been integral to 'supportive' work with young people

intentions towards them. This may pose a particular threat to facilities and practices which have previously been offered in terms of open access and voluntary participation.

Key points

- An alternative model of support sees youth as a time of 'being' and focuses on developing young people's creative potential.
- This model has been associated with open access leisure provision for young people.
- Since the 1960s one strand of this work has encouraged young people to critically engage with the conditions of their lives and has been concerned with issues of equality and power.
- It has been argued that recent youth policy has threatened this approach and has tended to redefine empowerment in commercialised terms and to reinstate a compensatory model of support.

5 Support as empowerment

In the youth work context, 'empowerment' has tended to have rather different associations than those that we identified in the extract from *Youth Matters*. Drawing on educational methodologies, it has seen youth work as a process of informal education. Tony Jeffs and Mark Smith argue that workers facilitate the informal education of young people through conversation and dialogue in the practice environment. Conversation pursued self-consciously by workers within the practice relationship is responsive to the everyday conditions of young people's lives and, through dialogue, seeks to extend knowledge and to provoke critical questioning of received reality (Smith, 1988, 1994; Jeffs and Smith, 1996). For Kerry Young (1999a, 1999b), informal educational interventions facilitate the development of a personal, moral philosophy and critical understanding. She identifies empowerment as the purpose of practice:

> when we think of empowerment as: 'supporting young people to understand and to act on the personal, social and political issues which affect their lives, the lives of others and the communities of which they are a part' (NYB 1990: 16), the suggestion is not only that young people be supported to oppose the external forces of oppression, but also, and importantly, that they have opportunities to examine the internal bridles and perceived powerlessness which underpin their sense of self and guide their actions in the world.
>
> (Young, 1999a, p. 88)

Interventions in this mould are not necessarily service specific. For example, they have been integral to holistic approaches to teaching, social work and probation, but as these services have been reorganised and become more rigidly formalised towards specific outcomes such as examination results, so the informal educational and empowering dimensions of support have devolved more completely to youth workers for whom this is the heart of their practice. Youth workers who conceptualise their profession in these terms attempt to offer facilities in which a set of relationships and an atmosphere can be created which encourage young people to relax, explore, challenge, question and learn with others.

The following example is from a mobile facility linked to a girls' school:

Youth worker (a):   I think the purpose of youth work is to – bring young people in – informal – educate them informally. But it's not just that. It's giving them freedom after school. Because at school ... they've got so many rules.

Although we have ground rules here, it's a little bit different. They can kind of be leaders themselves. And they can run schemes themselves, apply for funding, lead clubs, empower each other, we empower them. It's ... giving them more skills and what they want to do as well. Whereas at school they have to do the subjects. Here they can choose to come to the clubs. It's about choice ... And if they want to, they can get accredited. If they want. Everything is down to choice but we are here to support them and empower them in whatever they want to do.

Young woman: If you ever need help, and it doesn't have to be about getting out of the way of school and things like that, they are here. The youth mobile is here so that you can relax, and it's the basis of the student having a voice. Some teachers in the school are quite old fashioned and think that you are a student, you are here to learn, here to get an education and that's it. And then you come into the youth mobile and there's a whole different atmosphere. You're a person. You're a student, yes. But you are still someone. And they make that perfectly clear. That just because you look different, just because you act different, just because you are different in whatever, they always make sure you know that that's a good thing. That it's not a bad thing. It will boost your self-esteem and your confidence like nothing else.

(*EJ* Interviews, Location 5, 2005)

It is notable that most young people who use open access youth facilities value support which is non-specific and non-intrusive, which encourages them to pursue their skills and interests, and which responds conversationally to their questions and problems. Young people, including those defined as 'socially excluded', mainly think of themselves as 'normal' (MacDonald *et al.*, 2005). Like anyone else, they might encounter problems and difficulties in their lives, but this is normal. The type of help they seek is usually that which retains this sense of normality, which does not seek to label, pathologise or categorise them. As a trainee youth worker associated with the school based youth mobile project explained in relation to his own association with youth work:

My auntie died at a young age, and I was only about 14 or 15 and because I lived with her, she was like my mum, and I didn't come back to school. And one thing I can remember is [the youth project worker] ringing me. And that was the first person to ring. And that was the person who got me to come back into school and got me to get involved again. And so that's one point. I remember him.

(*EJ* Youth worker interview, Location 6, 2005)

The value of the phone call was in its humanity. The young person was approached from the perspective of human sympathy and it was because of this human contact that the later intervention around schooling was possible. When an intervention is designed only to address problems, it is possible to measure the outcome in terms of how far the problems were solved. Government has adopted this as a means of evidencing the impact of professional practice and thereby justifying public expenditure. In the example cited, the measurable outcome of the intervention was about schooling. However, that outcome could hardly have been achieved only in these terms.

In a short article designed to illustrate the difficulties of measuring the outcomes of creative intervention, Jeremy Brent (2004) described a piece of work which involved a group of young people building an arch as a centrepiece for a garden of remembrance. In this project, young people collaborated with the youth worker, with a sculptor and with each other to design, produce and communicate the nature of the arch. Empowerment in this situation was a collective process facilitating the expression of grief and deep feelings:

> One young man, whom I had seen self-anaesthetised with drink and drugs at the funeral of his brother (killed in a motorbike accident), was dripping sweat as he sawed through chunks of steel to give the arch the fruit of his effort. This was doing something, creating something, not just talking about it. It was the first time that I think he had properly grieved.
>
> (Brent, 2004, p. 71)

Brent is very sensitive about his approach as a worker in relation to this project:

> We could surmise the learning outcomes for the young people involved, but that feels almost sacrilegious. They were personal to them. I would not dream of asking them, let alone giving them a questionnaire to fill in ... The ... outcomes ... cannot be encompassed by any evaluation form.
>
> (Brent, 2004, pp. 71–2)

Here it is apparent that the interpersonal relationship which Brent as a practitioner had with the young people was prioritised over any formal conditions circumscribing his role and responsibilities as a professional worker. And yet he used this project, which he described as 'a powerful piece of youth work' (p. 71) to exemplify the best of his practice even while refusing the opportunity to delineate the learning and skills achieved. The importance of the practice was that a particular group of young people gained some agency, were supported to act on, rather than simply suffer, their grief (Thomson et al., 2002).

Professional workers can support young people in dealing with problems and issues without making their work problem orientated and by adopting empowering techniques. They often do so, as Brent did, from the viewpoint of relationship based knowledge about the individuals and groups concerned. It can be argued that government tends to approach young people differently, according to indices of deprivation or risk, as already or potentially a problem for themselves, their family and their communities.

Key points

- One strand of youth work has characterised it as a process of informal education, whose aim is to empower young people.

- This kind of work with young people is usually open access and avoids a problem orientated approach.

- It is difficult to assess the value of this kind of youth work within a framework of outcomes and evidence.

6 Targeting, specialisation and partnership

Given limited resources and the differences between groups and individuals, practice interventions in public and voluntary services have always been targeted and organisations have always to some extent offered specialist projects. Moreover, no public service has ever operated in a complete vacuum – there have always been cross-professional relationships. However, as Chapter 1 explored, in recent years moves towards policy driven and funding led targeting, specialisation and partnership have tended to shift decision-making power away from the imperatives of face-to-face practice, towards bureaucracies and organisational managers caught in a relationship with government in which organisational survival is tied to the delivery of outcomes. This binds face-to-face workers, within tight systems of accountability, to the targets contained in organisational plans. In this way, professional judgements are now constrained by explicit and externally defined boundaries rather than by responsiveness to the work in progress, as this social worker implied in an interview with Sarah Banks on the subject of professional ethics:

> A situation could happen like ... you've got ... little Johnny, for example [whom] you haven't seen for ages, and you've made an arrangement to go to McDonald's for tea and made arrangements to take him to the park and do something with him. And you know, it's important to him, he hasn't seen you for weeks. And then suddenly, child protection or something, somebody downstairs ... what's priority? Why should he be left? You know, you ring up and cancel. [And he thinks] 'well, I'm not important now,' because that's taken over ...
>
> (Quoted in Banks, 2004, p. 169)

Since targeting tends to favour short term initiatives, it can be argued that it undermines those workers who rely on long term relationship building to achieve their aims and objectives. In some cases, it appears that practitioners are struggling to reconcile their commitment to humanistic approaches with organisational directives. Here are two quotations from interviews with detached and outreach youth workers:

> The main issue would be [gaining] the infrastructure funding, you know, there are little pots of money around for say health and wellbeing, pregnancy, and all of this, but if you haven't got the infrastructure funding in place, then obviously your projects can't really run without that.
>
> [...]
>
> We are in the business of PR ... I don't lie, I don't say we've done this when we haven't. But if there's an audience there who don't give a damn about information on drugs or sexual health or whatever, but want to know what you've done about [something else] you kind of draw out what people want to hear ... So maybe one funder would have a concern about something, you would pull out the bits that relate to that to present to the funder.
>
> (Quoted in Crimmens *et al.*, 2004, p. 26)

If workers conform wholeheartedly to funding led targets then their power to prioritise on the basis of practice knowledge is forfeited. When they resist and attempt to continue with the approach which reflects their understanding of the practice situation, they must nevertheless represent the work in the required terms in order to maintain credibility. Such a process inevitably impacts on their own satisfaction with and understanding of what they are doing (Spence, 1996). Decisions about which young people need most attention, the priorities for relationship building and the nature of the help that might be offered to the young people in question are all affected. Moreover, in focusing attention on the objective problem or issue, attention is deflected from what might be other concerns in the young person's development.

An emphasis on targeting services can threaten the model of youth work as 'being there' for young people

The difficulties are faced mainly by workers who are attempting to work holistically in order to achieve particular outcomes, for the process of targeting is inevitably accompanied by a stress on the value of specialisation. The expertise which accompanies specialisation enables services to respond appropriately and effectively to issues relevant to young people and adds an extra dimension to the professional status of those who work with them. Specialist workers are more likely to work at the interface between different professions, to create inter-professional networks and to cross professional boundaries, than are generic workers within the professions. Thus a youth worker with a specialism in drugs or sexual health, might work closely with health professionals or might take a specialist youth work job within the health service in order to work with young people around drugs issues from a health perspective. Work targeted at issues clearly has a cross-disciplinary dimension and this is potentially a powerful position to inhabit in relation to the development of appropriate services.

However, the success of specialisation is predicated on the confident articulation of generic professional values and skills within each of the relevant professional disciplines. Creative partnerships between specialist workers from different disciplines depend on equality between workers, the mutual acknowledgement of the value of different discipline based knowledge and skill, and an equal commitment from different organisations to participate in the partnership arrangement (see the discussion of the complexities of multi-agency work in Chapter 1).

These conditions can seldom be met. Not only is there is inequality of resources, training and status between professions such as youth work and social work, but there is uneven commitment to the value of partnership working, made more difficult by competition to claim outcomes. For example, youth workers in the *Everyday Journey* project pointed out that, when they worked in partnership with schools, their efforts to support young school-refusers to return to the classroom resulted in improved outcomes for the school and were not credited to the youth project. Professional disciplines also work within different conditions and systems. So the structure of the police force means that police might be irregular and inconsistent in their attendance at partnership meetings, while social services might withdraw from interventions dealing with young people over the age of 16 (Coles, 2005).

Often the success of partnerships depends almost entirely on the goodwill of organisations and individuals involved and this is not always forthcoming. It has been suggested by some social workers and teachers that youth workers are not keen on partnership working and that they can be 'precious' about their interventions and relationships with young people (Crimmens *et al.*, 2004). Perhaps this derives from their preferred method of working holistically through negotiated relationships with young people, exacerbated by a consciousness that the professional status of their practice remains a subject of contention. Perhaps it is related to their perceived loss of autonomy in the current climate of practice.

Key point

- It can be argued that an increasing emphasis on targeting, specialisation and partnership undermines practitioners' capacity to be responsive to young people's needs, and challenges practitioners' autonomy and values.

7 Worker support

Dissatisfaction with the conditions of professional practice is a recurring theme in research with workers. They inhabit a world of uncertainty in which relationships between workers and young people have been decentred in favour of relationships between workers and their employing organisation. This impacts on both the nature of the contact with young people and the quality and type of help that can be offered. This has not gone unnoticed by some young people:

Kim: Over the years this place has changed the [project name] as well, I can't think of how to describe it without saying paperwork 50 times.

... It's like you come in and you expect things to be happening, like it used to, and they are just all sitting at computers and talking about paperwork.

(*EJ* Young People's Focus Group d, 2005)

It is no accident that as the shift has occurred, so too the language of support has gained greater currency with reference to the wellbeing and professional development of workers rather than young people. Relationships and help are a matter for human resource management from the perspective of the organisation:

Line managers are one source of support for you at work. They can give clear feedback on your work and help you to develop realistic work programmes and time management systems. The work we do is sometimes stressful. The supervisor needs to understand your stressors and offer appropriate assistance. This might mean giving you uninterrupted time and space to talk, sending you home to sleep, or insisting that you take the risk of trying a new piece of work.

(Turnbull, 2001, pp. 240–1)

It is possible that the stress identified arises partly from the divergent principles through which workers are attempting to support young people. At a formal level, they are being denied opportunities to develop supportive approaches which build on their experiential understanding of the needs and interests of young people, in favour of more contrived interventions in which organisational priorities, and the terms of reference for support, are predetermined. Workers are constrained to work within organisational policy, while at the same time continuing to attempt to build constructive relationships with young people as a means of winning their participation and voluntary consent. Where the young people inhabit an oppositional culture, are 'disaffected' or are involved in offending behaviour – and, after all, these are among the principal young people targeted for intervention – this can be particularly tense for workers.

Intensive targeting of young people with problematic behaviour patterns leads to a concentrated level of behavioural difficulty in groups. Attention is almost inevitably going to be given to problematic rather than positive behaviour in these circumstances. Working with targeted groups requires high levels of skill and a high staff–young person ratio, using methods which are focused on the behavioural problems. It is seldom acknowledged in the literature that targeted, specialised and partnership approaches might be undermining the efforts of workers to offer support to young people in a manner which is meaningful from within their own professional perspective. It is also seldom observed that under the direction of organisational priorities, they have sometimes been placed at the centre of an irreconcilable set of demands which they are required to manage as individuals, and that this undermines their professional confidence and job satisfaction.

Key points

- Many of those working with young people express dissatisfaction with the current conditions of professional practice.
- Changing policy priorities have increased levels of stress among workers and have impacted on the quality of relationships with young people.

Conclusion

Offering support to young people is and has always been intrinsic to the professional practice of those who work with them. However, this chapter has argued that such support is devised within a matrix of different interests. Practitioners must be aware of and respond to those different interests in order to sustain their work, and this is an ongoing task which shifts and changes according to the political and social forces impacting on organisations at any given moment. Political decision making which impacts on national and organisational policy making is particularly important in constructing the framework within which practice operates. The more clarity the government has about its aims and intentions for young people, the more public services or voluntary organisations dependent on government funding will be drawn into delivering those political aims. In a climate of close scrutiny of public expenditure, it is inevitable that the terms in which work with the young is undertaken will be managed more closely. Closer monitoring of professional practice means that support can no longer be self-evidently inscribed within practice. It is now a key feature of policy and, as such, it has gained explicit dimensions which are particularly orientated towards youth problems and the problems of young people in relation to contemporary issues of transition.

The move to a more explicit articulation of the meaning of support has sometimes been welcomed as offering professional workers opportunities to demonstrate the effectiveness of their practice interventions. However, for some it has shifted the locus of practice away from the face-to-face relationships with young people and towards the systems and power structures of employing organisations which are charged with delivering policy. This has created dilemmas, conflicts and tensions in some practice situations, as well as increasing workloads. No matter how workers strive to meet government targets, increase their specialist skills and organise partnership approaches to effectively support identified groups of young people around specific issues, it remains essential to construct working relationships with the young people in question in order to exert any influence. Many workers understand the creation of such relationships as the key to effective practice within a holistic approach.

Stress for workers arises from the difficulty of meeting targets without constructing relationships, from the difficulties of creating relationships within systems devised for objective professional approaches, and from the fact that the value of relational work is seldom recognised within the terms of evaluation. This is exacerbated by the underlying reality that the issues which are identified as problematic for young people, or in relation to youth in general, are often caused by social and economic forces which it can never be within a worker's remit to address.

The last word on support might follow the sentiments of youth workers who decided to enter that profession because of their own experiences as young people:

Lana: I know from my own experience of participating as a young person in youth work projects and stuff, that for me it was very much to do with being around other young people, and having adults around who were really good role models, who were enthusiastic about what they were doing. It was about just the chance to do something that was enjoyable and learn a lot more about yourself and build confidence. And I think confidence was a big part of it as well – just becoming confident in who you were as a person and how you relate to other people. And I did a lot of dance and community arts stuff and for me, being able to develop my skills in that was, as well, another thing that I really enjoyed. And being able to speak out; and being told that you had the right to speak out about issues that were affecting you, and to get the space for that. And to have, you know, people respect that as well, as you know, you weren't just given the space, but people were actually there saying, 'We value what you are actually saying, and we appreciate it and we want to do something about it.'

Sharon: It's like a testing ground for real life as well. You can go on and have a go, if you, in my experience, if you think you might be able to do these things and maybe in a youth work environment, it provides you with a safe space for you to have a go at doing it, to see if you can. With the support of other young people and adults as well.

Jim: There's a level of excitement about it all as well. People get to do something extraordinary, like trying to get a skateboard park set up. You know, it's exciting. It's doing something big and real.

Sharon: It's changing.

(EJ Workers' Focus Group a, 2005)

Ultimately, practice designed to support young people can never solve all the social problems associated with youth. What it can do is make the lives of some young people easier and happier, widen their opportunities for learning, help them address problems and issues as they emerge and encourage them in their efforts to gain agency in their own worlds.

References

An Everyday Journey: Discovering the Meaning and Value in Youth Work (2004–2006) unpublished research project, Durham University/Weston Spirit.
[Spence, J., Devanney, C., Noonan, K. and Thexton, W. (2007, forthcoming) *Every Day is Different*, report of the research project *An Everyday Journey: Discovering the Meaning and Value in Youth Work*, Leicester, National Youth Agency.]

Banks, S. (2004) *Ethics, Accountability and the Social Professions*, Basingstoke, Palgrave Macmillan.

Brent, J. (2004) 'Communicating what youth work achieves: the smile and the arch', *Youth and Policy*, no. 84, pp. 69–73.

Carpenter, V. and Young, K. (1986) *Coming In From the Margins: Youth Work with Girls and Young Women*, Leicester, National Association of Youth Clubs.

Coles, B. (1995) *Youth and Social Policy: Youth, Citizenship and Young Carers*, London, UCL Press.

Coles, B. (2005) 'Youth policy 1995–2005: from *Best Start* to *Youth Matters*', *Youth and Policy*, no. 89, pp. 7–20.

Crimmens, D., Factor, F., Jeffs, T., Pitts, J., Pugh, C., Spence, J. and Turner, P. (2004) *Reaching Socially Excluded Young People: A National Study of Street-Based Youth Work*, Leicester, National Youth Agency for the Joseph Rowntree Foundation.

Davies, B. and Gibson, A. (1967) *The Social Education of the Adolescent*, London, University of London Press.

DfEE (Department for Education and Employment) (2000a) *Connexions: The Best Start in Life for Every Young Person*, Nottingham, Department for Education and Employment.

DfEE (Department for Education and Employment) (2000b) *The Connexions Service: Prospectus and Specification*, Nottingham, Department for Education and Employment.

DfEE (Department for Education and Employment) (2001) *Transforming Youth Work: Developing Youth Work for Young People*, Nottingham, Department for Education and Employment/Connexions.

DfES (Department for Education and Skills) (2003) *Every Child Matters*, Cm 5860, Norwich, The Stationery Office.

DfES (Department for Education and Skills) (2005) *Youth Matters*, Cm 6629, Norwich, The Stationery Office.

Eager, W.M. (1953) *Making Men: Being a History of Boys' Clubs and Related Movements in Great Britain*, London, University of London Press.

Eisenstadt, S.N. (1956) *From Generation to Generation: Age Groups and Social Structure*, New York, The Free Press.

Freeman, F.L. (1904) *Religious and Social Work Amongst Girls*, London, Skeffington & Sons.

Furlong, A. and Cartmel, A. (1997) *Young People and Social Change: Individualization and Risk in Late Modernity*, Buckingham, Open University Press.

Gillis, J.R. (1981) *Youth and History: Tradition and Change in European Age Relations 1770–Present*, London, Academic Press.

Greene, S. (2003/4) 'Deconstructing the "unplanned" pregnancy: social exclusion and sexual health strategies in Scotland', *Youth and Policy*, no. 82, pp. 27–46.

Holman, B. (2000) *Kids At The Door Revisited*, Lyme Regis, Russell House.

Holmes, J. (2004) 'Inside Connexions', *Youth and Policy*, no. 83, pp. 30–42.

Jamdagni, L. (1980) *Hamari Rangily Zindagi: Our Colourful Lives*, Leicester, National Association of Youth Clubs.

Jeal, T. (1989) *Baden-Powell*, London, Pimlico.

Jeffs, T. and Smith, M. (1996) *Informal Education: Conversation, Democracy and Learning*, Derby, Education Now Publishing Co-operative.

Jeffs, T. and Smith, M. (1998/9) 'The problem of "youth" for youth work', *Youth and Policy*, no. 62, pp. 45–66.

Jeffs, T. and Smith, M. (2006) 'Where is *Youth Matters* taking us?', *Youth and Policy*, no. 91, pp. 23–40.

Johnston, L., MacDonald, R., Mason, P., Ridley, L. and Webster, C. (2000) *Snakes and Ladders: Young People, Transitions and Social Exclusion*, York, Joseph Rowntree Foundation.

Levy, N. (undated) *The West Central Story and its Founders*, Papers in Lily Montagu Archive, Jewish Museum, Finchley, London.

MacDonald, R. (ed.) (1997) *Youth, the 'Underclass' and Social Exclusion*, London, Routledge.

MacDonald, R. and Marsh, J. (2005) *Disconnected Youth? Growing Up in Britain's Poor Neighbourhoods*, Basingstoke, Palgrave.

MacDonald, R., Shildrick, T., Webster, C. and Simpson, D. (2005) 'Growing up in poor neighbourhoods: the significance of class and place in the extended transitions of "socially excluded" young adults', *Sociology*, vol. 39, no. 5, pp. 873–92.

Measor, L. and Squires, P. (2000) *Young People and Community Safety: Inclusion, Risk, Tolerance and Disorder*, Aldershot, Ashgate.

Melrose, M. (2001) 'Young people sexually exploited through prostitution' in Factor, F., Chauhan, V. and Pitts, J. (eds) *The RHP Companion to Working with Young People*, Lyme Regis, Russell House.

Ministry of Education (1960) *The Youth Service in England and Wales* (Albemarle Report), London, HMSO.

National Youth Agency (2001) *Ethical Conduct in Youth Work: A Statement of Values and Principles from the National Youth Agency*, Leicester, National Youth Agency.

NYB (National Youth Bureau) (1990) *Towards a Core Curriculum – The Next Step: Report of the Second Ministerial Conference*, Leicester, National Youth Bureau.

Parmar, P. (1988) 'Gender, race and power: the challenge to youth work practice' in Cohen, P. and Bains, H.S. (eds) *Multi-Racist Britain*, Basingstoke, Macmillan.

Pitts, J. (2003) *The New Politics of Youth Crime: Discipline or Solidarity?* (2nd edn), Lyme Regis, Russell House.

Robb, M. (2007) 'Gender' in Kehily, M.J. (ed.) *Understanding Youth: Perspectives, Identities and Practices*, London, Sage/The Open University (Course Book).

Russell, C.E.B. and Rigby, L.M. (1908) *Working Lads' Clubs*, London, Macmillan.

Smith, M. (1988) *Developing Youth Work*, Milton Keynes, Open University Press.

Smith, M.K. (1994) *Local Education: Community, Conversation, Praxis*, Buckingham, Open University Press.

Spence, J. (1996) 'Feminism in work with girls and women', *Youth and Policy*, no. 52, pp. 38–53.

Spence, J. (2001a) 'Edwardian boys and labour in the east end of Sunderland: welfare and work' in Gilchrist, R., Jeffs, T. and Spence, J. (eds) *Essays in the History of Community and Youth Work*, Leicester, Youth Work Press.

Spence, J. (2001b) 'The impact of the First World War on the development of youth work: the case of the Sunderland Waifs' Rescue Agency and Street Vendors' Club' in Gilchrist, R., Jeffs, T. and Spence, J. (eds) *Essays in the History of Community and Youth Work*, Leicester, Youth Work Press.

Spence, J. (2001c) 'Activities' in Richardson, L.D. and Wolfe, M. (eds) *Principles and Practice of Informal Education: Learning Through Life*, London, RoutledgeFalmer.

Stanley, M. (1985 [1890]) 'Clubs for working girls' in Booton, F. (ed.) *Studies in Social Education, Vol. 1, 1860–1890*, Hove, Benfield Press.

Thomas, T. (2005) 'The continuing story of the ASBO', *Youth and Policy*, no. 87, pp. 15–28.

Thomson, R. (2007a) 'A biographical perspective' in Kehily, M.J. (ed.) *Understanding Youth: Perspectives, Identities and Practices*, London, Sage/The Open University (Course Book).

Thomson, R. (2007b) 'Working' Kehily, M.J. (ed.) *Understanding Youth: Perspectives, Identities and Practices*, London, Sage/The Open University (Course Book).

Thomson, R., Bell, R., Holland, J., Henderson, S., McGrellis, S. and Sharpe, S. (2002) 'Critical moments: choice, chance and opportunity in young people's narratives of transition', *Sociology*, vol. 36, no. 2, pp. 335–54.

Turnbull, A. (2001) 'Using line management' in Richardson, L.D. and Wolfe, M. (eds) *Principles and Practice of Informal Education: Learning Through Life*, London, RoutledgeFalmer.

Urwick, E.J. (ed.) (1904) *Studies of Boy Life in Our Cities*, London, J.M. Dent & Co.

Wallace, C. and Cross, M. (eds) (1990) *Youth in Transition: The Sociology of Youth and Youth Policy*, London, Falmer.

Williamson, H. (2002) 'A Welsh perspective' in Roberts, K. (ed.) *Social Inclusion: Policy and Practice*, Stourbridge, Institute of Careers Guidance.

Wylie, T. (2004) 'How Connexions came to terms with youth work', *Youth and Policy*, no. 83, pp. 19–29.

Young, K. (1999a) 'The youth worker as guide, philosopher and friend' in Banks, S. (ed.) *Ethical Issues in Youth Work*, London, Routledge.

Young, K. (1999b) *The Art of Youth Work*, Lyme Regis, Russell House.

Youth Justice Board (2006), www.youth-justice-board.gov.uk [accessed 10/10/06].

Acknowledgements

Text

Pages 67–68: Kehily, M.J. (2002) *Sexuality Gender and Schooling: Shifting Agendas in Social Learning,* RoutledgeFalmer; pages 72–73: Batmanghelidjh, C. (2004) 'Working with vulnerable children and the importance of relationships and loving care', in Blake, S. and Francis, G. (eds) *Spotlight,* Issue 2, March 2004. Reproduced with kind permission of the National Children's Bureau; pages 94-96: Kirby, P., Lanyon, C., Cronin, K., and Sinclair, R. (2003) *Building a Culture of Participation, Research Report,* Department for Education and Skills 2003. Crown copyright material is reproduced under Class Licence Number C01W0000065 with the permission of the Controller of HMSO and the Queen's Printer for Scotland; page 107: BBC (2005), *Parents-know-best view 'outdated',* BBC News at bbc.co.uk/news; page 162: Canaan J.E. (2005) *Recognising the Need and Possibilities for Teaching Critical Hope in HE Today;* pages 168-172: Kehily, M.J. (2002) *'Sexing the Subject', Sexuality, Sex, Gender and Schooling: Shifting Agendas in Social Learning,* RoutledgeFalmer; pages 175-176: Kehily, M.J. and Pattman, R. (2006) 'Middle-class struggle? Identity-work and leisure among sixth formers in the United Kingdom', in *British Journal of Sociology of Education,* February 2006, vol. 27, no. 1, pp.40–43, Routledge. Reprinted by permission of Taylor & Francis Ltd http://www.tandf.co.uk/journals.

Illustrations

Page 20: © Lambton Street Fellowship Centre; page 23: © PA/PA/EMPICS; page 36: Copyright © Paul Box /reportdigital.co.uk; page 43: Copyright © Jess Hurd/reportdigital.co.uk; page 57: Dennis MacDonald/Alamy; page 92: Image by courtesy of ICA: UK (www.ica-uk.org.uk); page 101: Image courtesy of Citizenship Foundation; page 108: © Empics; page 130: © Harry Kerr/BIPs/Getty Images; page 130: © Jiri Rezac/Alamy; page 160: © Mary Evans Picture Library; page 179: Reproduced with kind permission of Milton Keynes Christian Foundation; page 191: Reproduced by permission www.paddydoyle.com; page 224: © John Powell Photographer/Alamy; page 236: © Joanne O'Brien/Photofusion; page 242: © Photofusion Picture Library/Alamy; page 243: © EGON/Alamy; page 265: Taken from http://www.childline.org.uk/extra/reports-canitalk.asp; page 272: © Getty Images; page 296: © PA/PA/EMPICS; page 306: © Rex Features; page 311: © John Birdsall/ www.JohnBirdsall.co.uk.

Index

Abrams, Philip 129

accountability
  and practice 55
  and target setting 26, 27, 28-9

Adams, R. 62-3

adolescence, ideas on the nature of 185-6, 198, 298-9

adulthood, transition to 10, 269-73, 292-5

advocacy services 273-4

agency of young people 70, 269-70, 271

Ahmad, Y. 37, 38

Albemarle Report (1960) 302

Alcock, Pete 199

Alldred, Pam 174

anti-oppressive practice (AOP) 64

anti-social behaviour
  preventative interventions 18
    historical examples of 21

Anti-Social Behaviour Orders (ASBOs) 24, 70, 230-1, 233, 293

AOP (anti-oppressive practice) 64

ASBOs (Anti-Social Behaviour Orders) 24, 70, 230-1, 233, 293

Asthana, S. 47-8

asylum seekers, unaccompanied minors 272-3

Atherton, James 190-1

attachment theory, and resilience 276

autonomy
  of teachers 165
  of young people 70

Axon, Sue 106-8

balkanisation, in education 165

Banks, Sarah 28, 30, 32, 310

Barnardo's 102, 241, 271

Barnett, Lesley 244

Bartlett, K. 91

batch living, in institutions 189, 190, 209

Batmanghelidjh, Camilla 76-7, 202-3

Beck, Ulrich 40, 73, 227

behaviour management, in residential care 209-10

Bethnal Green, study of family and kinship in 128-9, 130, 150

Big Brother 103

binary management, in institutions 189, 191, 203, 205

biographical perspective
  on professionals 36-7
  on teachers 165-6
  and the use of self 66-9
  on youth 6, 8

Black Report (1979) 192

Blunkett, David 100

Booton, Frank 21, 22

boredom, and memories of school 160

boundaries 5, 9, 55, 73-7
  encounters 76
  exchange 76-7
  and lead professionals 47
  and reflective practice 79
  and support 290
  and transitions to adulthood 271-2

boys
  peer popularity in school 175-6
  in reformatory and training schools 189, 197
  and sexual learning in schools 170-1

Bradford, Simon 29, 235

Brechin, Ann 83

Brent, Jeremy 309
British Association of Social Workers, Code of Ethics 64
British Youth Council 102
Brown, Gordon 100
Bulger, James 23, 230
bullying 264
Butt, R. 224
Byrne, David 134-5

Cambridge Association for the Care of Girls 21
CAMHS (child and adolescent mental health) multi-agency team 43-4
Canaan, Joyce 161-3
Care Standards Act (2000) 34, 205
Carnegie UK Trust/Carnegie Young People Initiative 91, 115
Caws, Frank 19-20
Cawson, Pat 258-9, 260, 274, 275, 279
changing experience of youth 5-6
Cherrygrove Intensive Support Unit 202, 204, 210
child abuse
  and help seeking 263-4
  in residential care 205, 208, 274
  and risk 252
  studies of abuse and neglect 258-60
  see also child protection
child poverty 132
child protection 23, 253-62
  changing discourses of 254-8
  and multi-agency working 42
  and participation rights 106, 114, 118
  and partnerships 42
  and prostitution 271, 272
ChildLine 265-6
Children Act (1989) 112, 192, 193, 255

Children Act (2004) 37, 112, 254
Children (Northern Ireland) Order (1995) 192, 193, 194
Children and Young Persons Act (1933) 22
Children and Young Persons Act (1969) 22
children's rights 41
Children's Rights Alliance 102
Children's Rights Commissioners 112, 113-15
Children's Rights Director for England 37
citizenship 100-5
  young people and voting rights 101-3
citizenship education 101, 102, 103
Citizenship Foundation 101, 104
civil disobedience 100, 118
civility, and boundaries 76, 77
Clarke, Charles 162
Clarke, Michèle 210
class
  and education 156, 159-60
    young people's experiences of school 174-7
  and individualisation 156
  and professionalism 35
  and risk 220
  and the social structural model of support 296-7
  and teenage pregnancy 180
  see also working class
Cleaver, Francis 89
Cleaver, Hedy 260
Climbié, Victoria 42, 44, 98-9, 255, 257, 260-1
Cohen, Anthony 127
Coleman, S. 103
Coles, Bob 232
collective support 302
Colton, Matthew 206-7
Colwell, Maria 260

communication, and multi-agency working 44-5

communities
anthropological approach to 127
breakdown of 130-1
defining 127-8
ethnographic studies of 128-9
and neighbourhood 7, 8, 124, 126, 127-31
and practice 135-6
and participation 89, 91

communities of practice 46-7

Communities That Care 238

community action 136

community care 128

community development projects 136

Community Safety Orders 232

community workers, and neighbourhood practice 141-3

comparative perspective on youth 6

competence, and skills 62-3

confidentiality
young people and help seeking 265-9
young people's rights to 106-9, 267

conflict of values 64-5

Connexions 10, 69, 97, 243, 244, 288, 290-1, 293

consultation
and power relationships 40-1
young people and poor experiences of 18

content knowledge 57

Convery, U. 194

Cooper, Andrew 269

Craig, Sarah 206, 208

creative intervention 309

Crick, Bernard 101

Crime and Disorder Act (1998) 23, 230

crime prevention, Positive Steps case study 17-18

criminal behaviour
young people at risk of violent crime 145
youth crime 133
and youth justice policy 22-4

Criminal Justice Act (1991) 23

Criminal Justice Act (2003) 233

Crimmens, D. 311

critical incidents, and reflective practice 79-80

critical practice 6, 7, 53, 83, 84

critical reflection/reflexivity 82, 83

cultural perspective on youth 6

curfews, and young people's risky behaviour 224-5, 229, 231, 232

custody
and residential care 211-13
young people in prison 186

Dalrymple, Jane 265, 274

Davies, B. 137, 151-2

Davis, J. 40

decision-making
and practice 54-5
and young people in residential care 202-3, 210
young people's involvement in 69-70, 90, 93, 94

defensive teaching 167

democracy
and institutional care 200
and participation 89, 100-5, 109

deprofessionalisation 35-6, 61

Deptford Green Secondary School, London 94-5

detraditionalisation 40, 70

Devanney, C. 16

Deverell, Katie 34

dialogic approach, and evidence based practice 60, 61

Dickens, S. 242

disabled young people 260, 274

  and lead professionals 47-8

Dispersal Orders 70, 231

diversionary intervention 233-40

  emphasising the positive 239-40

  factors contributing to risky behaviour 234-5

  and the 'vulnerability' model 235-6

domestic violence 132-3, 259, 260

drugs (illegal)

  drugs cultures in schools 158

  drugs prevention programmes in rural areas 145-6

  and risk taking 127, 226

Dumfries and Galloway Youth Strategy Executive Group 95-6, 96-7

Dumigan, Liam 201, 202, 203, 204, 206, 211

Duncan, Sylvia 44-5

Eager, W.M. 297

EBP (evidence based practice) 58-61, 63

Eby, Maureen 81

education 155-81

  alternative sites for learning 178-80

  and deprived neighbourhoods 148

  higher education 155, 160-3, 176-7

  marketisation in 165, 173-4

  and pedagogic practice 167-77

  in a post-industrial economy 155, 156, 157-63, 178

  and residential care 198-9

  and support 289

  see also schools; teachers

educational settings 8

effective practice, demonstrating 18

empiricism, and evidence based practice 59

employment

  and education 157

  and risk 219-20

  youth job market 133

empowerment

  and safeguarding 273-4

  and support 288, 289, 290, 304-5, 306-10

encounters 76, 77

English Children's Rights Commissioner 113

Ennew, Judith 91-2

epistemology

  and practice 58

  and reflexivity 82

ethic of reciprocity 70-1, 73

ethics

  of practitioners 32

  and target setting 26, 30-1

ethics of care 30

ethnicity

  and advocacy services 274

  Black writers and anti-oppressive practice 31

  and help seeking 264

  and masculinities in school 176

  and support 303

  and young people's perspective on neighbourhood 147

EUROARRCC (European Association for Research into Residential Childcare) 185, 197, 202, 203, 210

Evans, Helen 263

Every Child Matters report 98-9, 254, 255, 256, 267, 291

Everyday Journey research project 28, 29, 287-8, 294, 295, 299, 300, 301, 302, 308, 312, 313, 316

evidence based practice (EBP) 58-61, 63

exchange 76-7

experience, and expertise 69-73

expert knowledge
   and institutional care 202
   and interpersonal skills 37, 38, 47-8
   postmodern challenge to 70
   and reciprocity in relationships 73
expertise, and experience 69-73

Farrington, David 234
Featherstone, Brid 45, 263
feminist perspective on social work 31
Ferguson, Harry 260
Finlay, Linda 32
Fixed Penalty Notices 231-2
Fook, Jan 82
Forrest, R. 130
foster care 191, 196, 197, 204, 206-7
Foucault, Michel 8, 209, 211
   Discipline and Punish 196-7
   on governmentality 225-6, 258
Foundation for Parents project 179-80
Foyer Federation 243
Fraser, Derek 198
freedom of association, young people's
right to 106, 110-11
Freire, Paolo 31
friendship, and support 297, 300
Frost, N. 46, 47
Fry, Margery 198

Galvin, R. 227
Garrett, Paul Michael 257-8
gender
   cult of heterosexual masculinity 185-6
   female staff at Glenmona Resource Centre
   193-4
   and help seeking 264
   and the life course model of support 298
   and peer popularity in schools 175, 176

   and professionalism 35
   and resilience 278, 279
   and sexual learning in schools 169-71
   teachers and pedagogic practices 168
   young people and participatory projects
   116
Gibbs, J. 261
Giddens, Anthony 40, 69, 211
Gilchrist, Ruth 19, 22
Gilligan, Robbie 276, 277, 279
girls
   and help seeking 264
   peer popularity in school 175
   in residential care 212
   and sexual learning in schools 169-70,
   171, 172
   working class 157
   see also teenage pregnancy
Glenmona Resource Centre 8, 187, 212
   age of admissions 201
   reasons for referral to 192-3
   rights and young people in 195, 208
   Slemish House mission statement 195
   staff 193-4, 203, 204-5
   transmutation from St Patrick's Training
   School 193-4
globalisation
   and education 156, 165
   and institutional care 200
Goddard, Chris 261
Goffman, Erving 189, 190, 196, 203, 205,
213-14
Goodson, Ivor 36-7
Government Advisory Group on Citizenship
101
government policies
   and neighbourhood 131-5
   and participation 98-105

and partnerships 42-3
and practitioners 15, 16-17
    challenges from 31-2
    priorities 9
    'Respect' agenda 145
    on risks posed by young people 228-33
        and retributive justice 230-3
    target setting 25-8
    and teenage mothers 244-5
    and transition 292
    youth justice 22-4
governmentality 197
    and risk 225-6, 258
Graham, Gay 204
Green, David 94
Griffin, Christine 185

Hall, Granville Stanley 185-6
Hall, T. 270
Hallett, Christine 263
Halliday, J. 47-8
Hargreaves, Andy 165
Hargreaves, David 164
harm
    and help seeking 262-4
    safeguarding and protecting against 253-62
Harris, Jose 197, 198
Harris, Phil 199
Hart, R. 93
Havell, Cathy 243
health
    in deprived neighbourhoods 149
    and the moralisation of risk 227
Health Action Zones 244
Healy, Karen 35
HEFCE (Higher Education Funding Council) 160-1
Henderson, S. 145-6

Henrick, Harry 230
Hester, Marianne 259
heterosexual masculinity, cult of 185-6
Hetherington, Rachel 269
hidden curriculum 171-2
higher education 155, 160-3
historical perspective
    on institutions 186, 187-200, 201
    on practitioners 19-25
    on support and transition 295-302
HIV infection, and risk 220, 221, 222
HIV prevention outreach workers, and professionalism 34
Holland, Janet 40, 70-1
homelessness
    and domestic violence 259
    as a risk 148, 241-3, 252
housing, in deprived neighbourhoods 148
Hudson, Bob 272
human rights, and participation 91, 105-6, 109-11
Human Rights Act (1998) 239
hybrid services 10

identities
    and community 129, 131
    and neighbourhood 123
    and reciprocity 71
    of teachers 166, 168, 173
    university students 163
    and values 65
    see also professional identities
illegal drugs see drugs (illegal)
individual support 302-3
Individual Support Orders (ISOs) 233
individualisation 73
    and class 156

and education 177

individualism
  and reflection 81, 82
  and teachers 165

industrial schools 188-9, 197, 198, 201

industrialisation, and the origins of youth work 19-20

informal education 173
  and target setting 27
  youth work as 20, 136, 306

inmate role, in institutions 189

institutional narcissism 74

institutions 8-9, 185-214
  concept of a total institution 189-91
  EUROARRCC research on 185, 197, 202, 203, 210
  forms of surveillance in 196-200
  history of 186, 187-200, 201
    size and structure 198-9
    and the welfare/justice dilemma 191-5
    and youth justice 188-9, 191-3, 199-200
  practice in residential care 186, 213-14
  staff in 193-4, 203, 204-5, 209-10, 212-13
  young people in residential care
    care or custody 211-13
    and participation 210-11
    person-centred environments 205-7
    rights of 195, 207-10
  see also Glenmona Resource Centre

instrumental accountability 29

Intensive Support Units 201-2, 204

inter-agency collaboration 5
  and safeguarding 256, 267, 271

inter-agency learning 45-7

inter-professionalism 42-8

interdisciplinary approach 6, 9

interpersonal skills, and expert knowledge 37, 38, 47-8

interpretative approach
  and evidence based practice 60, 61
  and the use of self 66

intimacy, and boundaries 76, 77

Inventing Adulthoods 144-5

Irish Association of Young People in Care (IAYPIC) 208, 210

ISOs (Individual Support Orders) 233

Jack, Gordon 238, 255, 258

Jamdagni, L. 303

Jeffs, Tony 22, 224-5, 299, 306

Johnson, Kurt 241

Joseph Rowntree Foundation 29

Kearns, A. 130

Keeping Us Safe: Report of the Safeguarding Vulnerable Children Review 257

Kehily, Mary Jane 67-8, 73, 180

Kempe, Henry 254

Kennedy, Margaret 260

Kids Company 74-6

Kirby, P. 96, 97-8

knowledge
  and practice 53, 56, 57-61, 80
  and professionalism 61
  see also expert knowledge

knowledge economy 162

labour market
  and risk 219-20
  and transition 292

Laming report (2003) 42, 44, 255

lead professionals 47-8
  and protection 256

leadership roles, and support 298, 301

life course model, of support and transition 297-8

Listening to Children and Young People project 37

Little, M. 238

loving care, and boundaries 74-6

Lymbery, Mark 31

Mac an Ghaill, Mairtin 165

MacDonald, Robert 150

MacLeod, Mary 262, 265-6, 274

MacLure, Maggie 166

McRobbie, Angela 157

managerialism 35

  and evidence based practice 60

  in schools 165, 169

marketisation, in education 165, 173-4

Marsh, S. 117

Marxism, and radical social work 31

masculinity, cult of heterosexual 185-6

Mayo, Marjorie 128

Meagher, Gabrielle 35

media

  and practitioners 16-17

  and young people's riskiness 223-4

mental health services, and the transition to adulthood 272

Midlands region, and economic change 156

migration, and neighbourhood 126

Milton Keynes, study of young people's rights in 110-11

Milton Keynes Christian Foundation 179-80

Misztal, Barbara 76-7, 109, 200

mobility, and neighbourhood 126

money problems, and risk 222

Montagu, Lily 297

Montgomery, Heather 270, 272-3, 278

Moorehead, Mandy 201-2, 204, 206

moral panics

  and neighbourhood practice 146

and risky behaviour in young people 230

Morgan, R. 37

Morse, M. 138, 140, 141, 142

motherhood *see* teenage pregnancy

Mount, K. 238

multi-agency working 42, 43-5

  Safe in the City scheme 242

  and targeted support 310-13

Muncie, John 193, 199

Murray, Cathy 264, 265

mutuality 70-1, 83

National Association of Youth Clubs 140, 142

National Curriculum 155, 156, 164

national occupational standards (NOS) 61-3

National Strategy for Neighbourhood Renewal, *Children and Young People* 148-9

Nayak, Anoop 146-7

NEETs (young people not in education, employment or training) 236-7, 292

neighbourhood 7-8, 123-54

  and community 7, 8, 124, 126, 127-31, 135-6

  defining characteristics of youth work 151-2

  emergence of 130-1

  experiencing 125-6

  and migration 126

  and mobility 126

  poor neighbourhoods 131-5, 148-50

  and social policy 131-5

  street based youth work 151

  young people's experience of 144-50

neighbourhood practice 135-44

  aims of 143-4

  community workers 141-3

  and moral panics 146

  unattached young people 139-41, 143

Neighbourhood Support Fund 236, 237

neoliberalism

and the moralisation of risk 226-7

and university education 161

Newman, Janet 35-6

Nil by Mouth project 104

No More Excuses (Home Office) 23

Northern Ireland

Children's Rights Commissioners 112, 113

Include Youth organisation 204

Intensive Support Units 201-2, 204

Rathgael Juvenile Justice Centre 209-10, 212

Voice of Young People in Care (VOYPIC) 204, 207, 210

young people in residential care 201-13

youth justice system 188-9, 191-3

see also Glenmona Resource Centre

Norwegian Ombudsman 114

NOS (national occupational standards) 61-3

NSPCC (National Society for the Prevention of Cruelty to Children)

study of maltreatment 259, 263

Young People's Centres 268

Nutley, Sandra 35-6

occupational cultures, of teachers 164, 165

Ombudsmen, Children's 113-15

outcomes, and targets 29

Overing, Joanna 127

parental responsibility

and residential care 193, 211

Glenmona Resource Centre 195

parental rights, versus young people's rights to confidentiality 106-9

Parenting Orders 24, 230

parents, and practice 54-5

participation 7, 40-1, 72, 89-120

in action 94-7

benefits of 97-8

and citizenship 100-5

defining features of 90-2

and differences between young people 116

and empowerment 91, 100, 115, 116-17

and government policies 98-105

key legislation 105-13

'ladder' of 92

limits of 115-17

and power relationships 40-1

and the public/private divide 91-2, 109

types of 92-3

and young people at risk 238-9, 240-6

and young people in residential care 210-11

see also rights and young people

partnerships

and inter-professionalism 42-8

and protection 7

and targeted support 310-13

Parton, Nigel 254, 257, 260

Peabody Trust and Centre Point, Safe in the City scheme 242-3

performance measurement *see* target setting

personal values, and practice 63, 64

Pitts, John 22-3

policies *see* government policies

political campaigns, young people's participation in 100

political values, and practice 63, 64

Positive Futures 293

Positive Steps case study 17-18

positivism, and evidence based practice 58, 59

poverty

poor neighbourhoods 131-5, 148-50

young people's perspectives on 262

power relations

and critical practice 83

in education 164-5

and evidence based practice 60

in institutions 189

and inter-professional partnerships 43,
46-7

and professionalism 35

professionals and young people 38-41

and protection 258

and reflexivity 82

and risk 226, 246

practice 6-7, 53-84

boundaries 5, 9, 55, 73-7

critical 53, 83, 84

and decision-making 54-5

defining 53, 54-5

evidence based practice (EBP) 58-61, 63

and knowledge 53, 56, 57-61

neighbourhood 135-44

and process 56

purposive nature of 56

reflective 53, 63, 78-82

and relationships 65-77, 84

and residential care 186, 213-14

and safeguarding 260-1

and skills 53, 56, 61-3

and values 53, 56, 63-5

practice based evidence 59

practitioners 6, 15-49

and childhood/adulthood status in young
people 270-1

historical perspective on 19-25

impact of change on 15

and institutions 186

measuring performance 25-32

Positive Steps case study 17-18

professionalism and professional identities
16, 32-42

reflective 78-81

in residential institutions 9

responses to support 294-5

roles of 15

settings 15

worker support 313-14

pregnancy see teenage pregnancy

preventative interventions 18

historical examples of 20-2

youth justice 23-4

probation officers

and professional values 46

and professionalism 35-6

problematising discourses, on young people
and risk 223-5, 235-6, 238, 252

process

and practice 56

and reciprocity 71

process knowledge 57

professional accountability 28

professional boundaries see boundaries

professional identities 16, 32-42

and challenges from practitioners 31-2

community workers 142-3

contradictory forces impacting on 35-7

and inter-agency learning 45-7

lead professionals 47-8

partnerships and inter-professionalism
42-8

and power relationships 38-41

practitioner or professional 32-4

and use of self 66-9

young people's perspectives on 37-8

professional manner, acting in a 55

professional practice 55

professional values 63, 64

professionalism

and knowledge 61

and teachers 168

prostitution, as sexual exploitation 271, 272

protecting *see* child protection

PSE (Personal and Social Education) 172-3, 236

psy disciplines, and institutional care 200, 202

psychodynamic approach

and evidence based practice 60

and reflective practice 79

and the use of self 66

public accountability 28

public/private divide, and participation 91-2, 109

Pugh, C. 16

punishment, changing attitudes to 196-7

pupil referral units (PRUs) 38

pupils

experience of school 173-7

and informal teaching methods 167

pupil–teacher relations 172-3

see also education; schools; teachers

pure relationships 76, 77

quality practice, and target setting 26, 28, 29-30

race, and professionalism 35

Rapport, Nigel 127

Rathgael Juvenile Justice Centre 209-10, 212

ReachOut bus, West Sussex 138-9, 141, 142, 143

Reay, Diane 162, 173-4

reciprocity 70-3

and critical practice 83

and exchange 76-7

Reder, Peter 44-5

reflection 78, 81-2, 84

reflection-in-action 78

reflection-on-action 78

reflective practice 53, 63, 78-82

reflexive project of self 69

reflexivity 82, 83

and social learning in schools 170

reform, shift from punishment to 196-7

reformatory schools 188-9, 197, 198, 201, 203, 209

regulatory frameworks 5

relationships 65-77, 84

biographical perspective on 66-9

establishing boundaries 73-7

experience and expertise 69-73

reciprocity in 70-3, 76-7, 83

and safeguarding 274-5

and support 297-8, 299-301

and young people in residential care 202-4

see also power relations

religious orders, and institutions in Northern Ireland 189, 191

reprofessionalisation 35

residential care *see* institutions

resilience

promoting 275-80

sources of 276

respect, 'earned' 39, 40

restorative justice 23

retributive justice 230-3

Richards, M. 272

Ridge, Tess 262

rights and young people 105-15, 118
  challenges to young people's rights 106-9
  Children's Rights Commissioners 112, 113-15
  confidentiality 106-9, 267
  human rights legislation 105-6, 109-10, 112
  and the limits of participation 116-17
  in residential care 195, 207-10
  right to freedom of association 106, 110-11
  voting rights 101-3

risk 9, 219-47
  as a contested concept 246
  and defensive teaching 167
  defining 219-20
  governmentality and risk taking 225-6
  and HIV infection 220, 221, 222
  in late modernity 220
  and money problems 222
  moralisation of 226-7
  problematisation of young people's riskiness 223-5
  risky circumstances 227-8
  and safeguarding 251-3, 258
  tackling risks posed by young people 228-33
  working with young people to overcome risks 240-6
    homelessness 241-3
  Youth at Risk website 220-1, 222, 233
  see also diversionary intervention

risk society, and evidence based practice 58-9

Robb, Martin 279

Roberts, Helen 246

Rooker, Jeff 243

Rose, Nikolas 200

rural areas, drugs prevention in 145-6

Russell Commission 100

Safe in the City scheme 242-3

Safe Moves project 242, 243

safeguarding 9-10, 252-81
  empowerment and advocacy 273-4
  individual work 274-5
  promoting resilience 275-80
  and protecting 253-62
    impact of abuse and harm 258-60
    in practice 260-1
  and risk 251-3, 258
  young people's perspectives on 262-73
    confidentiality 265-9
    harm and help seeking 262-4
    and the transition to adulthood 269-73

St Christopher's Working Boys' Club 20-1

St Patrick's Industrial School 188-9

St Patrick's Training School 190-1, 192
  mission statement 194-5
  transmutation to Glenmona Resource Centre 193-4

Schön, D. 79

schools
  hidden curriculum in 171-2
  local management of schools (LMS) 156, 164
  memories of 157-60
  PSE (Personal and Social Education) 172-3, 236
  Record of Achievement portfolios 178
  school exclusions 38, 133
  social and sexual learning in 168-72, 173
  young people's experience of 173-7
  young people's participation in 89, 94-5, 96, 97-8
  see also education; pupils; teachers

Scotland
 Children's Parliament 102
 Children's Rights Commissioners 112, 113
 Nil by Mouth project 104
 youth justice system 24
Scouting movement 298, 299
Seagate drama project 137-8, 138-9, 140, 141, 143, 144
sectarian violence, campaign against in Scotland 104
self, use of 66-9
Separated in Europe Programme 273
service users, and reflective practitioners 78-9
sexual learning, in schools 158-73
Sharma, Ursula 34
Sinclair, Ruth 40-1
sixth formers, experiences of school 175-7
skills, and practice 53, 56, 61-3, 80
Skinner, Angus 200, 207-8
Smith, Mark 22, 27, 224-5, 299, 306
Smith, M.K. 66
sociability, and boundaries 76-7
social actors, young people as 41
social care, and evidence based practice 58
social constructionism
 and evidence based practice 59-60, 61
 and reflexivity 82
social exclusion
 risk of experiencing 237
 and support 308
 young people's perspectives on 262
Social Exclusion Unit 131-2, 133
 Report on Teenage Pregnancy 244
 Rough Sleeping 241
social structural model, of support and transition 296-7

social workers, and professional values 46
Sparks, Richard 239
specialist workers, and support services 312-13
Spence, Jean 19, 29
spoiled identities, of teachers 166
Springhall, John 229
Squires, Peter 225, 227, 232
Stafford, Anne 18
Standards in Scotland's Schools Act (2000) 112
Stanley, Janet 261
statements of competence, national occupational standards as 62-3
Stenson, Kevin 147
Stephen, Dawn 225, 227, 232
street based youth work 151
stress, and worker support 313-14, 315
subversive identities, of teachers 166
Sunderland Waifs Rescue Agency and Street Vendors Club 19-20
support 10, 287-316
 architecture/building metaphor of 289-90
 collective 302
 compensatory 289, 290, 293
 context of 288-90
 and empowerment 288, 289, 290, 304-5, 306-10
 individual 302-3
 inequality and difference in 303-4
 and policy 287, 291, 292-3, 294-5
 practitioner responses to 294-5
 targeted 287, 291, 310-13, 314
 and transition 292-5, 315
  historical models of 295-302
 worker support 313-14
 see also Everyday Journey research project
Supported Housing 244-5

Sure Start Plus 244-5

surveillance 8-9

   move from punishment to reform 196-7

   and reflection 81

   in residential care 196-200, 213

   and risk 246

Tanner, Karen 259

target setting 5, 25-32

   and accountability 26, 27, 28-9

   and boundaries 74

   challenges from practitioners 31-2

   and ethics 26, 30-1

   and higher education 161

   impact of 26-7

   and quality practice 26, 28, 29-30

targeted support 287, 291, 310-13, 314

teachers 8, 163-73

   cultures 165

   as implementers of policy 172-3

   and the labour process 164-5

   life history approaches to study of 165-6

   occupational cultures 164, 165

   and pedagogic practice 167-73

     and school and social learning 168-72

   personal experiences of 67-8, 163

   professional life of 36-7

   and young people's participation in schools 97-8

technical-rational responses, and evidence based practice 60

teenage pregnancy 244-5

   and education 178-80

   preventing 29

   and risk 244, 247

   and social learning in schools 169-70, 171

   and Sure Start Plus 244-5

   theoretical perspectives on youth 6

Thomson, Rachel 40, 67, 70-1, 180

Tisdall, E. 40

Training School Orders 192

training schools 189, 190-2

Transforming Youth Work (DfES) 26, 65, 289

transition to adulthood 10, 269-73

   safeguarding 269-73

   and support 292-5, 315

     historical models of 295-302

Trinder, Liz 58-9

Trudell, Bonnie 167

trust

   and boundaries 73

   decline in 39

   and target setting 29, 30

   young people's perspectives on 37

Tucker, Stanley 32

Turnbull, A. 313

Turney, Danielle 259

Ungar, Michael 279

United Nations, Convention on the Rights of the Child (UNCRC) 41, 69, 105-6, 109-10, 112

university education 155, 160-3, 176-7

   and sixth formers 176-7

Urban Streetz Smart project 138, 139, 140, 141, 142, 143, 144, 146

Urwick, Edward Johns, *Studies of Boy Life in Our Cities* 296, 298

use of self 66-9

values, and practice 53, 56, 63-5

Victorian philanthropy 186

Voice4Youth (V4Y) project 71-2

voluntary organisations, and target setting 25

voluntary work, young people's participation in 100

Vostanis, P. 272

voting rights, and young people 101-3

vulnerability 9, 293
   challenging 275-80
   and disability 260
   sources of 276
   and young people at risk 235-6, 239

Waage, Tronde 114

Wales, Children's Rights Commissioners 112, 113-14

Walkerdine, V. 177, 180

Waterhouse Report (2000) 205

Watson, David 30

Watt, Paul 147

Webb, Stephen 58

welfare approach to youth justice 22, 191-4

welfare and control debate, historical perspective on 22-3

welfare/justice dilemma, and residential care 191-5

Wenger, Etienne 46

Wetherell, M. 176

'what works culture' 35-6

White, Sue 45

Who Cares Scotland 210

Whyte, B. 18, 24

Williams, Raymond 128

Williamson, H. 48, 123

Willis, Paul 157

Willmott, Peter 128-9, 130, 150

Woodfield, K. 242

Woolley, Gemma 90

workhouses 186

working class
   communities 128-9
   culture
      and education 157, 175, 177
      and globalisation 156
   and early forms of youth work 19-22, 296-8
   neighbourhood 133
   and teenage pregnancy 180

YIPs (Youth Inclusion Projects) 293

YOTs (Youth Offending Teams) 45-6

Young, Jock 246-7

Young, Kerry 60, 63, 73, 76, 307

Young, Michael 128-9, 130, 150

Young People Now website 123

Youth Inclusion Projects (YIPs) 293

youth justice
   historical perspective on 22-4
   and individual intervention programmes 199-200
   and institutional care 188-9, 191-3, 199-200
   intervention based on the retributive justice model 230-3
   in Northern Ireland 188-9, 191-3
   punishment response 22
   welfare/treatment response 22
   young offenders and professional values 45-6

Youth Matters (government reports) 5, 70, 99-100, 291, 304-5, 306

YWCA (Young Women's Christian Association), courses for young mothers 178, 180